ECOTOPIAN ENCYCLOPEDIA

"Callenbach is the author of the 1970 book, *ECOTOPIA*, which has become an underground classic. In it he creates an imaginary country whose citizens have to grapple with a lot of survival issues we are all facing now. He has expanded this theme in another book, *ECOTOPIAN ENCYCLOPEDIA FOR THE 80's*, an A to Z guide to survival in the age of inflation."

San Francisco Chronicle

THE ECOTOPIAN
FOR

ENCYCLOPEDIA THE 80'S

A Survival Guide for the Age of Inflation

Ernest Callenbach

And/Or Press
Berkeley, California
1980

Project Coordinator — Peter Beren
Editors — Peter Beren, Leslie Carr, Candice Jacobson, Alan Rinzler, Patricia Rose, Leslie Strauss, Sayre Van Young
Illustrations — Courtesy of Bruce Brody, *Seriatim Magazine*
Cover and Book Design — Bonnie Jean Smetts
Paste-up — Phil Gardner
Typesetting — Aurora, Berkeley, California

Some material in this volume is drawn from a previous publication, *Living Poor with Style*, © 1972 by Ernest Callenbach. New material © 1980 by Ernest Callenbach.

Published and Distributed by And/Or Press, P.O. Box 2246, Berkeley, California 94710.

Printed in the United States of America by the George Banta Company.

First Printing   January 1981

ISBN: 0-915904-54-3

ACKNOWLEDGEMENTS

An author of any kind of book, but especially one such as this, is a kind of quilt-maker, who may perhaps claim credit for the elegance of the pattern, but not for providing the pieces of fabric that went into it. The information in this volume came from hundreds of sources and through the help of hundreds of people. In organizing it,. however, I was particularly helped by Christine Leefeldt, Alan Rinzler, Peter Beren and Candice Jacobson. Errors or biases it contains are, of course, my responsibility.

Someday we must have a much more extensive Ecotopian Encyclopedia—distilled from all the experience and knowledge we will accumulate over the next several proto-Ecotopian decades. It will reflect more of a comfortable, reasonably settled consensus on many matters which, in this first sketchy effort, I have had to leave somewhat vague or doubtful. Toward that end, I welcome suggestions for future editions.

E.C.

CONTENTS

ECOTOPIAN ENCYCLOPEDIA

INTRODUCTION

THE AIM OF THIS ENCYCLOPEDIA is to compress into one volume the basic essentials of Ecotopian living—to set forth, in a rather summary form, what you need to know in order to live as a sensible Ecotopian.

But what, you may well ask, is an Ecotopian?

Well, an Ecotopian is a citizen of a country that does not yet exist—except in the minds of people who hope, in one way or another, to someday bring it into reality. I described the imaginary country Ecotopia, in a novel of that name,* as an attempt to sketch a coherent, detailed, even mundane picture of what it might be like to live in a society that took ecological thinking seriously. (In fact, seriously enough that the region concerned— what had been Oregon, Washington, and Northern California—seceded from the Union in order to carry out the reforms it felt essential. We are dealing, in the novel, with the year 1999 A.D.)

Ecotopians are dedicated to the idea that, if we go about it right, our species may be able to inhabit our precious little planet indefinitely—rather than wrecking its biosphere and rendering ourselves, along with our fellow species, extinct. They therefore are devoted to "stable-state systems" and technologies which disrupt the natural order as little as possible. They do not believe in the old kind of Progress or expansion, but wish to live—personally and in the realm of technology and economics—in modest, reliable, nondestructive ways. They utilize renewable, biosource, biodegradable plastics for many purposes where we use metals, and their energy supplies are almost entirely solar-derived. They have managed to begin a slow diminution of population. To provide each other with the emotional sustenance so lacking in traditional competitive American life, they have expanded their family living patterns to larger size; and they have adopted employee ownership as the standard mode of organizing business enterprises (which are, by that fact, mostly small in scale and intensely personal in operation). Conscious of the underlying agricultural basis for all societies, they have installed recycling

Fu-tung Cheng

systems that return sewage (no longer contaminated with industrial heavy-metal wastes) in the form of fertilizer to the land. They have decentralized their governmental bodies, returning the basic taxing power— from which all other powers flow—to the local community. They are still mainly city dwellers but, instead of suburban sprawl made habitable only by vast hordes of gas-guzzling automobiles, they have developed compact mini-cities in which people get around by foot, bicycle, and mini-bus, and they have connected these mini-cities with fast, frequent public transit systems. They have de-emphasized centralized, heavy-investment types of art and entertainment such as movies and television, and have experienced a vast upsurge of popular creativity in which almost all citizens participate.

As the 80's proceed, these Ecotopian notions will almost certainly seem less and less bizarre. The impact of high oil prices will force the United States toward restrictions on internal-combustion engines reminiscent of those which the Ecotopians adopted for more principled reasons. Changes in the world balance of trade will make us learn to eat more sensibly, even if our dietary enlightenment must follow economic necessity. And, if we are lucky, we will adapt to changes in our technical and economic environment by making long-overdue improvements in our social and emotional environment, so that we can hope to live in a healthy and reasonably happy manner befitting the quite clever animals that evolution has contrived us to be.

But when I completed the novel *Ecotopia* it was rejected by virtually every major publishing house in New York. I subsequently had to organize friends into an entity called Banyan Tree Books to publish *Ecotopia* independently—which was, as it turned out, quite an Ecotopian thing to do, especially since it was then distributed by Bookpeople, an employee-owned company. The book, like some children, led a charmed life from the start. It was reviewed warmly by a wide variety of publications. But more importantly, readers began to tell their friends to read it; they gave it to people as gifts. And so, on this swell of word-of-mouth, utterly unaided by any advertising, *Ecotopia* percolated through the Ecotopian territory. In Oregon, a dedicated band of Ecotopians began *Seriatim: Journal of Ecotopia* to follow through on issues I had not been able to explore in depth in the novel and to raise new ones. Even in the eastern parts of the country, where any proposal for change can count on being greeted with derision, people who after Vietnam and Watergate had begun to doubt the viability of the Republic looked with interest at this strange secessionist book. And in time, especially after Bantam Books published a national mass-market edition, *Ecotopia* established a presence of sorts on the national scene. Reporters ventured to ask officials in the California state government what they thought of it; Huey Johnson, Secretary of Resources, who was in fact engaged in starting a quite Ecotopian program of reforestation, replied "We take it with playful seriousness." Later, editions appeared in France, England, Germany, Italy, Spain, Holland, Denmark, Sweden, and Japan.

This rather astonishing success is not due, I am well aware, to any overwhelming literary virtues of *Ecotopia*—though it pleases many readers as a story, even a love story (with a happy ending). But it happened to occupy a niche in contemporary thought which was waiting to be filled: a vision of what life would be like if we abandoned our exploitive attitudes toward the universe and began to try to live in it as if it were home. (The Greek roots of the word *ecotopia* are, indeed, those for "home" and "place"—so it makes a comforting name for a country, diametrically opposed to the sense of alienation and threat which so many Americans have about our country today.) It is a hopeful book, dramatizing in concrete, daily-life terms the fact that technology now exists to transform our way of living into sustainable and sustaining modes. It is, if you will, not science fiction but "politics fiction." My intention, of course, was to push readers up against a wall of manifestly possible alternatives so they would have to ask themselves: "Well, we could do all these things—*why don't we?*" And also to confront that other ancient question: "If not now, when?"

Ecotopia is full of quirky details—about composting toilets, and lumbering methods, and plastics chemistry, and the standardized sizes of food containers, and train stations, and cooking. In these details it shows its ancestry in a book I wrote some years before, now out of print, called *Living Poor with Style* (Bantam Books, 1972). Though I didn't clearly see the connection when I was first writing about it, Ecotopia is a place where *everybody* lives poor with style: lightly on the earth, damaging other life-forms as little as possible, keeping a clear eye on the things that make our lives worth living in themselves, rather than as adjuncts to machines, or corporations, or the process of capital formation—which sometimes seems as near to a deity as we come these days, at least leaving aside that commanding Prince of Darkness, the automobile.

This encyclopedia is a direct descendant of *Living Poor with Style*, and indeed much material in it, revised and updated, derives from that book—but seen now, so to speak, in a translation into the Ecotopian. Where the aim of the earlier volume was to help readers invent decent, satisfying life styles outside of (and often in direct opposition to) prevailing middle-class modes of consumption, this encyclopedia tries to provide information that will be useful in living a sensible and responsible life in an epoch of ecological consciousness and relative scarcity. Some of it will doubtless make more sense to people who have read the novel, but the encyclopedia is designed to stand on its own as a handy guidebook to survival in the 80's. Whether or not we ever achieve Ecotopia in any literal sense, in Tom Bender's telling phrase we are going to be "sharing smaller pies." We will no longer be able to ignore problems of fairness, to each other or the environment and

Fu-tung Cheng

posterity, in hopes that Progress will solve them.

But this is going to be a great and painful turning point in our history.

American society has always been "consumerist," teaching its people that the possession of goods is a major end of human life, and that the indefatigable application of the Protestant Ethic (or a sufficient amount of guile) would provide an ever-increasing quantity of goods. Members of the middle and upper-middle classes did indeed receive enough of the advertised goods to keep them quiet; members of the lower classes were brainwashed into feeling that if *they* hadn't, it must be their fault.

For 200 years, thanks initially to an easily exploited frontier and later the easy exploitability of underdeveloped nations, we got away with it. But, in the past decade, our Vietnam war deficits unbalanced our economy; competition from Europe and Japan curbed our markets; increased charges for oil deranged our energy supplies, contributed to our inflation, and increased costs for virtually everything we burn, build, or buy. What improvements in productivity our industries manage to carry out seem to be eaten up through increased social costs of the resulting unemployment and dislocation, or are invested in short-term speculative activity—"tax-loss" investments which do not increase productivity further.

In the 80's we will have to come to terms with the fact that our former profligacy can no longer be supported by economic realities. And, though it is seldom recognized, our economic problems and our ecological problems are intimately linked; indeed they are merely two aspects of one underlying problem. We may study (and attempt to solve) this problem equally in our private lives and in our political lives. The technologies and details involved are of course complex, and no single book can deal with them in any comprehensive way. But the principles are simple enough, no matter how people with special interests may wish to disguise them; though we ourselves may often resist their application, in the long run we must learn to live with them. If our national life can be looked at as a biological process, what we face is the prospect of "losing weight." People like to imagine that special diets, machines, or regimes will help them reduce, but in the end there are really only two alternatives: eat less or exercise more (or both).

The same principle applies in economic life. We are already being forced to "eat less" because the United States is no longer in a position to dominate the world's economy through control of the main trading currency, "the almighty dollar"; the Japanese yen, not to mention the German mark, is now considerably more mighty. Our goods must compete, in today's fickle world market, on terms which mean that our pay for producing them is roughly stable, or sometimes even declining: the tractor which we once sold in Argentina, paying our factory workers the equivalent of $10 an hour to produce it, must now compete with Japanese tractors at prices which mean we can pay our workers only

$9.50 an hour. What this will mean for the economy as a whole, when added to its increasing concentration, bureaucratization, and the high rates of profit extracted by its owners, is a slight decline in our "real standard of living," that is, the number of loaves of bread we can purchase with an hour's pay. As has happened in England since World War II, this belt-tightening is not likely to get drastic, but it is almost sure to continue for a long time. The prosperity of a sizable upper-middle class able to afford Mercedes cars and expensive restaurants should not delude us into believing that the nation as a whole has been thriving economically. In reality, America's average real wages have been declining since 1973. From 1979 to 1980 they dropped almost 8%, in fact.

The traditional view is that a healthy society must be an expanding society, and that advocates of steady-state economies are purveyors of economic doom. Such views fly directly in the face of recent reality. The fact is that for the last half of the 70's the US economy *was* very nearly in a steady-state condition: its overall output remained nearly stable, though of course individual sectors and industries grew while others shrank. This was hardly a period of economic catastrophe, except for people of very low incomes and for small investors in the stock market. (Those interested in future steady-state economics have begun to suspect that a stock market, whose operation depends on confidence in ever-increasing profits, is not a satisfactory way to distibute investment in such economies; the securing and retaining of investors has become increasingly prob- lematic for many firms, even profitable ones.)

In the 80's, we will doubtless continue to have some good years and some not-so-good years. What is crucial to keep foremost in mind is that the overall prospects for a slow but continuous "eating" of less can mean greater social and ecological health. Indeed, since wealth inherently means greater consumption, and hence more ecological destruction, more modest life styles are in fact

Fu-tung Cheng

the *major* means by which we can lessen damage to our environment. But the choices we face will not be easy, on either a personal or national level. We will have to revive our skill and ingenuity at making do with less—which, it so happens, increases feelings of self-reliance, resourcefulness, and pride. In short, we will have to *minimize* our consumption in ways that *maximize* our satisfactions. And that is what this encyclopedia is about: it's a handy compendium of ideas, principles, and information that you can use in coping with the problems and potentialities that the 80's will bring.

It is, of course, impossible to predict in any detail what styles will prevail during the 80's in dress or eating or political protest. I have tried, therefore, to avoid including material that is likely to "date" because styles change. (Since inflation makes it impossible to speak of prices in dollar terms that will be hopelessly outdated in two years, I have had to use other ways of referring to the value of things.) But a few items may seem strange to readers who came of age in the relatively placid 70's. I include material on political organization for instance, because I believe that the political life of the 80's is likely to be quite turbulent—perhaps not in the style of the 60's, but still involving a great deal of protest, mass movements clamoring for attention, and sometimes explosive and startling developments on various political levels. Many people are going to be hurting, and hurting badly, as the decade wears on; they will find ways of conveying this hurt to people in power, whether through mass demonstrations against the perils of nuclear melt-downs, or campaigns to attach "escalator-clause" indexing to pensions and wages, or perhaps even sabotage campaigns aimed at stopping the production and dissemination of carcinogenic chemicals. We live in a country where, although we luckily still have many democratic rights, the enforcement of those rights can only be secured through constant political struggles against oppressive secret police systems, exploitative economic and taxation systems, an electoral political system which is very slow to respond to needs for change, and a television and newspaper establishment which efficiently filters out news of people's demands—until they become so massive and explosive that they can no longer be ignored. These struggles went on through the 70's just as they did during the 60's, and they will go on in the 80's, taking new forms we cannot yet imagine.

But overall, it seems probable that we will move, slowly and haltingly, in Ecotopian directions. As far as visions of a livable future for the country go, Ecotopian ideas in fact seem to be the only game in town; other orientations aim merely at patching up features of an outdated and fatally vulnerable system—rear-guard actions attempting to stave off immediate disasters, but not coping with the underlying problems.

It is said that there is a Chinese curse, "May you live in 'interesting times'!" The 80's are going to be very interesting times. It is up to us whether they turn out to be a curse or a blessing in disguise.

• Quality paperback edition: Bookpeople, 2940 Seventh St., Berkeley, CA 94710; mass-market edition: Bantam Books, 666 Fifth Ave., New York, NY 10019.

How to Use This Book

This encyclopedia is organized by simple alphabetical order. Flipping through it at random is a good way to get a feel for how the material has been put together and for the different types of entries. Two kinds of cross-references help to tie the material together. Some items have, at their ends, notes like this: See BICYCLES. There are also some cross-references which are indicated merely by the capitalization of a word. Thus, in an entry about transportation, you may find the word BICYCLES in capitals, meaning that relevant information can be found under that entry. Some entries also have books listed at the end, which are good sources of fuller information.

Certain topics of undoubted interest and importance are not dealt with here because they are too complex for brief treatment, are amply dealt with in readily available books, or have rapidly changing features. These include such items as abortion and contraception, women's health, higher education, the draft, money market funds and other alternatives to savings accounts, camping, clothing, and recreational drugs. A good library or bookstore will provide easy access to current information in these areas.

No encyclopedia is meant to be read straight through. This one is intended as a household reference book to keep around and consult as need arises or to be read by fits and starts. While the book contains many general ideas, its basic purpose is to provide orientation and information about practical questions of daily, personal life we will face in the 80's as we struggle to survive, each of us contributing small fragments of Ecotopian living modes to the growing over-all pattern. Great oaks from little acorns grow, and great societal changes grow, in the long run, out of the small decisions that people make, in their millions, day by day. Let's try to make them right.

AGING

Demography (the study of populations) tends to be an engrossing but depressing subject. Its statistics derive from factors so slow to act, because they stem from the human generational cycle, that nothing much can ever be done about them in the short run. Educational administrators, for example, can only look ahead to the fact that during the 80's and part of the 90's, they will have declining school and college enrollments with a resulting erosion in budgets. And industries also ride the population waves, like surfers hoping to take advantage of the big ones.

For the next several decades, U.S. population will have an increasing proportion of older people. By 2000 A.D. more than half the population will be over 60. This will mean, of course, more retired people for the younger, smaller working population to support, through Social Security taxes and other means. And already we see steps being taken to lessen this problem: extension of working years by raising obligatory retirement ages, reduction of tax penalties on retired people who continue working part-time, and so on. While some such changes will work against the interests of the older people in the population, the fact that they will undoubtedly become more politically conscious of their numerical power will greatly soften political moves against them. And it will be good for the society and good for individual senior citizens if their productive lives can be extended. Many people do not survive retirement very long — particularly men, whose self-esteem has, in our sexist culture, been more tightly involved with work than that of women. Hobbies are often not a satisfactory substitute for gainful work, which for many people "proves" you are a valuable member of the human community.

We have also begun to understand the aging process better. Though we are still shunting infirm older people off to "homes," it is becoming clear that this kind of isolation, even if paid for through government programs like Medicare, is inferior to the kind of integration into communities that is being attempted in Scandinavia and, spottily, here. The central idea is that aging is a continous process we all go through (our physical peak, after all, is about age 18) and that there ought to be no point after which people are thrown on the junk-heap. Our energies, intelligence, wisdom, and judgment generally continue to be useful to advanced ages, if we arrange our lives so that they have scope for action. We are even beginning to understand that older people can continue to have active and satisfying sex lives. Their role in educating younger people should by no means be confined to their grandchildren (if they happen to have any) but should be made available on a wider basis. One interesting project combines a small housing complex, in which a mix of older and younger people live, with a child-care center, managed and staffed mainly by older people. The complex includes space for small enterprises (stores and workshops) to be run by its inhabitants, and the complex is near supermarkets and other sources of necessities. COMMUNITY GARDENS also offer a focus for older people's contributions to neighborhood solidarity and productivity.

People on pensions are the chief victims of

11

inflation unless their pensions are "indexed" through escalator clauses to the cost-of-living index.

Senior citizen centers are being established in many neighborhoods, to provide meal services, welfare service information, and other needs. Many religious groups have also maintained retirement centers for their members. Downtown hotels, close to necessary services, have often been converted to residential hotels for older citizens. And of course MEDICARE and MEDICAID programs benefit millions.

See DYING.

AIR CONDITIONING

The air conditioner was a virtually unknown appliance at the end of World War II. It is now one of our greatest consumers of household energy, used largely to correct the deficiencies of incompetent building design and construction. People have become convinced they cannot live without air conditioners, and so great is their habituation that they keep their dwelling windows closed, with their conditioner running full blast, even when the outside temperature is lower than the air conditioner thermostat setting—in other words, when they would get cooler faster by opening a couple of windows.

New buildings, even in hot climates, can be constructed so that mechanical air cooling is very seldom desirable. In old buildings, money spent on insulation will quickly be repaid in lower air conditioner operating costs (or in not having to rely on one at all). If you feel you *have* to have one, wire up a simple outdoor thermosensor to a dial you set at the same temperature you are asking your air conditioner to achieve, and arranged so that when the outdoor temperature is lower, a bell rings or a light flashes. (A good hardware store can sell you the parts and give you a wiring diagram.) Wire it so the only way to stop the signal is to turn off the air conditioner. In one experiment, householders with such devices cut their electricity consumption by 16%.

See COOLING.

AIR POLLUTION

Smog is only one type of air pollution, though perhaps the most familiar. It irritates eyes, rots rubber, affects bronchial and lung functioning, kills or stunts many kinds of plants (including orange and pine trees and grape vines), and generally makes life unpleasant for most species.

There is even evidence that some of its components, carbon monoxide and nitrogen dioxide, aggravate alcoholism and mental illness: mental hospital admissions go up on high-smog days. Smog attacks are especially hard on older people and the infirm who often suffer health setbacks, and even death. Smog is a severe problem in most American cities, not just those, like Los Angeles, which have special combinations of constant sunlight and huge amounts of auto exhaust. Even small cities, which these days may sometimes have more cars per capita than large ones, can have terrible smog if they are situated in bowls or valleys where wind circulation is weak. The ultimate solution is the elimination of the internal combustion engine, which is by far the **major source of smog, though oil refineries and** other industrial sources are also contributors.

Air pollution in the form of tiny particles ("particulates") is another major health menace. For a time it was believed that diesel engines were a desirable alternative to the gasoline engine, until it was established that they emit large amounts of particulates—which cause their peculiar smell and, as our noses have been trying to tell us, are carcinogenic. Auto brakes contain asbestos for cooling which is rubbed off into the air as particulates; as street dust, it is then stirred up by passing vehicles and inhaled into your lungs, where it is a potent carcinogen. (See CANCER.)

One particularly nasty aftereffect of industrial air pollution is acid rain, which now falls over much of this country and many parts of Europe. Sulfur emissions from factory stacks drift hundreds of miles and contaminate rain in distant states. The rain is so acid that it stunts forest growth, endangers agricultural crops, eliminates fish in lakes, and corrodes metal, paint, and even clothing. In the short run, it can only be eliminated by the installation of "scrubbers" to remove the sulfur emissions. In the long run, acid rain can be eliminated by turning to solar, methane, methanol from biomass sources, and other kinds of industrial process heat. (See SOLAR ENERGY.)

ALCOHOL

You can spend an enormous amount of money on alcohol, even if you're not a real juicer. The price of a fifth of Scotch can feed you for a week. But if booze is your thing, or you can't get anything you like better, the best general rule is simple: drink cheap standard-brand American wine, unless you live in a wine-making region where you can find even cheaper good stuff.

Wine. Wine has been around for several thousand years, but its virtues have only recently been more widely recognized in the US. In small quantities wine can actually be good for the health; it relaxes you and provides some vitamins, as well as some calories of food energy. It goes well with many foods, and can make the difference between just a meal and an elegant repast. There are many poor French or Italian households where the absence of wine would be as badly felt as the absence of silverware.

Except in small neighborhood liquor stores, you will now find all over America a reasonable choice of decent cheap wines. There's no mystique to wine buying, unless you get rich enough to become a connoisseur; in the beginning you can start out simply by finding a solid red wine that appeals to you. (A decent cheap white is harder to find.) The major California wine corporations produce wine that is undistinguished but drinkable; the little wineries produce wines that are sometimes superb and sometimes awful, and the prices of the really good ones, which often surpass good French wines in quality, have become ridiculous. The wise beginner thus sticks with the ordinary labels. This stuff is sent around to the East Coast in stainless-steel tanker ships, but a full-time staff of trained experts is engaged in keeping it at an even, mediocre level of drinkability.

Or you can make your own wine. It's legal to make up to two hundred gallons per year for your own home consumption and not for sale. That's a considerable amount of wine. It takes a source of grapes (or other fruit—plums, apricots, cherries, etc.), a large crock or plastic canister, and a lot of bottles and corks. However, home winemaking cannot reliably produce wine at a significantly lower price than gallon jugs of commercial wine, because of spoilage, wastage, and other factors. Unlike beer, where you really save money, making your own wine is for pleasure and not for thrift.

Beer. Beermaking was formerly frowned upon by the federal tax authorities, for whom booze is a stupendous source of revenue; but now, as with wine, you are allowed to make 200 gallons per year for your own consumption. (And in any case, no one was ever prosecuted for a little quiet brewing.) American commercial beer is such a flat, thin, weak sort of drink that the beer companies seem to be positively inviting home competition, as well as encouraging the increasing importation of German, British, and even Australian beers and

ales—many of which are delicious, substantial, and powerful (as well as extremely expensive). Home brew costs about a fifth of what store-bought beer costs. It contains much more alcohol than commercial beer; it has more vitamins since it isn't filtered to death, and it has a generally richer taste and consistency. You can make draft beer (flat) or fizzy beer—which can have more carbonation than commercial if you like it that way.

What you need for elementary beermaking is a large crock or canister, a lot of clean bottles (screw-top type won't work), bottle caps (soak them before using so the cork seals better), and a bottle capper; it also helps to have a hydrometer, and a six-foot piece of plastic tubing (one end stuck into a scrap of wood so it floats near the surface in the crock) to use in bottling. Here's the recipe: Put your crock on a porch or in a cellar where the fermentation smell won't bother you (or suspicious neighbors). Mix some hot water with a can of Blue Ribbon Malt Extract (available in dark or light at most large supermarkets); this takes work, as the extract is very sticky. Then add sugar in the proportion of five pounds of sugar to one can of extract (for ten gallons total crock capacity). After you've got the extract and sugar thoroughly dissolved in the hot water, add more water, sort of tepid, until you have the whole crock full of water that feels barely warm to the touch. Into this mixture put some yeast: this can be just ordinary powdery (not cake) baking yeast you buy at the grocery, mixed in a cup of the warm mixture to dissolve it better. But it's best to buy special brewing yeasts from one of the sources listed at the end of this entry. Stir the whole thing to distribute the yeast well. Cover the crock with some polyethylene sheeting, cheesecloth, or other cloth to keep out fruit flies—they love beer! Wait and watch about a week to two weeks, depending on the temperature, skimming off the fermentation scum if it gets very thick. If you live where there are cold winters, you'll have to do the fermenting inside, as the yeast will die in cold weather. When the small bubbles from the fermentation (you can see them by looking at the surface from an angle) have almost stopped, or when the hydrometer's red line has sunk to the surface of the mixture, siphon the beer into clean bottles and cap them. (Some people add about a quarter teaspoon of sugar to each bottle to increase the fizz.) Be sure not to fill the bottles too full; leave an inch or two of air in the neck to absorb the carbonization pressure. Cap securely and mark with the date. (If you have some small bottles, fill them so you can try them as samples to see how the batch is aging.) Beer improves up to six months in the bottle; beyond that there's no point in not drinking it. Generally two months aging in the bottle is about right.

After you've made a couple of batches in this elementary style, you'll be ready for the advanced class. This involves experiments to find which yeasts you prefer (some are top-fermenting, some bottom-fermenting, and they create subtly different tastes in the resulting product), with making ales and meads as well as beers, with using gelatin to clarify the beer before putting it in bottles, and so on. You'll find it best to follow the example of experienced home brewers in keeping careful records, so that when you've done something spectacular you have a way to repeat it. Home brewers are an intensely competitive lot, with their own techniques, their own tastes in sugar ingredients (there's raw sugar, honey, invert sugar, dextrose, lactose, etc.). If you can find one to apprentice yourself to, you'll be assured of a good start.

The chief cautions to be observed in beginning to make home brew are these: make sure your bottles are really clean, ideally using boiling water as a last rinse, and use a hydrometer, or at any rate don't bottle too early, lest your carbonation become excessive and your bottles explode. (You should not store home-brew bottles where they **might get bumped by children or passersby.**) If you're doubtful about a batch, put on heavy gloves, cover a bottle with a heavy rag, and open it very gingerly. If the **cap flies off and most of the beer spurts out uncontrollably, don't sit around** lapping it up; carefully open all of that batch and re-bottle it.

There is an art to pouring unclarified and unfiltered home brew: open the bottle carefully **and pour gently so as not to disturb the sediment.** Set it down slowly too. Treated in this way you'll find that your home brew is clear enough to satisfy most people, and it's a joy to real beer drinkers. Watch out for it, though! It contains almost as much alcohol as wine—about three times as much as commercial beer.

Mead. A medium-sweet mead can be a great delight as a switch from beer. Here's a recipe: 4½ pounds honey, ¼ ounce citric acid, ½ cup freshly made strong tea, some yeast, and nutrient if you use it. Mix the honey with about half a gallon of hot water. Bring to a boil and boil for two minutes (to kill any bacteria). Put into a crock or canister, add citric acid and tea. Add boiling water until you have a total of about one gallon. Allow to cool to

about sixty-five degrees and add the yeast (and nutrient). Cover with a polyethylene sheet or cloth, securing it tightly with a large rubber band. Ferment in a warm place for ten to fourteen days. Then pour into a large jar with a plastic-and-rubber-band cover (to keep air out but let gas escape). Leave there until all fermentation stops— probably a month. Then bottle and keep for a year. (Mead is a non-fizzy drink, so you add no further honey or sugar.)

Distilled liquors (whiskeys, gins, brandies, and so on) cost more to make per unit of alcohol, and home distilling can bring stiff prison sentences. However, you may be interested in store-bought hard liquor, even if it is higher-priced. Your best bet is vodka, which is practically nothing but alcohol and water; it's the easiest of all liquors on your system, since it has the fewest "congeners" (oils, sugars, and so on, which are abundant in brandies and whiskeys). There is very little variation in quality from one vodka to another, so buy the cheapest you can get. Often grocery-chain brands are good bargains.

One of the worst buys is pre-mixed cocktails, which are fantastically more expensive than the **straight stuff.**

A Guide for the Home Production of Fine Beers, by Myron Burch. Joby Books/Bookpeople, 2940 Seventh St., Berkeley, CA 94710.

Mail-order source for wine and beer-making supplies: Wine and the People, 907 University Ave., Berkeley, CA 94710.

ALCOHOLISM

Alcohol is by far the greatest American drug problem. We have many millions of alcoholics— people whose lives are dependent on alcohol, and who drink so much that their health is seriously endangered. Our death rate from alcohol-induced cirrhosis of the liver is staggering. And alcohol takes its toll on every level of society: in the **executive suite, behind the facade of the suburban** home, in the working-class neighborhood, as well as on skid row. A large proportion of our 55,000 auto dead each year is due to alcohol, along with hundreds of thousands injured or maimed. The judgment of most medical researchers directly familiar with drug use is that alcohol is a more dangerous drug than marijuana. It is especially hard on the liver, may help cause malnutrition, and doesn't do your head any good either. However, in small quantities, it promotes conversation—and even digestion (there is a dedicated band known as the Medical Friends of Wine).

Alcoholism, like addiction to other drugs, is a mental-health problem. Some states have a drying-out program in their state hospitals. But to really get off alcohol requires a total re-orientation of one's life, and can only be accomplished with a lot of help. Alcoholics Anonymous, an organization listed in the phone book, has much experience in coping with alcoholism, and seems to offer the most successful "treatment" so far.

There are about a million alcoholic American women of childbearing age, and their number is increasing, especially among teenagers. Maternal alcohol consumption can lead to brain deficiency in babies. Women who drink heavily should avoid pregnancy, and pregnant women should avoid alcohol.

Alcoholics Anonymous. Revised edition. Alcoholics Anonymous World Services, Inc., 1955.
Healing Alcoholism, by Claude Steiner. Grove Press, 1979.

AMUSEMENT, FREE

It's amazing how much goes on in our cities which you can attend free—but most people never hear about it, so they end up watching television. Here is where to find out what's going on:

Newspapers. Sunday papers, community or special-interest papers (see PERIODICALS AND NEWSPAPERS), and some dailies have listings of museums, special exhibitions, political meetings, lectures, plays, free or low-admission concerts (sometimes you can get student ticket rates or get in free by ushering—call the house manager at the theater), dances, movies, court sessions, city council meetings—all of which are either free or very cheap.

Bulletin boards. These can be found in libraries, around universities and colleges (which have the best informal communications of any of our communities), sometimes in government buildings. Announcements of many coming events will be posted here.

Posters. The poster as a commercial art form had practically died out a few years ago, but the use of arty posters to announce rock concerts in San Francisco led to a new flowering of the art poster. Some cities are belatedly following the European system and providing kiosks where posters for concerts, plays, and other cultural events can be displayed.

There are also many free amusements which do not get listed in any of these places, and you have to find out about them on your own, depending on your tastes and ingenuity. For instance, many

transit systems offer an all-day or all-weekend pass; with it you can travel anywhere on their lines, especially way out to the ends where the parks, beaches, and other interesting places are. Or you can ride around the inner city and get to know it better. Coastal and river cities have ferries which are cheap and fun; in general, anything that exists for everyday purposes can lend itself to inexpensive amusement.

You can visit all the parks in your city, large and small; it's likely that some of them are really beautiful and interesting. For instance, a botanical garden usually has a fantastic variety of exotic plants you'll never see elsewhere. Or there may be a rose garden, or a monster greenhouse where tropical plants grow and the air smells damp and strange. There may be a park with a lake where you can rent little boats and paddle around, or where you can swim in the summertime. There might be a harbor park where you can walk around and look at the elegant boats—which is a way I have spent many a lovely (or rainy) afternoon. Walking or bicycling around a park can be both restful and relaxing.

Many cities have free facilities that few citizens are aware of. There may be free tennis or handball courts in your neighborhoods. There are probably shuffle-board courts, and in parks with buildings there are probably table-tennis tables. Most cities have at least one public swimming pool with a small admission charge.

You can also get a lot of pleasure out of your city just by walking around in places you don't usually go. In fact, that's one of the original appeals of cities: there's a lot going on, a lot that you can see in a compact area, many possibilities open to you nearby. Don't confine yourself only to the areas you are familiar with, though of course you should use judgment (and if necessary make some inquiries) before venturing onto turf where you might encounter hostility. Some of the most interesting areas are those inhabited chiefly by people from foreign lands: Chinatown, with its strange groceries and imported tourist goods; districts where there are Russian bakeries with mysterious cookies and pastries; black neighborhoods with soul food or Caribbean restaurants; Italian districts with extraordinary resources of pasta and delicatessen foods. As the years go by, more and more of the world's inhabitants are living in the same colorless, timid, bland, middle-class way. It is chiefly in our cities that we can see remnants of the more vigorous and varied cultures from which our ancestors came.

See WALKING.

APARTMENT HUNTING

Sometimes an apartment can seem so appealing when you first walk into it that you forget to check it thoroughly to see whether it will really suit you. Here, therefore, is a handy checklist to run down when you're considering an apartment or house.

Space. Most people try to have one room per person—four rooms for a four-person family, and so on. (The strong American preference for this ratio is now causing our rooms to get smaller on the average.) But this standard is hard to find for large families, so members have to double up. Both for biological families and EXTENDED FAMILIES each member needs a private space for sleeping, entertaining, reading, thinking. But these private spaces can be small (only a bit bigger than a bed) if the common-use areas are spacious— say a good-sized kitchen and one very large main room (or pair of rooms connected with an archway or sliding doors). The higher the ceilings, the more spacious a place will seem.

Light. Sunlight falling into a room can brighten it up enormously, and give you a place to grow indoor plants. Sunlight is warming to sit or lie in. And if some of your windows look out on trees or a yard of some kind, better still. Skylights are often beautiful, and even if they leak (as they often do) they're a delightful source of additional sun.

Air. Especially in places that get hot in summer, you need cross-ventilation—windows at opposite ends so that air will move through.

Heating. Check to see if all the radiators actually work. In many parts of the country you'll be paying for heat in your rent, so make sure there is some! If there's a gas heater, be sure it's vented so it can't asphyxiate you.

Plumbing. There should be a sink in the kitchen; try both hot and cold water faucets. Look under the sink to see if the drain leaks. Go in the bathroom and try the toilet. Turn on the cold and hot water in the basin. Try the faucets in the tub or shower too. You can fix many small plumbing defects but serious leaks mean trouble, and living without hot water is like camping out all year-round.

Security. Everybody gets burgled sooner or later these days, but you can help make it be later by having a strong door on good hinges, with a proper lock. (You might even want to invest in one of the new pickproof locks.) There should be a window-locking device on all the windows, especially if they look out on the ground or on fire escapes.

Fire escape. On the second floor or higher, you need another way out if the hallway is in flames—a fire escape or a window out onto a porch roof. If a room is at the end of a long corridor, you might want to tie a heavy escape rope onto a stout hook near a window—and train children to use it if they sleep in that room.

Vermin. Check around for rat turds, stain marks on walls which show where rats or mice have been passing by, cockroaches, and so on. Most central city areas—and many fancy neighborhoods— harbor these unwelcome visitors. You can get rid of the rats, and most of the cockroaches, but it pays to know if they're there before you move in. Garbage cans should be the snap-top-type, so they're ratproof and dogproof.

Amenities. Many old buildings have pleasant additions which make life nicer. If there's a fireplace, find out whether it works. If there's a roof you can get out onto, that helps in the sticky summertime, and might offer space for GARDENING. Some big apartment buildings have garbage-disposal chutes, which are handy. In smaller places, a car-parking spot may be included. If there is no shower, and you like one, ask the landlord if he'll pay for the parts if you put it in.

Safety. One of the dangers of old buildings is peeling layers of old paint. Small children eat paint flakes, which gives them lead poisoning— leading to mental retardation and other illnesses. Check both walls and floors. Other common dangers are rickety stair railings or porch railings, gas leaks in stoves or heaters, cracked windows whose pieces may fall in onto children, elevator doors that don't work right, and areas that don't have working hall lights. It's also wise to check for places that make it easy for purse snatchers or other unsavory types to hide and pounce on people going in or out.

Let's say you have never looked for a place to live before. How to go about it?

Once you have some idea of a couple of neighborhoods you want to consider, do a little exploring. It's best to be able to use a map. But just wander around—on foot, or on a bicycle, or some other slow-moving way of travel. Use a crisscross pattern to be sure you don't miss anything. Stick your head into the stores; try to get some feel for "how people treat each other around here." Do they sit on their stoops or porches, do the kids play in the street? Ask people questions—about public transportation, about stores, about the school— whatever concerns you. And above all, ask everybody whether they know of any places for rent.

The best deals in housing are always gotten by word of mouth. You hear from relatives or friends that a good place is going to be vacant. Or you're talking to a storekeeper and he or she mentions that a relative has a place for rent. Give yourself as much time to look as possible, so you can take advantage of these informal leads. It takes weeks of steady looking to find anything you'll really like.

Places advertised in the newspaper or listed with realtors may be all right, but they will usually be more expensive and not so satisfactory as things you hear of by word of mouth.

There's another reason to try and find places directly: owners who advertise tend to treat their properties as businesses, so they add in all their expenses, may have tax lawyers and other expensive overhead, and end up charging more for a place than a small landlord does. Watch out for "For Rent" signs as you walk—these are usually used by small owners, or by people who rent out part of their building and live in it too.

Be careful of landlords or landladies who live there. They tend to keep their places in good repair, which is an advantage, but they also tend to be nosy—which is very unpleasant for tenants. Some old people, who haven't realized the sexual revolution that has taken place since World War II, will even object to overnight visits from women friends or men friends or just friends—though this is now permitted even in college dormitories! Best of all seems to be an owner who is retired and lives out of town, but who comes around occasionally to check on the building or fix things.

Always pay your rent by check (so you can prove you paid by showing a copy of the canceled check) even if the owner offers to give you a receipt.

If existing apartments do not fit your tastes or budget, you can live in places like lofts, warehouses, or former stores—which artists and others have been converting to dwellings in many of our central cities. It takes some competence in carpentry, plumbing, and wiring—but it can get you space, convenience, and style.

Pioneering in the Urban Wilderness, by Jim Stratton. Urizen Books, 1977.

APARTMENT REPAIRS

Generally the person who lives in rented places faces a sticky problem in dealing with owners. If you complain and get the owner to fix things up, the result may be a raise in your rent. And if the owner won't fix up and you go to the city health department, which investigates and forces the owner into making repairs, you may find yourself facing an eviction notice. Supposedly protective laws may not be much protection in such cases; only strong tenant unions, which are rare, offer much real help.

So, many tenants tolerate broken plaster, leaky pipes, dirty garbage facilities, missing window-panes, and other such problems rather than run the risk of being evicted. After all, even a beat-up house is better than no house at all—or a slightly fixed-up house at a higher rent.

There seems to be only one way to get around this vicious circle, and it won't work with all owners. Some of them evidently like to see people live in bad surroundings. But most are not really crookeder than the rest of us; they're just reacting to tax laws which make it positively desirable to let their buildings rot.

Here's why. First, owners generally make most of their money by buying a building, creaming off the depreciation allowance from their income taxes, selling in five years, and then buying another building and doing the same thing all over again. The value of a building doesn't drop very much if it gets more run-down, and unless it gets hopelessly dilapidated it can always be rented because of the housing shortage. (If the housing department declares it unfit for human habitation, many owners will just walk away and leave it; there are thousands of such abandoned buildings in any major city.) Second, if an owner makes any visible improvements or any inside improvements the city finds out about—the building's property taxes will be raised.

You have to approach your landlord or landlady, therefore, with a deal that won't cause tax trouble, and might even make a little more money when the building is sold. Basically, you offer to fix the place up yourself, if the materials needed are provided for you, in return for a written lease that keeps the rent where it is for a significant period (at least a year and if possible two). If you paint a sizable apartment, you are saving the owner in labor costs at least a month's rent. So the owner is ahead, and so are you since you've got a newly painted place but at the same old rent.

Or suppose there's broken plaster in your walls. To get a plasterer to fix them is expensive and might lead to a hike in the rent. But you can plug up the holes yourself, usually by getting the owner to finance about a dollar's worth of plastering compound.

Generally the owner will be distrustful at first of your ability to carry out such jobs. Tell him or her you can understand this, and that you'd like to do a small job first, like painting the bathroom, to show you want to do it right. Then get the owner in to look at the results and put it that now you need the rest of the paint for the other rooms.

Rotting steps and railings are among the most common (and most dangerous) defects of old buildings; they are also the hardest for individual renters to do anything about.

If a step is cracked or sagging, you can nail a piece of plywood on top of it to keep someone's foot from going through. (Use thin plywood or the step seems too high and people may trip.) Often you can patch up or brace a weakened railing. But if the whole flight of steps is sagging or rotting, it'll have to be torn out and replaced. With a bad owner, one possible (though of course illegal) way to get this done is to get the people in the building together, pick a convenient dark night, and deliberately pile weights (not people) on the stairs until they collapse. Then clear them off and notify the landlord that the steps have caved in and nobody can get in or out. To keep on renting the building, the owner has to fix the steps.

If there are dangerous conditions in the building, like falling plaster or wobbly stair railings, you may want to notify the owner in writing, by registered mail. This relieves you of legal responsibility for any injuries that may occur, and gives you grounds for a later complaint to the city, for withholding rent due to illegal conditions, and even for suing the owner. Neighborhood Legal Service offices may be able to help you in negotiating with the owner and preventing him or her from evicting you or raising your rent because of your complaints.

An owner is legally obligated to equip your dwelling with sturdy locks, sometimes of special types that make it harder to force a door or windows; broken window glass that makes entry easier must be replaced. It is important when you move into a new place to go over it from a potential burglar's point of view and do what you can to make entry difficult (and noisy, so that neighbors will be alarmed if you're not home). Most police departments have prevention officers who may be willing to drop by and advise you on ways to decrease the likelihood of being hit by burglars.

See REPAIRS, HOME.

APPLIANCES

It is now conventional for planners to assume that a new suburban house creates a total energy drain of some 24,000 kilowatts or the equivalent. A substantial part of this goes for heat, but the rest is for a vast array of energy-guzzling appliances and enough electric light for an operating-room.

People trying to live in Ecotopian ways will want to minimize their dependence upon appliances as well as their energy consumption. What is a reasonable minimum? In my experience: refrigerator, stove, radio-record player, blender, toaster, and iron (see separate entries for further information on each).

The energy consumption of appliances varies widely, and you should compare carefully the labels that most of them now carry, giving the figures. Over a five-year lifetime, you will spend more than the purchase price of most major appliances on the energy they take to run; so their energy drain is probably their single most important feature. Frost-free refrigerators, upright freezers, and air conditioners are particularly heavy energy users.

Since most appliances, like American cars, are constructed to last at least ten years (and refrigerators and freezers up to 15 or 50), on the whole you will get better value for your money—and in many cases more energy-efficient appliances—if you rely on secondhand sources. It takes some knowledge and care to be sure of what you're getting, or at least to minimize the risks (here again, see individual entries). But you may on occasion buy something new, and be asked whether you wish to buy extended warranty or guarantee coverage. Should you pay any attention to such questions? Obviously the local reputation of the dealer's repair department is an overriding consideration. But if you do not know the people you're dealing with, remember that guarantees and warranties are usually intended to protect the company which manufactures the appliance, not you. They promise to "replace defective parts" or something like that, but they protect the company from any other liability. So you will probably not only have to pay for shipping your appliance to the factory but also for the work of replacing the defective part. This usually costs far more than the part itself.

Second, a guarantee is only as strong as you are in enforcing it. If the manufacturer is two thousand miles away, you don't have any real chance. The local dealer will often disclaim any responsibility, unless you are a steady customer or look like you can cause real legal trouble. The Better Business Bureau, which is a kind of mutual-defense-league of local businesses, will tell you that all their members are respectable firms who always treat their customers fairly, and that they're sure nothing is wrong. Your only recourse, therefore, except in rare cases where you might sue in small claims court, is public exposure, and you don't have much chance of that unless your local paper carries a public-service feature. (Even some quite reactionary papers have daily columns in which readers can complain about unjust treatment from companies or government offices. The paper contacts the offending parties, and the threat of publicity usually gets justice done. Such columns are valuable even though they can handle only a small proportion of the fraud and injustice perpetrated on people. Try to get your local paper to set up such a column. They probably won't do it, but you'll have some fun hearing the excuses why they can't.)

If you are thinking of buying some appliance new—like a washer or refrigerator—you should consider Sears or Montgomery Ward. They maintain their own repair and service departments, and many people give good reports about their handling of breakdowns during the guarantee period.

But, in general, you had better not put much confidence in guarantees and warranties. The only case where it's worth time and money threatening or bringing legal action to enforce your warranty is with new cars—and no person trying to live in an ecologically responsible way should buy a new car except in very special circumstances. (See AUTOMOBILES, ALTERNATIVES TO.)

Modern manufacturers take a great deal of trouble to make sure that things don't last too long, so you can count on breakdowns. Insist on a dated sales slip with any appliance you buy new and keep it with the guarantee paper (or send in the guarantee postcard as directed). Then if trouble occurs within the supposed guarantee period, it can't hurt to check with the dealer. If the dealer follows the letter of the guarantee, you'll find that the defective part may cost $5, which the manufacturer pays, but you'll be stuck with the labor charges, which somehow come to $35. Unless you're in a small town where a dealer's reputation will suffer, many a dealer will not be co-operative even in replacing the part.

Whenever you buy an appliance, new or secondhand, insist that its serial number be written down on the sales receipt. Otherwise the store may deliver another model, an older or defective one, etc., and without the serial number to prove your point, no lawyer can help you get your money back.

In recent years (after a long history of unconscionable neglect) the federal government has taken some fitful steps toward promoting safety in consumer products, including appliances. While the government still probably spends a thousand dollars in subsidies for manufacturers for each dollar it spends protecting us from mis-designed and defective products, this new development is cheering. It was the Consumer Products Safety Commission that finally recalled the Firestone "500" radial tire and that forced manufacturers to stop putting asbestos in hair dryers (which blew the carcinogenic particles out into people's faces). If you have a question about some product, their toll-free number is 800-638-2666.

Appliances are, unfortunately, still being designed so that repairability by the user is made very difficult. One sensible criterion for whether to buy something is whether it looks like you could get in to see what's wrong if it develops trouble.

APPLIANCES, ELECTRICAL REPAIRS

Many simple devices like hot plates, waffle irons, toasters, hand irons, and hair dryers are basically just heating coils (or strips) in some kind of a case. They have a thermostat to keep them from getting overheated. Hair dryers and room heaters also have a fan to circulate the air they warm. Aside from cord trouble, the most common problem with these appliances is a break in the heating element. Over the years the heating coils or strips literally evaporate; also they get more brittle, and a jolt may finally break them so the current can't pass anymore.

To deal with these devices, first check the prongs on the plug and the cord to see that the wire is OK. Also check to make sure there is current in the receptacle you're using. A simple test is to plug the appliance into some other outlet.

If you have to open it up, be sure the appliance is unplugged. Sometimes the screws are visible. Sometimes some of them are under the nameplate or handle, which comes loose. Once it's open, shake it and look for places where the heating elements seem loose. They may also be loose at the terminals. You can reconnect broken ends by twisting them around each other firmly and squeezing with a pliers. (Make sure the twisted ends don't touch the metal case, or they'll short-circuit and give somebody a nasty shock.) This procedure won't last as long as a new element—which an electric shop can probably sell you if you have the model number—but it doesn't cost anything.

Lamps and other non-heating type appliances have several things that may go wrong with them. In order of likelihood: plug not making contact in receptacle (bend prongs a little); cord broken (replace); bulb not touching bottom of socket (unscrew and pry up tab at bottom); switch broken (take apart and put in new one).

For some other appliance repair hints, see REPAIRS, HOME.

How Does It Work?, by Richard M. Koff. Signet, 1961.

APPRENTICESHIPS

Many highly skilled trades are still learned by apprenticeship—a system which goes back to the Middle Ages, when boys were legally "bound" to master goldsmiths or weavers or whatnot for the years it took them to learn the trade. Skilled workers make more money than semi-skilled, but the real advantage of learning a complex trade and becoming a printer, machinist, carpenter, plumber, auto mechanic, electrician, and so on is that you can then find work anytime, anyplace, in any town or city in the country. You are good at something; you have a union card to prove it; you can always find a job, even in a full-scale depression. But you are not compelled, like many white-collar workers, to work full-time all the time, or to be nervous about keeping a boss happy. Some jobs are partly seasonal, like construction carpentry. Others are short-term, and when a project is completed you can lay off for a while if you feel like it. Part-time work isn't easy to find, but if you're good, you can sometimes work that out too, in small auto shops or other independent operations.

As automation spreads, skilled workers are needed more, not less—to build and service the machines used by unskilled and semi-skilled workers. Skilled workers tend to get jobs with more variety and challenge. And if you move around on the job, as many repair crews do, you get a fair amount of down time when you can drink coffee and socialize. You have a strong union to back you up in disputes and protect wages and working conditions. (Many craft unions are racist, sexist, and undemocratic, but all are under strong pressure to take in minority apprentices and women and be open to new members generally for

public-relations reasons if nothing else, so it pays to keep pushing.)

Being an apprentice is not much different from holding a regular job. You work a full, eight-hour day, alongside experienced workers who are supposed to help you pick up on how to do things. You get paid much less than they do during your first six months or year, but it's still well above a subsistence wage; and after that (on a pre-arranged schedule) you get periodic raises until toward the end you are making nearly what they make. Some apprenticeships last two years, some last up to four; in printing some last six. You have to take night-school courses too, between two and six hours per week. In theory the contract obligates both you and the company to carry out the full program for the prescribed number of years, but in practice you can quit if you wish; the company, however, can be held to its obligation.

The country has a chronic shortage of skilled workers, but there are less than 260,000 apprenticeships, and they are hard to get. The biggest apprenticeship possibilities are in the building trades. Neither the giant corporations nor unions have traditionally put much energy into apprenticeships. The companies often prefer to train semi-skilled people to run just their own machines at lower wages than an all-around skilled worker would earn; and the unions often prefer to keep down the number of members so that high wages can be secured. (In some corrupt unions you have literally had to be somebody's relative in order to get apprenticed!)

Apprenticeships are generally set up by a company-union agreement, and there is an actual contract that both sign, together with the apprentice (and the parents if the apprentice is a minor). To apply for an apprenticeship, you should first collect a number of character-reference letters, including at least one from a union member (more if possible). The best way to be sure of getting into an apprenticeship program is to have friends on the union committee, so it pays to do a lot of preparatory sniffing around to meet the right people. You should have finished high school, or at least two years of it; and you should be in good physical condition. Generally aptitude tests and a physical exam are required; many trades also require good school grades, since "working with your hands" takes more intelligence than many white-collar jobs. Age is not necessarily a barrier; some trades will accept you over twenty-four.

There are some fake "apprenticeships" set up by companies to get young people to work for low

One of the many small, decentralized apprentice shops in Ecotopia.

wages. States have apprenticeship agencies where you can check out a program, as does the US Department of Labor.

Information on apprentice programs in your area can be found at the state employment office.

ASPIRIN

Scientists don't yet understand how aspirin works, but it is the most widely used remedy for headaches, colds, and miscellaneous aches and pains. Buy the cheapest aspirin you can find, for there is absolutely no difference in brands—they are all the same substance, acetylsalicylic acid. To get the lowest price, buy the "house brand" in drugstores or supermarkets or health-plan pharmacies. Don't let brand names like Bayer's or Squibb's impress you. Aspirin is just aspirin, no matter what name it carries.

Many highly advertised and high-priced aspirin-based pills are around—Bufferin, Anacin, APC, and so on. They are all a waste of money. Some of them contain caffeine, some of them contain supposedly stomach-soothing drugs; but if you get sleepy from aspirins, have a cup of coffee; if they upset your stomach, try a glass of milk. (Milk is a good idea with aspirin anyway, because aspirin—especially when consumed with alcohol or citrus fruit juices—tends to make the stomach lining bleed slightly.)

Aspirins in large quantities are dangerous; they can be fatal to small children. Baby aspirins, which are flavored to make them appeal to young kids, usually come in tight safety-cap bottles which are hard for small fingers to open. But keep them locked up in a high cabinet anyway. (Along with all the other dangerous drugs and substances you have around.) Don't call them "candy" to get your kids to take them; they'll take them gladly, because they taste good. (A child who has swallowed a lot of aspirin needs prompt hospital attention.)

Don't over-rely on aspirins. If you find you're having persistent headaches or other aches, see a doctor. Some headaches come from temporary stresses, overtiredness, the coming on of a cold, or other temporary causes. But headaches can also come from eyestrain and serious threats to your health.

If you have had reactions to aspirin, there are alternatives called acetaminophens (such as Tylenol); they're expensive, but easier on your stomach.

AUCTIONS

If you are immune to crowd psychology, auctions can be a good source for furniture, rugs, clothes, books, and other things "too numerous to mention," as the traditional auction notices say. But you really need to know what you're doing—if you're easily stampeded, you can find yourself paying more for something than it costs new. In many cities permanent auction houses sell furniture and household goods weekly or even more frequently; occasional or weekend country auctions can be found too. Both types are listed in the classified ads of the paper. You can go around beforehand, look at the goods, and find out approximately when they will come up for bids. Then check a Sears catalog to make sure you know what a fair price is. Your game at auctions is to bid only on things you want, and to set a top limit for anything you want to bid on beforehand. I have attended auctions where bidders go completely crazy and bid up an old bicycle that isn't worth ten bucks to $50. On the other hand, working refrigerators may go for $20. But on the whole, auctions are far more time-consuming than secondhand stores. The lure, of course, is that you might turn up something exquisite at a reasonable price (if the antique dealers don't outbid you).

The dedicated auction-goer develops a fine feel for the bidding—when it is petering out, when it will go hopelessly higher, when you are bidding against a determined professional who may have a rich customer lined up, when you are bidding on a piece of junk that nobody else wants, and when somebody is bidding against you (a friend of the auctioneer?) just to push the price up.

AUTOMOBILES, ALTERNATIVES TO

The automobile was invented as a mechanical replacement for the horse and carriage. It introduced a degree of freedom of movement unprecedented in human history, and set in motion a profound transformation of our society. But the car, delightful as it might have been in a nineteenth-century land of wide open spaces, is really not appropriate for urban living patterns. It is, in fact, in that class of things known as "positional goods": things that are undeniably good to have, but only so long as only a few other people have them too; if they're too common, they interfere with everybody's enjoyment.

At present, so over-run is our nation with automobiles, we devote more than one-eighth of our total wealth to building, operating, maintaining, and policing them. Cars kill a half million of us every decade, choke the survivors with toxic smog, and wreck our cities as healthy and safe habitats for people. Reliance on an auto system of transport in a modern metropolis is biologically insane in a quite literal sense. We need a whole range of developed alternatives, and we need them fast: interurban rail and streetcar lines, rapid and frequent bus service, better taxis, a vast network of carpools. As individuals, we need to work out for ourselves non-car methods of getting around: BICYCLES, WALKING, use of existing PUBLIC TRANSIT. As citizens acting politically, we must confine and roll back the cancerous growth of the automobile system. Instead of spending vast sums from the public treasury to make life easier for automobiles and harder for pedestrians, we should reverse the process. Turn parking lots into parks with bicycle paths. Make streets narrower and curvier, or only allow buses and taxis to use them. Encourage zoning changes that integrate living, shopping, and working places into closer proximity, so cars aren't necessary to move from one to another. The outcome of our struggle with automobiles will be critical for our national survival. It's them or us.

American auto-makers have been slow and incompetent in designing light, energy-efficient cars to compete with such foreign makes as the Honda (whose small and inherently pollution-minimizing "stratified charge" engine gave it a substantial advantage in the late 70's over cars requiring catalysts or other complex pollution-control devices). During the 80's, we can expect a slow improvement as Detroit learns to build small cars that are competitive and durable. However, no improvements can ultimately save the automobile as our principal mode of transport. It is simply too expensive, in money and energy, to build and operate, and its subsidiary hidden costs are insuperable. Someday, looking back on the curious era from about 1910 to about 1990 in which the automobile rampaged over the American landscape, destroying or transforming everything

Photo of one of the more "ancient" Ecotopian alternatives to cars. It's not exactly mass rail transit, but it worked.

in its path, we will see the auto as a kind of metal dinosaur that reigned, briefly and inexplicably, and then vanished into the auto graveyards—the fossil pits in which future anthropologists will seek the secrets of our strange way of life.

Autokind vs. Mankind, by Kenneth R. Schneider. Schocken, 1971.

AUTOMOBILES, COSTS OF

Few of us realize it, since car expenses are spread out over time, but even in 1978 the average driver spent fully *one-quarter* of the average national per capita income on cars and trucks—and that was before the second gas crisis. Substantial numbers of us spend more on our cars than on either food or shelter. And under the battering of higher fuel and oil prices, higher interest rates, higher insurance premiums, and costlier maintenance, outlays on cars will be even more punishing through the 80's. To get a realistic idea of your own existing or future car expenses, run through the following list.

Initial cost. Even if you got a car free as a gift, it would cost huge sums to operate. And you must think of the purchase price in two ways to be economically realistic: first, if you borrow the money, add on the interest to the original price of the car; second, consider that the money you are putting into the car (as down payment or total payment) could also be sitting in a bank earning interest, whereas if you put it into the car it immediately begins to "depreciate." (Because of depreciation, as well as to minimize risk of a new car turning out to be a lemon, you should plan to keep a new car for around 100,000 miles. It is also the depreciation factor that makes it generally more economical to buy a used car, so long as you check it over thoroughly.) You need to think of a car's cost in terms of cost per person per mile. If you want a car for a carpool, a comfortable large car may actually be more economical than a four-person car, especially as the big gas hogs are now in oversupply since gas prices began to skyrocket, and you may find a used one really cheap.

Insurance. In most major cities these days, your insurance bill will run almost as much as the average cost per month of lifetime of the car itself. This is true even if you have an old clunker and carry nothing but the liability many state laws now sensibly require.

Repairs. You can't ignore these, though they're erratic. They certainly cost you more than gas, oil, and tires. And some, like regular tune-ups, are essential to avoid spending even more on gas. You'll go a couple of months without spending anything, but then you'll come to a job that'll eat up a hundred bucks. (If you can do your own work, of course, you can cut down such expenses by maybe half. But don't kid yourself if you're not an experienced mechanic.)

Gas and oil. People who have cars drive around a surprising amount—they tend to put in at least ten thousand miles a year. At current prices, this can mean a great deal of money; figure your expenses out on a monthly or yearly basis. (With recurring gas shortages, of course, the more you drive, the more time you will spend in gas lines too.) You can cut gas consumption by driving at lower speeds, avoiding or turning off air conditioners, cutting out unnecessary short trips, accelerating gently, and not idling the engine for more than a minute if you have the choice of turning it off.

Licenses and fees. Even if your car is so old it's down to the minimum rate, they cost you something. Your driver's license has to be renewed periodically. Then there are the little things: parking meters (and parking tickets), bridge and highway tolls, parking-lot fees. You may also have things stolen from your car (car thieves can open a locked car in about fifteen seconds) and, of course, the car itself could disappear. Or vandals may crack windows, tear off the radio antenna, remove hubcaps, or steal tires. You can insure against such losses (or take them off your income tax as a deduction) but you can't escape the aggravation.

The minimum operating costs of a car are thus probably considerably more than you suspected. On the average, our country spends about one-eighth of our total national income on automobiles (counting the costs of streets, highways, police, courts, jails, etc., along with your personal costs).

In fact, according to a fascinating calculation first made by Ivan Illich, if you total up the time you spend earning the money needed to run your car, and divide that into the miles you drive it, your *real* average speed is only about five miles per hour—jogging speed! The reverse side of this calculation, of course, is that by finding alternate and cheaper ways of getting around, you can liberate the time you now devote to earning money to support your car.

In the past, not having a car has tended to make one appear odd to others. The entire American landscape has been transformed, over the past 50 years, for the convenience of cars. There are even parts of Houston, Texas, that have no sidewalks, only auto rights-of-way. Two-thirds of the land area of downtown Los Angeles is concreted over for highways, streets, and parking—and all of our cities have been to some extent Los Angelized. But in the future, those who escape dependence on cars will be in the forefront of a national trend and will save themselves a lot of money besides. And when we can stop the government from spending billions of our dollars to subsidize the auto and highway construction industries, we will take a big step toward both energy and money saving on a national scale as well.

AUTOMOBILES, ENGINES OF

A car is not complicated as modern machines go. Moreover, car engineering and design have moved with astounding slowness, considering all the fuss made yearly about "new" features. In reality the current stick-shift car is the same machine as Henry Ford's Model A, except that it's bigger, more powerful, and extremely more expensive. All its major components are the same, though in a front-wheel-drive vehicle or a rear-engine vehicle a few of them are arranged differently.

Here are the basic parts:

The heart of the thing is of course the motor (1). Inside it, rapid explosions made by a gas + air mixture drive pistons back and forth. The engine gets its air + gas mixture from the carburetor (2). The carburetor gets gas from the fuel pump (3); it sucks in air from the outside. Because the engine makes a great deal of heat as it works, it needs a radiator (4) to get rid of the heat. To start, the engine is cranked by the starting motor (5), which draws electric power from the battery (6).

Cars use electricity for several other purposes besides lights. The explosions inside the engine are triggered by spark plugs; their current comes from the coil and distributor (7), which get it from the battery when you are starting the car; after the car is running, the generator (8) makes electricity for the plugs and also recharges the battery—which gets a little run down by the effort of starting the motor. The motor's energy gets to the wheels through the transmission (9), which is a box full of gears controlled by the gear-shift lever (or automatically in automatic-transmission cars). From the transmission, power is carried back to the rear end, sometimes called the differential, a set of gears which turns the wheels. (Front-wheel-drive cars and rear-engine cars transmit power directly from the transmission to the wheels.)

That's basically all there is to cars, except for the brakes, which are a separate system from the motor.

You should also know that the engine, transmission, and differential contain oil, to keep the parts from heating up and wearing out. The dipstick which the gas-station attendant shows you indicates whether the engine oil is at its proper level.

AUTOMOBILES, HAZARDS OF

The automobile is a deathtrap. It kills more than fifty thousand Americans each year. It injures and maims millions more. Clearly Detroit doesn't seem to care, for it continues to design cars putting profit ahead of every other consideration. (Ford, for example, used $200,000 as the value of each of the lives lost by its refusing to redesign the Pinto's lethal rear-end gas tank—apparently because that's the average they expected to lose in suits by survivors. The cost was not great enough to cause them to modify the cars.) Sit down in a car sometime and look around at the knobs, levers, bulges, and sharp edges. If you have an accident even at a "low" speed such as twenty-five miles per hour, you'll be flung into them just as hard as if you belly-flopped onto them from a building two stories high.

Does your car have tinted glass, which dangerously cuts down nighttime vision? Does it have overloaded tires, put on by irresponsible manufacturers who know that small, low-pressure tires may be overloaded even when the car has only a couple of passengers in it? Does it have an enameled top over the dashboard, causing a distracting curtain of glare on the inside of the windshield? Does it have a steering column that will stab you if you hit something solid? Does it have doors that are likely to fly open in case of even a "small accident," allowing you to be thrown out and possibly run over by your own or another car? Does it have head- and taillights which are invisible from the side? Something like three-quarters of the cars now on the road are defective in most of these ways, and more. Half of them will—before they reach the junkyard—be involved in accidents in which people are killed or maimed. If you own a car for very long, the chances are that you will find yourself in one of these accidents. And so numb have we become to the slaughter caused by cars that the killing of a pedestrian is not even manslaughter (much less murder) unless the driver was unusually and obviously negligent.

The typical new car has compulsory seat belts, which if used would save the lives of about two-thirds of the people who are killed in crashes. It has a padded dashboard, recessed instrument knobs, non-chrome wipers, and a few other safety improvements. But the car is still a deathtrap, and the automobile transportation system contains routinely accepted hazards far greater than we or our government would ever tolerate on airplanes or trains. If you drive, you take your life in your own hands—and also put it in the hands of negligent manufacturers, incompetent repair shops, profit-greedy dealers, and other drivers who may be drunk, overtired, drowsy on barbiturates, or venting some emotional crisis by "driving it off."

Ralph Nader, who probably knows more about auto safety than anybody outside the companies' research labs (and they aren't talking), does not drive a car. If you do drive, be especially careful in rural areas, where ambulances and other medical facilities are in short supply; you are four times more likely to die from a rural accident than from an urban one.

AUTOMOBILES, MAINTENANCE OF

Anyone wanting to work on his or her own car should get the shop manual for it, not just the owner's manual. (Sears sells them if you can't find one free somewhere.) Cultivate friends who are good with cars; help them out and see what you can learn from them. If you know somebody who has the same make of car you do, hang around and find out how he or she manages, what tricks he or she has learned. Or if you're still in school, take a course in auto shop. No matter what kind of life you end up living, you'll probably have to cope with cars sometime or other; so be prepared!

Gas. Fuel costs are a small component of the

overall costs of running a car, unless you drive a great deal. For ecological reasons, you should try to cut down on your driving. (See CARPOOLS, BICYCLES, PUBLIC TRANSPORTATION, WALKING.) But there are a few other ways you can cut your costs. First, buy a car that burns regular, not premium (ethyl) as regular gas causes less lead pollution than premium. Some old cars that originally needed ethyl will run on regular. (One reason to buy old cars is that they did not require costlier, and sometimes scarce, low-lead gas. But they cause more lead pollution of the atmosphere.) Four-cylinder cars burn less gas per mile than sixes or eights (engine work costs a lot less too). Buy your gas at a co-op station if you can find one; the price will be several cents a gallon lower. Or try to find out the sources of the off-brands in your area. Some of these are really regular-brand gas under another label, like Wilshire (Gulf), Seaside (Tidewater), Canfield and Fleet-Wing (Standard). When you switch brands, try to get about the same octane rating as you've been using; using higher-rated gas will waste money. But watch out for gas from small refiners; sometimes it's OK, but sometimes it may gum up your engine.

The smaller, lighter, and more streamlined a car, the less gas it will use. So don't carry around a lot of heavy stuff, and avoid roof racks, whose air resistance takes a heavy mileage toll. Air conditioners cut mileage about 15%; either disconnect yours or avoid using it.

If you live on something you can officially call a "farm," or if you own a boat, you can buy gas for non-road purposes and thus escape paying that part of the price which goes to taxes for highways and roads. The ideal situation is to have your own buried gas tank and private pump, as many old farms do; then you can get one of the local oil distributors to come around and fill it up from time to time, at a price considerably lower than you pay in gas stations. When you buy gas and put it in your boat at a marine fueling station, you get a receipt which you turn in as part of your income tax and get a refund. It is, of course, illegal to siphon gas out and put it in your car (it is also illegal for the oil companies to do some of the things they do). If you do siphon gas, for this purpose or in emergencies, use a pump, not your lungs, to get the siphon action started; many people don't realize that gas is a toxic substance (as well as tasting horrible!)

In recent years, cars with diesel engines have become common. These get considerably better mileage than gasoline-powered cars, and at one time diesel fuel was much cheaper than gas. The price advantage has diminished steadily, however. It has also been discovered that diesel exhausts, though they contain less smog-producing pollutants, have more fine particulate matter in them, which is cancer-causing; in time, therefore, diesels will probably have to be controlled in some way.

If you happen to live within easy distance of the Mexican border, you can obtain both regular and diesel fuel from the nationalized Mexican oil system for much less than we have to pay American oil companies. (It is usually desirable to buy premium gas in order to match the octane ratings of American regular.) The political lesson, of course, is that we could enjoy those lower prices too, if we followed the Mexican lead and nationalized *our* oil companies.

Tune-Ups. Regular tuning-up of your engine will increase gas mileage about 10%, and as gas prices rise this will be more and more worthwhile. Checking and, when necessary, replacing spark plugs and distributor points (like much other minor routine maintenance) is easy to learn; get a friend to show you how. You can also easily clean or replace dirty air filters, and replace oil filters. Adjusting carburetors takes some skill, as does setting the engine's timing, but millions of drivers do it themselves, and so can you.

Driving habits. You can save a lot of gas (and aggravation) by avoiding stop-and-go traffic. Aim to keep your speed steady—no jackrabbit starts, no sudden braking. Avoid unnecessary idling. Keep your top speed down to 55; beyond that, pushing air out of the way consumes extra energy and your mileage plummets. Don't open windows unnecessarily; it creates drag and cuts mileage, sometimes as much as an air conditioner does.

Oil. Unless your car is already burning considerable amounts, it is worth spending a little more to get good oil as this is what keeps the engine from wearing itself out. It's also worth it to change the filter. Ironically, the short-trip driving done by most cars is absolutely the worst way to treat an internal-combustion engine. Oil doesn't lubricate well until the engine is really hot—which takes up to half an hour, and many town-driving trips are only ten minutes long. Heat-control valves and automatic chokes tend to get stuck (experts estimate that half the heat-rise valves on all US cars are out of order). This increases the tendency of old engines to drip gas down into the crankcase where it dilutes the oil and forms corrosive acids. Cold engines also give lower mileage. We will never get free of these inherent drawbacks until electric or other motor systems are adopted, at least for city driving.

Engine wear will be cut down if you use "multigrade" oil. These are marked "10-30W," etc. They lubricate better in cold engines, still work in hot ones, and don't congeal too badly in cold weather. If you have a fairly new car, "extended service" oil is required when you're only supposed to change oil every six thousand miles. (If you read nothing else in your car-owner's booklet, read the section on lubrication and oil changing; it may double the lifetime of the car.)

Standard oils today contain many substances intended to control gumming, foaming, acid formation, and so on. Stay away from other additives and from stuff you add to the gas—they **won't save as much as they cost you. Re-used oil, which lubricates even better than new oil but has** lost its additives, used to be cheap and easily available (it was standard for the army). Now **drained oil is no longer recycled and filtered, so it is** practically impossible to find re-used oil, either for cars or other machinery. This situation is both a technological and ecological absurdity.

Various novelty oils have been introduced in recent years, and may increase your mileage very slightly (though not as much as buying radial tires). There is even a very high quality oil made **from vegetable sources; as petroleum gets scarcer** such oils will doubtless become more common.

Tires. Most of the small amount of innovation in the auto industry in the last thirty years has come from European research. Radial, steel-cord tires were in use in Europe for some twenty years before finally reaching us. These tires last about twice as long as nylon or rayon tires. They hold the road better in turns, they are more resistant to heavy impacts, and since they are tube tires they do not suffer "air-outs" if a tire tucks under in a crash turn, and because they take low air pressure they have a large "foot-print" to hold better on the road. (Do not mix radials and bias-ply tires on your car or handling instability will result.) Radials also roll easier and can thus give you several miles more to the gallon. Their disadvantages are that they cost more (though not twice as much) and that they make a little louder hum on the road. Because of these terrible drawbacks, supposedly, the American auto and tire industries kept them from us for two decades! Instead we were and are still offered the standard rayon tires, nylon tires which develop annoying flat spots at night, and fiber-glass tires.

Tire selling is a jungle operation. The Firestone Company went blithely on selling its "500" tires in massive quantities long after they were known to be defective, and small operations have no better standards. Whether you're an expert or an amateur, it is entirely impossible to tell what kind of a tire you are buying by the name and price. **Until strong government standards are enforced,** the only sane procedure is to buy tires at Sears or Montgomery Ward—dependable sources with straightforward descriptions in their catalogs. Pay no attention to labels like "premium," "first-line," and so on. These are just words; one brand's premium tire may be another brand's cast-off third-quality tire.

Most people on a low budget will put retread tires ("recap" is the better term) on their cars. A recap should run almost as long as a new tire before it wears out, but it costs only half to two-thirds as much. Buy recaps only through a mechanic or shop you trust; cheap recaps tend to wear rapidly, **may throw off the new rubber entirely, and can** otherwise cause trouble. A good recapping house will give you a written guarantee, usually for something like ten thousand miles.

Tires wear a little differently on different wheels, so rotating them is often recommended. This is a waste of money unless you do it yourself, because switching costs more than you save in rubber. (Don't rotate a new spare—save it so you'll only need three new tires.) If you notice one tire wearing badly, it might be worth the expense needed to realign the wheel—but you might be better off just to let it wear. New tires also need to be balanced, since they are often a bit heavier on one side and may cause an annoying bump-bump-bump as well as spotty tire wear.

AUTOMOBILES, PURCHASING OF

For many people, emotional and status factors are the critical determinants of what kind of car they buy. Under the impact of rising gas prices and other operating costs, however, this will **increasingly be a luxury. Already, EPA** mileage-per-gallon ratings constitute an important consideration for many buyers. (You will *never*, incidentally, be able to achieve the EPA figures, which are obtained under extremely favorable test conditions and by highly trained drivers; and even if you did, the high price of a new car obliterates its potential savings on gas, even at $2 a gallon.) Minimization of lubrication and other servicing requirements is also a selling point many people find important—though this is a two-edged "improvement" as it often leads to infrequent checks of the car's operating components, especially when self-service gas stations prevail, so that many people seldom look under the hood for months on end. You should **make a point of checking battery water level, oil** level, tire pressure, and the fan belt once a month. It's also important to wash your windshield and rear window; night glare contributes to many serious accidents.

Before you get close to buying any car, go to your local public library and study the ratings of both new and used cars in *Consumer Reports*. No matter what decision you finally make, you will learn a lot by doing so. Talk to friends who have cars of the kinds you're thinking of, especially about their service problems; the availability of good and reasonably priced service is probably the single most important factor in owning any car. (An experienced and trustworthy neighborhood **mechanic with low overhead is the ideal.**)

If you have learned how to give a car a thorough checking over, and utilize a mechanic to diagnose its engine, brakes, etc., you will always be wisest to buy used cars, and from private parties. Unstylish though it may be, a small, clean, American used car, bought after careful inspection by someone more knowledgeable than your friends, will give you the most transportation for your money, and the least aggravation about repair frequency and adequacy.

Buying a car from a dealer is like wading through a swamp full of crocodiles: some of them (the big new-car dealers) are fat and a little lazy, but they can still bite your leg off; the smaller, hungrier ones (the used-car dealers) will chase you over a three-foot wall. (See USED CARS for a checklist of things to be careful about.) Here are some auto sales tricks.

The bait and switch, commonly used in TV, radio, and other commercials, is luring the customer in with a very attractive low-priced deal that's really unheard-of—like a practically new car for half its original price. When you get to the **lot, the salesman or saleswoman confidentially** tells you that you can have it for that price, of course, but the block is cracked and the front suspension was wrecked in a crash. But over there in the corner is a real deal....

Inflated, fake asking prices are commonplace in selling practically everything, but because so much more money is involved in cars, they're more likely to impress you. The dealer simply puts a price on a car that's a couple of hundred dollars more than he expects to get for it. Unless you've been studying the *Blue Book* prices on cars, you may not know this—and when the salesperson tells you he or she can knock off $150, you may think it's a big favor. **You should never buy any used car without** checking the book (*Blue, Red*, etc.) price on it. **Don't just peer over the salesperson's shoulder** either: get a friend or service-station attendant to let you look at a copy—or try the library—so you can be sure you're looking in the right place and know what the numbers mean. Both "high" (retail) and "low" (wholesale) prices are given and assume that a car is in good saleable condition.

Although theoretically new-car prices are firmly fixed, in reality they're inflated prices too, partly because the manufacturers post inflated tickets, and partly because the dealer (unlike many used-car lots) will take your old car in trade. (It would be absurd to pay the ticket price for any new car.) But **then the amount of "discount" or allowance the dealer gives you on your trade-in is only one part of the calculations. Therefore, different dealers will give** you different prices on new cars, and it pays to shop around; you may save several hundred dollars, except on very popular foreign cars that are in limited supply.

Once in a while, a dealer will actually sell a new car at near cost—to win a bonus from the manufacturer, to meet pressing debts, or because financing the deal will bring a kickback on the financing. But auto selling is not an occupation which naturally develops one's generosity. Most "bargain" deals should be handled only with a forked stick, like a rattlesnake. The only ones I would trust are from co-ops, which can sometimes get you a new car for only a little more than the "official" (and probably fake) wholesale price.

Much of the trickery of car selling comes out in the paperwork. The salesperson will make you some deal on a scratch pad and then go in "to sell it to the manager." Well, it turns out the manager makes a few little changes which the salesperson **passes off as unimportant—but the contract is put** in front of you to sign anyway. The salesperson will try to pretend to be your friend; the manager is the creep. This version of the old one-two game can get quite complicated. Maybe the manager will even come out and "let" the salesperson beat him down to your price, in return for some slight changes in the financing—which, it turns out later, will cost you several hundred dollars extra.

Bushing is when the salesperson dickers with you, agrees on a price, and then before you sign writes a higher price into the contract without your noticing it. Make sure you look at the written price and make sure all blanks on the contract are filled in or X'd out—especially the trade-in allowance. The contract should also include all the extras, services, and repairs the dealer promises to make, spell out the guarantee if there is one, and contain all other elements of the deal. Anything not written in the contract is just hot air.

The highball is when the salesperson gives you a phenomenally generous trade-in allowance, gets you drooling over the good deal you're getting, and then suddenly notices a mistake. By that time, probably you're so set on the new car that you won't back out or will accept a lower trade-in allowance. Oddly enough, lots of people will fall for this, losing hundreds of dollars by a moment of confusion and hesitation.

The lowball is the same trick but working from the price—offering you a car at a very low price, and then at the last moment substituting a higher price.

Salespeople will try to discourage you from road-testing a car. In two-thirds of car sales they get away with this, ridiculous as it may seem. Any car you're discouraged from testing is probably a turkey. Don't even look at it.

Big dealers will often offer a guarantee of some kind (thirty or ninety days) on used cars. This means little unless they are also new-car dealers with their own shop where they can actually have your car repaired—usually not very speedily—when something goes wrong.

Whenever salespeople ask you to sign something, you can be sure it is some kind of contract, no matter what it may be called. Otherwise there would be no reason for needing your signature. Read the contract; get a cup of coffee from the machine, sit down, and tell them you'll see them in fifteen minutes. If they get to putting on the pressure, tell them you want to take it home and study it, or show it to your sister-in-law who's a lawyer.

The contract must contain the serial number and motor number of the car, and you should insist on comparing these with the actual numbers on the car before you sign. Not having these exactly right can cause you lots of legal trouble later and maybe even loss of the car, or you might not be able to get it registered. (Even a fancy-looking car can have a stolen engine put into it.)

There are dealers who will fiddle with a car after you've signed the contract but haven't yet picked the car up. They'll put on worn tires, switch to an older battery, even pull out a radio or other accessories. If you suspect you're dealing with a real crook, make a list of the tire numbers and note down all other equipment, so they realize you're prepared for trouble.

Cherries and Lemons: The Used Car Buyer's Handbook, by Joe Troise. And Books, 702 S. Michigan, South Bend, IN 46618.

AUTOMOBILES, REPAIRING OF

The going prices for auto repairs, especially in established dealerships, have become so astronomical that once a car is out of warranty it is essential to find a good independent mechanic to work on it. But you can also gain skill at diagnosing what is wrong with your car, and you can learn how to fix common small troubles that require no special skills or expensive equipment. Many evening schools now offer do-it-yourself auto-repair courses, some of them especially set up for women. (People who don't understand the fundamentals of cars are easy marks for unscrupulous repair shops.)

Any car needs a tool kit, but an old car even more. You should carry, besides the usual tire-changing tools and flashlight-pliers-screwdriver, several items that will often be useful: a pair of jumper cables to start your own or other people's cars, a piece of three-quarter- or one-inch rope to use in towing, a tarp, some old gloves for working in cold weather, some electrical wire and tape, and a set of extra fuses. Also some road flares to lay out in case of accidents, an eight-foot piece of clear plastic tubing with a squeeze pump to siphon gas and some kind of can to catch it in, miscellaneous old ropes for tying on cargo too big to fit inside, an old windshield-wiper blade for cleaning off dew, and a scrap of rigid sheet plastic for scraping off frost and snow without scratching the glass. If you live in snowy country, you'll also need chains and an old shovel for digging yourself out. Acquiring these will obviously take some money—another seldom-remembered expense of owning a car.

The best way to learn how to do minor repairs and maintenance is to work along with friends who have the same make or a similar car. But you can also get a repair manual from the library which will explain many repair operations, both generally and specifically, for most common cars. You should periodically replace spark plugs and clean and gap them in between changes; this is easy to do. Fixing worn wiring and fixing leaky water hoses are other common, easy jobs. You can change the oil if you have a way of disposing of the old oil without causing pollution; you can use a hand grease gun to lubricate some cars. If you have **generator trouble, you can pull it out and take it to** a generator shop for rebuilding. When switches go **bad, brake cables need tightening, or taillight glass** gets broken, you can almost always cope. And once you get used to working on your own car, you will probably gradually get more confident and skillful until you are doing everything but major motor work. And even that is within the competence of the ordinary person if you study the relevant manuals carefully, get any necessary machine-shop work done by a capable outfit, and have good general tool skills. It is a wonderful feeling to have torn down your motor and rebuilt it: now you *really* know what makes it go!

In driving around in a car you need to be able to tell whether it's running all right. Here are some common, obvious danger signals and what they mean.

Heavy, thumping noise; car may also bump up and down. A tire has probably gone flat or blown out. Don't brake suddenly; slow down and then pull over as far off the road as possible. Stop at a level place where the tire can be reached for changing. Open the hood, which is a sign you need help. Driving on a flat tire will ruin it and may damage the wheel rims as well.

Grinding noises, especially when you shift gears. Something is giving way in the transmission. If the car will run without making a really awful noise, put it in second and drive slowly and carefully to your repair shop.

Weak turning over, then nothing, when you try to start motor. Battery is probably "dead" (run down), unless wires are loose or broken. However, this does not usually mean you need a new battery. If a battery runs down because of a short or because the headlights were left on, it will usually work fine once it's charged up again (and any shorts fixed). A dead battery can usually be charged up **temporarily in any service station, and this should** get you home to a trusted mechanic. (Try never to have anything serious done to your car on the road—use makeshifts and stopgaps to get it back home to someone you know.) Stick-shift cars with weak batteries can be parked on hills where you can coast down a bit to start them; this may stretch an old battery's life a couple of months. But prepare yourself for the shock of buying a new one. If you like to keep old cars around, a cheap battery charger is a handy thing to have.

Steam coming out of hood when you stop; *probably hissing noise too.* The engine radiator water is boiling over. Drive into the first gas station. Keep the motor running and drive to the water hose. Open the hood carefully, and uncap the radiator *only* with a heavy rag protecting your hand and with your face turned away. Then very slowly run cold water into the radiator until the motor cools down.

Motors overheat for two main reasons: the **cooling system is clogged or it has a leak. (Some** heavy new American cars boil over simply from going up long steep mountain grades.) Incidentally, if the steam appears to stop before you get to a station, it may just be blowing away before you can see it. You need more water anyhow.

Brake pedal goes down slowly to floor when you push it. You've got a defective master cylinder in your brake system. Sometimes pumping the pedal will give you more braking power temporarily, but get it fixed right away; defective brakes cause many accidents. Often, especially if you're on the road, **you can get a gas station to fill up the brake-fluid** reservoir, and then you can limp home, pumping the pedal when you brake—but drive cautiously, and use the engine to slow down (by downshifting) as much as possible.

Brake pedal goes quickly down to floor. Your hydraulic brake system has failed completely, probably because of a bad leak. Instantly shift into the next lower gear, even if the gears clash as you do so (into "low" or "first" gear on automatic transmissions). The engine will then help you slow down. Try the emergency brake, but watch out, as it may make the car jerk or swerve. American cars really have parking brakes rather than emergency brakes, but they can save your life going down a hill if you use them. If this doesn't stop the car, and you're on a hill or about to hit people, run into a hedge or parked car or wall or small tree. It's better to ruin the car than kill yourself—or others—at the bottom of the hill!

Burning smell. This may be just the odor of air pollution, but it can also come from electrical wires heating up and burning their plastic or rubber covers. It can also come from leaving your hand brake on, or from tires which are badly out of alignment and twisting against the road as they turn. Stop and see if you can see the source of the smell. Hot wires need to be replaced promptly.

Smoke. If you smell or see smoke, stop and get out of the car immediately. Collected oil may be burning, or a gas leak may have caught fire. Unless you have a good fire extinguisher handy (*not* water) and really know what you are doing, get at least fifty feet away from the car. Don't go back till you're sure the fire, if there was one, has burned itself out.

Grinding, sandy noises, or a slight shimmy felt through steering wheel. These may indicate trouble in the bearings. Get a mechanic to listen.

Whining, shrieking sounds. These can come from fan-belt slippage, or from normal operation of some power-steering mechanisms.

Chattering of clutch when you start off. This may be annoying, but it doesn't hurt anything. Unless your clutch slips, which makes the car dangerous to drive, leave it alone.

If all this sounds like a lot to worry about, think again about whether you really need that car!

Parts. Every auto company spends a lot of money advertising that its parts are better than other companies' parts. This is a big joke at the customer's expense. Many parts in a car are manufactured by small feeder companies anyway—and the big companies seem to think they're all right then. With the exception of VW parts which are usually cheaper, it is a good rule never to buy "original" parts if you can help it. Parts for all US cars and for many foreign cars are available through Sears, Ward, and many small parts suppliers. In any case, make some phone calls before buying any parts—prices vary a lot.

Auto parts and accessories stores sell a lot of junky accessories, but their basic parts are pretty standard. If you know cars, you can save money by buying from wrecking yards, whose prices are usually just a shade under wholesale. They buy totaled-out cars, in which most of the parts are often perfectly sound and undamaged, for maybe a hundred dollars. Thus, although they're sharks and you have to know what you're doing, you can often get a good battery (take along a hydrometer to check it), radiator (make leak checks), tires, and specialized parts. However, wrecker prices on small parts are often more than from stores; anything that costs less than one or two dollars, buy new.

Collision repairs. One important reason to drive an old car is that you will not be motivated to spend large sums keeping it in mint body condition; if you collect some insurance when somebody hits you, you can hang onto the money.

Despite the great national campaign to strengthen bumpers against minor crashes, they are still very fragile. At the outset of the 80's, a 5-miles-per-hour angled crash into a barrier caused from $14 to $272 worth of damage; backing into a pole at 5 m.p.h. caused from $114 to $259 worth. A crash at 10 m.p.h. will totally ruin many cars from a safety standpoint and cause from $795 to $1036 worth of damage.

Finding a good, trustworthy mechanic is the single most important necessity when you own a car, especially an old one. Keep looking around. They do still exist. Ask all your car-owning friends.

When you're dealing with a mechanic you don't know well, be very careful. The auto-repair business is full of incompetents and swindlers who will "repair" things that have nothing wrong with them, damage things that were working OK, and charge you for things they didn't do. When you take your car in, get a work-order sheet filled out which says what is to be done. Never sign a blank order sheet, or you may find yourself paying for jobs you didn't want done. Ask beforehand how much a job will cost. Experienced mechanics have standard estimates for all common jobs and can tell you within a few dollars.

Try and find a mechanic who isn't a "rulebook mechanic" determined to put everything in factory-fresh shape. What you want is to keep the crate running at the minimum possible expense. You need a mechanic who is reliable, but who knows what is really necessary and what can be put off or not done at all.

If you have a serious disagreement with a mechanic about the work or the bill, you'll have to go to small claims court. Your state may have an agency intended to police abuses in auto-repair shops, and a complaint to them may solve your problem without your having to go to court. (It may also help to eliminate an incompetent or crooked mechanic.) There is also the federal toll-free number of the Bureau of Automotive Repair: 800-952-5210.

The Joy of Automobile Repair. Lancaster-Miller Publishers, 3165 Adeline, Berkeley, CA 94703.

A Women's Guide to the Care and Feeding of an Automobile, by Carmel Berman Reingold. Stein & Day, 1973.

B

BABY EQUIPMENT

There is no question that having children is expensive. But the amount of money spent for non-essentials, especially for babies, is staggering. Inexperienced parents who wander into a baby-supplies store are likely to come out with a ton of pink and blue junk that neither they nor the baby need. One of the great virtues of Dr. Spock's *Baby and Child Care* is that he explains inexpensive ways of providing for the essentials. And he points out some things salespeople try to push but you don't really need: pillows, booties, bath thermometers, and so on.

Here are the essentials:

Bed. Vaudeville family children slept in their parents' traveling trunks, but trunks and suitcases are only OK if they can't accidentally flop shut and suffocate the baby. Dresser drawers, big wood or cardboard boxes, and many other things will serve—all they really need is four sides and something soft but flat (not a regular pillow) on the bottom. Since being able to rock the baby helps when he or she is fussy, it's nice to suspend the sleeping place either by ropes or from some kind of bracket, like the beautiful old-fashioned cradles. And a simple cradle can be made out of any box by putting rocker pieces at each end. With any of these ideas, you can attach a string to the thing and run it over to your bed; many times a baby who wakes briefly can be lulled back to sleep with a few tugs on the string—without your ever getting up. Since getting enough sleep is the number one problem of new parents, such a device will richly repay the little trouble it takes to rig up.

Babies wet a lot, so their mattress needs covering with something totally waterproof. You can buy pieces of crib-size waterproof sheeting that has flannelette on both sides; it's washable, comfortable for the baby, and saves a lot of trouble. You also need some sheets (diapers will work fine when the baby is very small) and a couple of blankets. Make sure you have at least one very light blanket. Several light knitted or loosely woven layers are better than one deadweight heavy one.

Changing table. Since you'll be changing the baby's diapers constantly for something like two years or longer you need a changing surface that enables you to do it smoothly, efficiently, and safely. The best is a dresser that is kitchen-counter height; if it's table height, you have to sit down, which is awkward. The area should be big enough that an active older baby can't easily roll off of it. (All the same, you should never turn your back on any baby who can roll over, when you've laid him or her on such a raised surface.) Pad the top with rags or cotton batting, and tack a heavy plastic covering over the whole thing; on that, for comfort, you can lay a diaper or other washable cloth. Your supply of diapers and rubber pants should be stored right near the changing surface, along with other clothes. Make an out-of-reach place to lay the diaper pins while they're off the baby, so you don't panic when one disappears and you think it's been swallowed. Sticking them in a bar of soap keeps them in one place and makes the pins easier to slide through the fabric. Keep some cotton balls handy, for cleaning bottoms, and ointment for diaper rash, which most babies get sooner or later. The diaper pail should be next to the changing table; get a big one with a tight-fitting lid. (This is one case where plastic is best; urine is corrosive.)

Bathtub. A big dishpan makes an excellent bathtub, and you can use it on the changing table or on the kitchen counter. A kitchen sink and a washtub will also work fine. Keep the water slightly warm, not hot.

Clothes. In warm weather and in heated houses, babies don't really need much of a wardrobe. A couple of light shirts, a warm shirt or sweater, several sleeper coveralls (which come in terry cloth and can be worn day or night, leaving the child free to move but also warm), and maybe also some sleeping sacks (nightgowns that have closed bottoms, and are also good for going out in cold weather) are all you really need. But parents get a great deal of joy from dressing up their babies, and anything that leaves the baby free to move and not too hot will probably strike him or her as tolerable, and you as charming. A wool hat is a good idea for wearing outdoors in cold weather, since babies don't have much hair.

Transportation. Because your baby will go pretty much everywhere with you for the first months of life, you should pay a great deal of attention to how you plan to carry him or her around. If you live in a flat city area and have an elevator, a standard baby carriage may work fine. (The bigger the wheels, the easier to manage—try to find an elegant old-fashioned or foreign one.) If you plan to get into and out of cars or buses a lot, or have to go up and down stairs, a light, fold-up stroller is probably the best solution.

But maneuvering even a light stroller through doors and up steps is no fun, for either you or the baby. Many parents have begun adopting papoose-style carriers which strap on their backs like a campng pack. The baby sits there, looking around at the world, yet with the immediate comfort of the parent's contact and motions. (For babies who can't yet sit up enough for these carriers, there are belly-sling affairs which carry the baby right up against the parent's chest; these are especially convenient for the first months of nursing, since the baby is right at the mother's breast.) It takes a bit of practice to get used to carrying weight around, but if you like to be on the move and don't intend to let your baby tie you down, it's well worth it.

Young babies will usually sleep pretty much anywhere, but some parents like to get them in the habit of sleeping in some kind of car bed when they are out in the evening, or in a small sleeping bag. This also adds to your flexibility when children get older, because they will usually sleep happily anywhere, so long as they're in their familiar bag.

Miscellaneous. The first thing a doctor asks when you phone in about a sick baby is his or her temperature, so you need a rectal thermometer. You also need some cotton swabs for nose cleaning (babies don't learn to blow until after they can talk).

That's it, if you're breast-feeding. You need no bottles, sterilizers, warmers, nipples, bottle brushes, strainers, bottle caps, funnels, and so on. In fact, all you need is some vitamin drops which will be prescribed by your pediatrician. If you are nervous about weight gain, a scale is reassuring. Breast-fed babies normally gain more slowly than bottle-fed ones, and people may try to alarm you about this; make sure your doctor has plenty of experience with breast-feeding, because doctors unfamiliar with the process may lack necessary information and be unable to be supportive. If you need further support, advice, or information, contact the local chapter of the La Leche League— an organization of experienced mothers dedicated to helping you with any problems you may encounter with breast-feeding.

BANKRUPTCY

Businessmen and businesswomen go bankrupt all the time—when a new venture fails or an old one crumbles. But most people tend to think that "bankruptcy" is a terrible thing, like cancer, so they don't think of taking advantage of it as a businessperson would. You are "insolvent" in the eyes of the law if your liabilities (debts, including installment debts) are at least $1,000 and far exceed your assets. But you aren't bankrupt until either you or your creditors file a legal petition (which requires a modest fee) and a court officially declares you bankrupt. The petition must be filed in US District Court, and often legal aid is needed, costing sometimes some hundreds of dollars—though you may be able to get what's necessary from the Neighborhood Legal Service. Two appearances in federal court will be required, under a new law.

Although the "trustee" appointed by your creditors will pay off part of your debts by selling some of your property (like your car, any property you may own but don't live in, etc.), each state has a list of things that can't be taken away from you.

Generally this includes your "homestead," at least up to some fixed value, and personal items like clothes, tools, and some furniture; you can also specifically ask to keep certain other things. If you have been in business you can often keep the last month's wages due you from the business. Everything considered, it is sometimes to your definite advantage to go bankrupt and start over fresh.

You can only go bankrupt once in six years. You can also be prevented from "discharge" (release from debts) in bankruptcy if you conceal assets, refuse or fail to answer questions to the court, disobey a court order, obtain credit with false statements, or commit other frauds.

After you have filed a bankruptcy petition, don't discuss your debts with your creditors. If, in a moment of weakness, you promise one of them you'll pay "every cent I owe," your creditor may be able to hold you to it.

Sometimes a lawyer will set up an "arrangement" in bankruptcy, where you aren't actually declared bankrupt. This is a good idea if you are in some kind of small business, however unorthodox, and don't want to injure your credit or reputation.

Our bankruptcy laws are sometimes criticized as unduly liberal. (In medieval times, you went to "debtors' prison," often for life—a practice frowned upon by our founding fathers.) They actually function as a kind of national insurance system for individuals and small businesses that do not make it, spreading the creditors' losses around in as fair a way as possible, and getting the individuals involved back to some kind of productive work.

Bankruptcy: Do It Yourself, by Janice Kosel. Nolo Press, 1980.

BARTER

One reason not to throw things away is that you can probably trade them for something you need. (Not to mention that you reduce our output of garbage!) Bartering is an ancient and honorable American custom, and it is particularly valuable in an age of inflation for one simple but enormously important reason: since it doesn't involve much money, it can be kept outside the official economy, with its taxed wages, sales taxes, and other methods of siphoning off your resources.

You can barter items for other items, but you can also barter services. If you know how to do something—how to quilt or bake bread or do carpentry or plumbing—the chances are that you know somebody who needs to learn, and who can either teach you something in return, provide you some service (gardening? wood-chopping? driving you on some errands?), or otherwise "swap" with you. You can even advertise on bulletin boards. (Participation in organized barter "clubs" or services whose membership lists can be obtained by the IRS, however, can expose you to auditing and tax charges, since the IRS views barter as equivalent to money sales and has no compunctions about double taxation.)

Bartering also cements friendships in a way that buying and selling things for cash somehow just doesn't do. You don't even necessarily have to get a return on an item right away. Some experienced barterers know that if they say, "Well, just take it now—you'll discover something you can give me for it," they will seldom be disappointed. Barterers have to take each other's tastes and personalities into account; they have to deal with each other as human beings.

But the financial side is often gratifying too. If, for example, you go into a store to buy something new, you'll pay, let's say, $50 for it. Plus maybe $3 in sales tax. But to get that $53, you probably had to *earn* about $70 (considering the impact of income tax.) On the other hand, if you can find somebody who'll give you the item in barter, you "pay" for it with an item of yours on which you've already gone through the financial preliminaries; you are, so to speak, recycling your previous investment. So your effective outlay for the item you want is probably less than half of what it would be if you bought it new. And, depending on how you value your time, it might be even less if you trade a service for an object.

One of the reasons to grow vegetables, or keep bees, or raise chickens, is that they tend to provide you with more than you can use, so you have surpluses to use in bartering. That can be, in fact, half the fun.

Barter: How to Get Anything from Automobiles to Vacations Without Money, by Constance Stapleton and Phyllis Richman. Scribner, 1977.
Let's Try Barter, by Charles Morrow Wilson. Devin. 1960.
The Barter Book, by Dyanne Asimow Simon. Dutton, 1979.

BATHS (AS A PLEASURE, NOT A DUTY)

Most Americans conceive of bathing as a solitary occupation, like praying, aimed at making you as nearly antiseptic as possible. This is nonsense, because our skin is normally inhabited by millions of microbes. In fact, since skin is rather like bark (soft and porous), scrubbing its surface only reveals a fresh crop of microbes further down. The body is marvelously equipped to deal with microbes on its surface; tears, for instance, contain antibiotic substances. Too much washing with soap can remove the skin's natural oils, making it dry and stiff, or disrupt its natural acid-base balance, making it prey for fungi. All you really need is to remove sweat residues and any actual dirt you may have picked up. So the less soap the better. What you mainly need for joyful bathing is plenty of hot water. You also need friends: if warm water is pleasant for one body, the pleasures can rise geometrically when several bodies are added. Unfortunately, the standard American tub will barely accommodate two people. So you have to turn to bathing in streams or lakes where the water is often too chilly for much lounging about, or to hot springs or hot baths; or else you have to build your own oversize tub-pool. It ought to be something like three feet deep and perhaps five feet on a side, or round, like many commercially available hot tubs. Build it on solid ground or over a reinforced part of the floor; the amount of water will weigh two tons, more than enough to break through an ordinary floor and flood whatever is below.

The Japanese have thought most seriously and poetically about baths. When you arrive at a Japanese home after a long journey, you are first of all offered a bath; the Japanese know that a hot bath (in a deep tub) refreshes the weary spirit and soothes the tired body. The traditional Japanese bathtub is made of fragrant-smelling wood; you scrub with soap and a dipping basin, outside the tub; then, after rinsing off the soap, you soak up to your neck.

Most Americans take deep, hot tub baths only when they're sick and on doctor's orders (or in romantic movies, with lots of soap bubbles). But in recent years a hot-tub craze has swept California middle-class households, and in that state you can now buy wood or fiber-glass tubs in a wide range of prices, and with various types of heaters. (One ingenious system hooks up to your regular hot-water heater, and can be further linked with a solar heat source.) It is important to have a way of covering your tub with an insulating material, to cut down heat loss and thus minimize your water-heating costs.

These hot-tubs will probably spread to other areas with warm climates (they are best for outside use) but if you live in a colder place you could still build yourself a smaller Japanese bathtub or *furo*.

(As far as I know, they cannot be bought in this country.) This isn't particularly tricky, except for the heater. Build a box out of two-inch-thick lumber. (It need not be finished lumber; the roughness of sawed timber feels good.) You will have to design it carefully and put it together with large screws ("lag screws") because the weight of that much water will push apart a box that's just nailed together. Seal the cracks with caulking compound. It'll probably still leak a little; because of that and because of the problem of draining it, the best place for it is in a laundry room, converted garage, or other room with a waterproof floor and a drain.

You can connect it into your regular house hot-water system by use of a heat-exchanger and pump, or you simply buy an old water heater and let the hot water recirculate through it naturally. (For this system the heater hot-water outlet must be lower than the tub; otherwise you must install a small pump to circulate the water.) The heater thermostat may require some adjustment to avoid making the water too hot (most people like it at less than $110°F/43°C$).

With any bath system in which the water is retained, you must take health precautions against waterborne bacteria. Swimming-pool supply houses can provide you with a chlorine compound. And from time to time the tub needs draining and scrubbing.

After the kitchen, the bathroom is the most important room in the house. It's ridiculous that bathrooms are built hardly bigger than closets; see if yours might be enlarged by knocking out a wall, or perhaps adding a big bay-window alcove. A proper bathroom not only has a comfortable, deep tub (and a SHOWER, if you like showers) but it should also have plenty of room for taking off clothes and for sitting around and reading; it should have a big window that looks out on trees and green things, or a view of some kind. An ample supply of clothes hooks (which can be simply short dowel rods glued into a board) makes it easier for a number of people to use the bathing facilities at once; a good supply of large towels is also desirable. (You can buy towelling fabric by the yard.) A bathroom should have a slatted wooden bench, comfortable for damp bodies to sit or lie on, and big enough to double as a massage table. Make sure there are some plants—ferns generally love the moist air of a bath area. There's no reason for a bathroom to be all white enamel and antiseptic like a hospital. (But avoid colored or flower-printed toilet paper; it may cause inflammation.) If you wish to bar commercialism from your bathroom, remove the wrappers from soap and toilet paper before you store them. Whether you prefer natural wood or brightly painted walls, a soft rug or a cool smooth floor, consider the bathroom a meditation chamber. From water came all animal life on earth; the act of taking a bath is not only to get clean, but to restore contact with our primal element. A bath ought to be a joyous occasion.

BATTERIES

Auto battery prices and quality vary enormously: never buy a new battery from a service station—it'll probably cost considerably more than at Sears. Unless you have an automatic transmission, you can probably get started by having someone push you, or letting the car roll downhill, or by stopping somebody and running jumper cables from his or her good battery to your dead one.

Unfortunately, intermittent short-trip driving in town never gives a battery much chance to get recharged. If that's your main kind of driving, get a high-quality battery.

The strength of a battery is measured in "ampere-hours." Sears has a chart that tells you which of their batteries has the right rating for your car. In cold-weather starting, you'll need the full rating power.

As of 1980, no batteries had been developed that were really satisfactory as energy storage for electric cars, though elaborate studies had shown that a city transport system using electric vehicles would produce overall far less smog, despite the fact that oil-burning electric generating plants do produce some. The energy consumption and manufacturing and operating costs of individually owned vehicles are so large that ultimately they will give way to more intensively used vehicles: TAXIS, BUSES, and various kinds of streetcars and trains, probably all electrically driven.

In the 70's, small and relatively high capacity rechargable batteries were developed for use in small tools. While these devices were often quite convenient, the over-all cost of such systems in both energy and money were greater than those of cord-powered ones (partly because battery manufacture is itself quite energy-consuming). This is likely to be true for the indefinite future and for most battery systems. Directly harnessing wind power, for instance (say through mechanical connections to well pumps) is always preferable to converting it into electrical power and using that to run an electric pump. In fact, until full-scale photovoltaic electricity becomes available at competitive prices, it will *always* be cheaper to avoid electricity as a means of transmitting energy.

BEANS

Since pasta, potatoes, and rice are high-starch foods and may tend to make you fat, you need to learn about beans. They come in a delightful variety of forms and colors, and some of them will *not* make you fart, though there is no general rule about this—you have to experiment to find out which kinds your own digestive system takes to. The best protein suppliers are soybeans, which can be eaten in many different ways, including sprouted (this gives them even more nutritional value than they have as cooked beans).

Some beans really require the lengthy soaking recommended on the packages; others don't. Try different cooking methods and recipes until you find ways of dealing with beans that you really like. They are a fundamental low-cost cooking resource, and one that beginning cooks sometimes neglect. Combining beans with corn, as in much Mexican cooking, provides combined proteins that supply virtually all the needed amino acids, and many vegetarians therefore make a habit of eating beans and corn together.

BEDS (AND OTHER SLEEPING PLACES)

As the space quota for each person shrinks—which housing shortages seem bound to bring about for many Americans in coming years—it will be sillier and sillier to try to totally devote special rooms to sleeping. The "bedroom" is a particularly wasteful use of scarce space. It is generally used only about eight hours out of twenty-four; its floor space is generally far too big to be justifiable in terms of how much use is actually made of it. The only time a bedroom is really worthwhile is when it is used as one person's private space—where he or she retreats to read quietly, watch TV, talk to a friend, make love, sew, and so on. This kind of multiple-use bedroom makes sense in large households where privacy is hard to come by. But even then relatively little space is required.

A better perspective on sleeping accommodations is gained if we look back on two contrasting traditions. In the old Dutch farmhouses, beds were built into the walls as special alcoves, separated from the main room (in which cooking, eating, visiting, and everything else went on) by a curtain which could be drawn when you went to bed. These alcoves seldom had windows to the outdoors because glass was very expensive; modern counterparts usually do, partly for ventilation and partly because it's nice to be able to lie in bed and look out. To save further space, the bed was not low like ours, but high enough so that cupboards or drawers could fit under it. Thus both sleeping space and clothes-storage space were provided in an area of about four by six feet; even a small modern bedroom is around ten by twelve feet, plus a closet. Such alcoves can be built with doors, of course, and with a little strip of floor space along the front where you can stand to dress. Such "roomette" bedrooms would, if we had a rational building industry, be available through a catalog order service; you could build only your main room with its kitchen, bathroom, heating, and other facilities, and then bolt on a series of roomettes around the sides where you wanted them. You can sometimes adapt this approach to existing bedrooms by constructing an alcove around your bed. It should have a lower ceiling than the rest of the room, to mark off its special role (a hanging cloth of some kind will have the same general effect).

The Japanese have traditionally not had separate sleeping rooms. They sleep in a bedroll: mats and quilts are kept in a cabinet by day and laid out only at night. While this seems difficult from the privacy standpoint to most older Americans, especially where sex is concerned, societies which have lived in this manner have evidently developed ways of getting along; some young Americans who live communally have also found that sex is not necessarily always a totally private activity.

Anyone who has done any amount of sleeping-bag living will realize that this system has many advantages. For instance, so long as the floor is dry everywhere, it means that you can pick your sleeping spot according to your mood. Sometimes you might want to sleep near the fireplace, sometimes on the veranda to listen to the rain, sometimes on a couch; where a number of people are all bedding down in a large room, it means you can drift over to be near people you are feeling good about—you're not tied down to a piece of furniture.

Curiously, Americans have always been a lot more ingenious about sleeping arrangements in their cabins or summer houses than in their regular houses. All that's really essential for a sleeping place is a mattress or foam pad of some kind lying on a firmly supported piece of plywood. (Springs are expensive, usually bad for your back, and take up space.) This means that there is no reason why beds cannot be placed practically

anywhere. You can hang them by chains or heavy ropes or wires from the roof. You can build them as little high-up balconies (surrounded by curtains if you like). You can make double-deckers or triple-deckers. One clever friend of mine put his bed over his sink; he realized that any air space high up over a fixed object like a sink is just going to waste—so he built a two-by-four frame, nailed up a plywood sheet and a railing, built a little ladder, and had a bed without wasting any floor space at all.

The prospect for the 80's is that more and more people will be doubling up in houses and apartments. Families with many children have always faced this problem and sometimes have solved it by having three or even four kids sleep in a double bed. But this system doesn't really let the kids get the sleep they need, especially if one of them gets sick or is wakeful and keeps the others awake. The cost of plywood and foam-rubber mattress pads or reconditioned mattresses is low enough that you can build a bed for everyone. (You need a piece of five-eighth-inch plywood, two-by-fours for a frame to hold it up, a piece of one-by-three for a railing, and a mattress.) Often, too, you can find a corner of your house or apartment that isn't being used, where a bed can be built in—sometimes all you need to support it is some boards nailed into the wall studs. The addition of a skylight can often make a high-up space delightful for a bed-platform.

Beds can sit in alcoves, roll up, fold up against the wall, or go back into a closet like the so-called "in-a-door beds." Or you can have a bed platform which also serves as an eating or studying table or as a workbench.

In short, it is not necessary to be trapped by the orthodox idea of a bed. A bed is the nest of leaves or pine needles where you curl up for the night. It can be any place you like it, and made in any way you like it. It can have any kind of bedclothes you like—from a sleeping bag to a down comforter to the conventional two sheets, two blankets, and a bedspread. (Bedspreads to cover up ugly blankets are depressing; get rid of the ugly blankets instead.)

A Pattern Language, by Christopher Alexander, et al. Oxford University Press, 1978. Full of ingenious structural ideas for bedrooms and every other part of a living space.

BEEKEEPING AND FISHPONDS

The term "busy little bees" is not just a joke: bees are incredibly industrious, and if you provide them a decent home they will forage ceaselessly for you and provide surprisingly large amounts of delicious honey for practically no cost, in almost any region except heavily pesticided agricultural areas. Bees are legal to keep in many towns and some cities; if they are not legal in your town, you could probably organize a successful campaign to change the situation.

Besides, bees can be raised in indoor hives, as schoolteachers sometimes do for children's benefit. A hive can be attached to sit on a windowsill, so long as the bee entrance is a bee-tight pipe; it can even have a glass wall (coverable with a flap—bees don't like light in their hives) so you can check up on them. And of course a beehive will fit on many urban balconies. Beware, however, of locations near other people's balconies or windows, since bees returning at dusk are attracted by light. Rooftops are also good possibilities, but on hot asphalt roofs you must provide ample shade to keep the hive cool, and mount it on an elevated platform where breezes will also help cool it.

Bees not only produce honey, a delicious and relatively healthy sugar substitute and food energy source, they also fertilize many plants, including fruit trees, which are common in towns. People sometimes have an unreasonable fear of bees, but in fact if a hive is in a backyard away from pedestrian traffic it poses no danger to residents or passersby; your dog, if you have one, will soon learn to keep away from it. A careful beekeeper rarely gets stung, but it does happen.

Your local college may offer a course in beekeeping, and your library certainly has useful books about it. Best of all, however, is to find a beekeeper who is already doing it and apprentice yourself for a while. You can keep only a few bees, just enough to provide honey for yourself and friends, with very little work. But you may easily be tempted to get more bees, to learn the intricacies of the field, and to start extracting honey and selling it in jars—at flea markets or through stores—as a handy extra source of income. With sugar prices high, and many more people conscious of the pleasures of honey, the demand is likely to continue strong.

The reason fishponds are treated here along with bees is that bees have a short lifetime; around any busy hive you will have a lot of dead bees, and fish happen to love dead bees. Some people, as at the Farallones Institute Integral House in Berkeley, dig a fishpond (theirs is about ten feet square, maybe five feet deep, lined with black plastic sheeting to prevent water loss) and put their beehives next to it. The Integral Urban House also has a small home-made windmill which runs a pump to aerate and filter the fishpond water. Bluegills will grow in such a pond, but you may want to experiment with more exotic species— tilapia, carp, etc. Even if your county is urbanized, it should have a county agricultural agent who can give advice on ponds. If a fishpond is more than you want to undertake, you can always feed dead bees to your CHICKENS!

BICYCLES

Though some misguided souls still regard them as kid stuff, bicycles have outsold cars in the United States since 1973, and their place in our national life will surely continue to grow. The days of driving around the corner for a loaf of bread are over, and for many short trips the bicycle is becoming an increasingly common replacement for the car. This is true, astonishingly enough, even in places like New York City, as well as in small cities and towns; many people's lives are organized in such a way that most of the trips they make daily are less than a mile or so. This is easy range for a bicyclist, even if he or she is totally out of shape, which few regular bicyclists are, as riding not only develops your leg muscles but also gives your heart and lungs a workout.

For the rest of the world, bicycles are a prime smog-free means of adult transportation. In some compact cities like Amsterdam they not only out-number cars, but are a far faster, easier, and incredibly cheaper way to get around.

If your idea of a bicycle is one of those balloon-tired heavy-frame, unwieldy jobs that kids ride, drop by a bicycle shop and see what real bikes are like. The best ones are made of very light metal. You can pick one up with one hand and hoist it on your shoulder, so you can easily carry it up steps, into buildings, and so on.

Also, they have gearshifts (and usually hand brakes instead of coaster brakes). In flat places, a three-speed shift is enough. Where it's hillier, you may want a five- or ten-speed bike, which will get you up a steep hill with ease and allow you to adjust your pedaling to the terrain: you get the farthest with the least work if you keep your pedaling rate even. These are the bikes favored by the cycle enthusiasts you see zooming around in parks or on country roads. They're magnificent, colorful machines. Since a good bike should last you forever, the cost per month is still very low even for a seemingly expensive model. But a three-speed with coaster brake is the best and easiest-to-ride bicycle to start with.

Bikes need very few repairs. (In taking them apart, some axle and pedal nuts unscrew "backward.") You can easily fix everything except gearshift problems, and even these are cheap to have fixed in a shop. Buy yourself a bike-fixing guidebook, and you will spend virtually nothing on repairs—a pleasant change from car ownership. Oil everything about once a month, except for ball bearings, which should be coated with grease every few months. If the chain picks up dirt, take it off and soak it in oil.

Some people prefer to ride an old and beat-up bike because it is less likely to be stolen. There are plenty of car thieves around, of course, but stealing a bike is easy work for anybody with a bolt cutter that can nip off your chain and lock. Recently, therefore, fantastic new locks have been devised, which even a welding torch would have trouble cutting; they are large enough to clamp your whole bike to a pole or bike rack. If you buy an expensive bike, they're essential insurance. Police in smaller cities have a good record of recovering stolen bikes that have been previously registered with them, but you're still wise to keep your bike inside, especially at night, or at least out of sight of passersby. Europeans have ingenious hooks or pulley systems that suspend bikes by their front wheels in hallways or other unused corners; you can probably find a safe convenient place by adopting this approach.

Racks can be bought that clamp onto car bumpers and support a bike; you can make such a rack with a few boards and bolts. It gives you a drive-then-ride flexibility that can be very useful if you have a parking problem near your job. Folding bikes also exist that fit into a car trunk or a closet.

There's a good secondhand market in bikes, especially on the bulletin boards around colleges and universities, as thousands of students own bikes and sell them when they leave town. Bike dealers often have used bikes, though not so cheap. Sears sells a solid three-speed job for a reasonable price, so if you can't do better than their price secondhand, get one of those. For many years I have ridden an old Sears bike which is plain and durable and doesn't look worth stealing like one of those fancy Italian models. It also has handlebars designed for upright riding, rather than the curved-down handles which give more leg power but require you to lean forward.

You may feel that bicycles are all very well, but how do you haul anything with them, and what do you do about children? You'd be surprised what can be carried on a bicycle. The French were defeated at Dien Bien Phu by Vietnamese artillery whose parts and shells had been brought hundreds of miles through the jungles on thousands of Vietnamese bicycles. In European cities you may see a man balancing a heavy load on what seems a frail bicycle. But actually a bike can support a hundred pounds in addition to the rider. And for a small child you can bolt a seat on the back, complete with safety belt. These only cost a couple of dollars, and kids love them. If you also have a carrying basket on the front, you'll be able to haul at least one bag of groceries. Baskets, big enough to hold four bags of groceries, are used on downtown delivery service bicycles, if you really need hauling capacity! Bike stores, too, sell backpack bags for carrying books, clothes, lunch, and other small items.

In many cities you're required to have a bell or horn in order to get licensed. Bells are best because horns' rubber bulbs are soon torn off. It's a good idea to register your bike (the fee is usually nominal) as insurance against theft. Real insurance can be bought, but it's not worth the expense.

Even if you lose a bike to thieves once in a while, you'll still be saving money. After I had had my Sears bike for two years, for example, I calculated that compared to taking the bus to work I had saved five times what the bike cost me (not to mention the health benefits, savings on parking fees or tickets, etc.). At this rate I could have the bike stolen twice a year and still be ahead.

A couple of safety notes: although it may make you feel like a tank-driver at first, wear a sturdy bicyclist's helmet. Even in a minor spill your head can easily strike the ground (or a nearby car) with enough force to fracture your skull, merely by the action of gravity. And since car drivers sometimes don't notice bicycles as fellow occupants of the public streets, you could even get into an accident where you get banged against a car or thrown from your bike. In any such encounter, a helmet greatly increases your chances of coming through with only minor injury. (You should always ride defensively, of course, just as you drive a car only more so—never get into a position of depending upon a car driver seeing you. Be aware also that there are drivers who maliciously threaten bicyclists just for the fun of it. This is a form of criminal assault, and if you have the evidence and witnesses to prosecute such a driver, you will be doing bicyclists everywhere a great service.) If you ride at night, get a light that straps onto your leg and moves up and down as you pedal—calling attention to your position better than a fixed light. They're also small enough to fit in a pocket so they can't be stolen. A white reflector pointing forward or a headlight is also an important safety precaution, along with reflectors on the wheels (making you visible from the side). Keep tires inflated to the pressure called for on the sidewall; low pressure makes a bike harder to pedal, and too much makes it bouncy and gives a less firm grip on the road. In rain or snow, you'll need a snugly fitting coat, parka or poncho, and gloves.

The real triumph for the bike rider comes during rush hour, when the cars are stalled in long, tangled lines, or crawling bumper to bumper down crowded streets, looking for parking spots. Then you zip along freely, watching for drivers who open car doors without looking back, between and around the cars. At such times the bicyclist gets home faster than the car driver, and it doesn't cost anything. Nor does the bicyclist worry about parking spaces, parking tickets, driver's licenses, gas shortages, hubcap thieves, or people who like to scratch automobiles' shiny paint.

The Amsterdam Provos had a plan to stock the cities with tens of thousands of free bicycles which you could pick up anywhere and drop off anywhere. (During the night, the city would distribute them where they'd be the most needed in the morning.) This beautiful scheme was considered revolutionary by the property-respecting Dutch authorities, and their police went around locking up the free bicycles offered to the city by the Provos. But the principle is sound and its time will come. The American city as it now exists has been gutted to make it fit for cars. But someday our dependence on cars will be broken; our homes and jobs and neighborhoods will be given a more compact, people-oriented form, linked by less expensive and obnoxious means of transportation. We can hasten this happy time by pushing our local governments for more bike paths, for safely separated bikeways in dangerous traffic areas (European cities keep cars out with low curbs), and bikeways in scenic places. Also, encourage local merchants to provide bicycle parking racks; it lessens their patron parking problems.

A postscript on kids' bikes. The "Stingray" and its successors—balloon-tired, low-framed, small-wheeled, big-seated bikes—are strictly toys, as your child will soon discover if he or she tries to follow you more than five or six blocks on your full-size bicycle. With their chrome, fancy upholstery, and stick-type gearshifts, they are really just junior car substitutes, useful only for messing around on the

block. They are also tippier than regular bikes. If you want your kids to be able to go anywhere, get them real bikes.

A child's first bike should have a coaster brake. These are easier to learn to use than hand-operated brakes, where braking more strongly on the front wheel than the rear one can give you a spill.

Glenn's Complete Bicycle Manual, by Clarence W. Coles and Harold T. Glenn. Crown, 1973. The bike mechanic's bible.

Anybody's Bike Book, by Tom Cuthbertson. Ten Speed Press, 1979.

BIOREGION

The conventional boundaries on maps have very little real meaning, even as far as cultural and social divisions go. We need to begin thinking in terms that are related to the actual landscape and to the social "organisms" that inhabit it—groups of people defined by shared traditional habits, beliefs, economic relationships, and connections with the land. Our country is too big a unit for these purposes; its geography is too complex, and its people are at cross-purposes in too many ways. A county on the other hand is too small, and like a state is generally too artificial a unit. The bioregion is a useful intermediate concept: an area defined by natural, geographical features (most often a watershed—that is, the area drained by one group of rivers, and usually surrounded by mountains) and inhabited by plant and animal communities (and usually human communities too) different from those in adjacent bioregions.

Some bioregions are relatively compact. Ecotopia, for example, occupies the Cascade bioregion, which basically extends from middle California north along the Pacific Coast (continuing, really, into Canada). The humid Southeast also constitutes a coherent bioregion, as well as a sociocultural region. The Rocky Mountain area and the desert area of the Southwest are diverse enough that biologists subdivide them in various ways. Human habitation, like that of animals and plants, grades and overlaps depending on historical and political circumstances, competition pressures, climatic and technological changes. It makes less sense to try and think of a "state" like California as a single entity than as a series of bioregions, each with its own somewhat distinct culture and interrelations with the natural world. Sacramento may be the political capital, but there are two *real* capitals: Los Angeles for the heavily Spanish-speaking, water-importing, automobile-dependent southern

areas, and San Francisco for the northern areas which bear the imprint of Mediterranean cultures and are more localized into permanent relationships with agriculture and forestry, for which they have abundant water. But there are other, smaller bioregions within the existing map borders of California also: east of the towering Sierra Nevada range, people and biotic communities are more akin to those of Nevada and Utah (the Great Basin bioregion) and in the extreme southeast, bordering the Colorado River, there is an overlap with the Colorado watershed areas.

In time, we should bring our political boundaries into conformity with our bioregional-cultural boundaries. Otherwise, artificial political units such as states will be torn by unnecessary and unproductive strife, as is already the case in California over water supplies. A bioregion that is also an integrated political unit can organize its political life to match its natural resources, its trade patterns both internal and external, its community needs, and its long-term biological support systems (which are always, in the long run, agricultural). It can develop among its people a sense of shared values, shared problems, and shared destiny—a community world view that can be passed on from generation to generation and relied upon to orient people to their survival

necessities. In short, bioregional thinking can make the area where you live seem like home; and some feeling of rootedness, of identification with your own place, seems to be a basic necessity for human well-being. (See MAPS.)

BLENDERS

The blender is probably the small electric appliance most worth having around your kitchen. You can do everything an electric frying pan will do in a heavy iron skillet; you can do everything an electric broiler will do in your stove. But you can't make juices out of vegetables without a blender, and you can't make milk shakes easily. A heavy blender will chop up and puree practically any kind of fruit or vegetable. So you can produce mixtures as fantastic as those offered by a "juice bar"—celery and cabbage juice, plum and apple juice, apricot and pineapple juice. You can also make cheap baby food, puree broccoli soup, carrot cake and zucchini bread, walnut butter, sauces to pour over ice cream, and lots of other things. Blenders are simple machines which either work or don't, so they are relatively safe to buy secondhand if you try them out first. The new ones have variable speeds and other refinements, but all you need is one whose motor runs, whose top stays on, and whose bottom doesn't leak. (Ask to try it with a little water in it.)

BLOCK AND NEIGHBORHOOD ORGANIZING

To undercut the top-down organizing of the ruling class and its political parties and to give an explicit voice to the actual needs of American people, we need new structures: organizations on the job and organizations where we live. Neighborhood committees and block organizations are useful in bringing people together on a human basis: for cleanup campaigns, to bring pressure on the schools, to fight city hall for better services, money for parks or stoplights, and so on. They are also a way to combat the depersonalization of American life—the atomization that locks each household up by itself, isolated from its neighbors. In recent years they have been springing up by the thousands all over the country, in all kinds of neighborhoods, oriented to many different types of concerns.

To get started in neighborhood organizing, you need to find a few friends who want to help. Go around and talk to some likely-looking neighbors, and find out what they think needs to be done, what people will be organizable around. Try to put up a street bulletin board where people can pin up announcements, for-sale notes, and whatnot. When you get going, plan some kind of fun event (a picnic, potluck, free movie, etc.) and print a leaflet to drop off at each apartment and house—also including your ideas about neighborhood organizing.

Neighborhood organizing should be undertaken not as a duty but because it can improve your daily life and bring you into contact with new friends nearby. Don't fall into the trap of the kind of "canvassing" done by precinct electoral workers. You are not after votes—you are after minds and

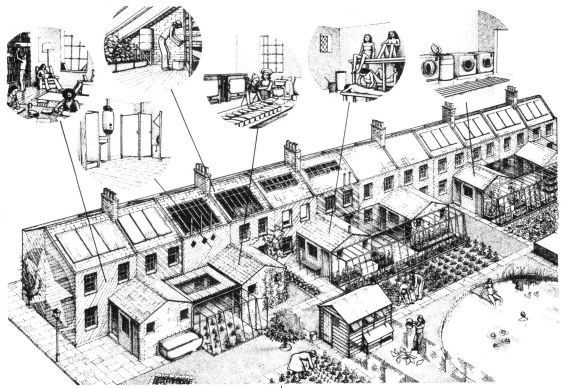

The "Autonomous Terrace," where neighbors cooperate to grow food, create shared recreation, and accomplish other shared needs.

bodies. And you can only make this fun if you operate in a small area. Even a precinct is too large.

Community organizing needs its own intelligence service to really improve conditions. Find out who has the power to make changes in your town and what kinds of pressure will make them move. This means analyzing the local power structure: who are the really important people in town? (Often they are hard to spot—they may include little-known owners of the major businesses or behind-the-scenes political figures.)

Your group should try to find sympathetic people who are good at doing research on the problems that concern you. In trying to improve slum housing, for instance, much tricky detective work is often needed to find out who actually owns a building. The real owners often hide behind anonymous corporations, use of lawyers' offices, trusts, and so on. But they can always be located if a thorough enough search is made. You will learn as much as you can about relationships between the corporations responsible for polluting your environment and the local officals who let them get away with it. The operations of your city housing and health departments and of the courts that handle evictions and time-payment cases—all need to be studied so that you can publicize corruption, make your demonstrations and leaflets carry the greatest impact, and minimize retaliations. In pressing for new health, welfare, or other social programs, you have to find out whose support is essential and whose opposition would be fatal. You also have to locate useful supporters outside your own group, such as reform-minded clergy or lawyers. And above all, you must find out where the money is and where it's going; for under capitalism, as the popular saying has it, there is indeed "a racket in everything."

Whenever people can become better educated and better informed, they soon find themselves in motion politically; little by little they begin to discover what is going on, they decide what is wrong with it, and they work to replace it with something better. In big ways and small, direct and indirect, we all participate in this political struggle. We owe it to ourselves and to our children, who will have to live in the world we create, to make our personal and collective political weight felt.

BOOKSHELVES

Most apartments and houses lack bookshelves, though they may have incinerators, dirty-clothes chutes, special silverware drawers, linen closets, and other storage facilities. This is one of the sad consequences of living in a non-reading nation. (Though our book sales have been rising rapidly, Americans publish, buy, and read far fewer books per person than the citizens of Britain, Japan, and various other countries. We also have fewer bookshops.) But books are important as free or cheap amusement, for information, and most of all for nourishment of the spirit. Per dollar spent, you get more hours of pleasure reading books than from movies, concerts, records, or restaurants. Once you begin to love books, you will begin to keep them.

The near-universal student solution is the board-and-concrete block system. This has the advantage that you can use any kind of boards you can get hold of; they don't all have to be the same type, length or even width. Variety and interesting wood is half the game: driftwood, used construction lumber, old pieces of shelving. With a half-dozen boards and about eight blocks (which you may have to buy at a building-supply firm) you can change the arrangement whenever you get bored with it. Large concrete blocks are a little more stable than the smaller red bricks; they're also cheaper overall, and besides, the holes are useful for holding pencils, letters, chopsticks, rulers, and many other little things that won't fit into your drawers. The blocks come in several shapes, hole patterns, and colors.

Always build considerably more bookshelves than you think you will need. You will soon fill part of the extra space with radio, record player, records, and boxes of small objects.

Board-and-block bookshelves can also be turned into benches for extra guests, or supports for one end of a table made from a flush door. If worst comes to worst you can burn them for heat, as Mozart had to do with his furniture when he lay dying in poverty in Vienna.

The Shelf Book, by Jon M. Zegel. Running Press, 38 S. 19th St., Philadelphia, PA 19103.

BORROWING

Sooner or later everybody gets into a position of having to borrow money. You may be undertaking some project that requires materials you can't finance yourself, or you may get clobbered by medical bills, or you may just run out of cash before you get paid on a new job. The problem is how to borrow on the least disadvantageous terms. Renting $100 for a year may cost you $10-12 from a bank, $12 from a credit union, $18 if it's part of a time-payment plan, and $36 or even more from a finance company.

What follows rests on the assumption that you have previously established your CREDIT in the community, which takes some time to accomplish.

Your strategy is to find a loan at rates as close as possible to regular bank interest rates—at which large loans are made for ordinary business purposes. Anything higher than that is an extra, and you are paying it because they think you are a "risk." You must therefore make yourself look like as good a risk as possible.

First, always try your bank. (Secretly you may wonder whether they possess good judgment if they would lend money to anybody like you—nevertheless, give it a try.) If you've kept a checking account there for a couple of years and haven't yet welshed on any bad checks, they will at least consider your application. Make sure you have what is called a constructive purpose to declare when they ask why you want the loan. Paying off or consolidating a group of high-interest time payments is a constructive purpose. So is buying appliances, furniture, a car, etc.—though a bank will not normally lend you anywhere near the total cost of an old used car. Repairing your house or buying equipment and tools that will help you earn money are also considered very constructive. Buying a new wardrobe or buying records are, regrettably, not constructive in the bank's eyes.

Credit unions are co-op banks; their members pool their savings so they can (though a paid professional staff) lend money to each other. Their loans are generally competitive in interest rates and sometimes better than those of banks (not to mention auto dealers) as well as easier to get, especially if you have been a member for some time and have a stable job. (Most credit unions will lend up to $2500 on your signature alone.) Credit unions are usually limited in their membership—to government or company employees, or grocery co-op members, or teachers—but you can probably find one you're eligible to join. (Some 36 million other Americans have.) It's good insurance against a sudden need for cash, either in a emergency or for some large purchase; if you move to a new town, find one and join it without wasting time. Try to apply well before you need a loan, however, since credit union loan committees often meet only once a week.

Credit unions can now issue "share drafts," which look like checks and work like checks: they enable you to draw against your savings, but until it's actually paid out your money continues to sit

there and pay interest. Loans from a credit union are often insured; if you die, the loan is paid off and your family is not obligated for it.

Recently Congress has enacted a bill to establish a co-op bank, a sort of large-scale credit union for co-operative enterprises, backed by government funds. This should make it possible for many new co-ops to get adequate financing and for established ones to expand sensibly.

Finance companies (or loan sharks as they are often known to their unlucky customers) will rent you money even if you are not a good risk or have a bad credit rating—but they will charge you plenty for it. Different companies may rate your riskiness differently, so shop around and see if you can get a better deal. Watch out for service charges and other extras; look in the contract to find the annual interest percentages and the total financing cost. Be wary of contracts that give the company a claim on your property if you have any. And find out what happens if you miss a payment.

Pawnbrokers, though you can sometimes buy from them at decent prices if you really know the merchandise in question, are a last resort for borrowing money. Their interest rates are utterly unregulated and can be astronomical. And of course if you can't scrape together the money to redeem your goods by the due date, you lose them. A pawnbroker will seldom lend you more than about 10 percent of the actual value of an object—or give you more than that even if you offer to sell it outright.

Friends who have accumulated savings they're not likely to need for a while are another possible source of loans. To avoid endangering the friendship, it is best to be businesslike: write your arrangement down on paper so each can have a copy, and plan a definite repayment schedule. Most friends will not expect interest, at least on a short-term loan, but it's a generous gesture to offer it anyway; after all, you'd have to pay it if you got the money from a bank. If you borrow money from a friend to put into some business venture, be especially sure to establish whether you simply pay back the money loaned or a split of the profits.

Underworld lenders connected with rackets of one kind or another circulate in depressed neighborhoods. If someone on the block offers to lend you money, especially in connection with some kind of deal, say thanks a lot but no thanks. The terms may sound tempting, but in case of a dispute you may end up dead.

A person who is borrowing money—from any source—may sometimes be asked to get a "co-signer." A car-purchase contract sometimes calls for a co-signer, and so may installment-buying contracts. When you co-sign a contract, or "sign a note" as it's sometimes called, you are just as liable for it as the other person is. You are, in fact, guaranteeing that he or she will pay and promising to pay yourself if the other signer doesn't. This is very different from just "signing a reference," as people sometimes call it. It might put you in debt for hundreds or even thousands of dollars.

It is wise, therefore, to sign notes only for members of your family or very good friends— people you'd really be willing (and able) to pay up for if necessary.

See also CREDIT.

Brand Names

American industry systematically tries to brainwash us into thinking that brand names hold a kind of magic: that Bayer aspirin is superior to other aspirin (although all aspirin is chemically identical), that RCA is better than Motorola, and so on. In fact this "superiority" consists of a high-priced advertising myth. There are minor differences among products, but the most famous brands are seldom the (slightly) superior ones, and they usually cost more. Buyers who trust big names like General Electric are buying TV air time with their hard-earned cash, not quality in the goods.

It is usually possible to figure out, if you want to spend the time and energy, which of brand X, Y, or Z is probably the best, because *Consumer Reports* runs elaborate scientific tests and publishes the results, with information on safety hazards, breakdown rates, etc. However, some excellent but little-known items never get covered by *CR* —like the McIntosh hi-fi or certain rare foreign cars, which some engineering freaks consider better designed and better made than the widely distributed brands (but which are also extremely expensive).

The only rule that makes sense about brand names is: be especially cautious about the "big brands," whose reputations were probably built some years ago, and are maintained chiefly through advertising. Look for new brands which are getting a reputation by word of mouth from people who know something about electronics, or cars, or whatever is involved. There is at least an outside chance that a new, small company, fighting for its life against the giants that dominate its field, will be run by people who take real pride in their product. (Later, if they are successful and expand, they too will pay more attention to overhead than to quality.)

Bread

Every cookbook has easy recipes for making bread, and if you really get into it, the soft, squishy abomination sold as "bread" in our stores will soon seem unfit for human consumption: you will be making your own special kinds of whole-wheat bread, rye bread, rolls, and so on. It always surprises people how easy it is to make bread: it just takes some mixing, some kneading (working the bread around under the heel of your hand), and some patience—you have to wait for it to "rise" (the yeast you mixed into it will grow and produce bubbles that will make the bread fluffy). Once you get into the basic routine of baking, you will probably branch out into all kinds of delectable (and cheap) pastries, cakes, pies, rolls, muffins— and will discover a good place to buy the many different kinds of flours. Don't be confined by the choices in a typical supermarket; there are lots more, and a health-foods store, though it may be unduly expensive itself, can probably tell you where to find a store specializing in grain products. By doing your own baking you also avoid the additives and preservatives of commercial bread. Homemade bread seldom remains uneaten for very long, but you can store it for a long time in the freezer or refrigerator if you need to—where all bread keeps best.

Even if you don't want to do any baking, you should pay some attention to the bread question, a major issue in our cultural life. American white bread has been getting steadily more and more like blown-up pasteboard, and many people eat it under the illusion that it is a more nourishing food than the facts indicate. There's no actual danger in eating ordinary white bread (except conceivably from some of the chemical additives that are put in to "preserve" it), but you should not rely on it as a basic food, even when it is labeled "enriched." Here is a rundown of the major kinds of available bread:

Whole wheat. Because this is made from the entire wheat kernel, including the skin where the vitamins and proteins mostly are, whole wheat is the best bread for you. It has a slightly pebbly texture which makes the most crunchy and interesting kind of toast, and it has enough body that it will hold together a juicy kind of sandwich. Beware of "wheat bread," which is made from mostly unenriched white flour—it doesn't taste as good, and it isn't as nutritious.

Enriched white bread. To make wheat flour white, the millers have to remove most of the nutrients from it; then they put a little back in and call it "enriched." Though many states still do not have laws requiring even the minimum restoration of nutrients indicated by the "enriched" label, this is an improvement over plain white bread. (Never buy white bread without checking the label.) Most French bread and rolls are enriched, but watch their labels too.

Rye bread (including pumpernickel, etc.). Despite their dark color, most rye loaves are mixtures of rye and unenriched white flours. They are still tastier than white bread, or course, and somewhat better for you; and some responsible bakeries are using all enriched flours.

Raisin breads and similar novelty products. These, often beloved of children, are unfortunately almost never enriched. Here, as in many other situations in the food industry, we can evidently only secure basically healthful breads for our children by enacting laws that will force the manufacturers to produce them. (If manufacturers voluntarily produced healthy products, they would have less "government regulation" to scream about.)

BREAKFASTS

America possesses a tradition of hearty breakfasts, and there was once much to be said for this, despite an unhealthy over-consumption of eggs, bacon, and butter. Recently, however, urban dwellers are tending more and more toward a "continental" style of breakfast—a roll and coffee taken on the run. Unfortunately, we forget that this style of breakfast evolved in connection with an early lunch, as in France, or a huge midday main meal, as in Italy. Unless you can arrange your life in some such way, you ought to eat a decent breakfast. And there are some relatively painless ways of doing so. Health-food enthusiasts eat tasty, concentrated cereal-nut mixtures ("Familia" is a Swiss brand, "Crunchy Granola" an American one) which you can also make yourself and save money: they usually contain rolled oats, whole-wheat flour, brown sugar, soy oil, honey, sunflower seeds, finely cracked raw nuts, raisins, raw wheat germ, and small pieces of dried apples or other fruits. You generally eat them with milk poured over them, and small pieces of fresh fruit

add to the taste. Most commercial granolas now contain large amounts of sugar; homemade will be better for you.

Since breakfast tends to be a rather regressive time of day, you may like things that you can suck up instead of having to chew: mix an eggnog by stirring a beaten egg into a glass of milk, and add a little vanilla or nutmeg. Or make a shake by stirring a few tablespoons of frozen-orange-juice concentrate into a mashed banana and mixing it into a glass of milk.

The traditional bacon-and-eggs breakfast is so heavy in cholesterol and fats (as well as the possibly carcinogenic nitrites in the bacon) that you should indulge in it rarely—certainly no more than once a week. Avoid butter in favor of margarine made with polyunsaturated oil, and use decent whole-wheat bread for toast.

Pancakes can be made with egg whites instead of whole eggs, or use "imitation egg," if you don't mind its additives.

Cooked cereals are available in quick-cooking form. They're nutritious, surprisingly inexpensive, and come in many different tastes and textures—from relatively gooey oatmeal to pebbly types such as Roman meal to really crunchy Irish oatmeal (a cheap equivalent of which is called "steel-cut oats"). You can sprinkle them with brown sugar, honey, cinnamon, granola, sunflower kernels, and add a dab of butter with some milk.

BUDGETING

Everybody has to bother with money to some extent—if you don't money is the one thing you can count on to disappear. There is only one way to make sure you can stretch your money till your next check. That is by dividing it into weekly or daily amounts, and then spending only that amount. Moreover, if you're trying to save some money, the same principle applies: you have to put aside the savings at the beginning and then divide what remains. Otherwise it will be impossible to get through to the end of the period with enough to eat, and you will end up borrowing, which will only make the next period harder.

Assuming you have a checking account to store your money (so you don't spend it too early, or get robbed), here's how you do it:

● When you get your check, deposit it in the bank; but hold back enough cash to live on for the first week.

• Pay your rent, utilities, telephone, car payments, and any other regular bills right away. If you're saving up, put that away too.

• Divide up the money that's left, in the bank and in your pocket, into the number of days or weeks you're budgeting for. The result is the number of dollars you have to spend each day or week. It will seem discouragingly small—and remember this has to cover everything: food, car repairs and gas, clothes, medicines, bus fares, children's lunches, and so on. So try to spread these expenses out over the month as evenly as you can.

• Buy your staple supplies (flour, rice, beans, spaghetti, dried milk, bread) in large quantities at the beginning of each week. That way you'll be sure to have enough food to get through the week if you need it. Buy more perishable things such as vegetables, meat, cheese, eggs, and fruit only after you've made sure you can last the week.

• Never "borrow" from next week's money. If you're going to need something that can't be covered by your weekly amount, save up by scrimping this week, so you can buy it next week.

• If you can be thrifty or lucky enough to come out at the end of a week with any money left over, you deserve to be able to spend it thoughtlessly—buy some luxury you've been wanting, or just blow it! The puritan minds tells you to carefully stash it away and get your fun out of counting it or something. That's not a very enticing sort of pleasure—and besides, the time to do your savings is at the beginning of the month, when you put a little aside in a credit union or savings account.

BULLETIN BOARDS

Luckily, our cities are so full of secondhand stores and other sources of old stuff that you can very often avoid buying new things. In addition, one of the great social inventions is the bulletin board, on which people post notices of things they want to sell or buy. Bulletin boards are commonly found around colleges, in laundromats, in supermarkets, nailed up outside stores, or even on houses. If none exists in your neighborhood, start one—pick a busy, heavy-traffic location and ask a storekeeper if you can nail up a board somewhere. Seed it with a few cards from your friends and see what happens. A careful buyer can always do better by buying direct from a previous owner than from a dealer. (Obviously you must give a careful tryout to anything you buy anywhere, but especially when you are buying strictly as-is.)

Don't confine your ideas about bulletin boards

to the buying and selling of objects. People can also advertise rides offered or sought, apartments or rooms to rent or share, things to barter, and so on.

BURNS

Cold water is a good immediate treatment for any burn. Light "first-degree" burns (as bad as a bad sunburn) usually need no further treatment, except maybe some cooking oil or cold cream (though a really bad sunburn can give headaches, nausea, and extreme tenderness of the skin). Blistered, deeper "second-degree" burns, and charred, twisted, no-feeling-left "third-degree" burns need to be treated immediately by a doctor. Face and hand burns may require special surgery, and may heal badly. Burns can result in serious shock and fatal infections. If a severe burn has clothing stuck to it, don't try to remove it yourself; the skin may come with it.

There is considerable evidence that a heavily negative-ionized atmosphere decreases the pain due to burns. If you have a household ionizer, you might put it and the burned person in a small room together.

BUSES

The lowly bus didn't get much attention as a mass-transit vehicle until new, sophisticated, "space-age" subways were built in San Francisco and Washington, D.C. When these turned out to be extraordinarily more expensive to build and run than anyone had anticipated (and didn't even work that well because their fancy electronics were incompetently designed), it began to be clear that buses will be a permanent and valuable part of any urban transit system. For one thing, they use the highways that have already been constructed, courtesy of the auto-highway lobby, out of the tax-payers' unknowing pockets. (Only about a quarter of the $338 billion spent between 1956 and 1979 came from gas-tax funds; the rest was a general subsidy from the public treasury.) Their routes, stops, and frequency can be easily adjusted to meet ridership needs. Given special reserved high-speed lanes, they can beat subway commute times (so could old-fashioned ferries, for that matter). And, while their operating energy efficiency is not quite so high per passenger as fixed-rail systems (trains and streetcars), if you add in the amounts of energy needed to build rail systems, the bus may even come out ahead. Many countries manage to build buses that are spacious, comfortable, quiet vehicles, even if General Motors, which effectively monopolizes bus sales in this country since federal transit-subsidy funds can't be spent abroad, hasn't yet been able to figure out how to do it.

The single greatest way to improve public transit, including buses, would be to force the people who control it —usually appointees —to use it. Short of that, transit activists, given new clout by the gas shortage and increasing passenger loads, have been mildly successful in needling bus companies for better service. But more is needed; particularly some type of regular funding that could assure mass transit of support as the highway lobby wangled support for highways. A percentage of local sales tax is one possibility, already used in some communities. Minnesota is considering giving a special income-tax deduction to bus riders. Under the Clean Air Act, some highway money has finally been diverted to city transit needs. Better bus service will become a hotter political issue as the oil problem worsens. For help: Environmental Action, 1346 Connecticut Ave. NW, Washington, DC 20036.

See PUBLIC TRANSPORTATION; TAXIS.

BUTTER AND MARGARINE

Butter is a major source of saturated fat, and its use should be minimized for both weight control and heart-disease reduction. If you do eat butter, the unsalted type is generally preferable, since salt masks off-flavors in butter, and butter to be sold unsalted thus has to be of higher quality.

Margarines vary a great deal in composition. You should look for those with the least amount of hydrogenated or hardened oils, and the fewest additives. Many supermarkets are now carrying such margarines, and if yours doesn't, phone the buyer and ask for it.

C

Cancer

One out of four Americans now dies of cancer, and cancer rates (after a period of stability) rose about ten percent in the years 1970-1976. New cases run about 765,000 per year, and more than 400,000 cancer victims die per year. In some types of cancer, such as lung cancer, rates have been rising drastically (80% of this is due to SMOKING which also causes bladder and pancreas cancer). Stomach cancer, on the other hand, has declined recently — no one knows why. Bladder, colon, and rectum cancer is down somewhat for women, but unchanged for men. Cancer of the pancreas increased sharply for some years after 1950, then leveled off; cancer of the uterus has declined steadily. Lung cancer will clearly continue to be an immense problem, but other types may also resume a rising curve; since the great increase in the pollution of the biosphere with carcinogenic chemicals began in the 1940's, we may now only be seeing the beginnings of their effects (cancers often develop only 20 or 30 years after exposure to carcinogens).

Cancer treatment, through surgery, X-rays, chemicals, hormones, and radiation, has improved somewhat; it now saves about one in every three cancer victims. Early detection greatly improves your chances of survival; regular physicals and self-exams are essential. While a great deal of attention and money have been lavished nationally on cancer, research progress has been slight. The conclusion of most researchers is that, whatever the precise mechanisms by which cancers begin and spread, the cause of at least three-quarters is environmental. (About 25% of the working population is exposed to toxic substances on the job.) Some of the mechanisms may be susceptible to control; detection processes will doubtless become more sensitive and accurate; the use of marijuana may be made legal to counteract the side effects of chemotherapy. Nonetheless, these improvements are marginal.

What obviously needs to be done is to decrease the factors in the environment that cause the disease in the first place. These are many, varied, and sometimes puzzling, but heavily industrialized states like New Jersey, New York, and Pennsylvania, in which huge areas are disastrously polluted in air and water, have cancer rates four times greater than Alaska's and twice Hawaii's. Particular areas with heavy concentrations of chemical, petroleum, and paper industries generally have high cancer rates. Many industries knowingly subject their employees and the public at large (see ECO-CRIME) to toxic substances. Some areas seem to have more smokers than others (city dwellers apparently smoke more than rural people) and thus have higher lung cancer rates. Some ethnic areas consume certain foods which are carcinogenic, as a type of Chinese pickle turned out to be. Colon and even breast cancers may be connected with increasing amounts of animal fat in the diet. (Breast surgery for cancer can now include reconstruction of breast tissue; Blue Cross will pay for such surgery.) Gradually cancer researchers are figuring out the particular causes of these variations, but the general lesson is clear enough: try to avoid being in places where carcinogens are plentiful in the air, water, and food; avoid foods, cosmetics, pesticides and herbicides, cleaning products, and other items which contain mysterious additives and chemical compounds likely to prove carcinogenic.

It is not true, of course, as some people conclude in despair, that "everything causes cancer." Almost *none* of the substances that maintained civilization until around 1945 were carcinogenic, but since then the vast expansion of the chemical industry has manufactured new substances by the tens of thousands. Most of these are not in fact carcinogenic, but our testing procedures to identify those that *are* carcinogenic are very inadequate. Through much more active government intervention, and through refusal to buy products whose ingredients have not been thoroughly tested, we can purge our environment of these dangerous compounds.

See CARCINOGENS AND MUTAGENS.

The Politics of Cancer, by Samuel S. Epstein. Sierra Club Books, 1978.

CAN OPENERS

As in most other areas of the house, a lot of the single-purpose utensils commonly found in kitchens are not really necessary. You can cut out cookies with a glass instead of a cookie cutter. You can roll dough, as our grandmothers did, with a broomstick or wine bottle rather than a rolling pin. You can poach eggs in any frying pan. If you are eating right, you will seldom need a can opener—but you will open a can occasionally, especially in the winter in cold climates. There's no need to junk up your kitchen with an eyesore chrome-plated can opener, much less to hanker after an electric can opener. Get a simple can opener from the dime store, or—if you really want to keep the signs of cans as inconspicuous as possible—a GI can opener from the surplus store. These are fiendishly ingenious gadgets hardly bigger than a nail clipper, but quite capable of opening cans if you have reasonably strong fingers. Be glad if it makes can-opening slightly unpleasant—that will motivate you to use more fresh and frozen vegetables, which are better for you (and frozen vegetables are generally cheaper than canned anyway).

CARCINOGENS AND MUTAGENS

A carcinogen is a substance that causes cancers to develop. Some, like dioxins, may do so even if present only in minute amounts, down to some "parts per trillion." A quick and inexpensive laboratory test, the Ames test, enables researchers to determine the carcinogenic potential of substances, and this resulted in the addition of many materials to the danger list—some of them widely dispersed in the biosphere by industrial or agricultural practices. Carcinogens are also often "teratogens," that is, mutation-causing; it is now believed that the hazard to our genetic material in this manner is far more dangerous than the cancer-causing effects, since it will have long-term effects on the species, whereas cancer simply increases the death rate but does not affect coming generations. Even if we are prepared to accept current cancer rates—or perhaps substantially higher rates—as the price for our technological life style, it is difficult to see what benefits could be "traded-off" against a deterioration in the genetic heritage upon which the species must ultimately depend to survive on the earth. Public policy must thus put the elimination of carcinogenic/mutagenic substances in the environment at top priority.

See CANCER.

CARPOOLS

People trying to save energy (and money) but who dislike ordinary forms of public transportation should explore the possibilities of car- or van-pooling, which began to expand dramatically in the late seventies. In most cities, there is a phone number posted near toll bridges or other concentration points of auto traffic so that people stuck in rush-hour traffic jams will notice and remember them; these numbers are for offices where you can enter your name in ongoing carpool programs or obtain names of people like yourself who are interested in setting up a carpool. The federal government also provides information about vanpools; write Vanpools, HHP-26, Federal Highway Administration, Washington, DC 20590. Pooling works only for people who have regular work schedules that they stick to, since the vehicle has to operate on a definite schedule. They are especially advantageous for people who live in outlying areas and commute downtown, where parking costs add to the other costs of operating your own car. But they are also used by people working in suburban or small-town jobs.

Some companies, universities, government organizations, and even public transit organizations have begun to organize carpools, for their employees, students, or the general public. Government grants are sometimes available to finance purchase of vans, if a suitable nonprofit umbrella organization can set up the scheme. A van makes it possible to carry substantially more people, or course, but an ordinary car will get your carpool started; later on, you may want to invest in a more comfortable van. (Or, if your group tends to expand, charter a full-sized bus.) In many small carpools, driving and use of car is rotated among members. In some, a driver is hired. There are carpools where snacks and drinks are shared on the way home, and hot coffee provided in the morning. Like buses, carpool and vanpool vehicles are entitled to use special or "diamond" lanes through congested points, which often makes your trip to work substantially faster than if you use your own car.

Almost half of our national energy supply is used in the gasoline to run our cars, and of this a large part goes for commuting. Thus, the potential energy savings of car- and van-pooling are spectacular. In time such pools will probably join public transit as the standard ways to get to work for most of the population living at a distance from their jobs. Special hazards to decide about before your pool goes into effect: how long to wait for tardy members, and your policy on smoking, radio-playing, and eating.

The concept of carpooling has been extended to long-range travel as well, by the National Carpool Association (Box 40403, Portland, OR 97240; toll-free 800-547-0933). This organization registers you as a member for a fee, and then makes available to you names and numbers of people going in the same direction as you are. You then contact them—they will include both would-be drivers and would-be passengers—and make arrangements that suit you both. You're never obliged to travel with anybody unless you choose to do so. Give NCA as much advance notice as possible, but usually a week will find you a ride or rider. Sometimes people share gas costs and driving; sometimes the driver charges the passenger a set amount.

Several thousand pilots of small planes also belong to this association. While small-plane travel is not as safe or as fast as commercial air travel, it is probably as safe as highway transportation, and of course you get to see the earth and what we have been doing to it from a totally different perspective. Most pilots seem to charge considerably less than commercial air ticket prices. Sometimes they will have to land in airports where ground transportation is not easy to get; inquire about this aspect of your trip.

CHAIRS

The Japanese say of Westerners, "They live on chairs," whereas in Japan people sit either directly on the soft tatami-mat floor or on large flat cushions. We are seldom conscious of it, but it is true that enormous amounts of our time are spent sitting in chairs of one kind or another: office chairs, kitchen chairs, easy chairs, car seats....

This is, obviously, not essential. You could, if you wanted to, furnish your place Japanese-style and live very comfortably. It might take your friends a while to get used to it (and to taking their shoes off at the door) but it would be a simpler and more healthful way of living than perching on chairs: getting up and sitting down would give your overall body muscles more exercise, and it would not crunch your internal organs as does sitting in ill-designed chairs.

Let's assume, however, that you are not prepared to go that far, at least not yet. You should still be thoughtful about your chairs and try not to have any around that are ugly; sitting in an ugly or uncomfortable chair will not do your state of mind any good. Unfortunately, American furniture designers seem to have a unique genius for producing awful stuff: bulgy, misshapen easy chairs and couches, hideous chrome-and-formica kitchen furniture, imitation Danish or Swedish furniture which somehow manages to be gross and ungraceful.

Therefore, you have to comb the secondhand stores very carefully. Couches are pretty much hopeless. You can find good old kitchen chairs, often with a rung or piece of back missing, but still sturdy and beautiful. Don't try to find "a set"; be happy with an assortment of beautiful different ones. Many old chairs have been coated with layer after layer of paint but are good solid wood underneath; see if you can find a chipped-off place where the wood is visible. (Paint remover will take the paint off, if you have patience.)

Easy chairs can be very nice to curl up and read in, but it is hard to find inexpensive attractive ones. The old leather chairs that our grandfathers sometimes had have all worn out and new ones are ruinously expensive. Chairs of a more recent vintage are mostly covered with cloth or plastic, often in ghastly colors. (A dark vinyl leather-like covering is now available which doesn't feel so clammy and is softer than most plastics. In dark brown or black, it can be tolerable.) The easiest and cheapest solution to the easy-chair problem— if you insist on solving it at all—is to find an old armchair whose upholstery is worn but whose springs aren't sticking out, and throw an attractive large piece of cloth over it.

If you come across a really beautiful heavy chair of simple design, it is possible, though it requires careful workmanship, to re-upholster it yourself— even in leather, if the shapes are not such that complex fitting is required. Study it carefully first, however; the more of the covering that can be attached with tacks, rather than by fitting and sewing, the easier the job.

CHEESE

Because it is a concentrated protein food and keeps a long time without refrigeration, cheese has been an important staple in European diets for many centuries. (Non-dairying peoples like the Chinese consider it repulsive.) Unfortunately, most cheese except low-fat cottage cheese is very high in saturated fats. Cheese comes in a fascinating variety of types—something like four hundred altogether—and is a source of the same kinds of protein you get in meat, fish, and eggs. Look around until you find a store with a good variety of cheeses; some stock nothing but cheddar

("American") and "process" cheeses. Especially avoid process cheese in little jars; it's largely water. Also stay away from pre-packaged sliced, cubed, or flavored cheese, which have ridiculously high prices. "Cheese food" is sometimes not too expensive, but it may not have much cheese in it — it can also contain dried milk, sugar, corn syrup, and who knows what else.

There are fancy imported cheeses that can become dear to a real cheese fancier (one of my favorites is a British item called Caerphilly) but you can usually find domestic versions that are excellent. Here are some of the main kinds to try.

Bel paese. A mild, creamy, light Italian cheese.

Blue. Named for its bluish streaks of mold; a very sharp tasting crumbly cheese, often put into salads. (Roquefort and gorgonzola are similar.)

Brie and camembert. Very soft, almost liquid when fully ripened, good for breakfast and dessert. Camembert has a sharper taste. Both have a crust which is edible.

Cheddar. Comes in a range of flavors, from mild to sharp. May be sliceable or almost crumbly, and varies from cream to orange color. It can be used in many recipes.

Cottage (or baker's cheese or ricotta). Lumpy texture and slightly acid milk flavor. Provides the lowest-cost protein of any cheese, with little fat, but is low in calcium compared to other cheeses and milk.

Cream cheese. Very soft, smooth white texture, though the best kinds (without added gum) are very slightly crumbly. Neufchatel is very similar, but is made from whole milk, not cream, so it's higher in protein and a bit lower in fat. (I also think it is tastier, and it can be cheaper as well.) Avoid Philadelphia brand cream cheese, which is overpriced because of its expensive advertising.

Edam and gouda. These Dutch cheeses come in ball shapes, covered with red wax. They both taste mellow and nutlike and are firm and sliceable. The gouda, which sometimes has a faintly acid flavor, also often has small holes.

Gruyere. Sharp, nutlike flavor and very smooth texture.

Liederkranz and limburger. Both these soft cheeses have a very strong flavor and smell.

Muenster. Semi-soft and creamy white inside, with a mild to mellow flavor.

Parmesan and romano. Usually cured for a year and grated for use as a seasoning in Italian dishes.

Swiss. Mild, sweet, nutlike flavor. Usually light yellow, with large holes, firm and sliceable.

All cheeses keep best for long periods in the refrigerator, but their taste is finest if they are eaten at room temperature. Cheeses go well with fruits and crackers as a dessert, and they can be mixed with practically anything else in sandwiches.

Some of the main recipes using cheese (aside from the familiar macaroni-and-cheese) are souffles, soups, fondues, and desserts (cheesecakes). Chopped up into small pieces, cheese is also excellent in salads.

Low-cholesterol imitation cheeses are available; they resemble a rather crumbly Monterey Jack.

CHICKENS

Considering that chicken-raising is perfectly legal in many towns and even in cities, surprisingly few people take advantage of this as a source of low-cost protein—both meat and eggs. It can also be a pleasure, and highly informative to children; and if you produce too many eggs for your own use, that gives you something to barter or to give to friends.

Raising a few chickens takes very little cash, very little time, and can use up kitchen scraps that you wouldn't want to compost (chickens will eat meat scraps, oyster shells, and various other kinds of refuse). Six leghorn hens can keep the average family in eggs most of the time. If you have a yard with long grass, they will consume quite a quantity of bugs, some grass and weed seeds, and will probably be sleek and beautiful, with an interesting social life. Like people, chickens do not seem as happy in small cages.

To get started in chicken raising, you need a sheltered warm place for the chicks, which you'll have to buy from a hatchery. (In cities a pet store can sometimes supply them, but at a higher cost.) A large wooden crate or even a big grocery carton will do for a dozen or so. In cold climates you will have to keep them indoors; if you keep them outdoors, make the box dog-proof and rat-proof. The easiest warming system is to get a 150-watt floodlamp bulb and suspend it over the floor of the crate—try about three feet above in ordinary weather. Make sure there is some shadow the chicks can get under if it gets too hot. Give them a constant supply of water and chicken mash; they eat more or less all the time. The water is especially important; if it runs out, the chicks will quickly die. Scatter wood shavings or some other absorbent material around to soak up the moisture from droppings. Chicks make a contented peeping sound when they are all right; if you hear them squealing piteously, they may be cold or hungry. They are normally very active and run around a lot; then they lie down in a huddle to sleep for a bit.

As they get bigger, you can gradually raise the lamp, since they need less warmth. By the time they have a more or less full set of feathers they can take spring, summer, or fall weather—but get them used to the outdoors gradually; don't just toss them out. You should start feeding them some mixed grain or cracked corn, about the time they get wing feathers. Strewing a thin trail of corn is a good way to get a chicken to go where you want it to. (Chickens are not very bright, but they are not as hysterical as turkeys. The one thing you can count on is their picking around at all small shiny or moving objects.)

There are several special necessities in raising chickens in town. One is to provide a securely fenced yard to keep out marauding dogs and raccoons. Another is to avoid keeping roosters, whose crowing will probably be considered a public nuisance by your neighbors. (Hens lay eggs without the presence of a rooster. If you feel this deprives them of happiness, you can keep your rooster at night in a cage too low for him to extend his throat straight upward, which he must do in order to crow at the dawn's early light. But of course this probably deprives *him* of some happiness!)

Chickens need a place to roost at night off the ground. They will sometimes adopt a convenient tree, or you can provide a roost made of 2 x 2's.

When the hens are nearing laying age (about five to six months) provide some comfortable nesting boxes. These should be well off the ground and have an entrance hole just big enough for a hen. Throw some straw or dry grass inside (make sure the boxes are protected from weather also and will stay dry). Collect eggs daily. The ideal system is to have an opening in the back of the nest box through which you can quietly put your hand to remove the eggs, even when a chicken is sitting there. In one rural commune with sophisticated carpenters, the laying boxes are built into the wooden fence of a large chicken run; the doors through which eggs are removed open from outside the enclosure, so the chickens aren't bothered at all. To encourage beginning layers to lay in the boxes rather than under a woodpile somewhere, some people put a darning egg (or a real egg) into the laying box when they think the hens are about ready. Early laying is irregular, by

the way; it takes some weeks or even months for a hen to get into the almost-one-per-day rhythm that a good hen can achieve.

The quality of eggs chiefly depends upon a hen's diet. If she is getting plenty of grass and bugs, they should have lovely orange yolks. Hens need cracked oyster shell as a source of calcium for the eggshells, once they begin to lay. Refrigerate your eggs, as they keep better when cool.

Sometimes a laying hen will get "broody." There are several schools of thought as to what to do when a hen begins to sit in the nest, to go out only occasionally to eat, and in short to become determined to hatch those eggs. The simplest is to let her do it, and the sympathetic reasons for this approach should be obvious. The trouble is that a hen who is allowed to go through the hatching cycle stops laying for a while. If you have a number of hens, they won't all get broody at once, so you may be willing to live with this phenomenon.

But some people match their own stubbornness to the hen's, and sometimes they win. They will pull her off the nest at every opportunity, immediately snatch away any egg she lays, put her in a wire-floored coop, and generally try to convince her that her natural instinct is a mistake.

When buying chicks, you face several interesting decisions. One is whether you want all females, all males, or mixed, which is cheaper. (There are uncanny persons who can tell almost infallibly whether a fuzzy little chick is male or female.) If you're interested purely in eggs, you might want to buy all females; if meat, all males. It is most educational to get a mixture.

There are several varieties of chickens available from hatcheries, and a great deal of special hybrid breeding and genetic research has gone into them. The leghorn is the standard all-white chicken, the workhorse (so to speak) of the poultry world. It lays white-shelled eggs, in case you suffer the delusion that they taste different. The leghorn's disadvantage is its dull appearance, especially if it is kept in bad surroundings and its plumage gets raggedy—which normally happens with good layers. Leghorns also tend to escape over fences, being light and better fliers than heavier birds. Hatcheries now have their own types of chickens developed for meat production, and these carry names given by the hatcheries. Most of them are white too, though they are developed by crosses from such attractive forebears as the New Hampshire (a chestnut-colored, dark-reddish bird; the rooster has iridescent blackish tail plumes; his neck feathers tend to be a lovely mixture of reds and golds) which you may still be able to buy if you look around.

Even in a large enclosure, chickens are prone to a poultry disease called coccidiosis which is transmitted through wet droppings and is thus most likely to spread in damp chicken houses or crowded pens. Birds with this disease droop and die; their livers have small yellowish pockmarks. Your county agent will probably be willing to come over and tell you if your birds have it, or you can leave a dead bird with him for analysis.

Vegetarians sometimes keep chickens just for the eggs, but most people want to eat the birds too. You may not find killing them easy, if you grow fond of them. You may not find it easy even if you don't like them, for in our automated and impersonal times everything is arranged so that people seldom have to face the fact that they are eating animals which have been specifically killed for that purpose. My personal feeling is that if you are going to eat meat—which I do—you should at least have had the experience of killing it yourself, so that you have firsthand knowledge of where your food is coming from.

The best way for an amateur to kill a chicken is the old hatchet on block. Make a quick, clean job of it—which means making sure the chicken's neck is laid out flat on the block. (Get a helper the first couple of times you try it.) Then hang the flopping bird up by the legs on a previously arranged rope. It will swing around wildly and spray blood a considerable distance; hang your rope out in the open somewhere. The flopping helps to drain the body of blood, which is a good thing.

There are several ways of removing feathers. The easiest for general purposes is to dunk the whole bird into a large pot of almost boiling water for a minute, shaking it around to get the water into all the feathers. Then hang it up again and pull out the feathers, largest first. They will come out in great gobs, but underneath you will find "pinfeathers" which refuse to come out so easily. They don't hurt the cooking any, but they do look unsightly, and you'll probably have to get out the worst ones with a pliers, since they're slippery. A good scald usually means you only have a few to deal with, however.

To remove the bird's innards, you should cut off the neck as short as possible, then reach in and loosen the organs accessible from the front. Then make a cut around the anus, reach into the body cavity, and pull everything out—intestines, gizzard, lungs, liver, and everything should come

out pretty much in a lump. Feel around to make sure you got everything: wash out the cavity, then feel around some more. Trim off the waste from the edible innards; skin the neck. (This whole process is known, for some weird reason, as "dressing.") Your bird is now ready to cook.

Chickens sold as "fryers" are generally young roosters. If they've been well fed, they are best eaten at about six to ten weeks old. A pullet that has been laying for six months or so is still pretty tender, but an old hen is chiefly good for stewing.

Incidentally, it is best to renew at least some of your stock every year. At the end of a laying year hens go into a molt period of four to six weeks; thereafter they lay again, bigger and stronger eggs, but fewer of them. Chickens kept breeding degenerate slowly, in a genetic sense; they get smaller and tend to lay fewer eggs. If you never bought any new hatchery chicks, your flock would theoretically revert, after many generations, to a "wild" type of bird. They would be tough, wily, and well adapted to survival, but they would horrify any proper poultry breeder.

CHILD-CARE SERVICES

Prospective parents sometimes blithely assume that ample child-care services exist, and that they will thus easily be able to return to work soon after having a baby. In reality, it is very difficult to find adequate care for very young children in most cities. Nationally, 85% of non-profit and 75% of for-profit day-care centers refuse babies under two years of age. "Official" institutions, though slightly more numerous now, are often cold and impersonal environments, with frequent staff turnover. Many home-based child-care operations are disorganized, lack basic necessities, or have tense and threatening atmospheres.

In evaluating a possible child-care situation, the first and most important thing is to honor your own psychological reaction to the place and people. If it feels comfortable and reassuring to you, it probably will to your child; if it makes you anxious and uncertain, it will probably make your child feel the same way. This overall sense is more critical than details, but you should also check out certain things about how children are handled. Make sure you visit long enough to notice, for example, how conflicts between children are treated. Are they suppressed instantly with a great show of adult authority? Are they allowed to run on for a while, but interrupted if things get too serious? Are they given total free rein? You should be comfortable with the general pattern. For babies, you'll also want to observe how toilet-training questions are dealt with. If you believe in a relaxed approach, you don't want a child-care situation where a great deal of pressure is applied.

Of course you will want to know what kinds of food your child will receive, since this will influence your own meal planning. Children love sugared foods, but a responsibly run center will minimize them, and will be sure to provide sufficiently high protein intake. Officially licensed facilities must meet state requirements for safety, space, and so on, but if you are dealing with a small private operation, make sure the children do not have access to dangerous streets, stairwells, balconies, or other lethal hazards. You may also want to check on TV policy; harassed child-care staff sometimes plunk children down in front of a TV for long periods. It is not at all necessary for a good child-care program to have a lot of expensive or complicated toys around (see TOYS) but the environment should be arranged to permit and encourage free physical activity with a variety of objects. Nor is "organized activity"—games, dances, and so on—essential; given the chance and materials, children organize a great deal of activity by themselves.

You may not choose to send your child to a regular child-care service, for economic or other reasons. It is important nonetheless to develop cooperative arrangements with friends or relatives so that you do not feel confined to full-time child care yourself. Develop exchanges with your friends from an early age on, so that your child gets used to the idea of being taken care of by other people. You will, or course, want to have some baby sitting in the evenings—and maybe you will even want to set up a formal baby-sitting "pool," where people keep track of the hours they owe and are owed, with a rotating secretary to make appointments, and so on. But it is daytime child care that is the most crucial to your welfare; so you need to develop a series of relationships with other parents with whom you can do informal exchanges. That way, without any money having to change hands, you can all gain important freedoms—and add to the variety of your children's lives as well. Sharing care of each other's children will also help to bring you closer to your friends. You might even consider starting a child-care service yourselves—it could bring in some income, and help to meet a pressing social need.

In time, child care should be integrated into our work lives—factories, offices, and stores should have facilities nearby so that parents can drop in for visits on their breaks and otherwise participate in their children's daily lives, and so that the children get to understand something of their parents' lives. Since the enterprises involved are benefitting from the work of parents, they should help to bear the costs of the child-care facilities, as is already the case in many other countries.

Good Day Care: Fighting for It, Getting It, and Keeping It, ed. by Kathleen Gallagher Ross. Women's Press, 1978. Canadian material, but excellent guide for US problems too.

CHILDREN

Children are a responsibility—both a moral and a practical one. But children are also among the most interesting people you can meet, if you bother to get to know them (your own or other people's). A lot of children are simply more fun to be with than most adults: more cheerful, more ingenious, more playful, more affectionate, more open. It's no accident that saints, artists, and other wise people have always paid attention to children—they know that you can learn as much from children as children can learn from you. Children are naturally free; they are full of the energy we all might have if adult life did not wear us down so fearfully, and they are full of mystery and surprises because they are not imprisoned by adult ideas and words and habits. Our children carry within them the only literal immortality we can have: DNA molecules bearing our genetic information, which will be passed on from generation to generation. But they also carry the immediate potential of the human race, so that in all our little acts of dealing with them we are helping create the freedom or the bondage of the next generation.

In earlier American life, children were considered an inevitable feature of almost everyone's existence. Even childless unmarried aunts and uncles participated in the lives of their nieces and nephews. It was a rare married couple that had no children, and large families (sometimes up to a dozen children) were common. With the availability of contraception, and the dawning realizations that children are expensive and that their presence sharply limits adult activities, the birthrate and family average size have both fallen. We are not yet to the point where our population has started a gentle decline, thus permitting less pressure on our resources, but we will probably reach it before the end of the 80's.

We have already entered an era in which childless people outnumber those with children. The political consequences are beginning to be felt in cities where school bonds, which once passed almost automatically, are being consistently rejected, and school boards are under strong pressure to cut budgets. (Some of this pressure, though, comes from parents who believe the schools are spending money on "frills," and want a return to reading, writing, and arithmetic.) And, since parenthood is no longer a near-universal experience, pressure is growing to take education out of the hands of the monolithic educational bureaucracy and, by some system of school "vouchers," make it possible for parents to choose among a marketplace of educational options for their children. Under this system, it is hoped, some schools would emphasize basics, some would have particular orientations toward special subject-matter areas, some would stress social development, some would be technical and scientific, some cultural. Thus, instead of trying as in the past to arrive at a state-wide, lock-step compromise educational program which nobody really is satisfied with, individual schools would be free to follow their own inclinations — and take the consequences in loss of enrollments if nobody liked the result.

Such developments, along with some parents' desire to educate their children at home, may help to reduce the isolation of children from ordinary life. Whatever their particular orientations, schools provide children with much of their early experience of the world; that experience needs to be as realistic as possible. In my view this means that in school children should be involved (just as they should be around their homes) with productive work. Schools should include gardens, workshops, and sidewalk "stores" in which their products are sold. Children should be expected to learn to manage these enterprises themselves, and to enjoy their success or suffer their failure. In a "primitive" society, children are present during most adult activities; they learn by observation and imitation, trial and error. When we can, we should also integrate our children into our real lives; but when we send them off to school, we should attempt to make sure that the school provides experiences which are not just rote learning, but learning enlivened and made compelling by its necessity in real activity.

As we engage in the political struggles required to achieve such changes, we need to keep in mind that children, who are naturally active, vigorous, optimistic, outgoing creatures, should not be ex-posed to chronic doses of adult political pessimism. It is no kindness to our children to bequeath them alienation and despair, nor will those attitudes be of use to them in trying to create the future when we are no longer around.

However, we know from the beautiful examples given us by many families whose radical parents have brought up children gracefully dedicated to the social struggle, that it is possible to be revolutionary without being bitter —to combat oppression without allowing one's spirit to be oppressed. We will meet many discouragements; but we need to show our children, by our example, that we will continue to fight gaily. We may lose a battle, or many, but we will not lose our liveliness, our human verve and spontaneity, which are the qualities that the struggle is about in the first place.

Our Children, Our Selves, by the Boston Women's Health Collective. Random House, 1979.

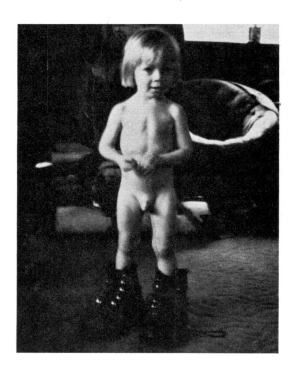

CHILDREN, TRAVELING WITH

Even children as young as two begin to be bored with what they can do around their own house, and parents commonly meet this situation by plopping them down in front of the TV. It's usually much better, for parents and children both, to get out of the house instead: to go visit friends, take a walk, go to a park or even the store. You don't really have to have a destination; small children are endlessly curious about everything, so any change of scene will intrigue them. One advantage of raising children in the country, of course, is that you can allow them to extend their "range" naturally: the bigger they get, the greater the territory they cover. A house in the country is usually surrounded by fields and woods where children can roam freely; in cities and suburbs they have to be restricted because of traffic and other hazards. Since the country is quiet, parents can count on hearing them crying if any disasters occur, whereas city parents can seldom let small kids out of the house unless they are in the care of an older brother or sister. (Middle-class parents are usually unwilling even to do that—so they have to trot along with kids whenever they leave the apartment. Small families could learn a lot from large families about how children can learn to be responsible for their smaller brothers and sisters.)

Small children who get used to being taken around with their parents learn how to deal with other small children; they get used to a variety of people and settings and situations; they learn that life is not just daddy and mommy. Carrying children around with you tends to break down the segregation that surrounds the young in our country; they get to see how adults behave and what adults expect of them.

By the time children are two-and-a-half or three, they need more activity and stimulation than even the most single-minded parent can provide, and you need to bring them into plenty of contact with other children—either in a child-care group, a nursery school, or just by exchanging them with friends who have kids about the same age.

CITY VS. COUNTRY LIVING

Admittedly, American cities have been hellish messes, and American young people often think about "going back to the land"—either to farm (often communally) or to live in small tribal bands, taking their inspiration from the original Indian inhabitants. One of the main advantages to living in the country, of course, is that you have more opportunities to use your natural ingenuity on shelter and food problems, so you can live very cheaply there; you may not have the city advantages, but you escape the disadvantages you would suffer by living at the same income level in a city slum. And you live in closer contact with the natural order and in a less stressful life-style.

But rejection of the city is a peculiarly American phenomenon; it doesn't occur in European countries whose cities are pleasant places, and where active, intelligent, future-thinking people find cities a congenial and stimulating environment. Not only that, but, as many entries in this book show (GARDENING, for instance), many wholesome activities directed toward self-reliance can be carried out in urban situations as well as in the country. It is possible to spend healthy time outdoors in city parks or on city waterfronts. City dwellers can learn to be conscious of the lives of their neighbor trees, plants, birds, and insects just as country people can: in any city vacant lot there may be fifty separate species busily surviving. COMMUNITY GARDENS often provide a springboard for a neighborhood to revitalize itself biologically, through planting of TREES and flowers. Every city window and balcony and roof can support luxuriant plant life. Once you start looking at your city environment as more than just concrete and glass, you may be surprised at the possibilities.

With the advent of expensive gasoline, a noticeable movement back to the central cities picked up speed. The cost and aggravation of commuting had become so great that many people realized they could afford stiff city rents or housing prices and still lead a better life—cutting down their dependence (and expenditures) on cars. With this resurgence of middle-class interest in the central cities, most of them have been getting back on their feet. "Urban renewal," which usually meant destruction of neighborhoods, has been stopped, and piecemeal regeneration is improving the quality of life in all kinds of neighborhoods. (See BLOCK AND NEIGHBORHOOD ORGANIZING.) Blighted waterfronts are being restored as parks and shopping areas; sometimes pollution control is even able to make bodies of water safe for swimming again. Department stores which had thought the future lay in even farther out suburban shopping centers are strengthening their old downtown operations.

Far from being just the dying end product of a decaying industrial civilization, cities have been the crucial element in human development since the very beginning of history. Jane Jacobs in her study *The Economy of Cities* (Vintage Books) suggests that even the beginning of agriculture came from the early neolithic cities.

Certainly in our world, the city is not only where the vast majority of us now live, it is also the source of most ideas (scientific, artistic, political, and philosophical—including environmental and back-to-the-land ideas). It is the source of jobs, money for development, political power. Most of all it is in the city that people have the characteristically urban human opportunity to mix with a great variety of others: to talk, to argue, to dream, to make contact with those whose minds fit with theirs, to plan, to scheme, to buy and sell. Our real problem is not to get away from or eliminate cities, but to transform them into ecologically and humanly satisfying places to live.

Romantic dreams about the easy satisfactions of rural life are usually espoused by people whose ideas of the country have been formed by brief vacations financed by city earnings. As a person who lived there twelve years, I can certify that country living is pleasant and soul-satisfying in many ways, but intellectually stimulating it is not. And, in actuality, living in the country tends to be harder materially than in the city; people are poorer, work longer hours, have worse medical and dental facilities, and even eat poorer diets. That's why so many poor people have moved into the cities since 1940. As big agriculture has prospered through government support and subsidy, the small farmers, especially southern blacks, have been driven out. "Tastes," people's preference for living in the city or the country, have really had little to do with it. People have gone to the city because they were not making it in the country.

Nevertheless, the determined band of young people who are moving back to the country find ways to survive. They do some farming, or work at odd jobs, or live on welfare, or sell dope, or have some secret income from well-to-do families. One promising arrangement is to work out symbiotic relationships between people who live in town and friends in the country. This makes possible exchanges of goods by barter, or bed-and-breakfast arrangements paid for in cash, or exchanges of living space for short or extended periods. Being *confined* to either city or country can be depressing, and we need to devise inexpensive ways of sharing living patterns between the two.

Mother Earth News, Box 70, Hendersonville, NC 28739. Aimed theoretically at the back-to-the-lander, actually covers both weird and practical projects feasible anywhere.

CLOCKS AND WATCHES

I am constitutionally dubious about "disposable" goods—things that are made so as to be unrepair-

able, and which you throw away when they start giving you trouble. But in timekeeping devices this is now the only reasonable kind for most people to have. The mass-produced Timex and Westclox timepieces keep better time than many expensive jeweled ones, yet they cost very much less. (There are only two or three kinds of insides, so you can buy the cheapest with confidence; they all run.)

If you happen to have an expensive watch and something goes wrong with it, a watchmaker will charge you a good bit just to open it up, blow on it, and find out what's the problem. So the lesson is clear: buy cheap watches and throw them away— usually they will keep time for five years or so. The same is true of alarm clocks. Avoid luminous dials—they give you a daily dose of radiation which can't do you any good. (Dials illuminated by a tiny orange bulb are okay.)

If you find alarm clocks ugly or just want to simplify your possessions you may want an alarm wristwatch. Small battery-powered travel alarms are available. There are also solar-cell-powered wristwatches, which never need batteries—the first real mass-market application of solar power!

Watches are a necessary evil at best. They interrupt and distort the normal passage of your own biological time and rhythms and impose mechanical standards that have no real meaning. The watch, like the time clock and the business suit, is usually a symbol of servitude. Try "losing" your watch once in a while—put it away out of sight somewhere. You'll probably find that you get through the day just as well without it—and it might be relaxing.

The "digital" watches which miniaturized electronics have made possible are a good example of technological hypertrophy, incidentally. Our actual experience of time is not second-by-second but in lumps or chunks, and usually when we need to know the time an approximation within five minutes or so is plenty accurate. A watch with hands provides us with an "analog" representation of time, which corresponds fairly well with our experience of it. A watch with numbers gives us superfluous digital precision—which our systems then have to translate back into the analog terms they live in.

See METRIC SYSTEM.

COFFEE

When coffee was first introduced into Western Europe, it was attacked as a degenerate substance; its imbibers gathered in coffeehouses, where the brew evidently encouraged intellectual conversation and subversive thought, for the coffee houses served as networks for the transmission of new ideas. Bach wrote a lighthearted cantata celebrating the forbidden joys of coffee.

Americans, with our unerring instinct for pleasures that do us no good, adopted coffee as our national drink, though we drink it very weak by the standards of most civilized peoples. Only recently have we grudgingly admitted that coffee is implicated in heart disease and various other disorders, and may even be mildly addictive. You should certainly keep your consumption to less than three cups a day; better yet is to switch to TEA, which contains about half the deleterious caffeine/thein compounds of coffee, and can also be a gourmet delight.

At the same time we have recognized the dangers of coffee drinking, coffee connoisseurship has spread among us. Elegant shops purvey exotic coffees (and teas), roasted in subtly different styles, along with a fantastic array of grinders, filters, and devices to make and serve the brew in. The search for the perfect cup of coffee can become as obsessive as the quest for any ideal—and as expensive. Most shops dealing in fine coffee will sell you half-pound quantities so that you can try out a lot of types. People also get into elaborate discussions about the virtues and drawbacks of various coffee-making methods, and of caffeinated vs. decaffeinated beans.

Most methods (except for espresso, which uses steam) have the common element of bringing together for about five minutes some not-quite-boiling water and some ground-up coffee, in a scrupulously clean container. You can perk it, filter it in a cone-shaped gadget, drip it, squeeze it through a cylinder of hot water, or even extract it in cold water overnight. The greatest difference is made by the cleanliness of your pot and the kind, quantity, grind, age, and condition of the coffee. You ought to fool around until you find a combination you like. (Boiling a little baking soda will clean the deposits from an old pot.) Store beans or coffee in airtight containers, and if ground, the ideal is to use it within two to three days.

The cream or half-and-half you put in coffee also has a great effect; if your home coffee isn't to your ideal taste it may simply be because you're putting milk in it instead. And be sure you're not putting in too much sugar.

Even if you've developed a taste for really strong coffee, it isn't necessary to turn to instant espresso or yearn for a full-scale Italian espresso maker. A specialized coffee store probably sells "macchinettas," little Italian pots you turn upside down, which make a properly hair-curling brew.

Instant coffee is about half as expensive per cup as real (or freeze-dried) coffee, and as it requires no apparatus but a cup and spoon, it does have advantages for people living very light and simply. Over the years its taste has improved, and there is some difference in taste between brands, so you may be able to find one that really suits you. (The one I like best, Cafe Salvador, is unfortunately available only in the San Francisco area.)

There are now instant coffee substitutes which taste quite coffee-like, and contain neither caffeine nor the methylxanthines which have been connected with benign breast cysts and possibly other health problems. To my taste, the best is Pionier (made from barley, figs, and chicory) and the next best is Bambu. Both are Swiss-made, and cost about as much as regular coffee per cup.

Coffee Lover's Companion, by Norman Kolpas. Quick Fox, 1977. Discounts health hazards, unfortunately.

COMMUNITY DEVELOPMENT

The domination of our economy by multinational corporations leaves us feeling exploited and helpless. They fix prices, produce defective products, abandon profitable plants because they make higher profits in lower-wage regions. So people are beginning to realize that community-oriented economic development may be a matter of sheer survival. It can also make neighborhoods feel more like home—economically, socially, politically.

Neighborhood-based enterprises can be responsive to a community's real needs and collective wishes. Rather surprisingly, the federal government is actually doing something to help them get started. The Department of Housing and Urban Development currently distributes $4 billion annually in Community Development Block Grants. These go to cities and counties, which are supposed to use them as seed money for enterprises that help redevelop community life and benefit low- and moderate-income people. Some of the money gets diverted into bureaucratic backwaters and corporate pockets, but some cities are making reasonable efforts to assist neighborhood programs.

The possibilities are endless: Starting new firms to generate jobs where people live (minimizing commute costs) or salvaging plants whose corporate owners have fled. Developing credit unions as sources of capital so that a neighborhood's money stays at home and works productively there, rather than going to a downtown or out-of-state bank. Refurbishing downtrodden housing or business premises, or just street clean-up, paint-up, tree-planting. Persuading businesses (bakeries, green-grocers, co-ops) to locate in neighborhoods that need them. Establishing local food production or processing facilities, recycling businesses, cooperative solar heating systems. Combatting crime through neighborhood alert programs. Improving local health facilities. Etc.

Community Development Block Grants: A Strategy for Neighborhood Groups, by Margaret Stone. National Economic Development & Law Center, 2150 Shattuck, Berkeley, CA 94704.

COMMUNITY GARDENS

Block associations have begun to turn eyesore vacant lots into mini-parks or ornamental gardens — giving a spurt of community spirit to run-down streets. But these days many city neighborhoods are sprouting not only private vegetable gardens but also community ones — either on city-owned land, or on land the city secures use of. Urban gardens provide a focus of neighborhood activity, increase residents' sense of participation in and responsibility for their neighborhoods, and lead to general clean-up and improvement. Sometimes these gardens are started by individuals looking for a place to grow things now that they are living in apartments. Sometimes public housing authorities start them, organizing and assigning plots, and on occasion providing basic preparation work. Some states and the US Department of Agriculture have offices that promote community gardening efforts. Often there are contests for best flowers and vegetables which cause a great deal of friendly excitement. And, though people initially feared vandalism from youths, frequently the neighborhood gangs are among the most avid garden-supporters and guard them faithfully. (If you start a neighborhood garden, make sure you include any local

gangs in your plans!) Gardens are particularly interesting to elderly people, often experienced gardeners with plenty of time for gardening work, which is health-enhancing on many levels.

If you're interested in starting a community garden, try to find a couple of friends to work with you. Then phone your city offices and ask for help. The USDA also maintains Cooperative Extension Service offices, with agents available to help you. Be persistent in asking about such services at city and county offices; the programs are new and phone operators may not know how to handle your inquiry.

The Complete Book of Community Gardening, by Jamie Jobb. 371 Irwin, San Rafael, CA 94901.

Spotlight on Community Gardening. Gardens for All, Bay and Harbor Roads, Shelburne, VT 95482. A monthly newsletter.

COMPOSTING

The fertility of our gardens would be greatly increased if we diverted most of our biodegradable kitchen wastes back into the earth. (Animal products, including bones, will biodegrade, but tend to attract scavengers.) The process is simple, and the results can be astonishing. The easiest procedure is to establish a trench in some part of your garden that needs soil improvement. Dig a trench about a foot deep and a couple of feet long. When you have accumulated a bucket full of kitchen scraps (a closed-top bucket enables you to accumulate them longer without decomposition odors) you deposit them in one end of the trench. Then go to the other end and extend the trench a foot or so, shoveling the dirt you dig up onto the garbage you have just deposited. This process will cover quite a lot of area in a year, and the deep digging produces great improvement in the garden soil. A drawback is that certain items (grapefruit rinds, for instance) may attract skunks.

A composting bin can be built of any kind of sturdy salvaged or scrap lumber. For a four-person household, a bin three feet square and three feet high will accommodate kitchen wastes, grass clippings, gathered leaves, animal or chicken manure, dried-out annual plants, etc. A plastic sheet used as a cover will prevent the development of a fly population, and will also increase the compost's temperature and thus speed decomposition; but you might prefer a tight-fitting wooden lid. Composting requires dampness; sprinkle some water onto the pile occasionally. An openable panel at ground level permits you to shovel out the finished

An "illegal" compost privy in Oregon. Users squat over a hole in the floor above the galvanized garbage can, which is wedged tightly against the underside. A scoop of peat moss is added after each use. When the can is full, it is set aside to cure before being taken to the compost pile. Clean, simple, elegant.

material, which will be soft, loose, and pleasant-smelling. Otherwise you should build the bin without a bottom, and remove finished material by blocking it up slightly. (In a warm climate, composting is rapid—only a couple of weeks.)

The same result can be obtained by using an old metal or plastic garbage can. Cut off the bottom, so you can remove finished material later, and punch a few holes near the bottom, to provide air. You can do composting in a circle made of wood slat fencing, inside a wall of old concrete blocks, or even in a plastic trash bag. (Add a couple of quarts of water to leaves, clippings, kitchen refuse, and some soil; tie the bag and shake it around every couple of weeks.)

Composting wastes can be mixed into soil and simply spread on your garden and dug in. They contribute plant nutrients as well as helping to improve soil quality. In time, fertilizer from the composting process in dry toilets will probably be legalized for use on food-producing gardens. This would permit a household with a large garden to become virtually a self-sufficient stable-state system for food production and recycling; it has been calculated, for example, that four persons' urine produces the nitrogen required as fertilizer for growing the vegetables they will eat in a year.

Extractive agricultural practices, highway construction, suburban sprawl, irresponsible lumbering, and many other forces are seriously depleting the earth's thin, precious layer of productive topsoil. Wherever we have the chance to build it up, or help our allies the grasses and plants and trees to stabilize and protect it, we must do so.

Everyone's Guide to Home Composting, by Robin Bem. Van Nostrand Reinhold, 1978.

Earth Manual, by Malcolm Margolin. Houghton Mifflin, 1977.

CONDOMINIUMS

Apartment renters generally resist the conversion of their buildings to condominiums, since it almost always increases their monthly outlay on housing by a substantial amount. (If you have a lease, you can probably stay until it runs out.) However, as with house ownership, the ownership of a condominium gives you access to the great American tax shelter: the fact that interest payments (which make up most of your monthly payments) are taxdeductible, along with your local property taxes. On balance, therefore, if your income is high enough to be significantly taxable, you might be at least as well off after condominium conversion— assuming, at least, that you have the necessary down payment and don't have to borrow it too. If your building "goes condo," it is imperative to obtain (with your fellow tenants) an independent engineering report on the structure, its wiring and piping, its heating system, its roof, and so on. As a condominium owner, you will share responsibility for all repairs that may become necessary. The owner of the building should be expected to provide in writing substantial warranties of the building's major components. It is essential to have a lawyer working for you (not the owner) in a condominium conversion; the documents are complex, the issues treacherous—far more so than in the ordinary house-buying contract.

Some condominiums are sold before they are built. It is risky to participate in such ventures, as you don't even know what standards of construction will prevail. In an established condominium you can inspect what you're buying—and have a structural engineer or house inspection service look it over—and also you can see what kind of community you would be getting into. Some condominiums cater to singles who do a lot of partying. Some have families with children, some don't. Some have good, cooperative relationships prevailing, some are hostile. Some may have restrictions on hobbies like ham radios, on pets, or on renting out your unit if you are away.

Condominiums may be harder to sell than detached houses, and they have not risen in value as fast as houses, though in central city areas favored by high gasoline costs, they may do so in the 80's. Operating costs in condominiums are very often higher than predicted, both because of inflation and other causes. If your total costs, square foot for square foot, would be even nearly as high as those of house owners in the vicinity, it's a bad deal.

But condominiums do offer amenities you would probably have a hard time providing for yourself: pools, saunas, squash courts, golf courses, boat docks. (Often these remain in the hands of the developer, who can and will raise the rent to the condominium owners association.) They may be attractively designed and landscaped—with less cost to you, and no maintenance and gardening duties to perform.

Before you get serious about a condominium, obtain the free booklet *Questions About Condominiums* from the US Department of Housing and Urban Development, Washington, DC. It explains possible legal pitfalls, dangers posed by unscrupulous developers, and critical financial factors.

CONTRACTS

Any paper a business or salesperson asks you to sign is probably a contract, no matter what it says at the top. Papers that are presented to you as "receipts" may be contracts. Never sign any paper until you've read it all and understand and agree with everything in it. A salesperson who tries to hurry you into not reading the contract is probably swindling you. Say firmly that you want to sit down and read it. When you sign a contract, you are promising to do everything it says—or take the legal consequences. If a salesperson is over-anxious for you to sign, there are probably parts of the contract he or she doesn't want you to see. Whenever any part of a contract is not clear, take it to a Neighborhood Legal Service office, or some reliable friend or relative, and talk it over. Never trust salespeoples' interpretations: they will say anything to make a sale and can guess what you want to hear. But in case of trouble, you will have no way of proving what the salesperson said—all that counts is what's down in the contract, on paper.

A contract will usually indicate the price of the object, your down payment if there is one, and the remaining price to be paid. Then the interest charges must be spelled out, as well as any carrying or service charges. Federal tax and sales taxes may be added. In some cases the seller may make you carry insurance on the items, especially in buying a car—but you should arrange your insurance elsewhere since the seller's is almost certain to have small coverage and high cost. Finally, the contract should show the total cost you will be paying. Look at this figure carefully: it will probably seem much larger than you expected from the sales person's pitch. If it is too high, say you have changed your mind and walk out.

Time-payment contracts will show the size, frequency, and due dates of payments. (The quicker you pay off a loan, the less it costs in interest.) They will also spell out what happens if you should miss a payment or stop paying. Usually this includes repossession, additional interest charges, garnisheeing of your income, and so on.

Never sign a contract where some of the blanks have been left open. If a blank doesn't apply to your deal, fill it up with X's. The seller should sign the copy he has shown you, right in front of you. If the contract papers disappear into a backroom with the salesperson just "to check," or "to get the boss's OK," they may come back with changes. Make sure all the copies read right and are the same. Then take yours home and store it in a safe place. If you ever have any dispute with the seller, the contract is the only legal weapon you have.

Merchants who sell on time are not all cheaters or sharks. If you can't make a payment, go around and talk to the company about it. They may be willing to extend your payments.

Contracts for work to be done around your house (if you own it) are especially dangerous, since they are often really mortgages on your property. Even where a small sum is involved, never sign such a contract. If you miss payments, your house can be taken away from you. Borrow the money from a bank or credit union if necessary, and pay by check.

Many swindlers thrive in the field of home improvements—roofing, aluminium siding and storm windows, termite work, and so on.

If you absolutely can't say no to a home-repair salesman and find you have signed a mortgage on your house, the Truth in Lending law now gives you three days of cooling-off during which you can notify the contractor (in writing) that you wish to cancel the contract. This cooling-off period, however, is widely misunderstood: it does not apply to any other type of contract, including contracts to buy a house.

COOKBOOKS

Some people collect cookbooks, others stick to one basic book and improvise from there on. And there are excellent cooks who have no cookbooks at all—but have a head full of recipes taught them by their parents and grandparents. You will find literally thousands of cookbooks in a big library, and even a small bookstore generally stocks a wide variety.

A beginning cook will want to have instructions available on the fundamentals of cooking: how long you cook meat, how to make a basic sauce, how to measure ingredients, how to bake bread, and so on. *The Joy of Cooking* by Irma S. Rombauer and Marion Rombauer Becker (Bobbs-Merrill) and *The James Beard Cookbook* (Dell Books) are two good standards of this type. Beyond that, you will want to begin to specialize. The foods of some special cultures may appeal to you. You may want to learn how to make casseroles that can be ready when you come home from work. You may be sick of your present diet and looking for something more interesting. You don't have to buy any cookbooks, however; go to your trusty local library and take out a half-dozen promising books; copy appealing recipes onto cards or into a notebook. Or go stand in a bookstore and jot down the essentials of a few dishes that strike your fancy. Most of all, when you eat something you really like at a friend's house, try to get the recipe. Recipe exchanging is a really basic kind of cultural exchange; by helping each other to eat better we render assistance that is real and stomach-felt.

COOLING

Many dwellings are not well insulated, and in hot weather they get pretty unbearable. For both economic and ecological motives, any habitation that's likely to remain standing for more than ten years is well worth insulating these days (see INSULATION). The result will be less heating expense in cold weather, and a more comfortable dwelling in hot weather, very possibly enabling you to avoid an energy-hogging and health-endangering air conditioner.

Besides, there are other ways of cooling your house. In the Southwest, people use an air cooler mounted at one of the main windows. It ought to be used in the tropical summers of the East Coast and Midwest as well. It is essentially a large cube-shaped box about the size of the lower half of the window, fastened to the house so that air can flow through it into the house. (A fan of any kind can be mounted on the windowsill, pointing in, to ensure a flow of air; remember to open a window at the other end of the house to let air out also.) Then inside the box, at the top, a drip system is installed, usually just fed by a garden hose: the hose is connected to a couple of rows of pipes (plastic pipe is cheapest) with rows of tiny holes in them. From these holes the water drips onto some kind of porous matting: the traditional southwestern one is made of aspen fiber, but you can also hang cheesecloth or burlap, strings, dense twigs—anything that will let both air and water pass through will work. The excess water is just left to drip down onto the ground. These contraptions will not of course cool air as much as an air conditioner, but they help a lot, don't cost anything to speak of, and use virtually no energy.

Sometimes one side of your place will face the sun, and get hot on that side. This can be pleasant and a good source of solar heating energy in the winter, but for the summer you need to build an overhang of some kind—check a solar architecture book at your library to figure the proper angle and thus how far out it should go. Shades inside won't help, because once the sun's rays get through the glass, their heat will spread around inside the house. You have to stop sun rays before they get into the house. If you can't manage a permanent overhang, you could put up some kind of bamboo shade or awning over the windows, or paste aluminum foil over the windows on the outside. Epoxy glue or rubber cement will hold pretty well if you clean the glass first and make sure to glue the edges down firmly. Face the shiniest side of the foil toward the sun so it reflects better. (Aluminum foil inside windows will help some, but it still lets the glass get hot and radiate heat into the room.)

Sheet aluminum is excellent roof insulation; in the Sierra foothills, where the summers are ferociously hot, every building has a bright shiny aluminum roof. Aluminum roofing is surprisingly cheap, too. If you can't stand the shine, paint it; the coating won't cut down its heat reflectance much.

It is also possible to make hot weather more tolerable by paying attention to the air circulation in your house, and by having a big fan to help circulate the air when you want it circulated. Houses cool down during the night; therefore, during several hours in the morning the inside walls and the air inside are cooler than the outside walls and the air outside. So keep your windows shut until the temperatures are about the same inside and outside. Once your house walls and ceilings have heated up thoroughly, it's likely to be hotter inside than in the shade outside, so it's to your advantage to draw the outside air in with a fan. Keep this up through the evening hours, perhaps even after bedtime. (Better yet, go sit outside in the shade, listening to the breeze blow or watching the clouds.)

The way to get a fan to push air through a house is to close all the windows but two: one where the fan is, and one at the other end of the house. Houses differ a lot in their natural air-circulation patterns; two-story houses are especially tricky. Sometimes you get the best results by putting the fan in an upstairs room, pointing outward, and opening a first-floor window that's in the shade and not over hot concrete. At any rate, if you point the fan in, remember you have to open something somewhere else so that the air can flow through the house; otherwise the fan only stirs up the air right in front of itself.

Many old houses, and houses built by people who pay proper attention to environment, are laid out so that shade trees protect them from the southern (noonday) and western (afternoon) sun. If you live in a very small house and in a very hot spot, you might consider what some Sierra trailer dwellers do: build a "tree"—an extra aluminum roof over the house, so that the sun's rays can't hit it, and air can circulate under it. This can be cheaper (and quieter) than buying and running an air conditioner, and of course it keeps off rain, so it might avoid a re-roofing job on the house. But try to relate the "extra" roof to the existing roof as a kind of echo—not just a flat platform over it.

As Bernard Rudofsky points out in his fascinating book *Streets for People*, the poorest Italian or North African town has streets which protect people from the sun in a way unknown in our American cities. Sun-filtering lattices and vines cover the Arab market streets; the Japanese use sliding cloth curtains to cut the sun's heat. But Americans just fatalistically accept broiling on hot asphalt and concrete as a natural part of life.

This isn't necessary. If we cared more about the life of our physical surroundings, we too could build shade-producing arcades like those built by the early Spanish settlers in the Southwest. Short of that, we can put up awnings or lattices made of inexpensive wood strips—in heavy snow country these can be made demountable for winter.

See AIR CONDITIONING.

CO-OP HOUSING

Apartment buildings are not always owned by private or corporate owners. In "condominiums" you buy an apartment (or duplex) from the builder or owner, and contribute to a building operation and maintenance fund that is supposedly managed by you and your fellow owners. (In New York, such apartments are traditionally called "co-op apartments.") Condominiums are being created by many owners of rental properties because they can be sold for very high prices.

But there are also true co-op housing developments—organized, built, and operated by co-operative societies, sometimes newly set up, sometimes offshoots of existing co-ops.

It is hard to get a co-op housing development going, and most recent ones that have succeeded have been managed by experienced co-op housing organizations such as the Foundation for Cooperative Housing at 230 W. 41st St., Bronx, NY 10471. Although co-ops are not able to produce low-cost housing in high-cost central city areas (only government subsidies can accomplish that), they are able to build cheaply and well in the surrounding gray areas. Their advantages are that they have no investors who skim off profits; they can build on a scale to take advantage of skillful architectural design; they create a sense of sharing and community among the people who live in them, and thus have few vacancies and low maintenance, utility, and recreation costs; they build equity for the owners and give tax savings over renting; they have lower closing costs and financing costs than ordinary mortgages; sale is generally easier; and because of co-operative maintenance, they preserve a high value in the property.

CO-OPS

You are lucky if you live in an area with co-op grocery stores—even if you don't shop there, since their presence counters the monopolistic price-fixing tendencies of the big chains. But the principles of co-operatives are far more important than their role in saving you money: they are a means of bringing the distribution of food under the control of the people who consume it. (There are also a great many producer co-operatives which help farmers market the food they produce.) A co-op is a democratically run organization with a board of directors elected by the membership; the board then usually hires a management staff. Some long-established grocery co-ops have become very large. This has given them the power to expand services greatly, but at a heavy cost in cumbersomeness and a loss of direct democracy. Consequently a new wave of small, more informal, bare-bones-services co-ops has sprung up, offering more personal contact and substantially more savings than their big cousins.

Generally co-ops price competitively with other stores (though in Sweden they aggresively undercut private-enterprise chains—a practice we should attempt to emulate here) and if they have a surplus at the end of the year, they divide it among the members according to their patronage amounts. The bigger co-ops and their associated co-op suppliers run their own testing and evaluating programs. They have home economists who can advise you on food buying and preparation problems, and they make available much useful nutrition and health-hazard information in the stores, and on the shelves, cans, and packages. Co-ops have taken the lead in reducing milk prices, enforcing accurate ingredient labelling, providing nutritional labelling, and showing price-per-pound information which enables you to cut through deceptive manufacturer sizing and pricing practices and see if the giant 79¢ package is a better buy than the colossal $1.59 package.

Co-ops have expanded into housing, where they have constructed and operated successful apartment buildings at low cost to the residents. They are also active in the health field. By emphasizing preventive care, they cut down on hospitalization and unnecessary surgery or drugs; by controlling their own health-providing organization and hiring its doctors, they have managed to put a lid on many medical costs. Co-ops also operate pharmacies at which drugs are available to both members and the general public at responsible prices.

If your area lacks a co-op, consider getting a group together to start one. It could have happy reverberations throughout your life. For information, contact the Co-operative League of America, 59 E. Van Buren, Chicago, IL 60605.

See FOOD CONSPIRACIES.

A Guide to Cooperative Alternatives. Community Publications Coop, Box 426, Louisa, VA 23093.

COST COMPARISONS

Business persons and middle-class people are always trying to be "rational about costs"—that is, trying to estimate whether one way of doing something is cheaper than another. Living this way is, admittedly, a drag; eventually you can become the Economic Wonder, judging everything dryly and arithmetically and seldom having any fun. However, such is the nature of our society that unless you are capable of calculating comparative costs you are being had, and frequently. Hence, if our schools were teaching us useful stuff, they would make sure we knew how to compare different courses of action in many real-life situations.

Take napkins, for instance. (Napkins? Well, why not?) You probably use paper napkins, like most Americans these days, and you have probably never thought about it much. If you have, you've probably guessed that your grandparents' system (cloth napkins that have to be washed and ironed all the time) is far too much trouble and probably more expensive anyway. You may say that even though you really like cloth napkins.

How to figure which is cheaper? You somehow have to arrive at the average costs. (Average in this kind of situation can mean either cost per meal or per week; it doesn't make any difference which.)

The figures which follow will be hopelessly outdated by the time you read them, but the principles of our calculations won't be affected. Low-cost paper napkins are about 70¢ for a package of 140. (The only cheaper ones are restaurant packages of five hundred.) That means the cost per napkin is about ½¢. If you have four people at table, that comes to about 2¢ per meal, 6¢ per day, 42¢ per week.

Cloth napkins which don't need any ironing can be bought for about $1, or four for $4. You can also make them, of course, and cut down the cost. They will need to be laundered about once a week. To figure the average cost of something like this, you must spread the costs out over time. How long, for instance, will those cloth napkins last? Obviously, it's impossible to say exactly, but you know it's going to be more than a few months; and you know it's not going to be for years and year. Let's just assume, therefore, that they'll last around a year. (They'll probably last longer, but what the hell.) The cost of washing them is also hard to fix precisely, since they just go into your general washbasket. But you can assign some rough guess to their share of the wash cost.

Now you're in a position to figure a comparative cost. If the cloth napkins last a year and cost $1

each, their average cost per week is about 2¢ each, or 8¢ per week for your family of four. The washing probably adds 5-10¢ per week, so your total cloth-napkin costs are around 13-18¢ per week.

Surprised? What you have just realized is that using paper napkins costs three of four times as much as using cloth napkins. This is the great power of knowing how to figure cost comparisons.

Now you know why people use cloth napkins.

Besides, using cloth napkins gives you the chance to make some weird and wonderful napkin rings or napkin holders. Clothespins painted different colors will work fine, but you can make much fancier and more elegant items: rings carved out of scrap pieces of beautiful hardwood, metal rings with etched or enameled patterns. These will identify each family member's napkin, in case you worry about germs; but if you really know a great deal about germs, you won't worry much. What our grandparents probably liked best was that each child had his or her own personal thing there on the family table, to use and take care of. Not a bad idea.

COUCHES AND SOFAS

There are many drawbacks to an ordinary couch. It is often so bulky that it gives a small room a crowded feeling. A full-size couch supposedly seats three people, but actually the middle person makes an obstruction so the end people can't talk to each other. (The old-fashioned two-person "love seat" is better for conversational purposes.) Many couches are either too narrow or too lumpy to sleep on comfortably, and their pillows don't make satisfactory sleeping surfaces even if laid down on the floor.

Couches that fold out to make a bed can be convenient, but they are almost always ugly, the beds are either too stiff or too saggy, and they cost a fortune unless you can find a battered one second-hand.

"Studio couches" are really low beds with some extra back cushions thrown in. They tend to slide out away from the wall the minute you lean on the cushions, but they are comfortable to sleep on.

In short, few if any really satisfactory cheap couches exist, and if you want one, you will probably have to make your own.

Luckily this is not difficult, if you liberate your mind from the conventional ideas. What you are after, presumably, is something you and your friends can sometimes sit on, sometimes lounge on, and sometimes sleep on. In short, a largish more or less flat surface, probably with a back along one side to lean on. This, like a bed, can be achieved with a large piece of plywood, some two-by-four lumber to support it, a slab of foam rubber or an old mattress, an attractive large piece of cloth, and some odd pillows to lean on.

You can make it freestanding and thus movable, or you can build it into a corner—which is easier, since you don't need so many legs. It's nice to do this near a fireplace so you can lie on it to watch the fire. You can make it practically on the floor, or higher. You can also hinge it at the back so it will tilt a bit for more comfortable seating but go down flat for sleeping. If you can locate the ceiling joists, you can even suspend your couch on ropes or cables so it can gently swing back and forth. You can make a storage box under it, or even drawers.

COUPONS, TRADING STAMPS

Coupons have pretty much replaced the "blue stamps" and "green stamps" of earlier decades as the supermarket chains' chief sucker-catchers; games are still sometimes tried, but are usually so transparently fraudulent that few customers are fooled. The "29¢ off" type of coupon is basically, of course, a device to persuade you to purchase something you had not planned to purchase. Once in a while you will happen upon a coupon at the time you really need something; and on other occasions, though you don't really need it yet, it's for something you're *sure* you will need later. In these cases, but only in these cases, it's wise to use the coupons, and doing so will also get you a bit ahead on INFLATION. At today's high gas and auto maintenance costs, it's never worth it to make a special trip to some store just to cash in on a coupon or two, unless you can combine the trip with taking advantage of advertised specials on things you use a lot.

Trading stamps, like credit card transactions, add to the overall cost of doing business, and these costs are passed on to you. You may therefore get slightly better value for your sales dollar if you patronize stores that don't indulge in such follies, especially co-ops.

CRAFTSMANSHIP

In my boyhood there was an old man in the town, named Mr. Womer, who lived in an ancient stone house and could fix anything. My father was pretty handy, but when he wanted something tricky done, or something done just right, Mr. Womer

A suspension bridge designed and built by local folks is one of many fine examples of Ecotopian craft work.

was the man for the job. He had a huge collection of tools; not just the usual basics, but dozens of different sizes of everything, all kept neatly in a series of toolboxes, all properly oiled and cared for. His house was very quiet, in the way some houses used to be before television; all you could hear, usually, was the ticking of several large clocks. Mr. Womer's workshop was in the back, behind the kitchen, which had a large iron wood-burning stove and worn blue linoleum. Mr. Womer knew, above all, how to assess materials, how to relate materials to tools. He carried and handled tools quietly, patiently, carefully, with a confidence that the tools would accomplish what he wanted. He was old and he was slow, but he was supremely competent. It was a joy to watch him work: to see him planning, marking wood, checking and re-checking dimensions, setting up tools, gluing, clamping, polishing, filling. Everything he did, fit; there weren't any loose joints. I imagine that the Japanese carpenters who built entire houses with mortised joints so that not a single nail was required must have worked in a similarly beautiful way.

At a certain point, this kind of competence becomes art; it becomes a satisfaction in and of itself. But this secret is not widely known. Aside from people who think of themselves as artists, it is mostly practiced by independent craftspeople who are tough and individualistic enough to have done their own thing over the years. You see them around, in their battered pickups: floating small contractors, carpenters, gardeners, fix-it persons of various kinds—eking out a living by doing something they love, and doing it well.

Thorstein Veblen told us as far back as 1899 that the spirit of craftsmanship had been killed by the industrial age and capitalist alienation; nobody any longer took pride in work, only in con-spicuous consumption. It is perfectly true that few people can take serious pride in the assembly-line or paper-shuffling work which most jobs involve today. But two developments show how hard it is to exterminate our stubborn desire to do something right: the great growth of home craftsmanship and do-it-yourself, on the one hand, and the seizure of certain possibilities in the machine technology by people who relate to it as creative artists, on the other.

Much do-it-yourself work is only aimed at money saving, which is good enough, if not too satisfying. But many people are turning to hand work because it is a relief and a contrast from the deadening, impersonal routines of the official world. You may shuffle papers or hold conferences or assemble parts by day, but by night and on weekends you can make things with your own hands that matter to you. Whether the work is called art or craft obviously makes no essential difference—people are making things that please themselves.

There are also people who seek to do creative things with advanced technology rather than out-side it—taking basically the line we associate with the Eames or Loewy traditions in design: that machine production is here to stay, and that it is interesting to try to use it artfully. Such activity transfers the spirit of workmanship from the actual making of something to the designing of it—with the actual construction ideally being done by automated factories. Although many of the resul-tant products are chilly and dull, done in the anonymous "modern" style, it is surely possible to use the machine manufacturing process interest-ingly. Designers and architects are really only beginning to confront this problem; they are mostly still caught up in an aesthetic that came in during the twenties—a kind of infatuation with

A kids' playground sculpted from ferrocement.

the machine and all its works which has now partly been transferred to computers.

The basic dilemma here arises from the fact that standardized whole objects (chairs, silverware, cars) quickly become boring, because we see them everywhere. It is only individuals who can make them non-boring, by transforming them and incorporating them into their own kind of context and structure. The unfulfilled job of technology in this area, thus, is to provide elements and units and materials that are malleable, that encourage multiform variations of use, that are in themselves multi-purpose. (It may even be possible to make plastic beautiful, though there doesn't seem to be much effort going in this direction.) In other words, if high technology is so goddamned clever, it must produce items that have the manifold uses and pleasant appearance we expect from an ordinary board or brick.

Incidentally, in the late seventies a style movement called "hi-tech" developed, involving the use of industrial products for domestic decoration. There is, of course, nothing wrong with this practice (and some instances of it are recommended in this book) but most of the products involved are actually very intermediate in their technological level. Also, because they are generally metallic, glossy, or plasticized, they are not very comforting for mammals like ourselves to spend much time around. It is not enough for domestic appurtenances to look good; they must also *feel* good.

CREDIT: INSTALLMENT PLANS AND PLASTIC MONEY

Installment Plans. Considering the variety of things available secondhand or through scavenging, bartering, or repairing, there are really not many items like appliances that one really needs to buy new, and the hazards of installment buying should make one hesitate even more. Time buying is least disadvantageous for people with sizable, steady incomes and most dangerous for people with irregular and low incomes. Even when both halves of a couple are working at decently paid jobs, they can find themselves desperately tied down by time-payment debts. So a rather old-fashioned attitude is best: don't buy anything new if you can help it; and try to save up the money for purchases beforehand. This isn't easy—but making payments isn't easy either. And by this system you avoid the risks and disadvantages:

● Buying on time costs you more. A new refrigerator that you buy on time doesn't just cost you 18% more than the cash price; check the *total* financed price, which sellers are obliged by law to calculate for you.

● Buying on time takes part of your income out of your control. Even though you may have money coming in, what you owe on payments isn't really yours. You must pay it, or the refrigerator will be repossessed and you will lose all your investment in it; worse still, your income can be garnisheed.

● Your payments can get so over-extended that you don't have money left to pay for food or to pay essential bills. When you always buy with cash, you can see the money in your pocket or checkbook: it's either there or it isn't.

When a merchant offers to sell you something "on credit," he is really offering you a loan. In the payments you make, you will not only have to repay this loan money, you will also have to pay a big chunk of interest: bigger than it would cost you to borrow that amount of money elsewhere. You always pay more when you get credit from the seller than when you borrow from a bank or credit union.

There is a great temptation to pay attention to only one thing about an installment purchase: what is the monthly payment, and can we afford it? For people with no money at all in reserve, it's hard not to get focused exclusively on this question, but you then get taken for much more than you would spend if you had the cash or could save it up.

Businesses make bigger profits from you through installment buying. For one thing, people buy things they would never buy if they had to save the cash. For another, if somebody walks into a store and plunks down cash for a color television set, the store makes only its markup—maybe half the purchase price. But if you walk in and buy that same set on time, the store makes its markup plus the store (or whoever carries the time-payment contract) also collects interest charges.

Besides, if you don't meet the payments they can repossess the set and sell it again, probably for more than its actual secondhand value (people think "repossessed merchandise" is a bargain), and at no cost except for the trouble of taking it back. There is also the danger that you may not get the legal notice they are supposed to send, and a marshall may come around and take your furniture, too, to cover the unpaid installments.

A good simple rule is never carry more than one time payment, if you must carry any at all. This way you keep down the hazard of getting over-extended, you minimize the amount of interest you lay out, and you'll be able to get a little variety into the way you spend money from month to month.

Remember that when you sign an installment contract, you are promising to pay all the installments due. If you miss payments and the store repossesses, you *still* owe most of the money. And probably you don't just owe it to the store, but the big finance company the store sold the contract to. Under new FTC rules, such holders of contracts cannot escape responsibility for charges of defective merchandise or broken guarantees or non-delivery as they formerly could. This includes credit-card companies, finance companies, and banks. This should destroy the former cozy relationship between predatory merchants and finance companies. You still, however, may be confronted by a creditor with expensive lawyers, not to mention debt collectors who can follow you to your work, bother your employer, and endanger your job, and finally garnishee your wages. In short, the chances are that you can lose a lot more through time payments than you gain.

The whole credit and installment-buying system invites cheating: it is surprisingly easy, despite all the detectives and credit-rating bureaus, to set up an installment purchase under a false name. Clever operators have been known to buy even high-ticket appliances and disappear with them, perhaps after making a payment or two. This is, of course, strictly illegal—and serial numbers make appliances easy to identify if they ever go in for repairs.

Plastic Money. Credit is the ability to borrow money when you need it. But the best time to establish credit is when you don't need it. Then later it will be available if you get stuck or suddenly decide to make some purchase for which you can't find the cash immediately. (Remember there is both the credit you obtain from banks, stores, credit-card companies, and loan companies, and also the informal credit you obtain through friends; see BORROWING.)

If you have had a regular job for some time, a checking account, a listed telephone, and some local references, you can easily establish credit with an oil company (inquire at a gas station). The next easiest is often a high-priced clothing store. Oddly enough, since such stores are generally approached by high-income people they are used to issuing credit readily. Use your card for a couple of small purchases (everybody needs socks and handkerchiefs!) and pay the account promptly when you get the bill. Once you have these to list on your credit application, you can ask to have your credit limit raised. This may mean filing a new applica-

tion (which is why you should keep a copy of the original one, so you can be consistent) but in inflationary times it is a good idea from time to time. Whether you will get it will depend on your job and address stability, your income, and whether you have overdrawn your checking account or had credit disputes; avoid both during the period you are establishing your credit.

It is now illegal to deny credit to women on the basis of sex or marital status or part-time employment or their husband's lack of credit. If you are refused credit, in most states you are entitled to know why, but the procedure of applying to the local credit-rating bureaus is cumbersome and must be carried out in writing. If a blot is laid on your credit, however, it is worth the trouble to find out why and to either correct errors in the records or settle whatever dispute is responsible for the refusal. If you are billed incorrectly on a credit account, question the billing in writing; until the matter is settled, not paying the amount in question will not affect your credit rating. Such disagreements must be resolved within 90 days after your complaint.

Once you possess credit cards, it is wise to use them as little as possible; they give some people the illusion of money-free purchasing. A simple rule is to buy some small thing on credit every six months and pay the bill promptly to avoid the otherwise staggering interest charge. Then your credit will continue to be available in case you do need it sometime.

There *are* several real uses for credit cards. One is to help in cashing checks; unfortunately, many merchants have taken to using the ownership of a credit card as an index to your general financial state. Another is to enable you to rent cars, which is now virtually impossible, no matter how much cash you offer as a deposit, without some kind of credit card. (You don't have to pay for the car rental with the card; you just have to possess one.)

If you are on the road a lot, obviously there are other ways in which a credit card can come in handy, though it's not essential—you can carry less cash and don't have to bother with traveler's checks. In ordinary life, however, the credit card and charge account are dangerous items. You may think you are strong-minded about not spending money, but restaurant owners with a business interest in human behavior have found that people spend about 30 percent more if they charge their bill rather than paying cash. Also, once you use a card in an emergency, you tend to get hooked.

Even if you don't actually spend more personally, the credit-card system causes customers as a whole to pay more. There are two reasons. First, because it costs a merchant money to honor credit cards (about three percent of your bill), he or she naturally raises prices at least enough to cover the costs. So everybody who patronizes credit-card establishments, whether by cash or charge, pays more than if the establishment did a strictly cash business. Second, and more important, the interest on late payments of credit-card bills is usually 18 percent. (The same applies to so-called "revolving accounts" pushed by department stores, Sears, and so on.)

In a money economy, everything costs money — even collecting money. The recording and transmitting of credit charges consumes vast amounts of labor. And despite the computers, mistakes are often made, so a secondary bureaucracy must be set up to handle complaints and irregularities and to police disagreements and frauds. This, of course, adds to the expense of the whole system and helps to drive the prices higher. But you can assume that it costs at least a couple of dollars for a company to make any contact with you — even to send you a brief non-computerized letter. Small amounts, then, are not worth the company's time to bother about, so many people have some success in simply refusing to pay small interest charges, engaging the companies in extended correspondence, and switching to another credit card if all else fails. The inefficiencies of the companies are so great that even in honest mistakes it can take years to get something straightened out — as people who have been billed for somebody else's purchases have discovered. (The only sure way to get attention from a human being is to punch out a whole vertical row of holes on the IBM payment card the computer sends you; this rings its bells and flashes for help.) Worst of all, the system has been introduced just at a time when most Americans (never an honest lot) have become aware of fraud, corruption, and criminality in the highest places and are more inclined than ever to get theirs if they can.

A DICTIONARY OF "CREDIT" SHUCKS AND TRICKS

Easy Credit Terms! = We will give you a loan to buy our inferior goods at outrageous interest rates.

Low Interest! = The highest interest the law allows (varies by states — may be up to 36 percent per year or even more).

Low Carrying Charges! = Charges that may be as great as the interest, or even higher, and cannot be legally limited.

No Payments for 60 Days! = We will charge you interest on the entire loan several months longer than usual, so your goods will end up costing you even more.

Save Now! = Buy now, and end up paying more later.

Nothing Down! = If we don't get it from you at the beginning, we'll get double from you in the end.

D

DAY CARE.   See CHILD-CARE SERVICES.

DISASTERS

City people are used to having specialists handle a large number of tasks which rural people generally perform for themselves: everything from domestic plumbing repairs to dealing with the consequences of storms. When services are not provided in the way they think fit, they feel helpless to do anything about it—except maybe to vote out some politicians, as happened to the mayor of Chicago when the city failed to clean up the snow one winter.

We need not only to cultivate the all-round resilience of country people who are accustomed to pitching in and improvising, but we should also give definite thought to possible disaster situations and prepare for them. Have a household meeting to discuss what should be done if there is a power blackout, or earthquake, or crippling snowstorm. Keep a flashlight with good batteries in some place where everybody can locate it, along with candles and matches. Be sure you know where the cut-offs are for your household water, gas, and electric supplies. Make a policy of keeping some kind of basic food such as rice or bulgar wheat in sufficient quantities that you could survive on it for a couple of days. And most of all, get to know your neighbors, since in emergencies collective action is almost always essential. See FIRES for special precautions in that area.

DISCOUNT HOUSES

Since World War II there has been a great growth in discount stores; they now exist in every city and sell a huge amount of merchandise of all kinds. Their prices are noticeably lower than the prices in regular appliance stores—though not as much lower as they used to be. Discounters avoid com-

pany price-fixing, where this exists in the open, by some kind of membership requirements. This usually means the customer will pay a couple of dollars for a card, but will save that amount on any substantial purchase.

In general, if you absolutely must buy something new and it costs more than about $20, you will save money buying at a discount house. Still, there are hazards. Since discounters are big-volume operators, they aren't much concerned with honoring guarantees or giving service on defective products. (Many don't even have service departments.) They'll try to stick you with time payments at high rates of interest to get back through the installments what they gave up on the price. Also, they may try to sell you inferior brands of equipment which look like the more expensive ones but which lack certain features. If you buy a Frigidaire because the discounter is selling it at less than an appliance store, you may get it home and discover it isn't the same machine you saw in the appliance store. Check model numbers and descriptions carefully.

This is even more important if you deal with a discount house that operates through the mail—you could end up paying shipping both ways on an item you don't want. And, of course, you can forget any guarantee (not that guarantees are worth much anyhow). But mail-order discounters can be very cheap; they also can be very slow! Generally you become a member by paying for a catalog.

Often co-operatives have "referral" arrangements with furniture and appliance stores which will get you a small discount. Recently co-ops and credit unions have begun to make discount arrangements on new cars, whereby you supposedly get the car for wholesale cost plus a few hundred dollars. However, you will have to sell your old car yourself—and you should still check around to make sure the discounter's final price is fair.

DISHES

The Western European bourgeois ideal was white china or porcelain dishes, shiny glassware, white linen napkins—and if you're lucky enough to inherit such stuff, don't be foolish and get rid of it: it's beautiful, like old jewelry. But for most of us, the problem is what to eat on day by day. Second-hand stores abound with plastic dishes and mass-produced dark china dishes that might as well be plastic, and old plates decorated with little flowers and tinted a faint pink. How to avoid them?

The first thing to keep in mind about dishes is that they don't all have to be alike. A table will, in fact, be more intriguing if every place is set differently. So don't trudge through thrift stores looking for "a set of dishes." Look for good individual items, but ones that really interest you. If they genuinely hit you, you'll almost always find that they also go together nicely—they may be different sizes or weights, but they'll have a common spirit.

Second, there's nothing wrong with a chip or two. A beautiful old plate is still a beautiful old plate, even if it's nicked. (Cracks, however, seldom stay mended, even with epoxy glue.)

Third, stay away from plastic—dishes and glasses both. Eating is one of the most personal, intimate things you do, so you ought not to corrupt it by eating from things that have a plastic look, feel, or smell.

People with small children may want to consider a new type of dishes which are actually glass, but virtually unbreakable; they won't break or chip even if dropped on a wooden floor. Unfortunately, they have a slightly glassy surface, but they do come in plain colors or reasonably attractive patterns.

DIVORCE

Our divorce rates now give you about a 50-50 chance, so it is unwise to get married without giving any thought to the possibility of divorce. Indeed these rates are a major motivation to consider a premarital contract (see MARRIAGE) which can avoid trouble, at least certain types of trouble, if you do separate.

In recent years, uncontested divorce has become much easier in many states and do-it-yourself divorce filing is common among people separating relatively amicably and without significant property to divide up. However, when children or property are involved, legal assistance is always necessary and desirable. Inflationary conditions, with a likely continued steep rise in real estate and a decline in the value of pension funds or other savings, make separation and divorce agreements more complex financially; expert tax advice may also be needed. When spouses plan to remain partners in holding property, the consequences of various contingencies need careful exploration so that risks and benefits are shared fairly. It is tempting, in a divorce, to try and get everything settled quickly so you can be rid of the whole mess. Many people make very unwise settlements when

they are in this frame of mind. Remember that divorce may be quick, but its consequences may be with you for the rest of your life. And once a divorce agreement has been approved by a court, it will be impossible to alter, except sometimes for child-support payments which can be changed if financial circumstances change (for the better or the worse).

Child-support payments are often set on an escalator basis. So are alimony payments, which are now relatively rare, but do exist—for ex-husbands as well as ex-wives. (The celebrated Lee Marvin-Michelle Marvin case indicated that sometimes quasi-alimony lump-sum payments may be won in cases when people have lived together for substantial periods without marriage, also.)

Legal help in divorce can be obtained from Neighborhood Legal Assistance offices or Legal Aid, and some co-ops have set up legal counseling services. In backward states where "fault" must still be proved even for a divorce that is really uncontested, a lawyer is essential. Unfortunately, getting married is cheap and divorce can be very expensive. A wise society would arrange things the other way round: getting married should be difficult and expensive, and uncontested divorce should be available simply by filling out a form and paying a filing fee. Marriage is, after all, a contract, and it ought to be dissolvable the same as any other contract, except where the state has a legitimate interest in the welfare of any children involved.

How to Get a Divorce Without a Lawyer, by David I. Levine. Bantam Books, 1978.

DYEING

If you come across clothes that appeal to you in every way but their color, they can often be dyed. Hideous pinks can be turned into almost any dark color; pastels can be covered up. You can't entirely obliterate flowery printed patterns, and you can't turn a dark color into a light one, but there are a vast number of interesting transformations you can work on clothes. It is also pleasant to give some color to items that are normally white, i.e., men's undershirts.

The dyes available in dime stores, such as Rit, are seldom used by weavers and other craftspeople who know good dyes; they are not available in subtle shades, they don't take very well, and they run onto your other clothes in the wash. To get dyes which perform well in these ways, you have to write away just like the weavers do to a company such as W. Cushing Co., Dover-Foxcroft, Maine; ask for their color book and price list. Their dyes are slightly more expensive than the dime-store brands, but well worth it. There are also many natural dyes: marigold and acacia flowers produce oranges and yellows, so do onion skins; coffee gives a reddish brown. Generally a lengthy soaking is required to extract the color, and then the fabric must be simmered for an hour or so.

Cotton and wool take dyes better than the synthetic fabrics, but you can dye rayon, acetate, and most other synthetics. Remember that all fabrics, but especially the synthetics, dry a good deal lighter than they look when wet. You can save the dye mix until your clothes dry; if they're not dark enough, put them in again.

Follow the directions carefully. Afterward, rinse the garments carefully and repeatedly—and hand-wash separately the first few times.

You need a large pot, such as an enameled one made for canning, which can take stove-burner heat. Don't use galvanized buckets or washtubs. A roasting pan is usually big enough. Make sure you've cleaned it thoroughly. The goods to be dyed also need to be clean; otherwise irregularities in color result. There are creative techniques for using irregularities—usually caused by dribbling wax onto the fabric—to make random patterns in fabric, but if you want even color, the fabric has to be clean.

Tie-dying is a fascinating special form of dyeing. If you bunch parts of the fabric together and tie them up tightly with string or elastic bands, little or no dye can get into the tied-up parts; thus they come out lighter. Since the whole thing involves many variables, you can't predict exactly what the results are going to be. This is the special fascination of the process: the generally symmetric, vaguely circular motifs are always different, always subtle.

You can't re-dye army surplus olive-drab. The reason is that the dyes used in army goods are excellent dyes. To get rid of them requires a process known as "digestion" which can only be done by a commercial dyeing plant; even then it doesn't get rid of all the underlying color, which tends to shine through the overlay of new dye.

DYING

Seeking to avoid recognition of our temporary status as living organisms here on our lovely earth, we relegate the process of dying to the social shadows. It happens "offstage," presided over by impersonal, professional, hired "others." Though more conscious attention has been directed toward it recently, by Elisabeth Kubler-Ross and others, dying is still a taboo subject for most of us, and hence we are often unable to deal with people for whom it becomes an imminent reality. But this means cutting ourselves off from an important aspect of our own lives—an aspect which then operates only subconsciously, if no less powerfully, until AGING or disease or accident forces us to confront it.

Counseling services are now available for families and individuals who are facing death. The process of recognizing and preparing for our own death is obviously an overwhelming challenge to our psychological resources, and we should not be ashamed of needing help. Nor should family members or others close to a dying person underestimate the severity of the strains they will be under.

After death, or in the process of dying, our natural counterforces fail and the microbes which normally inhabit our skin penetrate to the interior of the body. There they begin the slow process of breaking down the substances which comprise us, reducing them to other, simpler substances which later can be used again by plant or animal life. We may try to slow this process by lead-lined coffins or embalming, but in ten years or a hundred it will be completed nevertheless. We live as parts of nature, and we remain parts of nature after we are dead. Like a lowly microbe or stately redwood, we have a time to be born and a time to die—a natural cycle. We are sustained, like our fellow humans and our other fellow creatures, by feeding upon the products of previous cycles—just as we will directly or indirectly sustain those who come after us. We mourn our parents and our friends, for their lives were essential parts of ours. But we know also that generation follows generation without end. To ourselves, we seem strikingly individual, each person very different from every other. To a planetary observer we might seem more like the transient bubbles that make up an ocean wave, or the short-lived tiny fringes of the moss that covers a rock: a great web of human protoplasm covering the earth, just as the microbes cover our skin. In facing death, we also face the nature of life.

Our country, though it has a shortage of doctors and desperately unsatisfactory health care, is overrun by undertakers. Unlike doctors, they have not been able to organize and restrict their numbers so as to achieve a strong monopoly position, so they have to scramble after the available corpses and squeeze every last dollar out of bereaved families.

Their lobbies in the state legislatures have managed to obtain laws making it difficult and in some places almost impossible to die with dignity without bankrupting your family. America spends more on undertakers than on police or dentists.

If we learn more reverence for life, we must also learn how to deal more honestly with death. (Undertakers try never to use the word.) There are very few people who wish for themselves the full-scale nonsense of a typical American funeral—complete with embalming, "viewing" of the embalmed body, tons of flowers, a costly parade to the cemetery, and burial in a casket sometimes worth as much as a Cadillac. The fact that such funerals take place is due chiefly to the greed of the undertakers; they get away with it because of the guilty feelings of families who have not thought seriously about death and who are easy prey for the undertakers' hard sell. To someone expressing alarm at the idea of a $900 casket, they will speak of a simple burial as a "disposal plan."

The first thing to realize is that costly funerals are intended to make the survivors feel better. In fact, they are often authorized even when the dead person has specifically asked for simple burial. The reasons why family members will buy a costly funeral are complex. It reduces guilt they may feel at having treated the dead person badly; it softens the unconscious sense of relief at still being alive while somebody else is dead; it gives a chance for social display to prove the family can afford a good show; and it gives a dramatic focus for the expression of grief—a chance to weep, to feel desolate, to feel the loss (both to yourself and to others) which a death may entail.

Only the last of these reasons—providing an occasion for true mourning—is a decent and humane reason, and it ought to be the overriding concern behind our ways of handling death and burial. Mourning requires no pomp and circumstance and certainly not the presence of a gussied-up corpse. It requires only the gathering together of people who truly had feeling for the dead person and who wish to express it in each other's company. They can arrange a relatively formal event, religious or otherwise—or they can simply, like the Quakers, sit quietly and reflect on the life of the dead person, some individuals wishing to say something and some remaining still. Perhaps because flickering light and the immaterial, enduring quality of music seem magically appropriate, people often play music on such occasions and light candles. In many cultures which are less shy about the fact that life must go on, a wake is customary later—a drunken feast which gives expression to the life-force remaining and transforms grief at death into joy at living. We might do well to experiment with this example.

People should feel free to invent ceremonies that suit them and disregard commercial funeral practices. Death is a powerful emotional experience for those who live on; its impact ought not to be distorted by the vulgar tastes and sordid commercialism of the undertakers.

In America today most people still die in a hospital surrounded by chrome-plated equipment, hooked up to pumps and needles, watched over by dials and meters, sedated and isolated from their families and friends. The intention is humanitarian—to prolong life. But the effect is often to make a person's last days a nightmare of medical desperation, so that one dies like a medical phenomenon and not like a man or woman. In many ways it seems preferable to die at home amid your family and with your own things, thinking your own last thoughts about the adventure of life in a setting you love and feel reassured by. But this takes a great deal of strength. Also, doctors generally dislike it, and of course for some terminally ill people the care needed in their last days can only be provided in a hospital or, to follow the British example, in a "hospice," a home-like but medically equipped environment. Such facilities could and should be part of the neighborhood clinics which ought to constitute our basic everyday medical resources. It is particularly urgent to provide better visiting situations, so that family members can be with the dying person for more extended periods than most hospitals allow. The emphasis should be on preserving the quality of life until the end, without "heroic" medical efforts to extend it artificially.

What people need most when somebody has just died is practical help, moral support, and friends who are sensitive to their feelings. See whether you can pitch in with concrete assistance; don't wait to be asked. Children probably need to be watched, fed, comforted. Families may be swollen with relatives from distant places who need to be fed and housed. Mourners need to be kept company and, if they feel like talking, listened to. And, in all this, it is important to preserve a sense of ongoing life— not to distract people from grief but to give them the security they need to express their grief and thus transcend it.

As a reaction against the excesses of the undertakers, various types of funeral societies have been created across the nation. (You can get the address of one near you from the Continental Association,

1828 L St. NW, Washington, DC 20036.) You join these in advance for a small fee, and when the time comes they carry out the instructions you have given them. This saves your family and friends from having to confront undertakers at a time of grief and weakness, and can save very large sums of money. You will decide about these essentials:

Embalming? No religions commend this practice, though state laws used to require it. It means pumping the corpse full of preservatives and making it look "life-like" for viewing in the elaborate funeral services on which the undertakers make their big money.

Casket? A "container" may be legally required to transport bodies, but it may be surprisingly difficult to obtain a traditional and honorable plain pine box, without expensive handles or other "extras."

Burial or cremation? Both ground burial and cremation are very ancient customs—though cremation has only become common in America in recent years. Burial returns a body to the earth from which it sprang, and there is a certain poetic and ecological rightness in this, especially for people who have a strong attachment to the land or to the region they have lived in, or to a family whose members have customarily been buried in one spot. On the other hand, buying a cemetery plot can be very expensive.

Cremation, the burning of a corpse until it is reduced to a small boxful of ashes, has two aspects that appeal to many people. First, ashes can be scattered, which, like burial, seems an appropriate return of our mortal substance to the earth. Many legal obstacles used to obstruct this practice, but they have been struck down in most states. (People could easily circumvent them anyway, claiming to be taking ashes "back home" for interment.) Second, the fact that ashes can be scattered means that you don't have to buy a cemetery plot or an urn and a niche—for which cemeteries charge almost as much as for plots.

There are two alternatives. One is bequeathing your body to a nearby medical school, which will make it of service in the training of doctors. This is the only way to die without costing your family anything at all, in either money or trouble. Unfortunately, some medical schools are not interested, but it may be worth a phone call to find out. The other is do-it-yourself burial. The idea that people can be buried on their own or friends' land without any participation by undertakers is discouraged by every means of propaganda and law at the funeral industry's disposal. But until 50 or 100 years ago, almost everybody was buried either by church or family. It can still be done, except where city ordinances prohibit it, but there are permits to be secured and advance planning would be obligatory. In this as in other areas, our undertaking laws are one of the major insanities of our society, but they can sometimes be circumvented, and sooner or later must be directly challenged.

Social security pays a death benefit which may cover a funeral managed by a funeral society. Unions, credit unions, and lodges or similar organizations may also pay death benefits, and Workmen's Compensation insurance may also apply. Veterans theoretically can be buried free in national cemeteries, but most of these are full (check with the Veterans Administration).

The Hospice Movement, by Sandol Stoddard. Vintage Books, Random House, 1978.

On Death and Dying, by Elisabeth Kubler-Ross. Macmillan, 1969.

EATING

Humans are the deadliest predators on the face of the earth: we are capable of catching and eating any other creature. But we have grown so efficient (and perhaps so unnatural) that we no longer have to bother to catch our prey: we raise it in captivity, fatten it for slaughter. Nor must we gather acorns on the slopes as the Indians did and leach them and grind them into meal; instead we have vast agribusiness corporations whose employees plow and plant and harvest with gigantic machines. Few among us capture or grow any substantial part of our own food. Instead, we buy food in huge hallucinatory barns called supermarkets, where it is packaged in multicolored cellophane and plastic to keep from our consciousness—so far as that is possible—the facts of what we eat.

Children are not so easily brainwashed. Around the age of two, they become curious about food. They ask us what is that stuff we call "hamburger," and if we are not too evasive they get us to tell them it is ground-up cow meat. They look very doubtfully at a roast chicken, especially if they have seen live chickens at a kiddie farm or zoo. Often sensitive children at this stage will go through a vegetarian period. And they may also become fearful, for if big animals like their parents eat little animals like chickens, how are they to be sure that they are safe?

Eating is, thus, a far more serious business than most of us usually admit. Looked at from an overall ecological point of view, eating is the means whereby energy is transferred from the lower levels of food chains toward the top. The tiniest bacteria live in the soil, taking up and decomposing organic material; they are eaten by minute worms, which may be eaten by shrews or moles, which in turn are eaten by owls and hawks. Similar food chains exist in the oceans and other bodies of water: from microscopic plankton up to tuna and porpoises. Every creature which eats another smaller creature appropriates to itself the energy that has been stored up by that creature. It does this by decomposing its food into juices whose chemical components can be used as fuel or building elements in its own body.

For millions of years this process of eating and being eaten went on naturally upon the surface of the earth and in its waters. The wastes of each level of life became the raw materials of other levels of life, in a great chain or cycle. The dung of the buffalo nourished the grasses upon which the buffalo fed.

Humans, however, are largely heedless of the ecological cycle. We eat whatever we can get our hands on, and we carefully and idiotically wash our wastes down elaborate sewage systems into the rivers and ultimately into the ocean. Little by little, as the sewage of hundreds of millions carries its fertility away to the sea, our land becomes less productive and requires massive doses of chemical fertilizers to revitalize it. Our rivers become more polluted; the fish die. In the ruined cities of the past, historians now think we may see the price of ecological mayhem wrought by ill-considered irrigation schemes. And in the end, our cities and our great lush farmlands will go the way of those others: already the signs are visible in the steady dropping of underground water tables, in soil which needs massive doses of fertilizer, in the push of salty waters into new areas.

Eating is therefore of more than mere culinary or nutritional interest. Furthermore it is true that, quite literally, we are what we eat. Practically every tiny molecule in your body has been replaced in the past few years, in a steady process whereby your flesh and even the soft insides of your bones are renewed.

In themselves such reflections lead to no necessary conclusions about how we should eat; some people become vegetarians, some eat meat, some eat austerely, some become gourmets. But they put the kind of merely "scientific" advice we are given about diet and nutrition into a rather more intriguing light. And they give us a perspective in which we can think more lucidly about the American diet and its various hazards.

When you begin to think about changing your mode of living it is often easiest to begin with food—perhaps because food is such a personal matter and also because it's something you can easily control: if you want to stop eating meat, you can just do it. If you decide to engage in dietary self-defense, avoiding additives and preservatives and minimizing your intake of saturated fats, cholesterol and sugar, that is entirely within your power. Eating is thus one of the few areas of daily life where we do indeed possess the power to effect major changes; and it is no wonder that, in recent years, millions of people have done so.

(See EATING BETTER; REDUCING; VEGETARIANISM.)

EATING BETTER

There was a time when nobody worried about whether they were eating right. People's diets were fixed by tradition and by the fact that many foods were available only to the very rich. If you were of Hispanic background, you ate tortillas and other corn products along with beans; if you were black, you ate beans and greens and fatback; if you were Italian, you ate pasta with sauces; if you were Irish or Polish, the basic diet was potatoes; and around these basic foods each national diet used a small group of supplementary items: meats, cheese, vegetables, fruits, bread.

Nowadays, the traditional ways of eating are largely disappearing. Now almost nobody under thirty has been brought up in a really traditional way. American culture since World War II has become far more homogenized, nationally, under the impact of advertising, television, movies, and mass-produced products. The fried shrimp you eat in Chicago can also be eaten in San Diego and Boston; it comes frozen and pre-packaged (and even pre-breaded) from a factory in New Orleans.

But, oddly enough, people have at the same time become more confused about food. There are more and more fancy prepared or half-prepared foods around. There are thousands of "snack" foods, chips and dips and crackers and drinks, which look good but may have almost no food value and are expensive and heavily laced with additives, many of which are health hazards. People are worried and confused about the fattening effect of foods. The appeal of expensive meats and other foods has caused a downgrading of the basic, cheaper foods which every diet requires. Thus people pay too little attention to the food quality of the bread or flour or rice or beans that may be the foundation of their diets.

Worse still, in recent years the quality of many basic foods has actually *declined*. Flour-refining processes take out increasing amounts of the nutrients that originally grow in wheat or corn kernels, and the hulling and polishing of rice to make it look white removes its vitamins and other nutrients. (Surprisingly often, the best parts of foods, their most important nutrients, lie near the skin or surface.) When the American government exports surplus foods to underdeveloped countries, it makes sure the flour is "enriched" to put back the nutrients taken out in refining; it adds vitamin D to dried milk; it develops highly nourishing fish flour and basic protein foods; it even develops special cola-type drinks that are not just sugar and flavored water but actually have food value. But we at home are left to the tender mercies of the food industry and products that do not have to meet any positive healthful standards.

Now this is a terrible state of affairs. You ought to be able to go into any store, anywhere, and be sure that when you buy flour you are getting flour that has the fullest food value flour can have. You ought to be able to take it for granted that when you buy bread it's healthy bread, and not just a soggy concoction that's mostly air with about as much food value as wet cardboard.

To defend yourself against the perils of diet deficiencies, there are really only a few main points you need to know. Unfortunately, millions of Americans either never heard of these basic facts or have forgotten them along with a lot of other stuff thrown at them in school. In some instances, they have positively ignored them; as one student said, "I've lived on nothing but pizza and Coke for three weeks, and I'm still alive."

There are diets worse than pizza and Coke. All the same, you can't live long on a bad diet without endangering your health and your endurance. And if women try to go through pregnancy without eating decently, they may suffer real trouble themselves—and give birth to underweight, badly developed, or even defective babies.

Here, in as compact a form as I can make it, is what everybody needs to know about the nutritional side of eating:

In reality there is no food, not one single food of any kind, that is essential to human health. It even turns out that spinach, although it's one of the best green vegetables (along with broccoli, collards, etc.) and good to eat contains a form of iron which can't be assimilated by the human body—so all those children who had to eat spinach "for its iron" were doing so in vain. Carrots, although they are an excellent source of vitamin A, essential to good eyesight, are not the only source; nowadays margarine is enriched to provide more than enough vitamin A for everybody (butter also contains it).

In short, there is no reason to eat anything you don't like. The world is full of healthy foods, and if you have a varied diet you can be almost sure that you are eating well. There is no reason to fear food deficiencies unless you are among the people who are so terribly poor, uninformed, or badly brought up that they eat only a few things all the time. Even a simple regular diet can be perfectly nutritious, but constantly eating only a few basic items raises the chances that you will be missing some of the essentials. (There are forty-three substances, besides air and water, necessary to keep the human body functioning normally.)

Nutrition handbooks and guides and government publications are always coming out with authoritarian rules like "Eat all four food groups every day." These groups are: (1) milk and milk products; (2) meat, chicken, and fish; (3) vegetables and fruit; (4) bread and cereals. There is no earthly biological reason why you must eat meat at all (as long as you understand how to replace the proteins you would have gotten from it). Nor must you fanatically eat the other three categories every single day, as long as in the course of a week you are eating a balanced diet that includes plenty of all of them several times. A day is a short time in the perspective of most body processes. Your body doesn't punch a time clock. So what you really have to keep an eye on is relatively simple. (It's also simple to pass good eating habits on to your children who will then grow up to eat right and feed their babies right.)

An advantage in buying most of your week's food in one shopping trip (see FOOD SHOPPING) is that in making up your list (on paper, to avoid impulse buying) you can see whether you're getting a good variety of foods. Here are the essentials:

Milk group. Essential proteins—body-building and -repairing non-fat foods—are obtained from milk (dry has just as much protein as whole milk), cheese, yogurt, ice cream (not "imitation ice cream"). Although milk prices may seem sky-high to you, milk is still a bargain for protein food. Children and nursing mothers need about three cups of milk per day, or about five quarts per week. A family with two adults and two kids under eighteen ought to drink about fourteen quarts per week. However, a one-inch cube of cheese equals a cup of milk; yogurt is also a good substitute, so if you use them you won't need as much milk. (See MILK for other ways to cut expenses and stay healthy.)

Meat group. These are also largely protein sources: meat, fish, poultry, eggs, dry beans (especially soybeans), nuts, peanut butter. Meat is the largest expense in most American grocery shopping lists. Short of becoming more or less a vegetarian, therefore, the main problem in eating well but inexpensively is to devise meals which don't use much meat and which avoid the over-priced (because they're over-popular) cuts. So the basic strategy is to reorient meal-planning away from the conventional meat-potatoes-and-vegetable rut. This enables you to take advantage of the rich inexpensive protein resources of beans, fish, the more esoteric cuts of meat, and poultry. (In general, poultry is not only your best buy economically, but is also less fatty than meat, especially if you cut away skin and excess fat before cooking.) Expense has nothing to do with nutritional value in meat. (See MEAT for more on this.) Liver, kidneys, and other non-standard meats have about the same food value as lean steaks and chops, may have more than fatty ones, and certainly give you far more nourishment per dollar.

Vegetable and fruit group. These provide essential vitamins, roughage, and food energy. In the course of a week you should include some dark green vegetables such as spinach, collards, broccoli; some yellow ones such as carrots, squash, yellow beans; and some citrus fruits such as oranges, grapefruit, tomatoes. Even if you take vitamin pills (usually a waste of money), you need to eat some of each kind of food in this group. You should, of course, liven up your meals with tasty fresh vegetables when they're plentiful and cheap; but most of the year the basic routine will be buying frozen vegetables and cooking them in as little water as possible. (Their food value is about the same as the fresh ones.) Frozen orange juice is the cheapest citrus you can get; canned tomatoes and juice are fairly cheap all year-round. Raw fruit (apples, pears) with cheese makes an elegant continental-style dessert.

Salads are an especially tasty way of eating vegetables and are a whole subject in themselves (see SALADS). You can also simple munch on raw carrots, slices of green pepper, celery, cauliflower, tomatoes, and so on. Avoid iceberg lettuce, which has almost no food value.

Mashed or sieved vegetables and fruits are good for babies, as they provide iron. (Iron and vitamin D are the only substances not supplied in mother's milk.)

Bread and cereal group. The basic starchy carbohydrate energy foods come from this group, but a few of them also supply some protein. ("Cereal" here means grain, not breakfast food, although breakfast foods do come from grains.) Wheat, oats, rice, and other grains contain a good deal of protein originally; corn contains less. However, the process of milling the kernels (to give white flour or white rice) removes most of the protein and vitamins. People who insist on preferring white bread to whole wheat or white rice to brown are getting nutrient-deficient food. To counteract this, many flours, rices, and pasta products like spaghetti are now "enriched"—some of the lost nutrients are restored artifically. Look on the label: if it isn't enriched with B-vitamins (niacin, thiamin, etc.) and iron, forget it.

There is also a fifth official group, "other foods," which includes butter (and margarine), sugars, unenriched greasy bakery goods like doughnuts, cakes, cookies, and so on. You need not pay any attention to this group except to try and cut down on items in it; almost all Americans, rich and poor, eat too much of the foods in this group. Our *sugar* intake is scandalous and is a major reason for our national tendency toward overweight; also, it eats holes in your teeth and unbalances your metabolism. Fats are 40-45 percent of the average American diet, which is about half again as much as they should be. This is not only bad for one's health, but expensive besides.

Here, then, are a few rules of thumb (or stomach) for how to eat better under our debased dietary conditions:

Learn to read LABELS, not only to spot suspicious additives, but to notice the amounts of calories, protein grams, and saturated fats that foods contain per serving.

Drink non-fat milk; emphasize cottage cheese, yogurt, and other low-fat cheeses.

Cut down meat intake; emphasize chicken or turkey or fish.

Include plenty of dark-green vegetables, yellow vegetables, and fruits.

Eat decent whole-grain bread, and avoid rich, sugary baked goods, or other sugary foods.

Avoid high-calorie soft drinks, and minimize beer and other forms of ALCOHOL.

Following these simple principles will help you keep trim, since it reduces empty calorie intake. It will help keep you in basic good health, and if combined with sensible EXERCISE, will prolong your life.

See FOOD FADS.

Natural Foods Guide, compiled from the pages of *Whole Foods Magazine.* And/Or, 1979.

Handbook of the Nutritional Contents of Foods. US Department of Agriculture. Dover Books, 1975 (from USDA 1963 ed.) The source for most other nutrition tables.

Chemical Cuisine, C.S.P.I., 1755 S St. NW, Washington DC 20009. A handy chart for your ktichen wall, showing safe, doubtful, and dangerous additives.

A Consumer's Dictionary of Food Additives, by Ruth Winter. Crown, 1978.

Nutrition Survival Kit: An Antidote to Additives, by Kathy Dinaburg and D'Ann Ausherman Akel. Jove Books, 1978.

The Supermarket Handbook: Access to Whole Foods, by Nikki and David Goldbeck. Signet, 1976.

EATING OUT, WAYS TO AVOID

The proportion of meals Americans eat out has been rising sharply (and many of those "meals" are in fast-food places where the lack of vegetable and fruit foods makes for a badly unbalanced diet). But people living wisely and modestly should avoid eating out whenever possible—for reasons both of expense and nutrition. There are various strategies to avoid it, even if you are not a very home-centered person. One is to eat a big breakfast and a big supper. This will often get you through the day or else you may need just a small snack for lunch, such as a sandwich you can carry in your pocket, or some cheese and a piece of fruit. Or, you can avoid big meals altogether and, like our proto-human ancestors, have intermittent snacks all day— healthy foods, not junk. You can keep small supplies of food where you spend most of your time, or even make a habit of carrying food around with you. This is easiest if you carry a handbag or a knapsack or wear a coat with spacious pockets. Then you can get used to carrying a little food all the time—a bit of bread or hardtack, maybe a small can of sardines, a piece of cheese or salami: nourishing food you can if necessary make a meal out of, and not just a snack for emergencies.

The same idea applies when you go out on all-day expeditions. Never go to the zoo or the beach or on a long walk without taking food along. Get to be ingenious at making sandwiches. Remember, too, that in most places there is some kind of grocery store within walking distance. For the same money you'd spend on a couple of hamburgers, you can buy a loaf of bread, some cheese, maybe a green vegetable to be eaten raw (spinach or celery), and a quart of milk. For what you'd pay for a slice of pie or cake, you can buy several apples or pears or oranges. Carrying a good pocketknife means you can slice food up, open cans, open bottles, and generally cope with the problems of eating on the move; never be without one. (See KNIVES.)

ECO-CRIME

Our tradition of law arose several thousand years ago, in a much simpler world, when harm done to persons was directly observable: somebody hit you with a club, or stole your horse, or killed your sister. Such crimes are easy to define, obtain witnesses to, and prosecute. In our epoch, however, law based upon this tradition has been unable to cope with many harms because they are committed indirectly, upon large numbers of people, and usually by corporations whose individual owners, managers, and operators are shielded from personal responsibility for their actions by corporation law. In any true sense of justice, it is exactly as criminal to discharge cancer-causing compounds in the Mississippi River upstream from the drinking-water intakes of St. Louis and New Orleans as it would be to go out and club random people to death on the streets of those cities. The deaths involved are real and painful deaths in both cases; they have identifiable individual perpetrators. But, even though the cancer deaths are in fact far more numerous than the street-crime deaths, we have not tried to convict their perpetrators because the connection between the dumping of carcinogens and the individual deaths by cancer can only be established by statistical probability. (The evaluation of *all* legal evidence is in fact a matter of probability assessment too, of course; judges and juries must decide which witnesses are probably lying and which are probably telling the truth.)

The result has been that the law treats street criminals severely; "eco-criminals," people who order or authorize or commit damages and outrages against the environment and thus the public at large, have almost entirely escaped prosecution, or indeed even public moral condemnation. We have confined ourselves to attempting regulation of their activities by government agencies, which (usually ineffectually) try to limit the mayhem committed upon citizens. These eco-criminals are superficially respectable people, but it is time to recognize that criminals are criminals, even if they carry expensive briefcases and ride in company limousines. Criminal penalties—the spending of substantial times in jail, not just the payment of deductible fines—must be attached to the knowing commission of acts that kill, maim, or sicken members of the public. Until we have laws for this purpose, and enforce them, it will continue to be ourselves and our children who pay with our lives for corporate dumping of toxic wastes, for pollution of air and water, for the manufacture of unsafe products.

EDUCATION, COMMUNITY RESOURCES

In recent years new types of educational activity have proliferated in our urban areas. Somewhere in the shadows of most universities you will find a "free university" or education exchange of some kind. These organizations are basically coordinating and advertising entities to connect people who want to teach or study some subject. The classes offered range from highly technical matters like auto repair or computer programming to esoteric religious doctrines. The teachers who volunteer to teach them range from brilliant, innovative, restless souls to totally incompetent idiots: you are strictly on your own—you pay your money (most of which should be refundable after the first session if you decide to drop the class) and take your choice, without benefit of accreditation machinery. The material offered may thus be far ahead of traditional university fare, or garbled and out of date.

Community colleges are being asked to bear an increasing part of the load of educating students who have modest resources or do not wish to go to college away from home. They are not, of course, immune to the financial pressures of the 80's which are also grinding away at private and state colleges. But they cater to an interestingly varied student body, including people of different ages, work backgrounds, and motivations. Many courses are oriented narrowly toward direct job qualifications, but you can also contine your general education through a community college. Today, with jobs in top universities closed up, the staff at such colleges may be university-quality people.

Besides being a community-run school, this is one of the finest local-built schools we've ever seen.

Universities with budget problems have been expanding their extension divisions. These offer night and weekend classes in a wide variety of subjects; some of them are identical to university classes and are available for academic credit if you wish. They are taught by people with good academic credentials, who have the same range of quality as professors generally (teaching extension courses is a way for underpaid academics to make a little extra money). Extension divisions usually have correspondence courses available too, if you can't attend classes or don't want to. These are, of course, on a higher level than those offered by private correspondence schools, some of which are accredited and some not.

Many high schools, despite budget squeezes, still offer night school classes in vocational areas like auto shop or business and language skills, as well as regular academic classes you can take to finish high school if you dropped out to work. A few of them are still able to offer craft and hobby classes.

EDUCATION FOR SURVIVAL

The objectives of the official curriculum are defined and carried out in ways that prevent or inhibit students from using their minds to deal with the real issues and real needs of their lives. Nonetheless, it is still possible to learn a lot in school, and for any student who is going to be confined there for many years, it is senseless not to put it to whatever advantage you can.

Many essentials for survival with any kind of style are left virtually untouched by the schools, and it is up to us to learn about them from other sources. This book provides a basic orientation in certain areas, and indicates other sources you can turn to. But you might find it interesting to write out your own list of what you think it essential to know, just in order to get by decently in modern conditions, and to see whether your school offers help toward some of it. This might include a certain amount of technical information which is only taught, at present, to boys (and a few enterprising girls) enrolled in shop courses; how to use basic tools and work safely, how household electricity works, and what to do when it doesn't work. You may feel a grounding in "home economics" (dismal term!) is vital: how to cook basic nourishing foods, how to mend and sew, how to recognize frauds in stores, and how to figure unit prices of items. Your list might include social skills: how to find out about abortions in a hurry, how to complain to city hall, how to react to police harassment, how to defend yourself—judo, handling firearms. We all need to know how to drive a car, type, and so on. We need food-providing skills: how to garden, fish, dress game and poultry. Educators worry about "mere" skill training, forgetting that it is in learning how to do something useful to us that we practice the real essentials of education (analyzing situations, using our minds and their knowledge of reading, mathematics, physics, biology) and that attempts to teach such things abstractly are doomed to dullness, failure, and resentment. Thus a course in judo, for instance, requires an understanding of all the principles of mechanics (levers, forces, momentum) taught in physics courses—but how much more directly and personally!

Our education is strangely abstract and word-limited. It has no poetry in it, even when English classes analyze poems. The care of our bodies is almost a taboo subject: when discussed at all, it is taught in special classes, often segregated by sex. Most teenagers pick up a great amount of gossipy lore about skin care, sexual hygiene, and so on, but strangely few of us know much about first aid—despite the fact that automobile crashes are a constant feature of American life. Our schooling helps conceal from us that the human body is a vulnerable and delicate organism: it can drown, bleed to death, suffer heart attacks, and experience many other dangers which quick help might greatly alleviate. Yet only a handful of people have real experience and training, and school first-aid courses are almost all a joke. Schools should make sure that everyone knows how to administer sensible simple first-aid—and not only knows how, but has practiced it. Imaginative schools should stage "accidents" on the grounds and in hallways, to give kids practice in emergency situations.

But it is not only in danger situations that we ignore the needs of our bodies. Massage, for instance, is a great aid and pleasure to people whose lives make them tense and physically rigid, and who don't get enough exercise. Reducing salons, physical culture gyms, and massage parlors are all busily making money from massaging people. But massage is something that everybody ought to know how to do well, just as they ought to know how to make decent coffee and swim. It's not something you can learn out of books, either.

Perhaps worst of all, our schools do not teach us how to relate to each other in responsible, helping ways, but only in impersonal, competitive ways. Our education trains us for a life of alienation, conflict, loneliness. People brought up in prisons behave like inmates; they have been taught to. If we can achieve smaller schools, and if students can have a strong voice in running them so that they develop a sense of responsibility toward each other, we may yet turn back the awful tide of anonymity and unconcern. And if in our friendship networks and extended families and social and political groups we can practice direct care for each other, we may be able to develop the kind of direct personal solidarity that used to be found in large families, where everybody is educated by everybody else.

EGGS

Eggs are a prime source of protein; unfortunately, their yolks are also a prime source of cholesterol. For some people, though *not* for all, eating two eggs a day results in a pronounced rise in blood cholesterol, and conservative advice is to eat no more than three egg yolks a week. (Egg white can be eaten in any amounts you like.) This amount of egg is probably provided by the baked goods you eat, actually. So if you are trying to cut your cholesterol levels for your circulatory system's sake, you might want to switch to an "imitation egg" product. However, these contain various additives, so they are hardly ideal. You can, if you wish, run an experiment to determine if your system is sensitive to egg. Eat no eggs for six weeks and have your cholesterol checked; then eat as many eggs as you like for another six weeks, and have it checked again; then check it once more in six months. If the level is the same in all three tests, your cholesterol level is not being affected.

For most people, it is more critical to cut down on the amount of saturated fats consumed in meats and dairy products than it is to cut direct cholesterol consumption.

As this book goes to press, the effects of diet on serum cholesterol are under investigation. It is no longer certain that a low-cholesterol diet will reduce cholesterol in your blood. EXERCISE may be an important factor in keeping down cholesterol levels. It is certain however, that a low fat diet will keep your weight down, which does reduce heart strain.

EMPLOYEE OWNERSHIP
(WORKERS CONTROL)

Industrial enterprises of many kinds are being successfully run on a democratic rather than authoritarian basis through various systems of worker ownership and management. On the principle that those who do the work should have the power to organize and control that work (and bear the responsibility for making basic business

decisions correctly), such enterprises generally have an elected board of directors who appoint operating managers; the board is responsible to the company employee body in making its decisions about investment, acquisition of equipment, changes in products, etc. If the employees become unhappy with the direction board and management decisions are going, they can elect new directors and change it (as has happened).

This is obviously a very different system from that prevalent in US business, where absentee owners and management are free to run a plant in any way they can get away with. Workers control gives people real and direct influence on how their jobs are set up, what standards they work to, their hours and shifts, and so on. It gives them a direct stake in the company's fortunes. (Output productivity in worker-controlled enterprises is usually considerably higher than in ordinary enterprises, for that reason.)

Household basement workshop.

Employee ownership is fundamentally different from "ESOP's" or "Kelso plans," in which employees obtain non-voting stock that gives them no control over the company (though it may give them some stock dividends). Kelso plans in fact are usually entered into by companies as a way of raising capital without having to go into the market for it. They are sometimes preferable, for employees, to the ordinary outside ownership situation, but they are *not* employee ownership or workers control. "Participation" by union representatives on company boards of directors, which has become common in Europe, is also not workers control, since the union representatives have only a very small number of votes. But true workers control is being attempted as basic national policy in Yugoslavia, it is common in England, and it is spreading in the United States.

The reasons are many. Sometimes a company will decide to close a plant, and the local employees will buy it and keep it going, often at a handsome profit (to themselves, this time). Sometimes a strike in a small company will paralyze the operation to the point where the owners simply decide to call it quits, and the employees, usually through their union, make a deal to take it over. Sometimes new operations are set up on an employee-ownership basis by people who believe that's the way our economic system should be run, for both idealistic and purely personal reasons. (An employee-owned company obviously has much more personal and more important interaction among its people than a conventional company.) And as our population includes more college-educated people, it will seem more natural to them that if they are going to have to take menial jobs because that's all the jobs there are, at least they ought to have some say over how those jobs are run.

Operating a worker-controlled company is probably no easier than operating a conventional one; many problems faced are similar. The New School for Democratic Management, 859 Howard St., San Francisco, CA 94103, is a "business school" which holds week-long teaching sessions all over the country; write or phone 415-543-7973 for details.

Own Your Own Job: Economic Democracy for Working Americans, by Jeremy Rifkin. Bantam, 1977.
Democracy at Work: A Guide to Workplace Ownership, Participation, and Self-Management Experiments in the US and Europe, by Daniel Zwerdling. Assoc. for Self-Management, c/o 1414 Spring Rd. NW, Washington, DC 20010. This association also publishes a newsletter and organizes local chapters.

EMPLOYMENT AGENCIES

It's a good idea to try employment agencies before you get too desperate for a job—don't treat them as a last resort. Check the want ads and find agencies listing your kind of job. When you go to an agency, put on your job costume and behave as if they were employers.

Watch out for racketeers. Don't deal with agencies that charge a "registration fee" or other fee before they get you a job; legitimate agencies only get paid if they place you. Try to avoid agencies that demand exclusive representation—you may want to have several agencies try to help you. When you register with an agency, they will make you sign a contract. Read it very carefully. Especially check for penalty clauses; sometimes these allow the agency to charge you even if you find a job yourself, or even if some other agency finds it for you. Sometimes they obligate you to pay a huge fee if you accept a job and then don't show up, or if the job turns out to be intolerable and you quit, or if you're fired. Do not sign such a contract, no matter how much you need a job, or how "nice" the agency people are. (If they were really nice, they would delete these clauses from the contract, and put their initials next to yours in the margin.)

An agency that is on the level will set its fees as a percentage of your future earnings, like 50 percent of the first month's pay. But generally these fees can be paid in a series of installments, so you do have something to live on while you're paying them off. Make sure the interest rate on these installments is clearly specified—agency fees can be deducted from your income tax at the end of the year.

Some employers in effect use employment agencies as their personnel departments, and pay the fees involved. Watch for their "Employer Pays Fee" ads, but don't neglect the other agencies.

Racket agencies sometimes list juicy imaginary jobs in the papers, and then push you off onto other jobs when you show up—a kind of bait-and-switch operation.

Agencies are especially handy if you are looking for a job while you still have your old one, because that way you can't possibly answer an ad and have it turn out to be your own company. Using an agency may also save you a certain amount of duplicate filling out of employment forms.

After an interview with a possible employer, phone back to the agency and tell them what happened.

See TEMPORARY HELP AGENCIES.

ENERGY

A great deal of irrelevant debate has been carried on about what our national energy policy should be; in effect, we have had none, which means that the previous inertial patterns (of reliance on fossil fuels, much of them provided by OPEC nations at sharply increasing prices) have simply continued. Americans tend to assume that some easy technological fix *must* be available to save them from the hideous prospect of having to drive less, insulate their buildings, and generally conserve energy. And indeed technological developments may help, in time (see GEOTHERMAL ENERGY; SOLAR ENERGY).

The key to a new energy policy will be as much economic as ecological. What the OPEC nations have done is to restore the operation of supply-and-demand pricing to oil. Unless we revert to imperialist foreign policy and simply occupy Saudi Arabia (a move for which right-wing pressure is very likely to become strong as the 80's wear on) this means that the price of oil is fundamentally held in check solely by the alternatives we have for it. In the absence of strong conservation measures and the development of solar energy sources, oil prices are essentially uncontrollable.

Luckily, money spent on developing alternate sources turns out to be doubly productive. First of all, it does produce energy for us; second, it helps to hold down prices on the oil we must continue to import, and may even, in time, actually drive those prices down. This means that a rational national energy policy would spend money on solar and other alternatives even when their immediate price is considerably greater than that of currently available oil-based energy. Such a policy is like plowing money into defense equipment—it cannot be justified on an immediate basis (after all, nobody is landing on our beaches) but it helps ensure the future, and its payoff is considerably

The power grid is fed directly by windmills atop these high-tension towers, in this artist's conception.

more predictable than that of defense expenditures.

After the Three Mile Island nuclear plant disaster in 1979, the future for fission plants in the US has seemed dim, from both safety and economic standpoints. Without a solution to the wastes problem and operating safety problems, most states do not wish to have nuclear installations within their borders. And without heavy federal subsidies, utilities are skeptical of nuclear too. The prospects for fusion nuclear energy seem dim: the process has small net energy output (it consumes most of the energy produced just to keep going), requires immense facilities that produce large amounts of radioactive tritium (and stainless steel), and would tend toward centralization of generation, with consequent even greater transmission-line losses than we suffer today, when only about 30% of the electricity generated actually reaches the lightbulbs at the end of the line.

Because they offer the prospect of producing gasoline, plants to make synthetic fuel from our large national coal reserves will seem tempting. However, they require amounts of water so large as to involve the desertification of huge areas of the West, and they produce heavy pollutant effects in other areas as well, besides devastating the landscape through stripmining. In addition, the cost of the energy produced is likely to considerably exceed that from biomass sources.

See SOLAR ENERGY.

Energy Future, ed. by Roger Stobaugh and Daniel Yergin. Random House, 1979. Fundamental analysis of long-range factors—the basic document.

The Last Chance Energy Book. Johns Hopkins University Press, 1979. A popular, illustrated treatment.

ENERGY SAVING IN THE HOME

It may be hard to believe, but aside from your furnace (70%), your greatest energy outlay is probably for heating hot water (20%). Here are some possible steps: turn down the temperature on the water-heater thermostat to no more than 140°F/60°C; wrap your water-heater tank with fiberglass insulation batts (wear a mask or damp handkerchief over your nose and mouth as you work with fiber-glass); put insulation on pipes if they carry hot water outdoors or through a cold garage/basement or crawl space in cold climates; install a solar heater or preheater on your roof (get a solar-energy handbook from your library to check out the do-it-yourself possibilities). Federal and state tax breaks may make it possible to install

a solar water-heater and pay only a fraction of its cost!

Old furnaces clogged and coated with soot inside may become inefficient and need cleaning. A new fuel injection nozzle (many oil furnaces have wrongly installed ones) might cut your heating energy consumption in half. A "retention head" burner can significantly increase the efficiency of an old furnace and is much cheaper than buying a new furnace. Remember to close off the heat from unused rooms and close their doors. Storm windows, thermopane (double-glass) windows, or even just plastic sheeting tacked over the windows, result in remarkable fuel savings. Installing or improving ceiling and wall insulation generally pays for itself very quickly at today's fuel prices. So will insulating shutters, especially over large areas, that you close at night. And, perhaps most important and easiest of all— wear a sweater and get used to an air temperature of around 68°F/20°C during the day (drop it to 55°F/13°C when you go to bed). This is healthier for you, keeps the air from feeling so dry, and saves far more fuel than would seem possible, because those last few degrees of warmth are "bought" at a very high price in energy. The same is true of air-conditioner cooling; try to get used to a 78°F/25°C level.

Cooking energy requirements can be considerably reduced simply by eliminating pilot lights on gas stoves, which burn a surprising amount of gas since they run 24 hours a day all year. Matches are fine if you don't mind the trouble; electric lighters now come in most new gas stoves and can be fitted

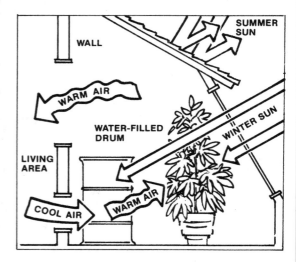

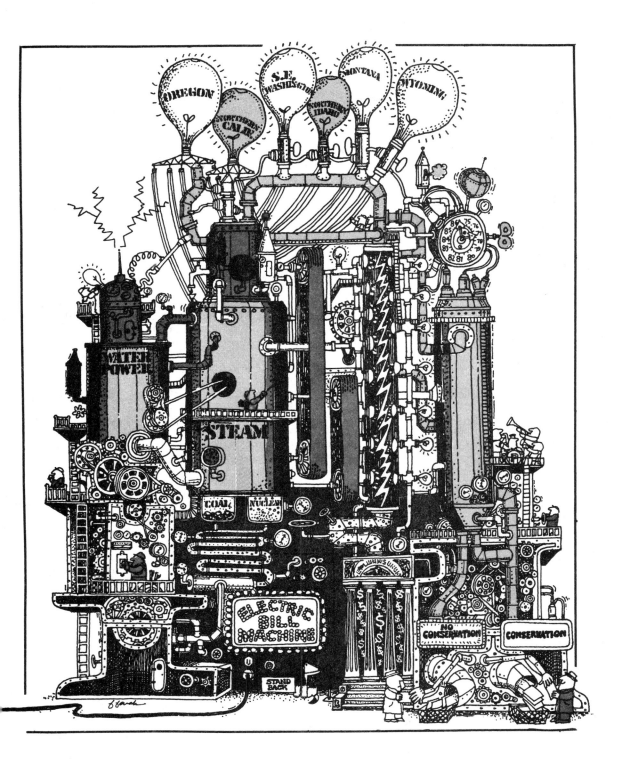

into old ones. (They are also standard now for gas water heaters and clothes dryers.) If you do a lot of baking, you may be able to improve the insulation in or around your oven.

Fireplace flues can carry away huge amounts of heat; close the damper whenever you don't have a fire going. (Better yet, replace the fireplace with a WOOD STOVE.)

Many houses lose a great deal of heat through the cracks around windows and doors. A careful job of sealing and weatherstripping is essential for savings here. A glassed-in porch also helps cut down heat losses when people go in and out. Windbreak plantings reduce a building's heat losses to the outside air.

If you remodel, or build a dwelling, "passive" solar heating can probably be incorporated into the design: that is, arranging things so that the winter sun shines into the living space (and if possible has its heat captured and stored in a quantity of concrete, masonry, or water) while summer sun is protected against by an overhang of some kind. With proper insulation, such design can reduce your total fuel consumption markedly. Depending on room arrangement and possible air circulation, the addition of a greenhouse connected to the living spaces can also provide a sizable portion of your house's heat requirements (and some vegetables besides).

Electricity savings are possible by avoiding electric heaters, by not over-lighting rooms, by turning lights off when nobody is using a room, and by avoiding high-wattage appliances like electric broilers and frying pans, hair-dryers, and irons. (Also, check new appliance labels for their energy-efficiency ratings, now required by law; compare brands and types.)

During the 80's, a large proportion of American dwellings will be equipped or retro-fitted with the above considerations in mind. We should undertake this transformation not just for money-saving motives, but because it befits us to live on the earth in ways that do the least damage through our energy-producing and energy-using activities.

About a third of American apartment buildings, especially older and thus less well insulated ones, have only one meter for the whole building's gas, and one for electric. The people pay for their utilities as part of their rent, and are thus not motivated to save energy. As a result, they use about 35% more than do people in similar apartments with individual meters. Unfortunately, the cost of rewiring and repiping buildings is so great that, even so, it is not economically

feasible yet, though one day soon it probably will be.

Some states have required utilities to establish "lifeline" rates for those who use little gas or electricity (including many old people living alone) who formerly were forced to pay higher rates than industries gobbling up enormous amounts. If your state doesn't have such laws, let your representatives know that it's about time it did. If it does, you may be able to cut your energy outlays substantially by cutting your usage a relatively small amount—enough to get under the lifeline maximum, and thus getting the lower rates.

Tips for Energy Savers. Pueblo, CO 81009. Free pamphlet from Energy Conservation Now.

EXERCISE

Exercise should be looked at as a potential pleasure, rather than a duty or a necessity: it *feels* good to use your body's remarkable physical capacities at something near their biologically intended levels of performance, rather than letting them moulder away through inactivity. Muscles that have some tone will not only look better, get your around better, and do your work better than will flabby muscles, they just plain feel better. Heart and lungs in shape to cope with substantial physical exertion are also in better shape for less strenuous activity; they give you a generous back-up capacity, which you can then happily and confidently call upon if you feel like exerting yourself by running upstairs to catch the phone, or going dancing, or making love. Getting plenty of physical exercise also, of course, keeps your weight under control, generally improves your skin, keeps your digestion in order, and makes you a more attractive and energy-filled person all around.

It does not, of course, earn you money, which is probably a major reason Americans have tradi-tionally paid so little attention to it. (Even now, only 15% of us get any serious exercise—a major cause of our bad state of national health.) But it doesn't need to cost you anything to speak of, either. The best activities for general conditioning are swimming, running, and active dancing. You can probably find a public pool, or a river or lake or ocean, in which you can swim free; for running your only expense (but it is an essential one) is a good pair of running shoes. You can dance anywhere there is a record player or tape recorder.

Swimming. More muscles are brought into play by swimming than in any other type of exercise, and the cardiovascular system is also given a good work-out if you swim seriously for 20 minutes or so. Learn a variety of strokes so you don't get bored. The key to successful and relaxing swimming is learning to breathe properly, which also reduces fatigue. If you don't know how to swim, take lessons at your YMCA or public pool. Swim fins sometimes are so much fun that they convince people that swimming is for them, and of course they are especially useful for snorkeling, for swimming long distances, or for use in rough ocean water. For swimming in chlorinated pools, small eye goggles are available.

Running. People can get hooked on running, and take to running marathons and other long-distance races; and as in any high-performance sport, this can result in knee and tendon injuries. But a moderate recreational runner with good shoes (especially if you can find park trails or other non-pavement places to run) should not encounter much trouble. Begin by a serious program of walking—not just strolling—and work up, alternating running with walking for a while, to develop your heart and lung capacity. If you have worries about your heart, a stress test can be arranged at most hospitals, after which you will be given a range of pulse rates to keep within; this is easy, and indeed in time almost automatic. For most people, running a couple of miles every other day provides a good basic conditioning program and only occupies about a half hour if you can do it in your neighborhood or near your job. But if you prefer, you can also just walk briskly. A daily half hour of stiff walking will keep you in fair shape, and in particular should make you begin to lose weight, though very gradually, if that is one of your motives.

Dancing. Courses in "aerobic dance" exist throughout the country; you go through minutely planned routines, like the dancers in musicals, which are contrived to give you strenuous cardiovascular exercise. You can achieve most of the same results by continuous active dancing at home, by yourself or with friends. A large mirror helps you to see possibilities for movements that will loosen up or use neglected muscles. The movements in exercise books, or practiced on television, can be turned into dance movements with a little ingenuity.

No matter what kind of exercise you like (and there's no reason, of course, to confine yourself just to one kind) the key is regularity. An exhausting burst of activity every two weeks is probably worse than nothing. What you need is a steady level of activity that you pleasurably keep up without feeling it's an obligation. Look for ways to incorporate an exercise into your regular daily life: run to the post office to mail that urgent letter, take the stairs instead of the elevator, use a hand lawn-mower instead of a noisy, gas-powered one, experiment with more physically fluid and active love-making (start out by dancing, and resist the temptation to jump right into bed!).

In any kind of exercise, it is important to learn to open up your chest and throat, which are often tight and constricted from stress and anxiety. This permits air to enter and leave freely and thus improves your oxygen intake and your body's general physiological efficiency. Various stretching exercises (like lying on a bed with your head and arms hanging down over the edge) will help. So will the simple effort to breathe more deeply and deliberately.

If you get more ambitious about physical activity, there has been a resurgence of interest in participant sports, as opposed to spectator sports, in this country. Groups and facilities abound for volleyball, racquetball, squash, track and field events, softball, touch football, etc. Many such sports involve little expense and provide the opportunity for socializing and making friends, as well as getting necessary exercise.

Don't deceive yourself that a little exercise will negate the bad effects of eating a high-fat diet or heavy cigarette smoking. But it has been found that jogging ten or twelve miles a week increases certain "lipoproteins" in the blood which seem to protect against heart attacks. In any case, regular vigorous exercise cuts your heart attack risk by some 35%, whereas stopping smoking cuts it by 30%. Why not do both?

If you are interested in burning off large numbers of calories, the best activities are jogging, jumping rope, cross-country skiing, and squash or racquetball.

A good deal of active exercise is necessary for children also, and you can no longer assume that urban children get it naturally, because so many of them spend a great part of their waking hours sitting at school desks, watching television, or being driven about in cars. (A great number of children also have bad dietary habits, which give them high cholesterol levels and tend to make them overweight.) Make sure your children get at least a half hour of really vigorous activity three or four times a week. Relatively intermittent energy output sports like baseball don't count. Basketball played *seriously* is good and so is soccer; tennis is only good for really skilled players. If an activity doesn't involve a lot of running, it probably doesn't give the heart and lungs a truly "aerobic" workout, which is what you and your children need.

Aerobics, by Kenneth Cooper. Bantam Books, 1972.

New Age Training For Fitness and Health, by Dyveke Spino. Grove Press, 1978.

Language of the Body, by Alexander Lowen. Collier Books, 1971.

Getting Clear: Body Work for Women, by Anne Kent Rush. Bookworks/Random House, 1973.

The Basic Back Book, by Anne Kent Rush. Moon Books/Summit, 1979.

EXTENDED FAMILIES

Through most of human history, the couple has been a relatively minor part of family structure, and the "nuclear family" as we know it—two people and their children, if any, often living at great distances from other relatives—was virtually unknown. In the long sweep of human history, the nuclear family will probably be seen as a very brief aberration, brought about by the special needs of industrial capitalism and the isolated suburban living made possible by cars, but insufficient for nurturing and supporting human beings. It is certainly in steep decline—only about a third of American households now fall into the old pattern—but it is not yet clear what will take its place. The corporations would in some ways prefer total atomization: every individual living in a separate cell in the beehive, and thus a market for a full range of appliances, prey to the commercial messages of more or less full-time TV watching. This model might even work if we had descended from solitary creatures like cats, instead of from our actual gregarious ape-like forebears. But in actuality we will probably move toward some new form of extended family—groups of a half-dozen up to perhaps fifteen people living together in one way or another, bonded together by ties of different kinds, sometimes blood relationships as in earlier extended families, sometimes religious convictions, dietary practices, and so on, and in some cases old established friendship connections. In such forms we will approximate the ancient groupings our species has relied on for survival: small bands whose variety of strengths and talents give great resilience against outside threats, and whose interior psychological life is rich and complicated enough to challenge its members' developmental potentials.

These extended families will help to reduce the present isolation and separation that characterize so much of American life. They will give children a secure world to grow in, but one with much more personal variety in their surrounding adults—to study, understand, and model themselves upon. They will relieve young parents from the severe emotional strains and practical stresses of trying to manage demanding babies or active young children entirely on their own; in a household or group of adjacent dwellings containing ten adults, baby-sitting or child-care exchanging works out much more naturally. Extended families give a warm surrounding support system for couple relationships and reduce our present tendency to put all our emotional eggs in one fragile romantic basket. They will give older people a continuing role in the social structure, and make caring for them in the home during times of weakness more feasible, rather than shunting them off to an isolated life in some institution. In turn, this will help them to maintain a productive orientation to life throughout their years.

Since the 60's, continuous attempts at experimenting with such new forms have been going on. Higher rents, higher gas prices, and higher costs for other survival necessities will, as the years pass, increase the advantages of living with other people—or immediately next to them, so you can share cooking, appliances, child-care, cars. Little by little, our widespread American aversion to dealing with other people will wear down, and we will find ourselves reinventing the wheel once more.

From experiments made so far—many of which have been at least as successful as marriages now are, on the whole, in our society—it seems clear that extended families must be based upon very strong ties and specific discussion of rights and responsibilities of each individual, not on just a vague idea that living together would be a good thing to try. Most of the formally organized communes that have survived share either strong religious or philosophical convictions, or an economic life which tie members together. (In emotional life too, necessity is the mother of invention; we learn to live together happily and productively when we *have* to.) But in some cases people have banded together on the basis of old friendships, and in some families brothers and sisters who would once have lived far away from each other are making it their business to live closer, sometimes buying property together, joining their friendship networks, helping to raise each others' children, looking after their parents, and so on.

Groupings of this kind have quite a different character when children are present than among people without children, since children constitute a great additional responsibility for the adults involved. In attempting to develop an extended family—a "family of choice"—for yourself, this factor needs very careful attention.

Many people in our society have been feeling the need for new kinds of groupings to supplement the nuclear family. The Unitarian church, in particular, includes many formalized groupings, throughout the country, aimed at producing family-type solidarity for their members.

EYE CARE

Comprehensive pre-paid medical plans of HEALTH MAINTENANCE ORGANIZATIONS include eye care—the checking of your vision every couple of years to make sure you are seeing all right, checking for glaucoma or other problems, examination for glasses if you need them, and provision of low-cost glasses. Medical schools and some universities have optometry departments where you can get eye care free or at low cost; they can usually direct you to a source of inexpensive glasses.

Elementary schools usually have vision-testing programs, but parents are the best persons to spot any vision defects a child may have. If you notice squinting or head craning when a child looks at TV, reads, or tries to see something across the room, it is a sign that something may be amiss.

Headaches can also be caused by vision difficulties.

The commonest types of vision problems are easy to correct with glasses. Nearsightedness, or myopia, is when you can only see things clearly closeup. Astigmatism makes things a little blurry at any distance. Generally only older people are far-sighted.

You may be able to find glasses that fit in happily with your personal style. If not, contact lenses are the kind of luxury it may be worth a good deal of economizing to indulge in. Teenagers can now get contact lenses prescribed by some optometrist. In recent years there have been great improvements in contact lenses (soft lenses, lenses that "breathe" better) so even if you were once told you couldn't wear them, you might check into it again.

Eyes that have been exposed to heavy dust, chemicals, tear gas, Mace, or other irritating things should be washed with water. Lie down and run it gently over the eye for at least five to ten minutes. Then keep the eyes closed for a while until they feel OK again. Severe exposure to Mace or tear gas can require medical treatment.

Eyelashes and bits of flying dirt will sometimes wash out, or you may be able to see them in the mirror yourself—use a clean handkerchief, and dab it against the object, which will usually stick to it and come away from the eyeball. Any really painful object in the eye may scratch the surface, and needs a checkup by an eye doctor. In such cases, be especially careful not to rub your eye, which could damage it severely.

FABRICS

In recent years fairly strict regulations have been issued by the Federal Trade Commission to control deception in the garment trade. New goods must carry labels stating the types of fibers in the goods, their percentages, and washing and drying requirements (or if dry cleaning is necessary). Stores may no longer remove these small labels or conceal them so that you can see only the bright, fancy advertising-type labels which don't have to meet standards of truthfulness. Of course, by the time the goods reach the secondhand store, all their labels except the store-name label have usually disappeared. You must, therefore, develop some expertise in recognizing fabrics.

Study Cloth. There is sleazy cloth and there is sound cloth, and you can get a feel for the difference. Good material is essential for clothes you can love; they have to feel right. If your reaction to something is "Well, it might be all right for some occasions," take that as a danger sign. Really good clothes will make you feel all right on practically any occasion: you can work in them, play in them, even sleep in them.

Cloth where the colors are woven in rather than printed on afterward is usually superior in other ways as well. And in general, cloth with a fine, tight weave is superior to cloth with a loose weave (unless the looseness is desirable for some special reason, like coolness in hot weather). Hold the cloth up in a strong light and look at it very closely on both sides, seeing how the threads run. Sunlight is best, since it shows true colors.

It is no mystery what determines the qualities of cloth—an enormous amount of research is done by the army and by private textile manufacturers to find out. The basic factors are these:

The warmth of a fabric depends on how much air it can trap within and between its fibers. Both thick and thin cloth are 60-90 percent air, and it is this air which keeps you warm. Wool, which has numerous tiny curly fibers, is the warmest, though some curlable synthetics are fairly warm. Warmth also depends on how well the fabric enables water vapor to evaporate from your body; there again wool is best. For outdoor garments like winter coats, a wind-resistant outer layer over a thick, soft inner layer is the best combination. This can be achieved, for example, by a sweater and jacket, a quilted coat, or a zip-in lining coat.

The feel of fabric on your skin depends upon several factors. If the fibers are hairy, like wool, it will feel warm. If the fibers are slick, like rayon or nylon, it will feel cool. If the fibers are thick, the fabric will feel scratchy, as in coarse wools. If the fibers are fine and tightly woven, the fabric will feel smooth, as in good cottons and some synthetics. Ironing makes cloth feel cooler because it squashes down the fibers so your skin touches more of them.

The drape of fabric depends on how fine the yarns are (the thinner they are, the softer the fabric and the more subtly it will hang). It is also influenced by the type of fiber; linen is used in tailored dresses and suits precisely because it is stiff. Sizing, water repellents, and other chemicals may also stiffen cloth. (Remember, in buying fabric by the yard, that the sizing will come out in the wash, leaving the fabric somewhat thinner and softer.)

The water repellency of a fabric depends on how "wettable" the fibers are—how fast they conduct water from the outside surface to the inside. Both wool, which is naturally slightly oily, and also some treated synthetics, shed water, but they are never entirely waterproof. Entirely waterproof things, like plastics, are unbearable to wear for very long because they trap perspiration inside and you are soon clammy all over; in really cold weather they are downright dangerous—they can lead you to freeze to death at temperatures in which wool clothing would be quite comfortable. Chemical water repellents don't usually last through a dry cleaning. Fabrics treated with them also get dirtier, since the repellents attract dirt. However, for a recent and novel development, see WATERPROOF CLOTHING.

Cotton. Washable, durable, easily ironable. Takes mending and patching easily. Available in every color conceivable; after long use the colors fade to soft, beautiful, subtle hues. Especially after some washing, cottons drape softly and are extremely good-feeling on the skin. Some cotton garments are now treated with resins that make

99

them wrinkle-resistant and cut down on ironing, but the formaldahyde-based resins used in treating some perma-press cotton are currently being tested for carcinogenic effects. Also, cotton burns rapidly; be careful of it around stoves and fireplaces.

Wool. More expensive than cotton, and usually woven in heavier fabrics, wool can be either in plain or "worsted" form; the latter has more tightly twisted threads and wears much longer. Wool is also woven into loose-knit fabrics called jerseys, flannels, and cashmeres. Good woolen cloth is springy when you squash it and hard to wrinkle. Unfortunately, wool has to be either hand-washed or dry-cleaned.

Labels in new goods which read "virgin wool" mean the wool has never been used before. "Reprocessed wool" has been used before, but not in clothes. "Re-used wool" is taken from clothes. (See LABELS.)

As wool takes up moisture from body evaporation, it appears to generate heat. The oil on natural wool is lanolin, incidentally, and adds to its heat-trapping abilities. And wool is fire-resistant; this is superior to making cloth fire-resistant with chemicals, which involves filling up its pores and making the cloth breathe less.

Many wool articles, such as sweaters, can be washed very carefully with mild soap in lukewarm or cool water; lay them out afterward on a towel to dry, making sure you dry them in their proper shape and size. (Wet wool can stretch badly, and heated wool will shrink disastrously.)

If you have something ruined by a cleaner or get into a dispute over charges, contact the Better Business Bureau. There is so much trouble with cleaners that the BBB will probably have an arbitration panel to which you can complain and perhaps win out.

Incidentally, it is almost never worth dry-cleaning a rug. Hang it up and beat it with a broom, or scrub it off with mild soap and lukewarm water. (Oriental and other wool rugs too.) Most rugs will shrink or discolor if dry-cleaned.

Synthetics. Chemists have produced a large number of synthetic fibers, some derived from renewable biological sources and some from petrochemical sources. Because they have slick fiber surfaces, where natural fibers have many little crooks and branches and protrusions, they do not hold water well and generally dry quickly.

Acetates and rayons are derived from cellulose, which comes from wood and cotton. They are generally strong fibers, and may be used as rein-forcing mixed in with cotton or wool. They burn and melt. Some forms need dry cleaning while others can readily be washed; check the labels. These fibers may sometimes be woven to look shiny and have a chilly plastic feel; they can however also be woven to resemble wool ("jersey"). Even in tight weaves, they tend to stretch (especially when wet) and do not hold stitching well. Since they are cheap, they are very widely used. And since they are biosource materials, they have a permanent place in an Ecotopian economy.

Acrylics (like the others below) are petrochemical products, and consume large quantities of nonrenewable oil and gas, both as raw material and as process heat, or electric power, and for some (especially nylon) large amounts of water are also required. Orlon is the best known acrylic. It is soft, reasonably warm, and lightweight, dries quickly (also burns and melts rapidly), and is machine-washable.

Nylons come under many different trade names. Nylon is the strongest fiber available (in thicker strands it is used for fishing line). It was the first drip-dry synthetic to be widely used in clothing. It usually has a clammy plastic feel because its shiny fibers lie flat against the skin, but nylon can be woven into soft, bulky forms suitable for light sweaters, or into jersey-type material. These tend to stretch, and take stitching badly. Nylon is useful chiefly in combination with other fibers, to add strength. It deteriorates in sunlight, and burns and melts.

Polyester fibers, which include Dacron, Fortrel, Polar Guard, and others, are strong and wrinkle-resistant. Dacron is used for sails because it is strong and never soaks up water. It tends to be stiff and uncomfortable in tightly woven fabric and often feels plastic. Polyesters are widely used blended with cotton; the resulting combination fabric can be machine-washed. They are also blended with wool for slacks, suits, and other hard-wear items which need dry cleaning. In the infamous "polyester doubleknit" form, they tend to droop and look sleazy.

Various other synthetics have been devised: Spandex which is quite elastic, olefins (polypropylenes) which do not absorb water and are used in carpeting and upholstery, sarans which are weather- and flame-resistant.

Although in time they will probably tend to be phased out because they derive from nonrenewable petroleum sources, many of these synthetics are useful supplements to the natural fibers, but they are seldom if ever as comfortable. In some garments, such as women's panties and pantyhose, synthetics are positively undesirable since they are not absorbent and concentrate heat and moisture.

"FAIR-HOUSING" LAWS

Since 1969, fair-housing laws have been on the books. Theoretically, these forbid discrimination in the sale or rental of all housing except where a family directly sells or rents a single-family dwelling, or where the owner lives in a small apartment building and rents out up to three apartments. Discriminatory advertising is prohibited. So is the practice of charging or asking higher rents or loans to persons of minority races. It is also illegal to say housing is unavailable when a minority person calls to see it, and then turn around and rent it to a white person. Real-estate companies are forbidden to discriminate in offering their services, and so is "block-busting."

Like any law, this one is imperfect in its application, and *sub rosa* discrimination is still prevalent (most commonly with small real estate operators, since big ones are easier to prosecute). Any person who believes he or she has been discriminated against can (1) contact a local office of the Federal Housing Authority or the Department of Housing and Urban Development, (2) phone HUD's fair housing hotline (800-424-8590) for advice, or (3) file suit in a local court, which is supposed to handle such cases quickly. It is important, obviously, to obtain solid evidence against the landlord or seller involved. This means getting witnesses to your actions and to the landlord's actions, which is often difficult to do. However, the landlords who are known to discriminate can be nailed if a racially mixed group of prospective tenants work out a suitable plan, especially if they can get help from a tenants' union or Neighborhood Legal Service office. By sending in minority-group and then white renters with witnesses, or with a lawyer, most of the landlord's tricks can be countered.

Processing of a complaint to HUD can take up to three months, so it will be of no immediate use to you in getting a place to live. However, if enough prospective tenants complain, or sue discriminating landlords, it will eventually force landlords to stop discriminating.

In recent years, because of the development of "singles complexes," a novel type of housing discrimination has arisen: against people with children. In some states specific laws have been passed against this practice, which is another way in which Americans isolate themselves from each other. An ideal community would have a healthy mix not only of races, but of old and young, families and single people, well-off and not-well off, most of them living in large households or adjacent dwellings as EXTENDED FAMILIES.

FATS AND OILS

Americans eat a great deal too much fat, and too much of the wrong kinds. Since fat is the most caloric of all foods, this fat consumption is a major cause for three quarters of our population being overweight (by a total of about 2.3 billion pounds in all, one clever nutritionist calculated). Some fat is essential for transport of fat-soluble vitamins, for insulation, and for energy reserve storage. But only a very bizarre diet indeed would lower your fat intake to dangerous levels. For most of us, the problem is to cut down *saturated* fats (meat fats, dairy product fats, chocolate, coconut, and palm oil fats) or *hydrogenated* fats (as in certain processed peanut butters, etc.) because these tend to raise blood cholesterol levels and thus increase the danger of heart attacks. *Polyunsaturated* fats (margarine, many vegetable oils, nuts, fish) should be substituted wherever possible, but because of their high caloric content don't overdo them either. Don't use animal fats for frying.

The effect of saturated fat and cholesterol consumption is offset to some extent by EXERCISE. Use relatively mildly processed oils, which retain trace nutrients and also simply smell and taste better than oils that have been heated or chemically extracted with solvents, though they will not keep as long. Buy only as much as you will use in three or four months, and keep the container out of sunlight and other hot places.

Experiment with different vegetable oils. Sesame oil is very light and good for sauteeing vegetables and for salad dressings. Safflower is another light oil, also suitable for deep-frying. Olive oil is standard for salad dressings and in Italian cooking generally. Peanut oil is a relatively strong-tasting oil.

There is no precise or legal meaning to the term "cold-pressed," which may merely mean "not solvent-extracted." Natural oils tend to be a little cloudy and are not filtered to remove their color.

FIRE

Of all household dangers, fire is the most terrifying. Anyone who has come back into the house to find it full of smoke (as I did once, when kittens had dragged a little pillow over a floor heater) knows the fear it brings. Some 300,000 dwellings burn in this country each year.

If there is fire in your house, even a small one, get the people (children and old people first) out of the place before you do anything else. The fire may be bigger and worse than you think. Fire can spread with lightning speed, blocking off exits or moving into new rooms. It can spread especially fast through curtains, shelves, and other light, easy-burning things. It can also spread over spilled cooking oil, paint, kerosene, and other inflammable liquids.

Then see whether you can reasonably do anything to stop it—either by pouring water from pots or hose, or by using a fire extinguisher, or (for small stove-grease fires) by pouring sand or salt on the fire. When a fire has gotten bad, don't be heroic and rush back into it, unless there are people to be saved—get out and call the fire department on a neighbor's phone.

Most people don't think seriously about fire, any more than about auto accidents—they think it can't happen to them. But you might save your children's lives by taking a little thought before-hand, as I learned to do from an uncle who was a fireman and had an eagle eye for hazards. First of all, look around the house to see how to get out of it in a hurry. If a fire starts at one end, can you get out the other—through another door, or a window, by climbing out on the roof and jumping down? If a fire appears in the hallway, how can people in the rooms get out? On upper stories, the landlord or landlady is supposed to provide a fire escape, besides the main entrance. If this hasn't been done, you may need to get a heavy knotted rope to keep near some window, so that people can slide down it to safety. (Find something solid to tie it to, if necessary screwing a big eye hook into a wall stud.)

Second, look around to see what you have handy to put out small fires with. Is there a bucket or really big pot always near the kitchen sink? Are there garden hoses that could stretch inside the house if needed? For electrical fires, grease fires, or burning liquids, can you afford a small fire ex-tinguisher that won't spread the fire? Are there blankets to use in smothering fires in clothing or people's hair?

Third, check through your place for unnecessary fire hazards: piles of old clothes or rags (especially greasy ones), woodpiles surrounded by dry grass, cluttered collections of stuff under the house or in the attic, anything burnable above or around a heater, water heater, or cookstove.

Fourth, teach your children fire safety from a very early age. Children seem to be practically pyromaniacs around four or five—they just love to light matches. And a surprising number of fires, both in houses and in forests, are set "by accident" through children playing with fire, usually matches. Keep all matches up high, out of sight. Show your kids how fire spreads, perhaps by setting a small, controlled fire. Teach them by example not to drop a match, even after it's out, on anything that can burn. (Don't throw matches into wastebaskets or garbage cans, which they may set on fire.) Let kids burn their fingers a couple of times, to learn by experience that fire is painful. You may even want to practice getting out of the house in a hurry. Many lives are lost when fires occur at night, and sleepy people don't move fast enough in getting out before it's too late. Remem-ber that many fire deaths stem from being overcome by smoke. If a room or hallway is full of smoke, drop to the floor and crawl. A damp handkerchief or washcloth over the face will also help filter some smoke. But move *fast*.

Television sets sometimes catch fire; keep them away from drapes and other burnable things, so the fire can't spread.

One of the few drawbacks of draped, loose-hanging clothes (kimonos, gowns, bathrobes, etc.) is that they may be a fire-hazard—you can catch a sleeve on fire over the stove, and some cottons and synthetics burn very easily. The best thing to do if your clothes (or hair) catch on fire is first to scream for help and second to smother the fire—by rolling up in a big coat or a soft rug or blanket. Fire needs air to continue burning. If you get badly burned and some of the fabric adheres to the burned skin, don't try to pull it off. Get to a doctor for treatment immediately. Never smoke in bed; you will incin-erate yourself if your drowse off and the bedclothes catch fire. See also WOOD STOVES.

FIRST AID

Training in first aid can help you save lives, especially in auto crashes, and may even save your own. It can also save unnecessary doctor bills. There is no shortcut to learning first aid, so you need to pick up knowledge and experience wher-ever you can. However, since situations arise where even a little information is better than nothing, the following recommendations might help in emer-gencies when no fuller information or better treat-ment is available. They have been condensed from authoritative sources (chiefly the Red Cross booklet

First Aid) and checked by doctors active in first-aid training. The reader is warned that first aid is not treatment. Any serious injuries need the attention of a doctor as soon as possible.

Head wounds, chest wounds, belly wounds, very dirty wounds, and wounds that cause severe bleeding or shock require more than immediate first aid. You must just stop the bleeding and then in most cases get the patient to a hospital immediately, no matter what the consequences. This is essential even when, in situations arising out of intense social conflict, it may result in police or political trouble.

Head wounds often cause bleeding that's difficult to stop. Because of the danger of a fractured skull, all head injuries beyond a simple bump should probably be seen by a doctor, who can check for fractures. Any period of blackout, confusion, stupor, or loss of memory means at least that a concussion has occurred, and possibly worse. Head injuries can have extremely bad aftereffects. If going to a local hospital may have political repercussions or result in police trouble, you can call other doctors or hospitals for advice, or try to take the patient to a hospital in a different part of the city; tell the doctor that the injury was caused by a fall from a ladder or something, and arrange to give a nearby address as the place of the accident, if possible.

Chest wounds may interfere with breathing. If air is being sucked in through the wound, smear heavily with vaseline and bandage heavily, to prevent air getting into the wound. A hand will do in a drastic emergency. Then get the patient to a hospital immediately.

Belly wounds can be severe, even if they don't look bad on the surface, because there may be internal bleeding. Shock, pain spread out over the belly, and rigid muscles when touched are signs of serious trouble. Back pain, vomiting, bloating of the belly, and general poor condition are also possible danger signs.

Here are a few of the things about which you should learn more in a first-aid course. (The American National Red Cross gives free courses — look them up in your phone book. Community organizations and schools also give training.)

When somebody has been hurt, try to find out from observers or the hurt person just what happened. Then you need to check all these things:

- Is the patient breathing?
- Heart beating?
- Bleeding?
- In shock?
- Developing an infection?
- Severe damage — broken bones, spine or nerve injury, head injuries?
- Conscious?

Above all, keep calm as you inspect the situation and decide what to do. It helps the patient actually to get better, and avoid the dangerous condition called shock, if you are able to reassure the patient that you know what you're doing. If possible, send someone for a doctor or ambulance, while you check:

Breathing. Learn to do mouth-to-mouth resuscitation. This is basically breathing your own breath into the other person. You must keep it up until he or she begins breathing again. Sometimes this takes a long time — even up to twenty minutes. Don't give up.

Heart. A strong blow to the chest will sometimes re-start the heart. First-aid courses also teach a kind of heart massage. You can tell the heart is pumping again by listening to the chest or by feeling the pulse.

Bleeding. The best way to stop bleeding is by pressing on the wound firmly with a sterile bandage, folded clean handkerchief, piece of underwear, or any other handy clean cloth. Do not try to use a tourniquet as they do more harm than good. Keep pressure on for at least fifteen minutes, and bleeding will almost always stop. Then a clean bandage, plenty thick to keep a light pressure on wound, should be applied. Don't pour on liquid antiseptics — they may burn the wound. Antibiotic ointments can be put on mild surface wounds, but not on deep ones. If the wound is not terribly bad and delay would not mean serious extra loss of blood, you can clean a dirty wound by washing it with clean water and mild soap before pressing on it to stop bleeding. This greatly lessens danger of infection.

Shock. Anybody who has lost a significant amount of blood must be treated for shock. Medically, "shock" means that because the body has been hurt, its blood vessels expand and thus there isn't enough blood to go around in all of them; the brain gets starved of blood, and the patient may pass out. Trying to prevent this, the heart pumps faster and the skin blood vessels clamp down to send more blood to the brain. So the signs of shock are very fast pulse (like one hundred per minute); skin pale, sweaty, cold; patient very nervous or even unconscious.

If you see signs that as much as four cups of blood have been lost, the patient may need a transfusion and should be taken to a hospital emergency room as fast as possible; it is a question of life or death.

A patient who seems to be in shock but has only slight injuries can be laid down with feet four to six inches off the ground and head flat. People who have merely fainted will quickly recover within a minute or two.

In mild cases of shock, without large blood loss, the patient should be put in bed to rest, watched carefully, and made to drink large amounts of fluids. If he or she has been taking fluids but doesn't urinate at least two cups every four hours, the kidneys may be damaged and a physician should be consulted.

A related and potentially fatal condition is hypothermia, or severe chill brought on by immersion in cold water, by severe winter exposure, or by wind chill—which can be dangerous even at seemingly mild temperatures. The body must be warmed gently, and kept protected from wind and further chill, for example in a sleeping bag.

Infection. A normally healing non-infected wound has a little rim of red, tender skin around it. Dangers of infection occur when a wound develops an abscess, like a giant pimple; a large red, hot, tender area spreads out around a wound; or red, tender lines appear in the skin around the wound. A fever is usually a sign of infection. Any of these conditions means trouble that can even result in death; a doctor should be seen as soon as possible. The usual treatment prescribed for infection is to soak the area in warm water four times a day for ten to fifteen minutes, and if the wound is in an arm or leg, to keep it raised as much of the time as possible. Antibiotic treatment is only sometimes desirable.

Deep dirty wounds can result in gangrene or tetanus, both extremely dangerous diseases, and a doctor should be seen after first-aid treatment. Black, dead, bubbly, or foul-smelling flesh around a wound is a sign of deadly gangrene, a life-or-death matter. To guard against tetanus ("lockjaw"), a "hot" patient can lightly puncture the skin of a foot with a clean nail, then go to a doctor and ask for a tetanus shot, not mentioning the other wound.

Aspirin (two tablets every four hours) will help dull mild pain. Patients who are terribly nervous— and not in shock or in danger of shock—can be given one shot of liquor (never more). Pain is a biological danger signal and you should not dull it until you are sure you know what is causing it.

The signs of a fracture are swelling, tenderness, misalignment of bones, and pain when moved. Broken bones should always be checked by a physician, who will usually take an X-ray and then "set" the break. Don't try to walk on a possibly broken leg, or use a broken arm. If you can feel or see a break in a rib, or suspect one, the patient should not be moved except by trained ambulance people, because of the danger of lung puncture.

Every household needs a first-aid cabinet with a collection of essentials in it, though obviously you can improvise for many requirements like bandages.

- Aspirin (hundred-pill bottles); buy the cheapest you can find, and keep away from children.
- Sodium bicarbonate (for "heartburn" or indigestion); cheaper than brand-name products with added ingredients, but works just as well.
- Calamine lotion (for bug bites, poison ivy, etc.)
- Adhesive bandages ("Band-Aid" brand is usually more expensive than others)
- Small tube of antibiotic ointment (no "burn ointments")
- Ice bag (for headaches, hangovers, injuries to joints and muscles—do not use a hot-water bottle or heating pad on such injuries!)
- Thermometer (if you have a baby, get the rectal type, and keep it washed)
- Tweezers for removing splinters

If you have children in the house, it's wise to write out, on a card kept in the medicine chest, the phone number of your local Poison Control Center; the Center can give you emergency advice if a child swallows something dangerous. You may also want to keep some syrup of ipecac, used to induce vomiting.

There's no use in keeping mercurochrome, iodine, or other antiseptics. Despite all the advertisements, no known drug is any help whatsoever against the common cold, which is a virus disease. Rest and a good diet are the best remedies. Nose drops reduce stuffiness, but can only be used two or three times a day. Non-prescription sleeping pills are so weak as to be useless; a small glass of warm milk and honey works better.

Here are a few miscellaneous first-aid pointers:

To stop a bloody nose, pinch the nose and hold for several minutes; this works better than cold packs or other remedies. If someone is bitten by a dog or wild animal, try to catch the animal for examination by a vet and a check of rabies records; otherwise a painful series of anti-rabies injections must be given. For frostbite, do not rub the frozen part with snow or ice, as that may damage the tissues; cover it with woolen cloth, and once indoors, soak in body-warmth water (not hot); a warm drink (not liquor) may help too. Don't put the frozen part near a stove or on a heating pad or on a hot-water bottle. For rattlesnake bite, experts differ as to whether to attempt suction over a small crisscross cut, or simply to run water over the bite and get the victim to a hospital. If you are way out in the wilds, the suction treatment may help; but be careful of arteries, muscles, and tendons in your cutting! Bites and stings from scorpions, spiders, bees, and wasps can cause intense pain; packing with ice, or soaking in cold water, is helpful. (Incidentally, those huge tarantula spiders which look so deadly are actually harmless to humans, though a few people may have allergic reactions to a bite.)

Emergency Medical Guide, by John Henderson. McGraw-Hill, 1978 (4th ed.).
The Pocket Medical Encyclopedia and First Aid Guide, by James Bevan. Simon & Schuster, 1979.
Family Health and Home Nursing. American Red Cross. Doubleday, 1979. Includes first aid.

FISH

Although the world's fishing fleets are pressing upon the resources of the continental-shelf fisheries (where most fish live), fish is still a good low-fat source of high-quality protein and many trace minerals. If you live where good fresh seafood is available, marvelous; if you don't, frozen fish is excellent and not too expensive. (Most people can't tell the difference.) You need less fish than with most meats, because there is very little waste from bones: none at all in fillets, which are lengthwise strips, and not much in steaks, which are crosswise slices.

You can also buy fresh fish by the piece, either a whole fish or a part, but usually without the head. The price is lower, but you do have some waste. A whole baked fish on a platter, surrounded by parsley, lemon slices, watercress, maybe little tomatoes, is an impressive meal, and if it is a bass, salmon, or other sizable fish you can make it go even farther with a rice stuffing.

Too many people fry fish, which tends to make it greasy and obscures the flavor. Broiling, actually, is the quickest, easiest, and one of the more delicious ways to cook fish. You can marinate it if you like, or just dab on a little butter or oil to keep it from getting too crisp on top. Salmon and some other fish are extremely delicate-tasting steamed or poached, especially with a sauce.

Fish is quick-cooking—broiling takes ten to fifteen minutes, baking twenty minutes to half an hour. Most people tend to overcook fish, letting it get dry inside. It is done when the flesh flakes apart easily with a fork and it should still look moist.

You may not have tried enough fish to know how much variety there is. The fattiest are salmon, butterfish, and lake trout. Next are swordfish, mackerel, tuna, catfish, buffalo fish, carp, and turbot. And lightest of all are sole, rock cod, halibut, red snapper, brook trout, and shellfish. The flavor differences between swordfish and salmon, for instance, are just as great as between steak and chicken. You may be delighted to find that your favorite type is among the cheapest—don't be afraid to experiment, even with smelt or sturgeon or fish you never heard of!

Many varieties of canned fish, both water-packed and oil-packed, are available, and can be relatively inexpensive sources of high-quality protein. Tuna is no longer as economical as it once was; if you are looking for something cheaper, try mackerel, a stronger-tasting fish which many people love. Watch for bargains in canned fish—sometimes you will find exotic items that are incredibly cheap and very tasty, like the "pica-pica" one of my friends used to gorge on—a hot-sauce fish of undetermined species, hailing from Southwest Africa; he bought it by the case.

Tuna, swordfish, and other large ocean fish are often heavily contaminated with mercury. These big fish, at the top of their food chains, concentrate contamination in their bodies; so it isn't wise to make them a very large part of your diet. You can eat as much as you like of smaller ocean fish such as sardines, herring, mackerel, etc.

FISHING

Strangely enough, there are fishermen (and -women) who do not eat their catch, whether because they have never learned to enjoy the taste of fish, don't know how to cook it palatably (simple broiling is generally best), or don't recognize it as a source of high-quality, low-fat protein. Sport fishermen and -women sometimes refer disparagingly to "meat fishing"—that is, fishing in hopes of catching something to add to their diet. But fishing, hunting, and gathering are primordial survival techniques of human beings and there is something to be said for staying in touch with them. Even heavily urbanized areas often have good fishing spots quite close by—in rivers, lakes, bays, etc. However, you may want to check with your health department about possible pollution hazards in local fish.

Anybody can bait a hook and throw a line in the water, and in small ponds filled with bluegills that is literally all that's necessary; the bamboo pole with a string and hook is all you need (and you can do without the pole in a pinch). Bluegills are widespread, and if you happened to be starving in the wilderness you could do worse than try to catch some. Catching larger fish is something else again, and you need to be instructed by someone who is experienced and actually catches fish; there are millions of active fishermen and -women in this country who hardly ever catch anything. Explain that you are not interested in investing in fancy equipment. Lots of people have rods and reels lying around the attic unused; you can probably pick up or at least borrow a set for nothing. Explain also that you wish to catch substantial amounts of fish, unless you are going on the more metaphysical but less productive kick of trout fishing—which, with its elegant paraphernalia of flies, super-resilient rods, and so on, is fascinating for other reasons entirely, such as the beauty of the cold mountain streams where trout live. If the bodies of water in your vicinity have not been rendered entirely uninhabitable by pollution, your teacher will be able to take you to places where people go who seriously wish to catch eating fish. There you may find whole families perched on a pier or bank, patiently fishing all day long—and maybe going home with enough catfish to fill a freezer for the winter.

There are other aquatic creatures you may wish to catch besides fish. Crayfish, which are small relatives of lobsters, abound in most streams and in irrigation ditches and lakes. You catch them by wading around turning over rocks; a small net and flashlight can make it easier. (They are most active at night.) As with lobsters or crabs, the standard practice is to kill them by dropping them in boiling water; you shell out the tails, which can be fried in butter or batter. Turtles make a tasty soup and can be easy to catch in some situations. Frogs, which are of course a great delicacy in fancy restaurants, can be speared with a long pole or netted; their legs are the only edible part.

Every state requires a fishing license, and game wardens will appear at heavily fished areas or on piers where sport-fishing boats dock, to check up. Certain spots, like piers built with federal money, are exempt from licenses. In general, you need to be reasonably enthusiastic about fishing to hope to recover the cost of a license. Fishing is not easy.

The best fishermen and -women I know, who are Japanese people in the San Francisco area, give a great deal of thought to it. And when they are fishing they are not just lolling around; they are paying astute attention to the behavior of their line, which is the guide to what is happening at the hook. Fishing is, no doubt, a Zen kind of activity; it requires patient seeming passivity, a sense of the critical moment, a non-verbal understanding of your role in the situation, and a comfortableness with your own predatory objectives. (See VEGETARIANISM.)

FLEA MARKETS.   See GARAGE SALES.

FLUORESCENT LIGHTS

The appeal of fluorescents is, of course, that they produce more light with less current than do incandescent bulbs, and as a result they've spread wildly throughout our homes and businesses. But they have so many disadvantages that I decided some years ago not to use them in my house. They make an annoying hum. In some cases they flicker. But more important, their light output is not spread out evenly over the spectrum like sunlight and incandescent light, but instead is concentrated in small "peaks" of intensity—lots of pink, then nothing much until you get to blue. (This unnatural character may explain their hypnotic effect in supermarkets and department stores.) Full-spectrum fluorescent tubes are now available, and though they cost more, they are what you should use if you don't mind the hum and flicker.

There is some inconclusive but frightening evidence that all fluorescent light is somehow harmful. It certainly is to plants (though there is a type of fluorescent tube, including the Gro-Lux and other brands, specially developed for indoor plants), and it has been vaguely connected with various human ills. Light can be thought of as "ingested." It passes quite readily through human tissue—as you see by holding your hand up to a strong light— and directly affects the nervous system through the retina. On the whole, therefore, it seems wisest to avoid fluorescents, and to make sure you get a modest amount of natural sunlight.

FOOD CONSPIRACIES

One way to spend pleasant time with your friends and/or to develop neighborhood solidarity, is to get a food conspiracy going. This is a group (usually about a half-dozen families works best) formed to buy food jointly—at farmers' markets and wholesale places—with the twin objectives of better food and less cost.

It is best to start with people you know, and then expand to take in new members if you feel like it. And you should begin by dealing with only a limited number of different kinds of food, or it can get too complicated and confusing.

The system basically works like this. Each week, one household does the shopping for the whole conspiracy: making the run to the farmer's market and bringing the vegetables and fruits back to the neighborhood at a pre-established time. (A station wagon makes the operation simple, since stuff can simply be set out on the tailgate.) Conspiracy members have previously indicated what they want on little slips of paper given to the people due to make the shopping run. Now members pick up their orders, pay the cost, and share their evaluations of both cost and quality. Sometimes the shoppers will have come upon fruit or other bargains too tantalizing to pass up, so you may be offered things you hadn't expected. But shoppers have to be cautious in this practice, and it seems best to make it their own responsibility: if they buy it, and nobody else wants it, they keep it!

Co-op groceries and some other suppliers will offer groups discounts on a considerable range of merchandise. This means you can buy staples such as rice in enormous bags, or a whole cheese wheel, or a case lot of wine....

The Food Conspiracy Cookbook, by Lois Wickstrom. 101 Productions, 1974. Directions for organizing a conspiracy, with recipes.

FOOD CONTAINERS

One of the most depressing things about the ordinary American kitchen is its domination by labels—ugly, loud, slogan-bearing labels that have no place in a pleasant, relaxed home. You can escape this tyranny of packages (for items you can't buy in bulk) by storing their contents in uniform jars or bottles with attractive hand-made labels. Save jars that have a reasonably acceptable shape and put salt, flour, soybeans, rice, lentils, and pasta in *them* instead of in the cardboard or plastic they come in. A way to make your storage jars more attractive is to use the kind of canning tops that separate into a disk and a screw ring; replace (or cover) the disk with something interesting and attractive—a cutout photograph, a piece of fabric, or anything appealing and thin.

The game of putting the advertisers out of your house can of course easily be extended beyond foods. Tear the wrappers off soaps—it helps the soap dry out, which will make it last longer when you use it. Unwrap toilet paper when you bring it home. Take the dust jackets off books (unless you plan to resell them). Put soap powder in a jar or can.

The beer can is perhaps the worst of all the American food containers. It is the sort of object that naturally leads you to toss it away wherever you happen to be. An aluminum beer can is practically indestructible—it will last for thousands of years. There must be a hundred billion beer cans littering our landscape by now. An ingenious process for producing plastics that decay when put in contact with wet earth has finally been developed, and should soon be applied not only to beer containers but to many kinds of food containers. Then you can throw them onto your compost heap instead of into your garbage can—truly a great step forward. In the meantime, take out your aggressions by crushing tin and aluminum cans and tossing them into separate containers so you can deposit them at a metal-recycling depot. (Glass bottles can also be taken to a recycling depot, but best of all is to avoid the No Deposit-No Return kind.) And urge your political representatives to pass "bottle laws" to encourage recycling and prohibit "disposable" metal cans.

FOOD FADS

Now that our traditional ethnic diets have come almost completely unglued, we run the danger of becoming prey to food fads. The only defense is to obtain a good basic grounding in nutrition, so that you can evaluate proposed diets for yourself. But a sound first principle is that any diet which is very extreme and limits your food intake to a few items is likely to be dangerous. A certain amount of nutritional safety lies in simply eating substantial types of different foods, which raises the chances that some of them, at least, will be providing both the basics and the trace substances you need.

Macrobiotic diets, for example, are especially perilous for people with liver damage (from hepatitis or cirrhosis) and can even lead to death. Their claimed purifying effects seem to reflect the calm which sets in from malnutrition. In the religious groups where they originated, these diets were used by monks as part of the process by which they demonstrated their devotion; in effect, if you survived, you were in. The brown rice which is the mainstay in these diets provides some protein and some starch and a few trace elements; it is far better than polished white rice. But eaten alone it will lead to scurvy, and the debilitation of such a low-protein diet will soon lead to other diseases.

If you want to experiment with minimal food intake, it seems best to do it outright, by fasting. Many Americans eat too much anyhow, so an occasional fast of a day is unlikely to hurt you. After you pass through the stage of feeling desperately hungry, you will get a hunger high. But you should be careful to keep up an intake of liquids (fruit or vegetable juices) to avoid drying out your system. Fasting for more than about forty-eight hours causes substantial changes in your intestinal bacteria and gastric processes, and when you start eating again you may suffer serious indigestion; so begin slowly and with easily digested foods. Always check with your physician before fasting for more than one or two days.

There is, of course, no particular danger in believing that blackstrap molasses, or yeast, or yogurt, or wheat germ, or rose hips will help to solve your health problems. These foods are perfectly good for you, in any reasonable quantity. But you should not adopt them as the basic staple of your diet, and you should avoid purchasing them in stores or in specially prepared forms where they cost a great deal.

In the 1970's, probably deriving mainly from Linus Pauling's advocacy of the curative powers of huge doses of vitamin C, a craze for "megavitamin therapy" developed. Our understanding of the effects of vitamins in quantities greatly exceeding those from dietary sources is of course limited, but there is strong evidence that they can be seriously harmful. It is reasonable that our ancestors, who consumed large quantities of fruit throughout the day, may have had the capacity or the necessity to consume considerably more vitamin C than we generally do. Other vitamins, and also trace minerals, should be used with great caution. Luckily, researchers interested in the effects of such substances on metabolism and other body functions are beginning to gain recognition from the scientific and medical community, and their work should gradually lead to a much better understanding in these areas.

Most Americans consume more protein than they actually need. Liquid proteins and other concentrated protein sources are thus not requried as supplements for a diet that has normal variety and ample amounts of other nutrients. Severe medical disorders can result if you make such substances the major element in your diet for any substantial period. (See REDUCING.)

Actually the most dangerous food fad in America today is the fast-food diet: hamburgers, French fried potatoes, milkshakes. These foods are heavy in animal and other fats and in salt. (They do provide some protein and carbohydrates, but the lettuce in hamburgers must be disregarded as a green vegetable.) All in all, therefore, the MacDonald's diet is substantially sub-par. It is time for ambitious entrepreneurs to start chains providing food that is fast but *good*: the Sixty-Second Salad, the Yummy Yogurt Bowl, the Speedy Sprout Special. If we're going to go out and gulp down commercially prepared foods, at least they ought to be nourishing!

Pre-mixed and prepared or processed foods constitute another commercialized food fad. The food corporations have discovered that, as more women work outside the home, and as single households proliferate, there is a huge market for foods you don't have to do anything to, except perhaps heat. Almost every element of a standard meal can now be obtained pre-cooked, from the canned or frozen soup course through the TV-dinner main course to the frozen-pie or prefabricated pudding dessert. These foods are, of course, generally at least twice as expensive as preparing your own, and they are loaded with additives, sugar, and salt. "Instant breakfasts" are particularly to be avoided, since they're basically non-fat dried milk powder with flavoring and a thickener, plus a few cheap vitamins. Here are things you can mix into milk: malted-milk powder (thickens it, flavors it, and may add vitamins); protein powder (may also give a vanilla flavor); molasses or honey; chocolate or cocoa; instant coffee (with most brands, dissolve it first in a few tablespoons of hot water); jam; orange juice.

See EATING BETTER.

FOOD POISONING

We are surrounded (and indeed inhabited) by bacteria of many kinds, and no matter how stringent food inspection practices are, some of them come along with or get onto our food. They can multiply and cause food poisoning if we allow certain conditions to exist. Surveys have found, for example, that about a third of our refrigerators are set above 45°F/7°C, whereas 40°F/4°C is required to keep bacteria from multiplying. Put a thermometer in your refrigerator occasionally, and if necessary adjust the temperature setting.

Meat and poultry kept at room temperature after cooking will support rapid bacterial growth in an hour or two. This goes for chicken salad, ham salad, and tuna salad, and sandwiches made from them for lunchboxes as well. Our digestive systems cope pretty well with moderate amounts of foreign bacteria, obviously, or we would never have survived at all. But not taking proper refrigeration precautions means exposing yourself to salmonella poisoning. Another practical consequence is that in planning a picnic, you should either use an ice chest, or utilize foods such as salami and cheese.

The most dangerous kind of food poisoning is botulism, which can arise from dented or damaged canned goods. Don't buy such cans, and if the contents of an opened can look or smell funny, throw them out; don't taste them, since botulinus toxin can be fatal in very small amounts.

Staphylococcal contamination of food can occur if you prepare meats while you have an open cut on your hand. You should also attempt to keep the preparation of meats and poultry separated from work on vegetables and salads, since cross-contamination can otherwise occur.

As will be clear from all this, cutting down your use of meat also cuts down the need for certain kinds of safety precautions in your kitchen, and thus simplifies your life.

FOOD SHOPPING

There are a few basic rules to follow in shopping for food. (Though as with all rules, it's fun to break them once in a while.)

Avoid buying food any place but a grocery store. Stay away from restaurants, drive-ins, hamburger stands, sandwich trucks, and so on. Food you buy in a store is usually less than half as expensive as food prepared for you—and it's usually of better quality. (If you are dying to try some restaurant, eat lunch, not dinner—you'll get the same food, but usually at a much lower price.)

Avoid buying in small stores, except for occasional bread-and-milk purchases during the week. The best buys are in the supermarkets in middle-class neighborhoods, and you should buy your week's food there even if it involves an expedition. Prices in small neighborhood stores can be as much as 25 percent higher, and quality is generally lower. The exceptions are specialized green-groceries, bakeries, and so on—which, if they are run by people who care, can offer higher-quality merchandise than the chains, though often at somewhat higher prices too.

Eat before you shop. If you're hungry,
statistics show, you will end up buying more, and more expensive stuff, whether you have a list or not.

Never buy pre-sliced meats or cheese (except maybe bacon, which is an extremely expensive luxury item, probably bad for your health, and hard to slice yourself). The slicing and slick packaging can more than double the price per pound.

Never buy canned baby food. Babies can and will eat all kinds of food if it is simply mashed soft enough for them—which you can usually do with an ordinary fork. If you have a blender you can mash up anything from asparagus to zucchini. Some adult foods, like applesauce, mashed potatoes, and scrambled eggs, are perfect for babies as-is. Canned baby food is one of the worst buys in the entire American supermarket. Some of it is loaded with sugar or salt; some of it contains additives. The only real excuse for buying it is if you have a craving for one of those weird combinations yourself!

Never buy soda or candy when you're shopping, or between-times either. The amount of money that Americans waste on soft drinks is staggering. They have little food value; they make you fat; they rot your teeth. But most of all, they cost like hell. If you can't resist your kids' requests for sweet drinks, mix them up fruit juice with a little extra sugar in it.

Plan your shopping to last for a week. Make a list and stick to it. Buy all your basic foods at once; make sure you've got enough to last you the week. Then you can always pick up milk and bread, and chicken or fish when you can afford it, as the week goes on. The less often you go into a store, the less you will spend.

Buy good food in small quantities. One of the depressing things about scrimping to stretch your food budget is the feeling that you never get anything that's really top quality. It's better, therefore, after you have laid in your stock of rice, beans, potatoes, and so on, to buy fish, meat, cheese, and other expensive foods with an eye to quality rather than quantity. It will make you feel better to eat a half-pound of good broiled halibut than a whole pound of greasy hamburger.

Eat non-standard meats. Your family may not have prepared kidneys, lungs, spleen, liver, heart, brains, etc, but that doesn't mean they aren't good. Look around in your cookbook and try some out. It's not true, for instance, that heart has to be marinated or cooked for hours; if cut into quarter-inch slices, it can be fried in a few minutes and tastes delicious in any kind of tomato-and-onion sauce. Brains, which are high-protein foods, can be cooked with scrambled eggs. Organ meats, however, have even more fats than other meats, and you should probably eat them only once a week.

Don't eat out of cans. Canned vegetables are almost always tasteless compared to fresh or frozen vegetables. You should buy vegetables that are in season whenever possible, of course, when they will be cheap and good. Don't go too much by appearance with vegetables or fruit; sometimes the biggest, shiniest fruit is also the blandest and mealiest, because it's been grown by hurry-up irrigation. Also, most fruit is picked early so it can be shipped to market before ripening; your best buy is a smlal quantity of fruit that's on the verge of perfectly ripe. (Don't buy more than a day's supply of ripe soft fruits such as apricots and plums.) Vegetables and fruits are healthy foods and you can hardly eat too much of them.

Don't be taken in by "convenient packages." Everything that is pre-packaged or pre-measured costs more than the same thing in bulk. Thus you pay more for tea bags, for cereal in individual-portion boxes, for potato chips in small bags, and so on. Manufacturers also use fancy packaging and odd-size containers to deceive you. (See PACKAGING.)

A couple of further tips for supermarket shopping: Buy house brands—the cheaper brands labeled by the supermarket chain or co-op chain itself; the cans are packed by the same companies whose stuff you get in name-brand labels. In canned goods, buy Grade B; it's as tasty as Grade A, just not as perfect in appearance. You pay a lot extra to get all-perfect fruits, especially; and if you can find cans labeled "broken pieces"—of peaches, pears, and so on—they are cheaper still. Some frozen vegetables are always cheaper than their fresh counterparts no matter the season; peas and green beans and corn-off-the-cob, for instance—especially when you buy them in bulk bags rather than the small square cardboard packages. (Never buy name-brand frozen foods; they're considerably more expensive than house-brand frozen lines.)

Try to leave your kids at home, or shop in a supermarket with some sort of childcare facilities. Otherwise they will be after you, with their television-brainwashed minds, to buy expensive sugared breakfast cereal, candy, and so on. Supermarkets have discovered that some parents can be bulldozed by children into buying practically anything—toys, pop, candy, gum—if it's displayed low down where the kids can't help seeing it. Stores that do this deserve the shoplifting they get. Train your kids to understand that toys are special things that are bought on special occasions in toy stores, where they are generally of better quality and cost less.

Should you watch for "specials" in the supermarkets? Unfortunately, since it's a drag, the answer must be yes. Some of them are "loss leaders"—items widely advertised at genuinely low prices which drag the customers in and then the store can nail them with a lot of their stuff at regular prices. These are less common now, when "discount" pricing prevails, but they can still be worth taking advantage of. Most specials, however, just reflect temporary small downswings in costs, perhaps because of fluctuations in crops, or some kind of finagling on the commodity markets. It is depressing to feel you have to pore over the ads and then plan your eating around the specials. The smarter you are about your food buying generally, the less you need feel compelled to watch specials. (See STOCKING UP.)

People who live alone have special shopping problems because the packaging and pricing in supermarkets seems to be done with a family of four in mind. The temptation is strong to turn to TV dinners and other quickie meals, but these are expensive for the amount of protein and other important nutrients they contain, and they tend to have a lot of sugar, excess salt, gravies, and other drawbacks. They are also boring compared to simple meals you can fix for yourself. So the best thing is to fight your way through the packages. Unwind the wires and take what you need from the asparagus and broccoli bundles. Get the grocery checker to cut a carton of eggs in half. Ring for the butcher and have him or her package the half pound of meat you need. In time, since so many people are now living alone, such actions will get the message through.

Freezers, those trophies of the appliance-mad society, are drastically over-rated. A freezing compartment in a refrigerator is a convenience; you can preserve frozen foods in it that you bring home from the store, freeze bread to keep it for a week, keep ice cream for a while, and make lots of ice. However, a separate freezer is only worthwhile if you grow large amounts of your own food or have access to really cheap sources. Otherwise, since a freezer takes a surprising amount of current and a good amount of capital to buy, unless you get one for nothing or very cheaply, you will probably be losing money all around.

Also you may tend to *waste* food: only a freezer that goes down to zero degrees Fahrenheit (-15°C) will preserve foods for more than a few weeks without their nutritive value dropping considerably. It takes a good deal of planning and care to use a freezer efficiently. You have to constantly put the new stuff on the bottom, so as to use up the older first. You have to be very careful about wrapping and packaging foods, which will quickly dry out if not in airtight containers. You have to mark everything so you can tell what is inside the wrapper. Frozen foods deteriorate rapidly once thawed, and should never be refrozen unless they have been thawed in the refrigerator.

There is a special freezer-meat swindle which many people fall for. Usually half a beef is advertised at some fantastic bargain price; but when you show up, it turns out to be a bait-and-switch operation—you are shown some grubby old carcass at the low price, and switched to some fine meat nearby at a much higher price, plus heavy installment payments. Then when you actually get your meat you may be in for some nasty surprises: you may really have gotten grubby meat; you may get short-weighted; you may get two front quarters (more bone and fat, less good cuts) which the dealer considers half a beef. Even without being cheated, you will end up with about half the original weight after cutting and trimming, so the price per pound will double. The "USDA" grade stamps may have disappeared or may turn out to be Standard, Commercial, Utility, or even Cutter or Canner. You will feel like you're eating crow instead of beef.

Besides, you should reconsider the amount of meat you really want and need to eat—from economic and health viewpoints (see FATS), and also in view of the fact that we should all attempt to get more of our protein from vegetable sources. (See VEGETARIANISM.)

FOOD STAMPS

If you're trying to live in an ecologically non-destructive and low-income style, you may very well be eligible for food stamps. The stamps can also help out on those occasions which many people face at least once in their lives, when they're really totally out of resources — the food stamp program is supposed to provide stamps quickly, so you don't starve, after a single interview. Though the program has often been regarded as hostile to students, in principle if you are available for 20 hours of work per week, you are eligible.

Eligibility is determined basically by your income, from which you deduct certain standard items like earned income, Social Security payments, child care, and excess rent costs. You cannot possess cash, savings accounts, stocks or bonds, or other liquid assets in excess of a certain amount (it was $1,750 in 1979 and will probably rise just about at the rate of inflation); people over 60 get an allowance that is almost double. If you have an expensive car, some of its value may count as a cash asset.

Food stamps were formerly paid for in part by users. Now they're simply given away. This helps some people who are very poor to use them. The income level of eligibility has, however, been lowered, so some people who are only fairly poor can no longer get stamps. The program has been improved from the standpoint of older persons, many of whom are desperately poor: stamps now apply for meals in communal dining facilities, for meal delivery services, and in restaurants that have contracts with state or local agencies. And you are no longer required to register for work until 65 — now it's down to 60.

Food stamps may be used only to buy food — not household supplies, vitamins, or foods intended to be eaten on the premises, such as at a lunch counter. In states with sales tax on food, food stamps may be used to cover such taxes. When checking out at a supermarket, be sure to separate your food items from non-food items and inform the checker you will be paying with food stamps; otherwise the whole check-out may have to be repeated.

Your local welfare or unemployment office is the best place to begin inquiring about possible eligibility for food stamps. The program is run by the Department of Agriculture's Food and Nutrition Service, which has regional offices in major cities. If you have trouble, try to locate a Neighborhood Legal Service for help.

FOODS, COOKING METHODS

Some vegetables are just as good raw as they are cooked, and you can experiment with them in SALADS or simply add them to appetizer or dinner menus: peas, beans, jicama (a Mexican root vegetable with a deliciously cool taste), zucchini, carrots, broccoli, cauliflower. Any type of cooking severely reduces the vitamin and mineral content of vegetables. So does peeling, since a large proportion of nutrients lie just below the skin.

For vegetables that must be cooked, *steaming* is better than boiling. Various kinds of metal baskets are available that sit inside any pot with a close-fitting top. Small bamboo steaming racks can be found in Chinese housewares stores. Use only enough water to be sure it doesn't entirely boil away — usually a half-inch will be fine. Vegetables taste and look better when they've been cooked only just enough — they should be a little crisp and chewy. Light varieties of fish, such as sole, are also good steamed.

Frying should be avoided whenever possible. It adds fat calories to your diet even if you use polyunsaturated vegetable oils; adding batter may pose a cholesterol problem and adds still more calories. Your objective, presumably, is to taste the fish or meat or chicken that you're cooking and not the batter, so the best procedure for most such foods is one of the following methods.

Broiling adds no fat (or only a little, if you rub some oil on top to prevent charring), allows fat contained in the food to drip out, and produces a tasty but only slightly crisped surface on the food. It is also the simplest cooking method, requiring no special pans, spatulas, or clean-up of the grease that gets spattered around by frying.

Pressure-cooking is an energy-saving method of cooking tough kinds of meat (such as tongue) in a relatively short time while also conserving food value. But unless you cook such meats a lot, or want to use a pressure-cooker for sterilizing canning jars (a task for which a very large enamel pot is really better anyway), you can probably do most of what a pressure-cooker would do by ordinary steaming.

Baking or roasting in an oven can be used not only for roasts and poultry, but also for Irish potatoes, sweet potatoes and yams, and casserole dishes. It is particularly nice to do in cold weather, because the heat created by the oven helps warm the house.

If you do a lot of cooking, especially for large groups of people, you may find a *food processor* worth the money (and clean-up time). It will do many things that a BLENDER can't, since it is strong enough to handle meats, nuts, and other relatively tough foods. If you like Oriental dishes, you might be especially interested in a processor, since it will chop, slice, and shred things much faster than hand chopping. On the other hand, such work is a good way to take out aggressions....

FRIENDS

In an alienated and fragmented society like ours, with the family faltering and love relationships (or even marriages) increasingly tenuous and often temporary, our friendships become all the more precious. Yet, curiously enough, few people give any systematic thought to their friendship patterns. A healthy friendship support network can help us through life's worst crises, and can make everyday life more interesting, varied, and productive. Sometimes, on the basis of well-established friendships, we can enter upon living experiments with other people, in joint or neighboring households, to help fill the void left by the disappearing nuclear family (see EXTENDED FAMILIES). In these new situations, we can establish new enterprises, or undertake challenging adventures, that we would never have been able to manage alone.

The emphasis in American society has always been individualistic, leading to our familiar national posture of "looking out for Number One." But now that there is no more frontier to escape to, and not even any more open road to flee on, we must come to terms with living with each other. Our psychological literature is full of books on solving internal personal problems or the problems of our couple relationships. It is time to turn this narcissistic focus outward, toward our friends and toward our interrelationships with society. It is largely through our friends that we cling to our particular ecological niches in the world. We need to pay attention to our friendships and to nurture them; they are one of our chief survival mechanisms.

Romantic love and friendship are in some ways opposing values, as people discover who fall madly in love and find themselves abandoning their friends — "well lost for love." The romantic tradition — nowadays hopelessly degraded by the wholesome eroticization of our society by advertising — implies that passion should suffice for happiness, that the ideal state of human life is continual enchantment with a beloved. But enchantment is transitory and founded on fantasy. Unlike friendship, it cannot long survive the realities of day-to-day life; unless love is founded on friendship, it is doomed to be temporary. Moreover, the friends we abandoned yesterday turn out to be badly needed when our lover abandons us. We are better off, thus, to regard the qualities important in friendship (trust, loyalty, equality, mutual regard) as the foundation of our lasting relationships, to which passion is an occasional delightful ornament.

The Art of Friendship, by Christine Leefeldt and Ernest Callenbach, Pantheon, 1979, Berkley paperback, 1980.

G

GARAGE SALES, YARD SALES, FLEA MARKETS

A major recycling channel, these methods of selling used items can be found in practically any community. Generally you get the best deals in garage or yard sales, especially when somebody is moving and is anxious to get rid of stuff before moving day. You have to develop a quick and ruthless eye to avoid spending too much time on any individual collection of junk, and it helps to have a half-formed shopping list in your mind for such occasions. But the main joy, of course, is in finding the things you didn't remember you wanted until you saw them. And then there is also the joy of haggling, which most people seem to expect.

Classified ads in some local community papers are used to announce garage and yard sales; often people put up notices on bulletin boards, as well as on telephone poles on the day of their sale. Beware of "permanent" garage sales, which are really secondhand shops, with correspondingly higher prices.

Flea markets are generally worth the trouble only if they are held by some organization on a very occasional basis. The regularly established ones are mainly filled with secondhand dealers selling the same tired collection of battered tools, old radios, overpriced antique jewelry, and well-worn kitchen implements. (Some of them also offer "hot" clothes, cameras, and electronic stuff.)

GARDENING

City people, as well as those in smaller towns, are turning increasingly to gardening as a source of wholesome and inexpensive food (not to mention pleasant recreation). A surprising number of city dwellings have backyard, balconies, or roofs where food can be grown either in the earth or in planter boxes, tubs, etc. The chances are that you can borrow or pick up free a spade, rake, hoe, and watering hose; you can probably find scrap lumber to use in constructing planter boxes, and a vacant lot somewhere will provide a source of soil — though it may need plenty of compost, steer manure, and other conditioning materials to bring it up to a standard your plants will like. Your local sewage plant probably has fertilizer sludge (usable on all but root vegetables) available for the hauling; dig it in during the fall. You may also be able to find free mulch material, which greatly decreases watering and garden care: sawdust, lawn clippings, rice hulls, etc. Good gardening books abound; look in your library. Also talk to some experienced gardeners in your area to find out what kinds of vegetables thrive best under the conditions of your locale and soil type and which are prone to diseases or insects. Keep your first growing experiments to good bets.

Some plants, like zucchini and other squash, are virtually indestructible and produce unbelievable yields. Most people have success with tomatoes, peas, beans (though these may need dusting with rotenone or other natural-source pesticide), carrots, lettuce, and corn. All these foods taste immensely better fresh. Even if you use no pesticides on them, wash before eating, since city air contains lead and other toxic materials.

You should like digging to be a successful gardener (even though, once you get your garden soil in good condition, mulching can greatly decrease the need to disturb the soil). This is especially true for soil that hasn't been worked for years, which will be packed down so solidly that nothing much can grow in it. To turn unworked earth into a garden, you have to spade it over thoroughly, down as deep as your spade can reach. Throw on some fertilizer or manure and some compost (rotted leaves, twigs, etc.) or peat moss to keep the soil from packing down again. Then in a day or so spade it again, and rake it before you plant. Notice whether it has worms: numerous active worms are a sign of good soil (worms provide aeration and drainage, and their castings are superb fertilizer; in fact, worms are being used to treat sewage wastes). Get started with COMPOSTING as soon as you start thinking about gardening. A small, inexpensive soil-testing kit is useful to check the acidity of your soil.

You might also save some room for a spice garden. And fruit trees are a nice thing to plant, too. They take some years to produce any fruit, so

others may reap the benefit of the trees you plant (just as you are reaping the benefit of trees planted by earlier generations). But the cost of a bare-root fruit tree is hardly more than the price of a bunch of cut flowers, and there's something particularly satisfying about planting a tree.

Your trees are likely to produce more fruit than you and your friends can eat ripe, so you should lay plans for drying some of it. Wire racks laid in the sun on a roof, and protected by screen or cheesecloth from birds and insects, will serve, but more complex devices and methods also exist. Again, check at your local library for more information.

In recent years, great advances have been made in productivity on small plots, using techniques of deep digging (two feet deep!), raised beds, and close planting to keep down soil temperatures and conserve moisture. These techniques are sometimes called the BioDynamic or French Intensive methods.

The City People's Book of Raising Food, by Helga and William Ostrowski. Rodale Press, 1975.

Basic Book of Organic Gardening, ed. by Robert Rodale. Ballantine, 1971.

The Organic Gardener, by Catherine Osgood Foster.

Vintage Books, 1972.

Practicing Plant Parenthood, by Maggie Baylis. 101 Productions, 1975.

How to Grow More Vegetables Than You Ever Thought Possible on Less Land Than You Can Imagine, by John Jeavons. Ecology Action, 2225 El Camino Real, Palo Alto, CA 94306.

New Sunset Gardening Book. Lane Publishing Company, 1979. A reliable, standard, comprehensive guide.

Seed sources: The usual range of garden varieties, and some novelties, are available from Burpee Seed Co., 300 Park Ave., Warminster, PA 18974; Joseph Harris Co., Moreton Farm, Rochester, NY 14624; Stokes Seeds, Buffalo, NY 14240; Farmer's Seed and Nursery Co., Faribault, MN 55021. For unusual Oriental vegetables: Tsang and Ma International, 1556 Laurel St., San Carlos, CA 94070. For exotics and other special items: J. L. Hudson, Seedsman, World Seed Service, Box 1058, Redwood City, CA 94064; Nichols Herb and Rare Seeds, 1190 De Pacific, Albany, OR 97321; Johnny's Selected Seeds, Box 15, Albion, ME 04910; Sanctuary Seeds, 1913 Yew St., Vancouver, BC, Canada V6K 3G3.

GEOTHERMAL ENERGY

Only a dozen or so miles beneath the surface, the earth's interior is very hot; in some localities this hot layer is much closer to the surface, close enough to heat underground water and produce either hot springs or steam geysers. Generally these areas are in regions where there has been volcanic activity; in the United States, most of them are in the Pacific Coast region. The original inhabitants of this country regarded the hot springs as holy and health-giving, and in Europe, hot springs have been developed as health spas. In recent years, the potential of such areas for energy-production has been recognized; Italy, New Zealand, and California now derive substantial amounts of electric power from geothermal plants.

The process is essentially simple: wells are drilled (by oil-well-drilling techniques) down several thousand meters to very hot areas. Natural steam then comes up the wells, often in great quantities; it is piped from the wells to nearby generating plants where it is used to turn turbines that generate electricity. The condensed steam, and the mineral salts that come up with it, are then re-injected back down the wells, so that the stream and watershed pollution associated with the process is very slight. The Geysers area just north of San Francisco will shortly be producing the equivalent of San Francisco's entire electrical demand, and geologists have recently begun to think that the tappable area there is far more extensive still.

In areas where hot rock that can be reached by drilling contains little water or steam, water can be injected down into the rock, where the heat turns it into steam.

Geothermal energy is particularly promising from an Ecotopian viewpoint because it requires only standard technology, which is entirely available right now; it is reliable; it has no public health dangers associated with it as do nuclear energy, coal, and oil — which all pollute the biosphere or threaten dangerous releases of radioactivity. With halfway decent design and management, geothermal energy is unpolluting; the necessary installations can be made to blend into the natural landscape. While it is inherently inferior to decentralized electricity sources such as photovoltaic cells or wind power because it requires high-voltage transmission lines to carry electricity from the steam fields to the cities where most of it is used, nevertheless geothermal energy is a major and immediately available alternative to conventional electricity generation methods.

A few lucky communities, such as Klamath Falls, Oregon, or Reykjavik, Iceland, are located in hot-springs areas which can be tapped for the heating of homes, schools, pools, etc. There, hot water is circulated through the equivalent of public steam pipes, and virtually no oil or gas back-up is required. In fact, in Iceland, geothermal heat is used to heat greenhouses for the growing of bananas, Iceland's third largest export!

GREENHOUSES AND SOLARIUMS

If you think greenhouses are only a rural possibility, think again. Even if you are a high-rise dweller, if you have a balcony with southern exposure you could convert it into a greenhouse. If you live in a house, of almost any kind, the chances are that you can add on a greenhouse that will help

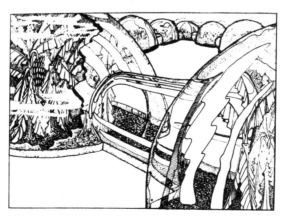

An Ecotopian greenhouse farm of the future.

heat your dwelling and provide you with a place to grow vegetables.

In new construction, architects are slowly becoming smarter about taking advantage of the sun's energy through both "passive" designs (arranging windows, overhangs, and heat-storing masses of concrete or masonry to catch heat when it's needed and keep it out when it isn't) and "active" designs (arrangements that pump heat from one place to another), as well as hybrid designs. But in any remodeling of an old structure, you should consider carefully how to incorporate greenhouse-type features. The essentials: to allow heated air to rise through the house, the greenhouse should be at the lowest possible living level; to store heat efficiently, it must have a strong enough foundation to support not only earth containers for plants but also a concrete floor or row of water-filled barrels. To control hot air movement and build-up, it must have ventilation openings to let outside air enter, and doors into the house living areas which can be closed. To prevent excessive heat, in summer, the greenhouse needs shades or overhangs or a deciduous tree, and often a steep angle of the double-glass walls.

In some states, lending institutions now give very favorable loan terms for money to install solar or other energy improvements. If a greenhouse is added as a solar-heating device, it may be eligible for substantial tax write-offs. This use alone may make it worth doing. But rows of planter boxes, even in a small greenhouse, can support a surprisingly productive vegetable garden. The plants will also help to humidify your air, which is especially healthful in winter.

See GARDENING.

HARDWARE, IMPROVISING

It is nice, of course, to be able to repair and build things "like a professional" — to buy the right replacement parts or hardware, to fit and machine things to fit exactly, to attach them with the best screws and clamps and brackets. But this can be expensive, so the home fixer, who is trying to make improvements while still not spending any money, must be alert to the possibilities of improvising at every level.

The key to this is to be bold. You will get nowhere by trying simply to cut corners — you'll end up with tawdry results. What you need to do is to think big, and you may come up with something really beautiful. There is always more than one way to do things, and sometimes the usual way is not the most attractive or interesting. It is possible, by developing a sense of innovative design, to build and fix things without a great deal of the usual money-eating expenses.

Here, for instance, are possible alternatives to a number of basic hardware items.

Hinges. You can use a nail or dowel coming from the frame into the swinging door, window, or whatever. Or combine big staples and nails. You can also use pieces of inner tube, leather, or other flexible and durable substances, tacked on like hinges. Better yet, use a sliding door — a piece of plywood running between strips of wood — that doesn't need hinges.

Latches. In parts of the country where wood is used for everything, like the Pacific Northwest, door and gate latches are made with a wooden bolt sliding in wooden guides.

Clothes hooks. If you have a wooden wall, or a wooden strip running along the wall, drill holes in it and glue in dowels.

Toilet-paper holder. Find a small Y-shaped branch; carve it to shape with a pocketknife and screw onto the wall (the same idea, but with a bigger stick, works for paper towels).

Cupboard doorknobs, and other hand grips. Use small, odd-shaped pieces of driftwood or weathered wood.

Broken windows. In places where it makes a burglar's entry easier, broken glass should be replaced. But in other locations you could preserve the old glass by taping the crack (outside and inside) with some fiberglass-reinforced wrapping tape. A whole roll of this is expensive; try to beg, borrow, or steal a few feet of it. (Package-wrapping stations in warehouses, stores, and offices have it.) No other kind of tape, except Mystik tape, which won't let light through, will stick to glass for any length of time. Clean the glass carefully where the tape will be; make sure it's dry before you stick on the tape.

A window that has been broken out so it can't be taped can be replaced with plastic sheeting taped or tacked to the frame. This is not a very satisfactory alternative, although people in cold climates cover all their windows with clear plastic in winter to cut down heating bills. Look around instead for substances that might take the place of glass; clear or colored rigid plastic, thin plywood (cardboard is useless as soon as rain hits it), even a piece of enameled metal.

Best of all is to get the owner to pay for the glass and putty if you do the work. It takes only a few minutes to learn — the essentials are to clean the frame carefully and measure the window dimensions exactly so that the glass shop cuts the pane to fit precisely.

Curtain rings. With a pair of pliers you can improvise rings out of clothes hangers; they can even be made to spring shut on the cloth so no sewing on is required. Generally rings are better than sewing the cloth into a wide hem and then sticking the rod through — even if the hem is very big, it still tends to bind, but a ring system slides easily.

Suspending things. Hardware stores are full of hooks, wires, rods, buckets, bars, and so on, but you almost never really need anything but nails — and even nails can often be replaced by a hole. If, for instance, you want to hang up something on a wooden cabinet, you can drill little holes in it, run strings or wires through the holes, and knot them inside. You accomplish three things by such an alternative to the conventional hook or whatnot: you liberate yourself from the standard way of doing things, you keep ugly chrome-plated or plastic junk out of your house, and you save money. Your imagination, once liberated, may lead you to do quite beautiful things: braiding colorful strings to hang up paper towels or toilet paper, using pieces of tree branch as coat hooks, building special little racks of driftwood or scrap wood for spices or candles or writing materials, planting small plants in the cavities in rocks or driftwood, hanging pots and pans from twisted pieces of very old rusty metal, and so on.

Rod supports (for curtain rods, shower rods, towel-roll rods, etc.).   Make V-shaped supports by tacking two small pieces of wood to the wall, or driving three or four nails in a U-shape.

See APARTMENT REPAIRS and REPAIRS, HOME.

HEALTH INSURANCE AND HEALTH MAINTENANCE ORGANIZATIONS

The fact that traditional single-doctor, single-patient medicine is not really satisfactory has finally become clear to almost everybody. Most doctors now prefer to practice in groups, to share hours and specialties and support staff. And the experience of such organizations as the Kaiser Permanente network of health plans has shown that the general health of large groups of people can be most efficiently served (with consequent lower costs) through plans emphasizing preventive medicine with regular check-ups, group practice by the physician staff, and financial arrangements which do not encourage unnecessary hospitalization or surgery (both of which are rampant in American medicine).

When medical treatment *is* necessary, especially in the case of hospitalization, the costs are so catastrophic that health insurance is practically obligatory. Still, only one state, Hawaii, has compulsory health insurance. There over half of the premiums are employer-paid, and there is competition between health care organizations to help keep costs comparatively low.

A consensus is developing that most medical services should be delivered through such organizations. But the national health insurance programs likely to secure Congressional approval in the 80's are essentially bailouts of Blue Cross and Blue Shield. They will provide no real improvement in preventive medicine practice, nor will they control medical costs. They may improve somewhat the proportion of costs paid by insurance — which has been little better than a third.

More comprehensive and prevention-oriented health care practiced in neighborhood centers and clinics, backed up by hospitals, is the kind of step we will ultimately have to take to obtain a humane, reasonable and person-centered health system. Representative Ron Dellums of California has introduced an alternative plan which would work and is gaining support. It provides for democratic community control of many medical services.

HEAT, INDOOR

Owners of rental dwellings are obliged by law to provide reasonable heat, and if you don't get it you can file a complaint to the city authorities or deduct from the rent the cost of heating the place yourself. But if you don't want to go that route, you may be able to improve the heating situation a little by yourself.

Air leaks around windows. Before cold weather comes, if possible, fill up the cracks. From the outside, where they are exposed to weather, the best thing to use is some kind of putty or sealing compound. (In cold country, some people just cover the whole window area with sheet plastic.) From the inside, practically anything will do — torn up newspapers soaked in flour-and-water glue and tightly forced into cracks, then painted when dry; rags dipped in some old paint and stuffed into cracks. Tack weather stripping around doors so they close tightly.

Radiators that don't heat up enough. Hot-water radiators sometimes fill up with air; then the hot water can't get into them. Get a valve key from a hardware store (or the landlord) and open the valve so air hisses out. When mostly water comes out, close it again. This may have to be done often, and if so only an automatic valve will permanently cure the problem.

Steam radiators also have a valve, which may be clogged. Turn off steam at the main turn-off handle. Unscrew the valve and clean out its little hole with a piece of fine wire (a very thin hairpin or a needle may work). Blow through or shake it, to get the water out. Steam radiators also have to be leveled just right. If they have just one pipe coming to them, they should slant down toward it just a little. You need a level to make sure, as the whole building may be tilted. Two-pipe radiators should slant toward the return pipe (the one without a turn-off handle). You can stick thin pieces of wood, linoleum, etc., under the legs to get them at the right angle.

Gas heaters that don't work. The commonest trouble with wall or floor heaters is that their pilot-light thermocouple (which generates current to run the thermostat) is shot. Replacing it will cost money, but it is not a complicated job and hardware stores have recently begun to sell replacements. Turn off the gas at the meter, then remove the thermocouple and take it along to the store to be sure you get the right replacement.

Electric heaters. Electricity costs far more than gas for a given amount of heat. But an electric heater may be justifiable in cases where you just want to heat one small room and leave the rest of the apartment or house cool. Secondhand heaters can easily be found in good condition or with easily repaired defects, such as dust collected in the thermostat. Heating a whole house electrically has been reasonable in the Northwest, which benefited from heavy federal hydroelectrical subsidies, but will soon be rediculous even there.

Kerosene and other room heaters. There are cheap kerosene heaters which are attractive in an old-fashioned way, but they have two disadvantages: even if you use deodorized kerosene, the heaters still smell, and as they don't have vents, they tend to fill your room with polluted air. You can really only use them like the old potbellied stove: they're OK for drafty rooms when you are sitting right next to them. But you can't rely on them for regular heat; to use kerosene for that, you need a bigger heater vented through the wall or roof.

Turning on stove to give heat. When all else fails, you can use an ordinary stove to heat at least your kitchen. The best way is to turn on the oven and leave its door open, with the broiler door open a crack. But you also get quite a lot of heat if you turn on several burners *and put big pots of water on them.* This has two effects: the sides of the pots become "radiators," and the water vapor from the boiling raises the humidity which makes the air feel warmer, as in a steam room. (You don't want to do this too much in a tight room, as excessive steam may loosen plaster.)

The healthiest temperature for human beings is around 65°F (18°C), but most Americans find that chilly. Many American houses are kept around eighty or even eighty-five — temperatures so high that they dry out your nasal passages. Oddly enough, people tend to overheat the most in cold climates — in New York, for instance, you may come in from zero weather to a blazing hot apartment where you immediately break out in a sweat.

Rather than overheating your home, put on a sweater or wear two shirts or even wear long underwear. You also cut down the shock of going outdoors into the cold. You will conserve surprising amounts of energy and, if you are paying for your own heat, you'll save a great deal of money because those extra degrees of heat are very expensive.

A thermostat not only helps keep the temperature steady, it also saves fuel. Whether you have a gas heater, a kerosene heater, or a furnace, it should be on a thermostat. Then keep the thermostat set between sixty-five and seventy (18-21°C). Turn it down even lower at night.

In country situations where wood is abundant the best way to heat is with a metal stove. But many city dwellers also find wood heating economical. See WOOD STOVES.

HERBICIDES.   See PESTICIDES AND HERBICIDES.

HOLIDAYS

Our traditional holidays are actually debased versions of very ancient festivities. Christmas goes back to the Roman festival of Saturnalia, and beyond that to pagan celebrations of the winter solstice — the time when the sun reaches its lowest point and the days are shortest, after which we can look forward to the coming of spring. Easter is our spring festival of rebirth, usually falling a little later than the spring equinox, and Thanksgiving is the fall equinox festival, though we celebrate it at a considerable lag after the equinoctial point. Midsummer Night's Eve is still celebrated in Scandinavia; it is the summer solstice, or time of the longest day and highest sun. In prehistoric times and indeed up to the Middle Ages, our Western European ancestors celebrated these pagan holidays as periods of fertility rituals, sometimes sacrifice, and often sexual license. In Ecotopia, they customarily signal the opportunity for a brief vacation from monogamy and are the occasion of major regional fairs.

The sexual side of traditional holidays has been diverted in our times into two main other kinds of excess: eating and buying, both of which tend to become unpleasant obligations. At Thanksgiving you are expected to eat too much; at Christmas you are expected to give too much; on New Year's you are expected to drink too much — and pretend to be happy, when in fact you may well be feeling pretty dismal. (In actuality the winter holidays are the heavy suicide season). It seems impossible simply to abandon these degraded festivities, though people do sometimes try to boycott them. What we need to do is to recapture their original ceremonial meaning: their celebration of the phases of our yearly cycle here on the earth. We depend on this eternal cycle just as totally as our forebears did, from the agricultural standpoint, even though only a small number of us are actually engaged in planting and harvesting. As we utilize solar energy to a greater degree, we will be more conscious of our dependence on the sun. A certain due gratitude to earth and sun would seem then to be as much in order for us as it was for our ancestors. Surely we can be inventive enough to devise some new expressions of it.

There are also some other traditional holidays we might want to revive or rehabilitate or re-emphasize:

Iroquois Indian Dream Festival (mid-January). During this festival people were thought to be out of their minds and thus not responsible for their actions; they went around masked, smashing things, and generally evening up old scores.

Valentine's Day (February 14). This was originally much sexier than our commercial greeting-card version — on this day birds and animals were thought to choose their mates, so humans did likewise, by magic or games of chance. If you want to take the risk they took in Rome, the first person you see on this day will be your true love. Or you can draw names out of an urn.

Holi (Hindi spring fire festival). This involves bonfires, bright clothing, and squirting colored water at passersby.

Walpurgis Night (April 30). This is when the forces of evil are abroad in the land — witches, demons, and their modern equivalents. To keep them away, bang on pots, ring bells, and light a big fire with a friction spark. (The spark won't work if any of the lighters have committed theft, adultery, or murder, so you had better keep matches handy.) In the true Druid custom, you would then eat cake, drink, and draw lots; the loser is torn to pieces and thrown into the sacred fire, while the rest grab burning sticks and run around screaming, "Burn the witches!"

May Day (May 1). This is a double-faced holiday, one side sex and the other politics. For the sex part, you need lots of dancing around a maypole and much nearby grass and woods for the celebration of fertility rites. For the political part, you need to remember that the tread of thousands of parading workers' feet has often struck terror into the hearts of the bosses, raising the specter of general strikes and the revolution.

Dragon Boat Race (early June). This is in honor of Ch'u Yuan, a dissident Chinese scholar of the third century BC. When his proposed reforms of a corrupt court fell on deaf ears, he jumped into the river. This festival commemorates the search for his body — with gaily decorated boats, drums and gongs, and a lot of racing back and forth. However, there is no goal and no judges, so the day becomes an occasion for picnicking, drinking, and assuring that yin and yang are in balance.

Bastille Day (July 14). In 1789, the French people stormed the hated Bastille prison and destroyed the records of the police, as oppressed peoples have done since and will do again. In France, celebrating begins the previous evening with music and dancing in the streets, followed by fireworks and more dancing the next day.

Day of the Dead (November 2). In Mexico and other cultures where wakes are regarded as an occasion for showing that life goes on, it does not seem strange to celebrate the dead. This day in Mexico is a picnic day; people stream to the cemeteries, long before sunrise, with candles, flowers, and food. For the dead (though the living eat it) they bring candy, cakes, and so on — made in the shape of skulls — and poets and musicians write and sing of death.

You may also find some of the traditional religious holidays to your taste. Modern religions tend to be bland, commercialized, and banal, and they try to make their holidays pretty much like everybody else's. If you want holidays with more guts, you'll have to find an old-fashioned religious group that still takes ritual seriously. They exist.

HOLISTIC HEALTH

Traditional medicine tends to isolate us from the functioning of our bodies and to put responsibility for curing disorders onto a doctor's shoulders. (Responsibility for *preventing* disorders is not considered part of medicine; that is classified as "public health," and about one-fifteenth as much is spent on it as on conventional curative medicine — despite the fact that such advances in our general medical welfare as have been achieved are almost entirely due to public-health measures.)

In reaction to this pattern, recent years have seen a considerable growth of interest in nonconventional healing and preventive systems, from acupuncture (whose biochemical mechanisms were only elucidated in 1979) to biofeedback, herbalism, hypnosis, massage, iridology, etc. Experience with and evaluation of these techniques has not yet proceeded to the point where a firm consensus on their value exists, though many people have found them effective, and certainly the atmosphere in which they are administered is generally itself a support for the body's own healing energies. The doctrines involved are complex; some have long traditional histories; some are likely to prove susceptible to scientific analysis in the near future, others not. The literature on these doctrines is extensive, and of highly varying quality. Two good introductory works are listed below.

My personal view is that many of these disciplines are useful for maintaining good health and for dealing with certain kinds of chronic conditions, but persons facing an immediate and serious health crisis should first, or also, consult a traditional doctor — many of whom are beginning to understand some aspects of holistic medicine.

It is noteworthy that "folk medicine" — the lore upon which most humans, in industrial or nonindustrial societies, actually depend for their day-to-day health care — has never forgotten that "disease" has nutritional, psychological, and environmental components, as well as microbial, physical, and chemical aspects. In a sense what we need is a new folk medicine, adapted to our conditions and incorporating what "scientific medicine" has discovered. The holistic health movement is heading in that direction. See MEDICAL CARE.

The Holistic Health Handbook, compiled by the Berkeley Holistic Health Center. And/Or Press, 1979. Extensive bibliography.

The Herb Book, by John Lust. Bantam, 1974. A complete dictionary giving identification characteristics and traditional and new uses.

HOME EDUCATION

One reason America's school situation is so tragic is that the problems we are asking the schools to solve can hardly be solved once children have reached school age: a child's basic mental capacities and attitudes toward life are well formed by the age of three. Thus, a child who is going to be curious and alert about how things work will be that way on his or her first day of school; a child who is going to go through life without ever figuring out what is going on will usually be that way on his or her first day too. What we are doing, really, is asking the schools to salvage the latter type of child as far as possible, and to give the former whatever encouragement they can.

The fundamental tasks of education must be begun by the parents, and they begin as soon as a baby is born. Though they never slack off entirely, they diminish by the time a child is four or five. When a child actually reaches school age, his or her "educational character" is largely formed.

It is within the immediate grasp of every parent to attend to the pre-school education of our children. This doesn't mean giving them lessons; it doesn't even necessarily mean teaching them numbers or the alphabet. What it essentially means is to show them how to use their minds. And there is only one way to do this: show them how you use yours. Children learn, like adults, chiefly by example. Here are some ways you can try to put this principle to work without beating your brains out trying to "be a teacher." (Remember that children only pick up on things they see are fun; if you go into some kind of agony trying to do something *to* them, they will accurately perceive it as a bum trip.)

Talk to them as if you were "talking to yourself." If you talk to yourself while you're doing things, this will be easy. If you don't, just try thinking out loud to them, whenever you're dealing with them or when they're hanging around: while you're doing housework, while you're fixing something, while you're laying out some food. It doesn't matter if it's a complete explanation or just a word here and there. What counts is that you are telling them what is going on, and why, and how. (Especially how.) You'd be surprised how many basic "educational" lessons this will get across. For instance, if you talk to your child (even a child of two or three) while you mix a cake, he or she will learn (1) that pleasant things like cake can be made out of things that don't look terribly impressive, like flour and water; (2) that making a cake requires a certain sequence of steps in order to work; (3) that you use special tools or utensils or appliances to accomplish things, like mixing and baking the cake; (4) that processes take time, like waiting for the cake to get baked; and perhaps most important and subtlest of all, (5) that you can act upon things in the world and get them to respond to your desires — that if you understand them, you can control them, and that you can do them better or not so well depending on your understanding.

Get them to help you. If you're an efficient type, this takes a lot of willpower, because small children's "help" often seems like interference unless you are willing to pay close attention to what they are trying to do, go along with it to some extent, yet still carry them along on your own project. But it can be fun, if you relax about it. Try it when you have plenty of time, and on projects that don't have any deadline or urgency — you don't want a child around if you're trying to stop a water leak that may flood your apartment! But if you're just putting a wheel back on a tricycle (children love to see you fix their own things, of course), by watching you and helping you, your child will learn (1) that tools have special names — ask for things and point to them when you need them; (2) that different tools have different purposes; (3) that there are causes and effects — the wheel fell off because the cotter pin broke, and a piece of wire in its place will hold the wheel on again; (4) that things have parts, and these parts are related—to replace the wheel, you have to remove the hubcap; the cotter pin or wire holds the wheel and the axle together.

Read to them. Having books, magazines, and newspapers around the house will show your kids that the printed word is important and interesting. Get children's books from the library. Take children along to the library as soon as they can walk around and look at the books there. Get them used to the idea that there are mysterious and fascinating things to be found out through reading.

Cut down on TV. It's not so much that the contents of TV programs are bad for them (though some of them certainly are). The real problem is that kids who spend most of their time watching TV don't get the chance to develop ingenuity through having to learn how to invent games with other children. They get used to being entertained by others — to sitting and waiting for things to happen, rather than making them happen. So it's a good idea to pay attention to how much TV your children watch, even if you can't bear to pay attention to what they watch. One hour a day is certainly plenty — it's probably more than your child spends directly relating to you. And try wherever possible to expose kids to the real contributions of TV — instant coverage of stupendous events like the moon landing, and such excellent children's programs as *Sesame Street*.

Writing. Let your children watch when you have to write something — a letter, a list of things to buy at the store. Let them play with your pencils and paper. Get them to tell you stories and write them down (sometimes their drawings have stories in them). When they get old enough to read a bit, write down notes and stick them up on the wall.

The names of things. Our world runs by words; if your child becomes curious about words and good at using them, it's an immense advantage. See if you can make up rhymes or word games with the names of things around the house or in picture books.

Numbers. A child who sees parents using numbers will know what they are used for — adding up a budget, seeing how much an installment plan will cost, planning the dimensions to make something and how to measure and mark the parts, reading prices in the store on shelves and cans, and so on.

Drawing. Most young children naturally like to draw. If they are given any chance at all, they will draw themselves, their parents, their pets, their street, their house, and so on. They will also draw their dreams, imaginary stories, and strange fantasy scenes. Unfortunately, most schools have limited facilities and allow little time for drawing. Only a few very good teachers understand that through drawing a child can come to understand and learn just as well (maybe better) than through other kinds of learning. So at home give your children plenty of paper, crayons, pencils, and even paints if you can afford them. The cheapest kind of paper you can buy is called "newsprint"; an art-supplies store or a large stationery store will sell it. The easiest-to-get free paper is computer printout paper, which any friend who works in a big office can probably get for you. It has numbers on one side, but is big and great for drawing. Supermarket paper supplies are almost always too expensive. The only exception is reams (five hundred sheets) of typing paper.

For older children, one of the most important things you can do is to keep books of various kinds available in the house. And there are two special kinds of books every household needs, for children and adults both:

Dictionaries. Anytime you put something important on paper — a letter, a petition, a plan — you'll need a dictionary to check spellings and meanings. Besides, a dictionary can be a fascinating kind of reading. Get a good big one. The *American Heritage Dictionary*, available in paperback, is the best I have found at present: it has good design and printing, and beautiful illustrations; its handling of usage standards is very complete and it frequently gives derivations of words. Many special children's dictionaries are available; check with a children's librarian for recommendations.

Encyclopedias. Never buy an encyclopedia of any kind from a door-to-door salesperson, no matter how sweet the deal sounds, no matter how beautiful the encyclopedia, no matter how good it might appear for your children! You will end up paying several hundred dollars for the set, much of it in interest and carrying charges. But you can phone a couple of used-book stores and find encyclopedia sets, probably of the identical edition, for modest prices.

Before you spend money on encyclopedias, however, drop in at your public library and talk to the children's librarian (or the reference librarian, if you're thinking of a set for yourself). They know which encyclopedias are satisfactory and which are junk; ask their advice, and look through the sets they recommend to see if they suit you. Many households, even intellectual ones, are well enough served by a single-volume job, the *Columbia Encyclopedia*, which can be bought easily secondhand. It is authoritative, fairly complete, and so big and heavy that it's much better than telephone books for seating kids at the table.

HOSPITALS, COUNTY

Nobody likes county hospitals, because they are huge, impersonal places where you feel lost and wonder whether anybody will bother to take care of you. But actually their medical work is reasonably good these days — most of the staff doctors are young and are working in the hospital because they see it as a way of helping humanity rather than getting rich quick. Outside medical experts who have investigated medical care in big county hospitals in Los Angeles and Oakland have found that it's acceptable, although conditions are crowded, nursing staffs are short, food is terrible, etc. The worst part is dealing with all the applications, offices, and the endless waiting. Before going to a county hospital, try to get the name of a doctor who works there and call for advice; then ask for him or her when you get there. Try never to go to a county hospital without a friend who can go to bat for you, keep you company, get you snacks, and generally help you out. Clinic outpatient services are far less good than hospital services — and sometimes very expensive if you have to pay for them.

If you have any income at all and are not on welfare, the county hospital will bill you, possibly far more than regular private doctors' rates!

County hospitals must treat anyone who comes in, whether he or she has any money, health insurance coverage, or any other resources. Some privately run hospitals in a county are used by the police to take emergency cases to, and you can go there under your own power too. But unless you can prove you're able to pay the bill, or are in clear and immediate danger of death, many hospitals will refuse to help you. If you are without money or insurance coverage, therefore, make sure that whoever takes you in, waits around to see what happens — it may be desirable to take you to the county hospital rather than wait for often delayed city ambulance service.

Under new programs to decentralize mental illness treatment away from big hospitals and back into the communities, city hospitals have psychiatric units for people going through mental crises (see MENTAL ILLNESS).

HOSTELS

Although the hostel movement is not as well developed in the US as in Europe, there are still a surprising number of hostels available (also in Canada). These are generally stripped-down accommodations offering a bed, toilet and bath facilities, sheets if you have no sleeping bag, and sometimes shared cooking facilities, for a very low cost. Hostels are often run by YMCAs or similar organizations, but some are privately operated. They can be found in cities and in beautiful rural settings, surrounded by forests, beaches, and hiking areas. While some are sexually segregated or feature other restrictions, others offer family rooms, pleasant communal living rooms with fireplaces, and are generally looser now about who sleeps where and with whom. A greater variety of people uses hostels now than in earlier times when their clientele was mainly penniless students on backpacking tours. For further information: American Youth Hostels, Building 240, Fort Mason, San Francisco, CA 94123.

HOUSE BUYING

In the late seventies, houses (and other real estate) became so expensive that relatively few people are now likely to generate the down payment and income required to buy one. Buying a house has become possible mainly for those folks who already have one that has risen in cash value, so they can sell it and then put the money into another house. This situation is already forcing people to consider puchasing houses jointly, usually by forming a mini-corporation for that purpose. In time, houses that have become too expensive to find buyers will gradually be broken up into smaller units that people can afford, either as rentals, condominiums, or cooperative apartments, but this will be a very slow process involving changes in ZONING laws.

In the meantime, you might conceivably find yourself in a position to buy (perhaps a CONDOMINIUM), and here are the elementary facts about it (but also discuss the process at length with friends who have done it). Real estate agents work for the *seller*, not you; so when you go to an agent's office and say you'd like help in finding a house, keep in mind that the agent's friendliness has a perfectly business-like basis: he or she only makes that juicy commission if you can be pursuaded to buy. A competent agent can calculate or help you calculate what effect buying a house at a given price will have on your tax situation; can tell you how to verify the property taxes that have been paid on the property (but generally *not* what taxes may rise to once you have bought the property, usually considerably more than what was listed on the tax rolls before the sale); and how different methods of financing will affect your payments. Financing is supremely important because a small difference in interest percentage (or "points," interest paid in advance to persuade the lender to give you the loan) can make a serious difference in monthly outlays. It is even more important if — and this is rare among Americans, but does happen — you stay in the house for more than a few years and pay off a substantial part of the mortgage. (Generally, by the way, there are interest penalties if you sell within five years. For that and other reasons, such as loss of your "closing costs," you should not buy a dwelling if you don't plan to remain in your present city for a considerable period.)

In the early years of a mortgage you are paying almost nothing but interest charges, and building up a very small "equity" in the property. Nonetheless, home ownership is generally advantageous from a tax standpoint since you can deduct all interest charges from your income at tax time. (It is mainly this tax policy, and not some mysterious propensity toward house ownership in the American heart, which has made house ownership so common in this country.)

You must, of course, maintain a house after you buy it, and this takes considerable time, money, and work. It helps to be handy with tools and mechanical matters generally, and to enjoy spending a certain portion of your free time fixing up your abode; if you don't, a house can become a real burden.

Stay away from "land contracts" — widely used in the Chicago area and elsewhere — which soak you with enormous interest charges, make you vulnerable to instant foreclosures, and leave you without the advantages of FHA guarantees. And study the situation carefully. Check with the city to find out whether a highway is planned to go through your property or nearby. Check the schools, the street lighting at night, the garbage, and other public services. Look into the tax bill — don't take the realtor's word for it (call the assessor's office). Before you sign anything, talk to your lawyer. (A paper innocently called a "bid," "offer to buy," or "deposit receipt" may really be a contract to buy.) Be sure to check the fire-insurance situation. This is now a difficult problem in many central city areas. Many insurance companies have "red-lined" such areas and refuse to write policies there. The rule here is either get the policy before you sign to buy the house, or (which is usually easier) insert a clause in the house contract which makes it conditional upon your getting insurance. That way the seller's real-estate agent will have to help you get it.

If you already own a house and are thinking of selling it, it is essential to get a tax accountant or tax lawyer to help you. The tax laws provide capital gains loopholes intended for rich people who sell property and want to keep the money they get from it; and here, for a change, little people can usually use the same loopholes — but only if they get expert help.

However, beware of relying on a real-estate agent for such needs. In fact, you can sell your house yourself through advertisements in the local paper; hire a lawyer to go over the sales contract for a couple of hundred dollars, instead of the thousands you as seller would "normally" pay a real-estate agent. It is one of the best-kept secrets of the real-estate game that the 6% commission is not sacred or fixed in law; you can negotiate with potential agents and set either a lower commission or a set fee in dollars. Realtors have been in effect skimming an enormous tax off real-estate transactions, and in fact contributing very little which the multiple-listings service (a cheap enterprise to operate) doesn't do. Shop around for a selling agent, it you feel you need one, who will give you a favorable commission or agree to accept a fixed sum.

For information on condominiums, see CO-OP HOUSING and CONDOMINIUMS.

HOUSEHOLD HAZARDS

Many recently developed cleaning and polishing substances are dangerous, especially to children. Dishwasher detergents usually contain TSP, a caustic that can painfully damage eyes and digestive tracts. Furniture polish in spray containers, which children may squirt at each other, can cause blindness. Cleaning liquids may be colored and packaged to be "attractive," and children may swallow them with lethal results. Simplify your supply of cleaning products to a few necessities, and keep those in a locked storage place if you have small children.

Here are some other items which irresponsible manufacturers produce that endanger their users: some color TVs give off dangerous radiation— don't sit closer than ten feet from one. Many hair dryers emit tiny asbestos fibers, which cause cancer (EPA has a toll-free number to advise if your model is dangerous: 800-638-8301). Some vaporizers used to make steam for coughs contain boiling water which will scald you if the vaporizer is tipped over. If small rugs lack non-skid backings, sew on jar rings. Gas floor heaters, whose grates get extremely hot, brand waffle patterns on tender children's flesh; if you have a baby just beginning to crawl, build a fence of some kind around the heater; after a bit teach the baby about moderately hot things by letting him or her touch them and saying "Hot!" at the moment of contact. This ensures you will later get real attention when you say "Hot!" about something really hot.

Children's cribs and playpens with wide-spaced slats allow children to stick their heads through and get stuck. Fireworks, even though supposedly illegal in most states, still cause many injuries each year. Ladders are often rickety from bad design or age; when you use a ladder, make sure it's solidly placed.

HOUSEHOLD PESTS

Some parasites live on our bodies (like lice); but there are other creatures that just like to live near us—eating our food and sharing our shelter and heat. It has been estimated that there are as many rats in a city as there are people (though nobody has ever taken a complete rat census).

Because rats, roaches, flies, and other pests live on your food, the only lasting way to get rid of them is to stop feeding them. You can trap them (cheese won't work, by the way), poison them, swat them, and so on—but as long as their food supply remains, each dead one will soon be replaced by a thriving young one. And you will have to spend more money on traps and poisons.

If you have to use household pesticides, keep them stored in a high, safe place away from children, especially if they are in spray cans which kids love to play with. Follow the label directions carefully, and remember that farm workers have died from exposure to these substances. Never let the spray get on dishes, utensils, or pets. If it does, wash it off immediately with plenty of hot. soapy water and rinse well. If it gets on food, throw the food away. If it gets on your skin or clothing, wash thoroughly as soon as possible. Never breathe insecticide spray or let it touch your eyes; keep the doors and windows open if you have to use it. Keep it away from aquariums (it kills fish) and pet food or water. If you use poison baits against rats, make sure children and pets can't get at them; many children die from rat poison each year. (See PESTICIDES and HERBICIDES.)

Rats and mice. Rats live in woodpiles and bushes around fancy surburban homes just as happily as in slum basements and sewers. Some rats and mice live wild, eating natural foods, but they will sometimes come into houses, either through holes or open doors. Rats seem to enter sewer systems through roof vents; sometimes they try to come up through toilets and drown.

Close off all the holes by which they can get in. Holes in plaster walls are best filled with spackle wall-mending mixture spread over some wire mesh, or steel wool dipped in spackle or plaster. Stuffing holes with paper or cardboard just gives the rats chewing exercise. Holes in baseboards or wooden walls that you can nail into are best closed by nailing on a piece of metal—a flattened tin can or a piece of roofing or whatever's handy. Make sure doors and screen doors shut properly. In summer, make sure open windows have screens— rats are just as capable of climbing up or down a fire escape as people are. (If the owner won't provide screens, nail on any old piece of wire mesh.) If there are big cracks under your door nail a board along the bottom to make the crack too thin for a rat to pass under. Don't be discouraged about keeping rats out—anybody with a hammer can prevent rats from getting into a living space.

Second, store your food in containers that rats can't gnaw through. This is a good idea anyway, because food keeps better in airtight containers. Put your rice, flour, bread, cereals, and other loose-packed foods into painted snap-lid coffee cans, big pickle jars, a tin bread box, or at least a ratproof cabinet with a tight-closing door latch on it. Rats are busy, active animals and need a lot of food. If they can't get at it, they will go away to other places where they can. Also, you should try to get together with your neighbors and building owner to get rat-proof garbage cans, for many rats survive solely on garbage. A neighborhood clean-up campaign to get rid of junk piles and other trash will help too. Rat infestation is grounds for breaking a lease, if done soon after you move in.

It is one of the shames of Congress that when a rat-control bill was proposed, many members of

Congress treated it as a joke. If your representative was one of these, you might want to pack up a big dead rat in a plastic bag and send it off. And if your local government is unresponsive, some live rats in the city council meeting room might get them to see a little light on this subject.

Cockroaches. Roaches are always looking for a good place to hide through the day. If you don't give them too many places, you'll have fewer roaches. Sometimes they live in cracks that you can close off or stop up; they may live under shelving paper in kitchens; sometimes they live under cabinets or other furniture that you could raise off the floor on bricks, to let the light in.

They also like damp places—bathrooms or under leaky sinks. Shaking boric acid (buy it in a drugstore) into their hiding places is the cheapest and safest way to kill roaches, but it costs money and here again, the real answer is to stop feeding them. They quickly become resistant to pesticides. Boric acid takes a day or two to work; then you wipe it up. Although it is not a carcinogenic chemical poison, boric acid is dangerous, even fatal, in large doses; so keep it out of the reach of children.

Unfortunately, it takes very little to keep a cockroach alive. It will eat small crumbs of food which you can scarcely see—so if you have children, you may have to get used to sharing your house with a few roaches. They will be, in effect, cleaning up the tiny shreds of cereal, toast, baby food, and whatnot the children spread around a house. You may feel better about it if you take the time to look at cockroaches carefully; they're really quite marvelous creatures, superbly adapted to their way of life. Their smell is actually the worst thing about them.

You can keep cockroaches off tables by setting each leg in a tin can that's been carefully washed to get rid of the label and all the label glue (cockroaches can't climb a slippery metal surface). People sometimes hire exterminators to come around and poison the roaches in their apartments or houses, but as long as the food supply remains, the roaches will come back to live off it. The best single way to keep down cockroaches: wash the dishes and take the garbage out after supper (cockroaches feed at night).

Ants. Generally ants come into your house for the same reason as roaches—to eat the food you have provided for them, in the garbage, the sink, the food-preparing area, or in cans or jars left open. The way to control them is to stop feeding them. There may still be a few around from time to time, foraging and looking for food you've missed, but you can probably stand that. It's better than going the expensive poison-spray route, which can poison you and your children. Never spray a vegetable garden to control ants, for some vegetable roots will take up the poison and you'll eat it. In some cases, ant stakes driven into the ground around a house will control the ant population fairly effectively. If you have a real ant problem—they're eating up your trees or biting your children—call your local public health department and get some advice. Otherwise it's easiest to regard ants as nature's way of cleaning up your garbage and returning it to circulation in the biosphere.

Fleas. Fleas live by sucking blood, and if they can't get enough from your pets, they will bite you. There seem to be two ways to get rid of fleas: by killing them on the pet (with a bath and dip, a flea collar, or flea powder) and/or by spraying them in the furniture and on the floors with an insecticide. Unfortunately, flea collars are dangerously poisonous, both to the pet and to children who might touch them. Some flea powders work, others don't; evidently some breeds of fleas have become resistant to them. Call your local Humane Society or veterinarian and ask what they use (many flea powders are dangerous to cats and puppies). It is unwise to begin spraying poisons all over your house just to get rid of fleas. In cases of bad infestation, it's better to take the infested rugs or furniture outside, beat or vacuum them thoroughly, and leave them outside for a week, away from passing animals or humans the fleas could feed on. This should interrupt their life cycle without spraying. If you are forced into spraying, move to a friend's place for a few days, until the pesticide has become less dangerous.

Flies. Wherever there is a lot of manure, garbage, or other decaying matter, or food lying around, there will be flies. If the manure is from your own animals, try to collect it and put in on your COMPOST pile, where the temperature (and the black plastic cover you should use) will keep flies away. Wet manure breeds many more flies than dry; arranging your animal pens so manure falls on straw helps dry it out fast. As with rats, securely closed garbage cans are a big help against flies. Screens and screen doors are your basic defense; usually they are required by the local housing code, so the owner of your building should provide them. You can trap flies on flypaper or similar chemical devices, but remember to keep these well away from food-preparing or eating areas—

otherwise you may poison yourself more than the flies.

Bedbugs. They are very hard ot get rid of, and spraying seems to be the only sure way. They are often resistant to some insecticides, so you have to use sprays containing deadly malathion—or pyrethrum, not so dangerous, but which needs to be applied several times. You must get the slats, springs, and bed frame thoroughly wet. Spray the mattress separately—get it wet but don't soak it; be sure to get spray thoroughly into crevices and tufts. Spray the baseboard all around the bed, cracks in the wall or floor, and any place nearby where the bugs might hide. Let the sprayed mattress dry thoroughly before sleeping on it; double sheets might not be a bad idea either, for a week or two.

I

ICE CREAM

A quiet revolution has taken place in ice cream in recent years—probably due to the persistent interest of dope smokers who often manifest an overwhelming desire for really good stuff! Your neighborhood may now be graced by an establishment that sells first-class ice cream made with natural ingredients and free of additives, artificial flavorings, thickeners, cellulose, and salt. Stay away from big chain operations, and if they won't tell you what's in it, don't buy it.

Generally, the heavier ice cream is, the better, because then you're buying food and not air; but of course the heavier brands are deservedly more expensive. Ice cream really ought to be sold by weight (about a quarter of the ice cream sold fails to meet minimum weight standards, which are lax enough in themselves). Ingredient labeling has also been lax in most states. Happily, therefore, making your own ice cream is an old-fashioned treat that is coming back. Look for a cheap hand-cranked ice-cream maker. There are simple recipes in many cookbooks; true ice cream contains cooked syrups, eggs, cream, sometimes gelatin, natural flavorings, salt, etc.

From a health standpoint, low-fat frozen yogurt or fruit ices are preferable to ice cream. Fruit ices contain no fats or mysterious artificial ingredients—just fruit, fruit juice, and sugar.

INCOME TAXES

If your income is entirely wages subject to withholding and your medical expenses are no more than average, you have no way to improve your tax situation, and may as well fill out the "short form" and forget it.

On the other hand, if you have other kinds of income which are reportable (i.e. *not* from Social Security, tax-free bonds, or illegal sources), there are almost bound to be ways you can reduce your taxes if you are willing to file a "long form." It means a rigorous habit of saving receipts during the year, keeping an expense diary, and an evening or two of mind-twisting work with figures; but most families can come up with enough deductions to make it worthwhile. A tax expert will probably be well worth the fee you pay—in organizing your information for the highest tax advantage and in telling you what limits to observe in claiming deductions. Certain amounts are regarded as legitimate by the tax auditors, and if you stay within those you'll probably get by. The fee of your tax preparer is itself a deduction for the following year.

What happens if the Internal Revenue Service questions your tax return? Something like two percent of all returns are now audited. First, they will get in touch with you, informing you that they think you owe them more money. This may be said on some kind of mass-produced form, rather than in a letter. Like any businessperson, you are free to proceed as if an honest mistake or difference of opinion is all that is at issue. You or your tax preparer will write back or go to the IRS office and argue with them, using whatever evidence you can muster. If that doesn't work, they send you a "ninety-day letter," which is another form saying you have to pay up. You can, however, appeal this decision to a higher-ranking auditor by writing or calling at the office. And if that doesn't get you anywhere, during your ninety days you can still appeal to the Tax Court of the US, which has branches all over the country. It costs only a small fee to argue your case before the court, and you can find out how to file by asking at the IRS office. If you lose, you have no alternative except to pay up—though businesspersons with a lot at stake can go into appeals court. To the amount IRS says you owe, they will add an interest charge.

Don't be shy about itemizing deductions. Deduction possibilities are put into the tax laws (for things like house interest) to gain middle-class support for the giant tax rip-offs of the corporations. A business manager who did not take total advantage of such possibilities would quickly be fired. As long as this attitude dominates our society, you are foolish not to claim everything you reasonably can. Nor do you necessarily have to keep elaborate records to justify your deductions; there is less than a one-in-eight chance you will be asked to show records. If you are audited, you may not be able to substantiate some of your claims and will have to pay up. (But always save the checks by which you've paid medical bills and other major deductible expenses.)

Incidentally, you may be able to take advantage of depreciation allowances yourself. If you have bought any tools or equipment which produce income, you can deduct part of their cost each year. You can also depreciate your car in this way if you are required to own it for your work, or use it at least half the time for income-producing purposes. In general, since the tax laws are written to help business, you are best off if you can set yourself up as some kind of small business. Then your expenses for transportation, publicity, phones, rent, and so on are all deductible. You can even give yourself an expense account if you're careful about it, and take customers out to expensive dinners like the high spenders do. You can also buy at trade discount. But you must make sure there is some real business involved somewhere in the enterprise. This may not be as hard to arrange as you think; some of your favorite activities can sometimes be set up as businesses.

Businesses also know that in cases of special hardship the IRS will extend the date of your payment of taxes at modest interest. There is a special form you have to fill out, but this is a lot cheaper and simpler than borrowing money from a bank or credit union.

INFLATION

Whatever the causes of inflation (Vietnam War deficit spending, higher costs of oil, drops in our industrial productivity, or whatnot) it will probably be a permanent feature of our lives. Our economy and its almighty dollar are no longer so almighty. The pain of this new fact will be borne in upon us throughout the 80's, in the form of higher prices and lower "real wages"—that is, lessened purchasing power for each hour of work. The real wages of many American working people in fact dropped slightly, after discounting for inflation, during the last half of the 70's. It seems likely real wages will continue to dwindle during the 80's. Without intending to, we seem to have achieved nearly the "steady-state" or stable economy necessary to halt our formerly ever-increasing depredations on the environment (and therefore on our posterity). One of the major objectives of our public and private lives in the 80's will be to learn to live with this situation—which actually has both ecological and economic good sides.

In highly inflationary conditions, money is more visible as the rather abstract thing it is, and people learn how to think about it in different ways. The "cost of renting money," or interest, becomes a major focus of attention in any financial transaction. People with cash savings—a rather small part of our population, actually—become acutely conscious that an inflation rate of 15% per year makes any money you store in an ordinary savings account at 5% actually *shrink* by 10% each year. So they try to put it in long-term savings certificates (which pay around 8%, but cannot be redeemed for six years or more without interest penalties). Or they explore "money market funds," which generally pay interest that just about equals the inflation rate; they resemble stocks and stockbrokers know about them; they're also advertised in the *Wall Street Journal*. Or they put money into municipal bond funds, which pay lower interest but are tax-free, or (if they have $10,000 to invest, or can pool with others through a bank) into six-month certificates that are insured and also pay about the inflation rate.

Some people with sizable amounts to play with not only have tried to keep pace with inflation, but actually to make their money grow in "real" terms. A few folks with time, inclination, and a certain amount of luck can make money by buying and selling stocks. However, small investors unable to move investments into and out of the stock market rapidly have been losing substantial amounts of money in recent years. It seems likely that, in a more or less steady-state economy, the stock market will behave more and more erratically, since investors can no longer count on over-all growth.

Some people have also invested in gold coins or gold itself, or in jewelry, art works, rare objects like antiques that seem likely to increase in value, and so on. Personally, I think gold objects and jewelry are particularly stupid as investments. They carry a 100% mark up: something you buy for $1,000 can be sold the next day for only $500. Moreover, gem quality has been dropping steadily. In a period when gold prices have risen spectacularly, it is tempting to acquire some. But prices may plummet in the future, and in any case you earn no interest on such investments. Speculating in gold or art can be fun, but you should recognize that it's a form of gambling, and only invest money you could afford to lose.

Under the impact of our general shortage of housing, real estate prices rose dramatically in the late 70's. Since we have no decent national housing policy, scarcity will continue and prices will almost certainly continue to rise faster than inflation. This may be especially true in urban areas, as rising gas prices will slowly cause a re-concentration of people in more convenient city areas, or at least slow down or halt the movement of people to the distant suburbs. Tax policies favoring real-estate investment mean you can, for your own residence, deduct from your income tax the interest portion of your mortgage payments (which means almost all of them); for rental property you own, you can deduct depreciation as well as operating expenses. Property taxes are also deductible. In computing your possible financial picture if you buy real estate, remember that you should usually "leverage" as much as possible — that is, use a minimum of your own money (in down payment) to get the use of the lender's money during the period you are waiting for the property to appreciate (and, for rental property, "depreciate" — in tax terms). If you have excess cash beyond your down payment, you might consider buying another property. But you also need to calculate that the amounts you put into down payments are, by that fact, not sitting in a fund somewhere drawing interest; this lost interest is, in a sense, one of the costs of your owning the property.

These esoteric fiscal considerations are, incidentally, a perfect illustration of how our tax policies distort our national investment and productivity patterns. If you simply wish to buy or build a house and live in it for the rest of your life, you are badly out of step and will be penalized, or at least not helped, by the tax laws which fundamentally work in favor of speculators. Nor are tax assessment policies favorable to the thrifty, handy owner-builder. If you manage by hard work and ingenuity to build a wonderful dwelling for a fraction of the cost a contractor would charge, you will still be assessed the market price, and your taxes may be so high you can't afford to live in the house. (People contemplating owner-building may be wise to make their houses so weird-looking that assessors will give them a low figure.)

However, doing it yourself is generally a way to save money, and especially so under inflationary conditions when the prices of skilled labor and professional services have risen much faster than wages. Since inflation has pushed many moderate-income people into higher tax brackets, you may actually have to earn $1,000 to pay for a plumbing job that costs $650; but you could do it yourself for $100 or so, including the cost of the instruction book you get from Sears or your public library!

(Home maintenance or improvement expenses are only deductible if they're needed in your first weeks of occupancy to bring a dwelling up to normal standards, or in special cases of solar-energy equipment installation; for these, you may not really save any money by doing it yourself. Check the situation in your area for solar tax incentives.)

In general, and not only in terms of inflation, you should not pay any debts until you absolutely have to, since this allows your own money to sit in the savings account as long as possible. It is unwise to use a higher than necessary tax-withholding rate to build up a refund with the IRS; this is simply giving the government the free use of your money all year, and depriving yourself of the interest it would earn. If you are self-employed or have outside income, make sure you do not overpay your quarterly estimated income-tax payments. And where possible postpone deductible expenses — medical outlays, charitable deductions — until late in the year, allowing the money to work for you as long as possible.

Borrowing, of course, usually costs you more than the inflation rate and on charge accounts can be as high as 18%. However, if you happen to be able to borrow at 12% and are in the 40% tax bracket, the deductibility of interest means that the actual cost of your loan is only 7.2%. In such situations, "the cost of borrowing is negative" — which is one reason why real estate and other upper-middle-class financial activity has not been badly hit by inflation, especially when added to the fact that 7.2% will be paid off, as the years pass, with increasingly cheap dollars. Sustaining this kind of investment strategy, of course, takes a healthy steady income to start with, to put you in that 40% tax bracket; and if anything disrupts that, your financial house can collapse almost instantly.

Inflation in general makes the condition of many people ever more perilous financially. Thirty-seven percent of American households have no savings whatever, and another 16% have less than $500: in other words, more than half of us essentially live moment-by-moment financially. It is no wonder that high and rising costs of the basic necessities are driving many of us to desperation. On the other hand, elaborate statistical investigation suggests that inflation actually damages the very rich the most (because they hold more assets which are losing their value) and the poor the next most; the upper-middle-class, home-owning group actually gains slightly but it is also the group that screams the loudest and attempts, by attacking government programs that aid poorer people, to push still more of the burden of inflation off onto the less fortunate.

INFORMATION, HOW TO FIND

Nobody can possibly remember all the information needed to confront life's nasty little problems. In fact a good education chiefly equips you with tools for locating information when and as you need it. (Most of the information you memorized in school ten years ago is hopelessly outdated.) One basic information source is the LIBRARY—but except for those which provide telephone reference service, you have to go there to use the resources.

With persistence and a certain amount of imagination, you can track down much useful information on the telephone; doing so can save you many wasted steps, bus fares, or car rides. Don't hesitate to phone a store and ask if they have something you are looking for. If you are trying to find out something that a government office might be able to help with, look under "United States Government" in the phone book; you'll probably still have to phone their information number and ask for help, since many agencies are listed in confusing or obscure ways, have just changed their names, or are not listed separately at all; most big cities have far more federal offices than you would suspect. If you get nowhere this way, phone the office your congressional representative maintains in your district; it has a staff of people who are knowledgeable about what the government does or doesn't do in your area, and may be able to give you individual names of people to call. The same goes for city councils; your representative needs your vote, and maintains a staff that is supposed to keep you happy and thus get that vote; make them work for it!

A special information service for toll-free numbers is maintained by government agencies and many corporations: 800-555-1212. Try it if you need to contact one that doesn't have a local directory listing.

If you are interested in some special field, you will soon find that there are two kinds of information-providing machinery. One is the "official" channel of printed publications, brochures, lectures, books, etc. This serves well to disseminate information widely, but it is always fairly slow. Consequently another "unofficial" channel develops. Among scientists, for example, personal exchange of drafts of papers, telephone calls, and personal letters constitutes the real, living means by which people keep up with what

others are doing. By the time a paper reaches actual publication, it's stale news. And in every field, "networks" of active workers exist, tied in to each other by these informal means. If you want to be absolutely abreast of "the state of the art," therefore, you must find some way of tapping into these circuits. This is not easy unless you have something to contribute which the people in the network will find attractive and interesting too. A substitute is to subscribe to one of the journals which provide prompt access to recently published documents and reports; two excellent ones are:

Co-Evolution Quarterly, Box 428, Sausalito, CA 94965.

Rain, 2270 N.W. Irving, Portland, OR 97210. For information sources particularly relevant to many of the concerns of this Encyclopedia, a free directory called *Consumer's Resource Handbook* is available from the Consumer Information Center, Dept. 532 G, Pueblo, CO 81009. Your state government may also have a department of consumer affairs, consumer protection, or some similar entity. If it doesn't, it should—governments maintain extensive and expensive departments to help business, and we, the victims, deserve equal treatment.

INSULATION

Insulation (and other forms of energy conservation) would enable us to save—and thus in effect produce—far more energy, at much less expense, than we could produce by nuclear or synthetic fuels technology. At the outset of the 80's, however, it was doubtful whether we would prove smart enough as a nation to grasp this simple yet tremendously important fact.

Many individuals and businesses have certainly grasped it, however, as can be noticed from the shortages and high prices of insulation materials. It is relatively easy to calculate the pay-off times of spending X dollars on insulating your ceiling or walls; even at current fuel prices it usually works out at between three and five years. Considering what else you might do with any money you happen to have, this is a sensationally profitable investment. Merely insulating your attic will save about 8% in your heating bill. Moreover, tax credits are available to motivate you even further. And some utility companies, finally beginning to see that they can't expect publicly subsidized nuclear power to rescue them, will even come out to look your place over and give you advice. (It will not necessarily be very professional. If a really big job

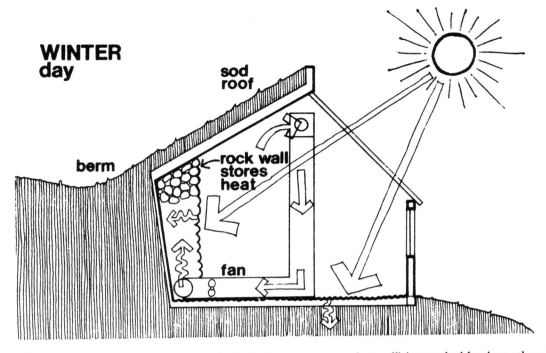

WINTER day

sod roof

berm

rock wall stores heat

fan

Schematic of a greenhouse using the earth as its insulation, a common and very efficient method for the northern exposure of many buildings.

is in prospect, try to find an architect or engineer with substantial solar design experience.)

Insulation comes in basically two forms: loose and in batts. The loose form is sometimes a spun rock material, which is fireproof, and sometimes recycled paper in shredded form, which has been fire-treated. Unfortunately, the borates which are used to coat the paper particles tend to come off after a while, and the paper shreds will then burn. This is a hazard mainly around electrical connection boxes in the walls and ceilings where heat can build up, or over ceiling lights mounted flush. It may be some faint comfort to know that, if you are likely to have trouble from such sources, it will almost certainly happen in the first couple of days after installation; so if your house doesn't catch fire by then, you're probably okay. But the sensible procedure is to build little boxes around these hazard points and keep shredded paper insulation outside them—use fiber-glass (without paper covering) there.

Loose insulating material has the great advantage that it can be blown into already constructed walls. Fiber-glass in batt form is fireproof, but can only be installed over ceilings or in walls under construction. Since tiny glass fibers come off the material and can be drawn into your lungs where they are carcinogenic, you should always wear a mask and minimize your exposure to fiber-glass. Don't tear or pull at it any more than necessary, and wear gloves (the fibers can enter your skin and are irritating).

Batt insulation is given ratings according to how much heat it will keep in (or out). The higher the R number, the more insulation value you get. Your city building department can advise you on what level is wise for your climate; again, if you are planning a sophisticated solar-heated system, find expert solar-experienced people to advise you.

With suitable insulation around the north side of a structure, and large double-glass windows on the south side (with insulating shutters to cover them at night) a house can derive much of its space heating from the sun, especially if the sunlight hits a large mass of concrete, stone, or water (say rows of metal barrels) after it comes through the glass.

It is almost as important, in older houses, to seal cracks as it is to insulate ceiling and walls. Install weatherstripping around doors, and repair or replace sills that allow air passage. (A lighted candle or incense stick will show where air is flowing in.) Seal up cracks around doors and windows where they meet the plaster of the walls. If you have a fireplace, make sure the damper shuts tight when it's not in use; if it won't, use a piece of metal to cover the fireplace opening (plywood might catch fire if you put it on before a fire is entirely out).

J

JOB HUNTING

At some point in your life, you'll find yourself in the "job market," trying to sell your labor power, talents, and energy.

Like basketball, job hunting is a statistical game, and your chances of success are improved if you can manage a lot of shots. Here is a brief summary of the rules.

Don't panic. If you are desperate and take the first thing you can get, you'll probably soon regret it and be looking around for something else. Therefore . . . .

Hunt jobs when you don't need one. The worst time to hunt a job is when you are desperate; like everything else, jobs are easier to find when you don't really need them. If you have been laid off, don't delay going to the unemployment office to apply for your benefits (see also UNEMPLOYMENT). You can also save yourself some money and therefore buy yourself some time by moving in with family or friends if you suddenly find yourself out of work.

If you have a job that will end in a few months, use up some sick leave or vacation time in hunting for other jobs, long before you're actually laid off. When you don't need a job right away, you can talk relaxedly with potential bosses. (On the other hand, a totally blasé attitude turns bosses off; they want somebody who is good enough not to worry about being out of work, but who is eager to do the right job well.) Once you really need a job and haven't found one, you tend to get more depressed and anxious every day. It is supremely important to try and fight this because it tends to make you seem less "employable" to interviewers. Hunting early also solves the otherwise difficult problem of whether to take the first job that's offered or to take the chance of telling the employers you want to look into other possibilities (which may lose you that job)—if you're still working, potential new employers know they have to give you something better or they can hardly expect you to make a change.

Make deliberate, planned use of your network of friends. Since most people work at something or other, practically everybody you know is a source of potential job information. Moreover, the really interesting jobs seldom get advertised; they're filled by word of mouth by friends of the people who already work there. So when you are job hunting, sit down and systematically phone everybody you know, letting them know you are looking, and asking them to pass on leads to you. Don't be shy about it: everybody needs a job sometime! Ask friends if they know anybody else you could call who might have job leads. Write down everything so you can come back to it later. Don't forget your relatives, and if you live in a city that still has a working political machine, get hold of your precinct captain and see if he or she can help you out. If you belong to any churches, ethnic groups, clubs, hobby organizations, etc., try to get the word out through them too.

Concentrate on what you have to offer. The awful question "What can you do?" terrifies most beginning job seekers, and a lot of pretty experienced people too. Employers often take the view that if you haven't already done whatever it is they want done, you can't possibly do it; and it's very hard to counteract this attitude. But it may help a little to sit down, before you get into the actual action of seeing possible employers, and outline your capabilities as you see them. (Not as you think some potential boss should see them.) Many people who fear they "can't do anything" are extremely capable, but just not in ways they connect with jobs: you may be extremely good with children, or an ingenious con artist, or superneat and orderly, or love to talk with people. The problem is to find some kind of job where some of your capabilities—the things you really like doing and do well—can be put to use. (Otherwise you are just selling your soul and your time.)

In brute fact, however, the only job an inexperienced and untrained young person can usually get is clerk, typist, or laborer. Such doors into the business world are, as Shakespeare said of the grave, hardly as broad as a church door, but they sometimes have to serve.

Know what the company or organization does. The atmosphere of a place is strongly influenced by its products, and it is good to work for a company whose output you respect, or at least don't consider a positive menace to society.

Case the prospective job place. Sometimes it is possible to look the place over before applying, and maybe even talk to some of the people you'd be working with. Coffee rooms and cafeterias are semi-public; walk in and have a cup. Don't be afraid to tell people what you're doing—they're usually glad to open up and give you some pointers. That way you can get a pretty good idea of what the atmosphere is, and you can stay out of jobs that would be real grinds. You may even be able to find jobs in places where you like to spend time anyway—as a waitress or waiter in a coffeehouse, a clerk in a specialty store or bookstore, a guide or guard in a museum, a boat repairer in a yacht harbor, and so on. It's worth a lot to work in a place where the other people are interesting to you, and where the nature of the work and the supervision are such that they don't constantly rub on you: do the supervisors monitor you by watching or listening to your calls? Can you physically move around without having to get permission? Are the supervisors or fellow workers mostly narrow-minded types or more loose and tolerant? Every company has its own "climate," and you should stay out of those which are unpleasant to you.

Resumes. In most any kind of work, it's a good idea to prepare a resume—a sheet listing your name, address, and phone number at the top, together with what kind of job you're seeking, and then detailing your experience in previous jobs and your schooling. Unless you've worked steadily, it's best to arrange your jobs by categories and leave off the dates (you can mention these during the interview). Arrange your schools in order, showing what you concentrated on. You should type up the resume very neatly and make copies. It's useful to leave some with influential friends, to send to companies that might have a job open, to submit to employment agencies, and so on. It gives you something to hang onto when you walk into an employment office.

Be Prepared. Applying for a job takes time, and you have to be ready to spend it, or don't bother applying. Remember it's part of the statistical game. You'll have to fill out each company's forms, whether you present them with a resume or not. You'll have to answer each interviewer's questions about why you left your previous jobs (don't bad-mouth other bosses—sound loyal but discouraged about prospects, etc.), what you did with your time in between jobs, why you want the job with this particular company, what you plan to do with your life, and so on. Follow directions— that's one of the basic requirements for any job. You may have to take aptitude tests, typing tests, psychological tests. You'll have to give references, too: either previous bosses, teachers, or other respectable people who will give you a good plug if asked. (Make sure you check with them first, and don't be afraid to ask whether they would give you a good recommendation—nobody needs false friends in job hunting.) If you are hunting a new job while still working at your old one, be careful: the prospective boss may ask whether your present boss knows you're looking, and if not will worry that you may leave him in the lurch too.

Always carry a working pen with you when you are job hunting, both to fill out forms and to jot down things that might be useful later. Keep a record of your interviews and contacts in a notebook or on file cards so you don't get mixed up as to what you or the interviewer said.

Dress for the part. You are seeking a role in a game, and only certain costumes are allowed. The president's son or daughter may wear pants, ruffled shirts, and a velvet coat, but except in advertising, films, and a few other "creative" industries, the safe bet is to look conventional-Amurrican; suits for men and women in status jobs, and plain but attractive though less formal wear for others. (If you really want a job in a certain company, find out how its employees dress by dropping into the company cafeteria or watching them come out after work.)

Know what a personnel officer is. It may make you less nervous about interviews if you remember that the personnel people in most companies are only screeners—they sift out the applicants; supervisors actually make the real decisions. Personnel departments are often staffed by people who couldn't make it in the production departments and have been sent to pasture in personnel where they can't do too much damage. They still have the power to turn you down if you come on in some way they don't like, but they aren't geniuses who can read your mind. Offer a firm handshake, talk to them in a lively but businesslike way, not deadpan. Sit quietly in your chair, look them in the eye as much as you can, don't smoke unless invited to, and be two or three minutes early for interviews. It is not a bad thing to be a bit nervous in interviews. If you're too cool, they may decide you don't really need the job.

Develop a credible explanation for your job gaps and general past. In earlier times, employers were very suspicious of anybody old enough to work who didn't have a continuous job record. If you had an unexplained three-month gap they'd figure you must have been in jail or something, or at least that you must be unreliable in some way. Now so many folks are in and out of school, traveling around the country, taking special training, setting up small business enterprises for themselves, and whatnot, there is no need to be embarrassed at the idea of explaining what you've done with your time when you weren't working. So write down a job history and develop stories for any gaps in it. Use your imagination — work it all out in detail; give it reality in your own mind, and it'll have reality when you tell the personnel interviewer about it. Stick to the truth where possible, obviously—if you went back to school or got specialized training, say so, even if it isn't relevant to the job you're asking for.

CETA, Civil Service, and Work-Study Jobs.

CETA and *Civil Service* positions require a different kind of job hunt from the steps outlined above. They often do not demand a special set of skills, and the particular qualifications necessary may be within reach of even those looking for their first job.

There is one great advantage in civil service jobs for people who live unorthodox lives: they are obtained through a system of objective examinations. Therefore, if you are good at taking tests you will probably score high on the civil service exams, and will soon be offered a job, as the highest-scoring people have to be called first. A variety of federal, state, and local government jobs require virtually no qualifications except a high score — many positions in the Post Office, for example, and low-level jobs in many other offices. Welfare workers, for instance, are often people with a BA but no special training.

Generally people in civil service jobs work hard — in the Post Office, for example, hours may be long and hard, and some jobs, like being a carrier, take a great deal of physical endurance. But the pay is not bad, and you have the satisfaction that you're doing something useful. And civil service jobs are normally secure against vindictive or sanctimonious bosses. It is even possible now to wear long hair in the post offices of many cities, since persistent longhairs who were fired fought their cases through to high courts, winning rulings that insured as long as you keep the mail going through, you can look as you please.

It is also generally possible to come back to a civil service job if you have left it for a while for a good reason, such as going back to school, traveling, or having a baby.

Information about federal civil service exams can be obtained at the Post Office information desk; for state jobs, try the state personnel department or employment department in your area; for city jobs, try the city hall information desk or personnel department. Such examinations are open to all and without fee, but you do have to go, fill out the forms, and make an appointment for each exam.

The programs through which government attempts to "mop up" unemployment when it gets too severe change continually. In principle, none of the programs are ever allowed to become *too* effective, because capitalism as we know it requires a substantial pool of unemployed people whose existence keeps pressure on wage levels, which would otherwise rise. But they are there, and can sometimes offer interesting, though temporary, opportunities.

The *Comprehensive Employment and Training Act* mainly provides jobs in the public sector — with county offices, city departments, school districts, etc—though efforts are being made to involve private industry. Some 3.3 million people were in CETA programs at the beginning of the 80's. Basically, the federal government subsidizes the agency to hire and supposedly train you. Naturally the agencies prefer to hire people, often college graduates and even some with advanced degrees, who can do the work with little or no training, but happen to be unemployed—as large numbers of highly educated people are going to be in the 80's. The jobs range from typist and clerk positions to gardeners, firefighters, dispatchers, janitors, and social welfare workers of various kinds, often doing very challenging work. Pay is generally low, and is set partly by how many dependents you have; the national average was $8,500 a year in 1979.

To qualify for a CETA job you must have been unemployed or on welfare for a given amount of time (it depends on the position in question) and state unemployment offices or county administrative or personnel offices can tell you how to find out what jobs might be available. There is, of course, a substantial amount of paperwork and red tape involved, as with any government program.

In previous years, CETA job-holders were able to hop from one job to another. New legislation now limits you to 1,000 hours in one year (35 weeks of full-time work) and 2,000 hours in any five-year period, and 78 weeks in public service employment. There is now supposed to be more emphasis on training, retraining, and upgrading of skills, especially for youths.

A somewhat similar program exists on campuses, called *Work Study,* to help students with limited financial resources support themselves while going through college. The government pays 80% of your wages, which makes you a very attractive part-time employee unless you are totally incompetent! Contact the financial aid office of your college to learn about the possibilities. Work Study is a great way to get some work experience before you get out of school.

JUICE, FROZEN

Beware of "imitation" juices—these may be in the same supermarket freezer section as frozen juices, but they're really just sugar and water and orange flavoring with a few tiny shreds of orange floating in them. Their sole food value is in a little vitamin C, but you should get that (in much greater quantity) from real oranges, real orange juice, or tomatoes.

Even standard bottled orange juice is not really fresh orange juice; it's made by adding water to concentrated orange juice, usually with some coloring matter. Like the cheaper frozen juice, however, it is extremely good for you. The tastiest way to get orange juice (and some extra food volume as well) is to eat real oranges.

KITCHEN CLEANLINESS

You will wash your dishes, of course—because it's unpleasant to eat off dirty ones, not because dirty ones breed microbes. You'll wash washcloths and towels because otherwise they get musty and mildewy. You'll scrub down your table and food-preparing area because otherwise they get encrusted with old juices and crumbs and attract cockroaches. But your main objective in all these cases, and indeed, in every case involving routine household cleanliness, is primarily pleasantness and only secondarily sanitation.

Building code regulations, in providing a hand-washing place next to the toilet, are on firm ground; this is a means of interrupting the cycle of feces-to-hand-to-mouth by which certain serious diseases, like typhoid, and certain annoying things, like worms, can be transmitted.

The television commercials and house-beautiful magazines persistently spread the idea that a kitchen ought to look like a hospital operating room: all antiseptic and covered with white tile, white enamel, and white formica. Many people are now prepared to admit, however, that the kitchen ought to be a comfortable room and as pleasant to look at (and be in) as any other room. Indeed there's a good case for making the kitchen the central room of the house, as it used to be. It's warm, a family with children spends a good deal of time there, and besides, eating is a central family activity; it's silly to have food preparation locked away into a separate room out of sight. If we didn't still cling to the old puritan suspicions that body functions were somehow disgusting, we'd be more prepared to allow the chopping, mixing, and cooking of food to be part of "real life." And we wouldn't tend to regard garbage as disgusting either since it is merely the leftover substance which we return, if we are living with ecological good sense, to the earth. (See COMPOSTING.)

In short, there's no reason to try to make your kitchen "spotless." A kitchen without any spots is a place where nobody can feel at home. You have to pay *some* attention to cleaning up your kitchen, but not too much. Here are the essentials:

Dishwashing. The more one-bowl or one-plate meals you cook, the less dirty dishes you wind up with. You will also cut down on dishwashing if you get into the habit of washing out bowls and pans you use in food preparation as soon as you're done with them, while you're waiting for a pan to heat up or something. Use a dishpan rather than washing dishes under hot running water—it saves considerable water-heating energy and also considerable water. Certain things should not be washed at all—heavy iron frying pans, for instance, should only be wiped or rinsed to preserve their "seasoning." And don't dry your dishes—dish towels just spread bacteria around.

Garbage. Fancy garbage pails are a perversion, in my opinion—designed to conceal from you the existence of slops. This concealment soon leads you to forget to empty the pail, which in a few days becomes genuinely foul. The best solution I know is to use grocery bags, stood in a corner somewhere, for non-recyclable items, and have a series of cardboard boxes for recyclables: glass, aluminum and tin cans, and newspapers. Compostables can be accumulated in a sink strainer and/or a bucket with a top. Peelings, skins, rotten leftovers, dry bread, and so on should go here.

Cities are now having great trouble finding places to dump their incredible amounts of garbage. They have in the past dumped it in the oceans or rivers, filled up marshes with it, and generally flung it around the world. We are now finally realizing that many of these practices are ecologically unwise, and besides they use up space that's valuable for other purposes. Garbage is seldom used to build hills and mountains. Landfillers always think garbage is ideal to make things perfectly flat. But in reality hills make a landscape more interesting, break the wind, provide skiing in winter, give varied habitats for growing things, and generally add to the variety of the world. Recently the Japanese have begun to compress garbage into building blocks (coatable with plastic, asphalt, or steel). We are experimenting with ways to burn it in power-generating plants, to capture the methane gas it gives off in landfills, and otherwise tap garbage as a resource. But the only real and lasting solutions are to reduce the amount we generate in the first place, and to separate it at the source into its recyclable components.

Work surfaces. A kitchen needs a good chopping block or other cutting surface for cutting up meat, vegetables, and fruit. Very beautiful handmade hardwood cutting boards can be bought, or you can make one of your own. Maple is the wood traditionally used in butcher chopping blocks, if you can get it. Even hard maple, though, will soak up some juices. It's a good idea to disinfect any cutting board occasionally, with some Clorox in water, followed by a thorough rinsing. Direct sunlight is also a disinfectant, so when you get into a new place, wash the cutting board and lay it outside for an hour, which also will give it a good smell.

Sunlight and air are natural allies in keeping a kitchen sweet-smelling and comfortably clean without making it your lifework. Use open-front cabinets, with things stored in attractive jars rather than advertisement-laden boxes; most boxed foods last much better if damp is kept away from them. Don't pile up fruits in a deep basket where the ones underneath may get rotten without your noticing it. (Keep fruit out of sunlight which makes it mealy and *doesn't* hasten ripening.) Bread and vegetables, however, keep better in a damp atmosphere, as in the refrigerator.

Disinfectants, cleaners, etc. Most households have enough cleaning agents to clean a hotel. In reality you need very few: soap or detergent of some kind for washing dishes and clothes; a cleaning powder for removing greasy spots on dishes, pans, and floors; and ammonia for washing floors, toilets, windows, refrigerators, stoves. (Clorox, another washing compound, is ridiculously expensive—other brands of the same substance can be bought if you don't like ammonia. Never mix ammonia and bleach, by the way, as a deadly poison gas results.) If you really need a more powerful cleaning compound, buy "TSP," which is the working ingredient in most spray-on cleansers. (Be careful: it's a caustic, and dangerous to eyes.) Cleaning agents are often colored, perfumed, and advertised as containing fake "secret new ingredients," as a way of selling them at double the price.

KNIVES

A few of our essential artifacts go back to the beginnings of human history, and knives are among them. People have used knives (first stone,

then metal) as long as they have been human. And we use knives constantly, many times a day. (Not to mention the intense symbolic role that knives play in our fantasies and dreams.) You might think, then, that people would insist on having really beautiful knives that could aptly assume their important place in our lives: after all, it is well within the capacity of modern designers and factories to manufacture elegant, inexpensive knives. But most stores sell junky knives and most people use junky knives, or knives that look fancy but can hardly cut butter. If you are used to seeing knives only in ordinary hardware or variety stores, you should visit a specialized knife store sometime. This will give you a new perspective on knives and prove to you how awful-looking most people's knives are—which is too bad, since an ugly or unbalanced knife is a constant nagging annoyance, whether we realize it or not.

Although the variety of shapes, sizes, and styles in a big knife store will seem bewildering, there are just two kinds of knife the average person needs: a pocketknife and a fair-sized knife with which meat, bread, leather, rubber, small pieces of wood, vegetables, and other things can be cut. A knife with a blade about eight inches long can be used in the kitchen and also carried around with you in a sheath on your belt, for camping. The well-known Bowie-type sheath knives are very strong; they have a protective hilt and usually a six-inch blade, although an eight-inch version exists which is known as the "Arkansas toothpick." A knife made of good carbon steel can be re-sharpened for years and will retain a keen edge. Carbon steel can discolor from food acids like tomato juice and it can rust if left wet. But this doesn't hurt its cutting ability, and you may like the irregular dark patina that develops; or you can keep it burnished with metal polish or steel wool.

Much stainless steel, though it is a fine metal for other purposes, is not a suitable material for knives. It will not hold an edge, and it is hard to sharpen. Its chief virtue is the familiar American consideration: it's shiny and stays that way. You can thus use a stainless-bladed pocketknife without worrying about drying it out when it gets wet.

To carry around with you, a pocketknife is practically a survival tool. Some will do any light mechanical job, except hammering. Knives are made with screwdrivers, bottle openers, can openers, corkscrews, augers, files, saws, scissors, tweezers, and even toothpicks. The Swiss army knife, which is available in a wide range of sizes and complexities, is solidly made, although expensive. Being a stainless steel job, the one thing it can't do terribly well is cut. It's red and has "Officier Suisse" stamped on the blade, but there are many cheap imitations, so watch out.

What you need in the way of knives of course depends on many factors of taste, and some people just like to have a lot of knives around—there's no denying that a wide assortment of beautiful knives is lovely to have in your kitchen. The shapes of knives are like the shapes of boats and other artifacts that have been around the human scene for a couple of thousand years: they have been varied and refined over the centuries to the point where very elegant knives indeed are available, along with the commercial junk. Knives vary in balance (how their weight is distributed), heft (their total weight), and handle and blade shapes, which affect how they fit your hand and working habits. You should not settle for a knife that doesn't look and feel right to you. The manner in which the handle is fixed to the blade needs special attention. Is it firm enough to take heavy stresses? Is the metal binding around the handle ends, if there is one, flimsy? If there is no hilt, is there a rounded, projecting heel on the blade so that your wet hand can't slip onto the blade? Are there places where cracks may open up to catch food particles and moisture? Does the brass or bronze or other metal of the handle go well with the color of the blade?

Price is not a reliable indication of the quality of a knife, although no really good knife is cheap. You can pay a great deal of money for a practically useless stainless steel knife, but you can get a carbon steel knife that will last you for decades for only a few dollars.

It's characteristic of our culture that America has given the world the electric carving knife. This battery-driven abomination saws meat up instead of cutting it, often giving it a raggedy, half-chewed look. It is egregiously plastic-ugly, and it makes an annoying noise. It is dangerously jumpy on bones, hard to clean, prone to breakdowns, and in short just the kind of thing to make life a little more complex, noisy, and expensive.

Sharpening knives is important to keep them in good health and serviceable to you. Do not use wall sharpeners or other grinder-type sharpeners unless you are experienced with knives and can tell if they are in proper adjustment; otherwise you may grind away your blade and never get it sharp. Anyway it's better to get a sharpening steel—one of those long, thin, rodlike devices. Or you can use a small stone—they are cheap and come on wooden handles making them convenient to hold in the hand so you can strop the blade on them. Buy one in a specialized knife store, and use it as they tell you to.

There's more to using a knife than just hacking away. Peer into the kitchen of the next Chinese restaurant you're in and study their technique of chopping vegetables with incredible speed and precision; if you are a real vegetable eater you may want to get a chopper as well as a knife. Get somebody who really knows how to carve to show you the joints in chickens and things like leg of lamb. One secret of carving an odd-shaped piece is to slice off one side to give you a flat side; then put that on the bottom.

Knives and Knifemakers, by Sid Latham. Collier Books, 1973.

L

LABELS

After some decades of prodding by consumer organizations and co-operatives, the food industry has been compelled by government regulations to attach informative nutrition labels to its products. Use of these labels is essential if you are to understand what you're eating and what its benefits and hazards are.

The labels must first of all indicate what the ingredients are—often very difficult to guess without the labels—and in their order of volume. Thus, a prepared food which contains more sugar than anything else (a common occurrence) must list sugar as its first ingredient, followed by water, flour, salt, and whatever else it contains. All preservatives, additives, and colorings must be listed; unfortunately, flavorings (which are often artificial chemical compounds) have been exempted because they supposedly constitute "trade secrets." If you find unnamed "flavorings" listed on a label, therefore, the best plan is to avoid the product.

Food labels must also provide a summary of the nutritional value of the product. This includes numbers (per serving) for the protein content in grams, the calories, and the FAT content—not always, unfortunately, separated into saturated and other types of fat. (See also NUTRITION.) Vitamin and trace mineral content must also be indicated. For many of these items, the label indicates what percentage of normal daily requirements you get by eating one serving (whose size is specified) of the food.

"Generic labels" on canned goods and other supermarket products mean simplified labels for non-advertised lines. These are generally sold at somewhat lower prices, reflecting some savings on advertising but mainly lower-quality contents (sometimes they are also used as loss-leaders to lure customers into a store). Co-op products and many "house brands" of the supermarket chains are usually better buys.

Informative labeling is also required on clothing: the component fibers must be listed with percentages. Manufacturers must also provide labels indicating proper cleaning procedures for a garment. It is easy to mix up clothing items, so you should leave these labels attached. (See FABRICS.)

Although small pieces of yardage don't come with them attached, larger pieces of fabric must also be accompanied by labels telling what's in them and how to care for them; fabric stores must supply these to you upon request.

See APPLIANCES for information about the energy-efficiency labels now required.

LAWYERS

Every society must have some means of settling disputes without recourse to personal violence. But the operations of the law, like every other institution in a society, tend to favor those with power and influence and to penalize the poor. A certain chronic injustice thus pervades our legal system. However, when large masses of people become conscious that they are being oppressed, and that their opportunity to obtain justice has been severely curtailed, they lose faith in the legal system and the society that maintains it—and a revolutionary mood begins to pervade the society. This happened in the US in the 60's, a time of widespread riots on the part of poor and powerless black urban dwellers. In response, the federal government began to try to provide some legal aid to people without substantial financial resources—and thus, in effect, with no real access to the law.

The result was a government entity now called the Legal Services Corporation. It maintains regional offices and several hundred legal service branch offices nationwide. They are available to help people without much money in many ordinary and day-to-day legal problems: rental disputes, welfare rights, Social Security and disability problems, credit and consumer issues, divorces, and so on. They also attempt to improve the general situation by suing companies in "class actions" when huge masses of people are systematically cheated, and by fighting cases that can establish important precedents. They will not, however, defend you if you have been arrested. (Neither will Legal Aid, another legal service organization with offices in many cities.) In that case you must find a private lawyer or turn to the public defender's office.

When you need a lawyer. If you're under the illusion that reasonably smart people can handle all their affairs without ever needing a lawyer, forget it. You could need legal help if:

• Someone serves a legal paper on you, indicating you are being sued.

• You are arrested for an alleged crime (serious or not).

• You are involved in an injury or property damage claim as in an auto accident. (Don't sign anything or talk to anybody until you've seen a lawyer.)

• You buy or sell real estate.

• You sign a contract, deed, will, or other legal paper. (See WILLS AND PROBATE.)

• You are involved in a contested divorce or one involving property or children. (You can "do your own" uncontested divorce.)

The only time it is reasonable to act as your own lawyer is in certain political trials where you are really being tried for your ideas. Even then, informed and experienced people differ as to the desirability of having a lawyer.

Fees. Even just a half-hour discussion of your case with a lawyer will cost something, since most lawyers don't give free advice any more than doctors give free treatment. Relatively standard fees have been developed for most legal services.

On the other hand, lawyers get "contingent fees" for many kinds of work—personal injury cases, will breaking, and other little chores. On this basis, if the lawyer wins for you, he or she pockets a third to a half; if he or she loses, you aren't out anything at all. (Make sure of your liability for court costs in a written agreement with the lawyer.)

"Minimum" fees are usually arbitrary and may be far less in the town or county next door. If so, you can probably dicker with a lawyer to go down somewhat. A certain amount of long-stifled competition is finally entering the legal profession. Lawyers are now free to advertise, and they do, though the prices they advertise are solely for routine work. This competition, and the fact that people have been coming out of law schools in huge numbers, has reduced the cost of certain legal services. (We have about ten times more lawyers per capita than England, a much less suit-prone society—from whence, by the way, our fundamental "common law" derives.) Also, it is at last possible for lawyers to practice in prepaid groups the way doctors do; they can, for instance, serve groups like unions and co-ops. Since this

promises better and cheaper legal service to people with little money, look around and see if any organizations in your area have group legal services. But beware of some "legal clinics." If sponsored by a law school, they may indeed resemble a low-cost medical clinic. Others are simply law offices specializing in easy, standard jobs like uncontested divorces, but charging high fees for everything else.

Choosing a lawyer. It is not easy to find the right lawyer for you. As with any service, begin by asking around among your friends. They may have a lawyer they can recommend. (If they have lost a lawsuit, they may recommend their opponent's lawyer!) The local bar association will give you the names of several attorneys active in the kind of work you need, but will not make recommendations; these attorneys may have a special low half-hour consultation rate, so ask about it in advance and agree on how much you will pay to talk to them.

As with doctors, it is okay to "shop around" for a lawyer—but each consultation will cost you. Never get into a relationship with a lawyer without getting clear on the financial deal. (And don't be panicked into retaining a lawyer you don't feel comfortable about; legal emergencies can usually wait at least 24 hours.) Even people with middle-class incomes often simply cannot afford to undertake a legal action because its likely costs in fees outweigh any gains they could expect if they win.

Honest lawyers will never promise to win a case for you. They can't get you out of a legal contract you have signed, like an unfair settlement deal, just because it's ridiculously unfair (and you shouldn't have signed it in the first place). They can't make your husband or wife come back to you—or even make an ex-husband keep up with his child-support payments unless he has a regular job he really wants to stick to. They can't help you go bankrupt more than once in six years. In short, they can't change the laws just for you—though in recent years when Congress has been badly constipated, much of our social progress has been achieved through the courts. But they can help you skin by with the least legal trouble possible, as wealthy people's lawyers do.

A good lawyer will try to keep you *out* of court, incidentally. A trial, even if you are unquestionably in the right, is a game of chance (the judge or jury may not believe you, despite the evidence) and it is bound to be extremely expensive. A good lawyer, who knows how to use threats and how to negotiate settlements, can often get most of what you would get even if you won in a trial.

Just having somebody who is "your lawyer" is an immense psychological advantage in your life. It makes you feel you aren't entirely alone and helpless; if you get in a jam your case will be argued correctly; you have somebody who can explain the system to you and prevent it from screwing you.

LIBRARIES

Ironically enough, you can learn much more in a library than you probably will in school. Finding out how to use a library may easily be the single most important eductional resource you can have, and it will help you throughout life. You could never remember everything you may need to know—the essential, therefore, is to be able to find out things when you need to. Moreover, a library is just a good place to know about. (The atmosphere created by a large collection of books is unique in the world.) And once you know how to find things in a library, you open up gigantic new frontiers of both knowledge and feeling—for in books is distilled the entire mental and emotional history of the human race. Whatever you might want to know, the chances are excellent that somewhere in your library there is a book that can tell you.

But how to find it?

Walking into a big library can be a forbidding experience. Many libraries were built to look like train stations or government offices, with huge pillars and lots of marble. But they are public institutions, open to all. And inside every library you will find pretty much the same kind of arrangement, so that once you are familiar with its parts, you will be able to use not only your own library, but libraries in other sections of the city, nearby university libraries, and so on.

Information desk. This is usually near the entrance. Someone there can explain how to get a library card so that you can take books home, and can help you find things or figure out how the library system works.

Reference room. The chief purpose of the reference room and the reference librarians is to help people "look it up." The reference room contains encyclopedias, atlases, almanacs, directories, guides, bibliographies, and other books useful in tracking down information. It may have telephone books from many cities or even other countries. If you want to know how many sheep there are in New Zealand, or the address of a company in France, a reference librarian can show you where to find out. If you want to find some biographical information, the reference department can tell you where to look. It's absolutely amazing how much sheer information is packed into the reference room of even a small city library. (But usually only the main branch has a special reference room or reference desk.) You can obtain information from reference librarians over the phone in many cities, and sometimes even after ordinary library hours. *

The heart of the library is its card catalog. This will be a collection—often a whole roomful—of cabinets with little pullout drawers containing cards listing hundreds of books. Usually there is one set of drawers arranged alphabetically by the names of authors, and another set arranged by titles of the books, so you can look in whichever one is more convenient. Sometimes catalogs also include a section arranged by subject. That way, if you are interested in clocks, or cars, or revolution, or music, you can find a whole collection of books that may be useful to you.

The call number, which also appears on the spine of the book itself, is your guide to where the book is located; write it down, along with the author and title, on a piece of scrap paper, or on a checkout card if the library uses them. Show it to a librarian and ask where the book is located.

Some smaller libraries have "open stacks"—that is, all their books are arranged on shelves open for browsing. This is a lovely way to spend time, and not nearly as dangerous for your pocketbook as browsing in a bookstore! As you wander around finding your own book, you will come across books which you would never have thought of looking for, and which will give you whole new areas to think about. Take the books you want to the check-out desk, where they record your borrowing of them. Some books you can keep for a month, some for shorter periods. The date by which books should be returned will be indicated on the card in the pocket on the inside cover of the book. Return books in time, or you get fined. (The library is the essence of communal sharing.)

Really huge libraries generally have "closed stacks," where you hand in a call slip or check-out card and then wait until someone retrieves the book from the stacks for you. In such libraries you'll be given a number, and when it lights up on a

---

*For example, on the West Coast you can call the Weekend Library Line Friday, Satruday or Sunday evenings until midnight: 415-540-0222.

board over the sign-out desk, that means your book has come out. (It may take ten minutes, sometimes even more.) Then the people at the desk will check it out for you.

Libraries often have special departments too. There may be a section for phonograph records, which can be checked out and taken home just like books. There may be a children's room, where books and records that are specially appealing to children are available. There may be an audiovisual department from which you can borrow films, slides, projectors, even videotape cassettes. There may even be a place to borrow tools. Magazines may be kept separately in a periodicals room; when they're about a year old, they are bound in heavy covers and stored in the stacks for later reference use. Newspaper rooms are also common—a useful place to check ads for jobs or places to live.

Books are the central means by which our society stores and preserves its culture. People talk about information retrieval and computers and other electronic wonders, but except perhaps in a few easily organized and super-specialized scientific fields, the place to find information is still going to be libraries, as far as we can see ahead. The stock-in-trade of libraries has been described as a "compact device capable of storing up to two million bits, serially arranged but capable of rapid searching by the human eye either unaided or aided by an index, transmissible through the mails at low cost, storable indefinitely without deterioration, reusable without accessory machinery, and remarkably inexpensive; sometimes referred to for short as the B.O.O.K."

But what is most important about books is that they are the repositories of the best (and some of the worst) that human beings have felt and thought over centuries. They come from every culture and every continent; they have been written by saints, scientists, dictators, criminals, poets, visionaries, bankers, chefs, revolutionaries, musicians, and madmen (and -women). They contain, for better or worse, the wisdom of the species. Knowledge is power, and libraries are where knowledge is at.

In this "post-Proposition 13" era, your library is probably suffering from budget reductions that restrict its hours, cut down its acquisitions of books and magazines, reduce its staff, and so on. Support the library's requests for funds to the city government. Libraries give more real return for the citizen's tax dollar than any other expenditure. Make sure your city representatives know it.

See INFORMATION, HOW TO FIND.

LIFE-CYCLE COSTS

The initial cost of something is only a part of its true cost, and sometimes (as with a light bulb) it's only a fraction of what you will pay to use it. To assess the real economic impact of a purchase, a full accounting is necessary and includes: capital cost, i.e., what it costs you to use money on that item and not keep it in the bank (or, alternatively, how much you pay in interest to finance it); operating costs, some of which—like berth rental for a boat, or the extra electric consumption on a no-frost refrigerator—may in reality be greater than the investment in the object itself; repair and maintenance costs; and finally disposal costs. These costs must all be assessed over the expected life cycle of the item. Then, dividing by the lifetime, you can obtain a true yearly cost. It is almost certain to be much larger than you expected!

Governments as well as individuals often refuse to acknowledge true life-cycle costs, and attempt to ignore them or deliberately hide them among other outlays. This makes systems which would be absurdly over-expensive if honest cost accounting were applied (nuclear energy's disposal costs or the automobile transportation system's pollution costs) seem acceptable. We must learn to stop this kind of sleight-of-hand in our economic life and avoid it in our personal lives.

See, for a painful example, AUTOMOBILES, COSTS OF.

LIGHT BULBS

Three giant corporations (GE, Westinghouse, and Sylvania-General Telephone) manufacture almost all the light bulbs in the US, and a very good business it is too. High profits from the bulb business, which they practically monopolized for many decades through false-front "competing" companies, kept GE going until they could get their hands on price-fixed, high-cost turbines and nuclear generating machinery, which keeps them happy these days, despite a few setbacks such as suits for anti-trust violations and having their officials thrown briefly into jail for price conspiracies.

Most light bulbs are made to burn out in 750 hours. There are some bulbs produced which burn much longer—1,500, 2,500, even 10,000 hours. The catch is that the longer the life, the less light a bulb puts out. (There is no way around this: it follows from the physics of lamp filaments.) Moreover, the cost of lighting your house is mostly in your electric bill, not in the cost of bulbs. During its 750-hour life, a bulb eats up electricity worth five or six times what the bulb costs you, depending on where you live. Research has shown that even in situations where companies have to pay in labor time to have a bulb changed, they are still better off using standard-life bulbs. The government, after an extensive congressional investigation in 1966, adopted 3,000-hour bulbs for places where burnouts would be dangerous or troublesome, such as toilets, stairwells, and basements, or where replacement is very expensive, as in clock towers. This was a triumph of sorts over the bulb companies, who didn't want to make long-life bulbs at all, but the ordinary user is still better off buying standard bulbs. You get more light output from one 150-watt bulb than from two 75s, by the way.

It is not getting easier to find standard bulbs. Many retailers have switched over to "soft-white" or other novelty bulbs which have a special inside coating and carry a higher price, though they give off no more light. (Generally they give less, in fact, though their diffuseness may be an advantage for a few special close-work situations.) The companies are steadily working to get rid of the lower-price standard bulbs so they can sell everybody only soft-whites.

If your bulbs are burning out too fast (and especially if several of them burn out at once), it is probably because the voltage in your area surges above the standard 120 volts frequently. If this happens, bulb life is seriously shortened. It may then be necessary to use bulbs rated for 125 volts instead, although they will give somewhat less light; you can find these at electrical stores. But the so-called "long-life" bulbs will cost you far more money in your electric bill than quite a number of early burnouts.

The way to save money (and energy) on lighting is to turn off your lights when they're not in use, and to keep the general illumination level down to what is really essential—your house doesn't need the bright lights of a hospital operating room! You can probably cut 15% off your electric bill (and help confound the power companies' projections of increasing demand) simply by developing the habit of turning off lights when you leave a room.

LIVING SPACE

Our lack of a sane national housing policy, and the concomitant spectacular rise in real estate prices, means that Americans will increasingly have to share houses and large apartments too expensive for most people to afford alone. This trend has an important positive side: it will force us to replace the declining "nuclear family" with new quasi-family living arrangements (see EXTENDED FAMILIES). It will also force us to re-evaluate our traditional (and wasteful) habits of arranging our living spaces.

How can you live better in cramped quarters? We can take some tips from the Japanese, who have learned how to live in more jammed-in conditions than Americans will face for many years, if ever. Most Japanese can't afford to devote any one space to just one function. So they don't have a dining room, or even a stationary table—they store a light table on top of a cabinet and only bring it down for meals. Their walls are lined with storage cabinets—sometimes mounted high enough to keep the floor underneath free. Then what space there is can be used for anything. You can bring out sleeping quilts and any space in the house becomes a bed. You can bring out pillows and any place in the house becomes an area where friends can sit and socialize.

We can also learn from boats, whose designers have become extremely ingenious at compressing things and combining them. In boats there is a storage place for everything—if there wasn't, things would roll all over the boat in a storm. And the tiny living spaces in boats are enormously appealing.

Sometimes, if you own your house or have a permissive landlord, you can actually change the arrangement of space in your house. Many walls are "non-bearing"—they don't hold up the roof or the story above—and can be removed without weakening the structure. Or you can knock the plaster off the studs or make an archway. One thing that makes a house feel comfortable and interesting is when you can see more than a few feet into it. This is why a big mirror, or a large window, makes a small room much more tolerable.

Outside spaces can be rearranged too. You might turn a flat roof into a roof garden or sunbathing area. If you can get a rooftop to yourself, you can construct a little outdoor sleeping shelter. By building a fence out of recycled lumber or driftwood, you can make a small private garden or play yard; sometimes you can enlarge a window into a door to give better access to the outside.

Moving costs money as well as trouble and work, and it disrupts your neighborhood friendships and contacts. So if at all possible, it is better to rearrange your present dwelling rather than move—even if you have to put a little money into it. Beware of moving too often for too little advantage.

There is no particular reason why houses should be built in permanent room shapes at all. Some bold architects have therefore proposed flexible systems of housing whereby the inhabitants could safely, cheaply, and easily transform their room arrangements as needed. It is, for example, easy to imagine houses where the floor carried all the heating, water, sewage, and electrical ducts, and the roof/ceiling served as another fixed element, supported on a central pedestal or on corner posts. Then the walls, with their doors and windows, would not have to hold up the roof; they could be made of light construction blocks or panels that you could glue into place wherever you wanted them.

Then, if you didn't like the idea that kitchens are small rooms cut off from the rest of the house, you could make your kitchen the main and largest room in the house—as in the traditional farmhouse, where the kitchen was the source of both food and warmth. If you wanted to make three bedrooms where only two had been, you could rebuild the walls to suit your needs. If you wanted to do away with a door, you could block it up; if you wanted a new window, you could stick one in. "Primitive" people who build houses of mud have long had this kind of flexibility—why shouldn't we?

It is also imperative, of course, that we develop means of constructing living space through truly industrial methods rather than the semi-industrial techniques now used. Through extrusion or other standardized, continuous-production-process means, we could obtain "rooms" that could be bought and installed on site by people themselves, and modular-sized appliances and other necessary equipment would be available to fit them. If such

One of the most incredible living spaces anywhere: "The Dolphin Embassy." It was designed as a combination living space for both people and dolphins.

housing is not soon developed, the United States will become in another few decades a nation of trailer-dwellers, since the mobile home (i.e., a substandard house on wheels) is the only kind of house people of average incomes can now afford to buy.

Decorating. Once you have finally found a place to live that suits you, and it has at least the bare essentials, how do you make it home?

In a commercialized society like America, people quickly get into a stereotyped pattern of thinking about their houses, and they tend to blindly follow the guidelines laid down by advertisers and commercials. Thus they begin to imagine they must fill up their houses with all manner of junk which some ad writer has said will make them happier.

Obviously, you can't be happy following somebody else's guidelines; you have to find your own. And the way to begin doing this is, simply, take it easy. Instead of hurriedly throwing into a new apartment all the things you could possibly "need," try to concentrate on bringing into it only those things you really love and absolutely must have. Give the new place time to develop its own spirit—don't try to make it resemble the last place you lived, or look like your friends' or parents' houses, or like something in a magazine.

In fact, the best thing to do when you've taken a new place is to go over with nothing but a cushion and just sit down quietly for a while in each room. Look around at its windows, walls, ceilings, floor. Notice how the light falls, and what you see out the windows. Listen to the noises. Feel how the air circulates. Don't be in a hurry to fill it up in your imagination; just concentrate on the spaces and their feel. You should never fight a house, you should fit into it. See if you can judge what the place "wants" you to do with it. Is its light made gruesome by a coat of pea-green paint? Would a little painting of cabinets or door and window trim give some life to the interior and link one room to another? Can you provide special places for the furniture you're bringing in, so it will feel at home and not crowd you?

It is easiest to make a house express you, and thus suit you, if you take a "simple living" approach. According to this way of doing things, we should dominate our goods, and not let our goods dominate us; in arranging dwellings we should strive for elegant simplicity, for lightness, for grace. We should be aesthetically economical— which usually means financially economical too, except that sometimes you will want to do or buy something which looks simple and plain but turns out to be expensive. In the long run it is better to have a few really good things in your house than to clutter it with a hodgepodge of cheaper stuff; for the good things will serve you better and there is more about them to love. A simple living approach should not mean austerity or denying yourself pleasures; it means making sure that your pleasures are real ones and satisfying ones, and that they are your own and not just castoffs from television and magazines.

Real luxury consists in having about you the things you need and love, and nothing that interferes with or cheapens them. If you treat your dwelling with this kind of careful respect, it will repay you with a sense of repose, shelter, and peace.

Here are some ways you might begin inhabiting a new place in a good spirit.

Once you have done any painting you have in mind, consider repainting some of your furniture, even if it isn't strictly necessary; a little paint of similar or related colors can make it look like it really belongs there. If the windows have good shapes, you might avoid putting drapes or curtains over them; you could paste on rice paper or other decorative paper, which transmits a soft, delicate light but gives you privacy. If there are places where it would be nice to be able to sit on the floor (like in front of a fireplace, or in a corner) try to find a soft secondhand rug; on it you could also keep some pillows, with covers of cloth whose colors work interestingly in the room. Cover up any bare hanging light bulbs—the cheapest way, and an attractive one, is with big paper lantern globes you can find in Chinatowns or import stores.

Also try to bring into your house reminders of the natural world outside, so that you remember the house is, after all, a part of nature. You may be sick of driftwood or shells, but the world is full of strange leaves, sticks, rocks, moss, and lumps and shreds of this and that; if something strikes you as having some mystery or beauty about it, bring it home so you can look at it patiently.

Don't be afraid of "bare walls." A plain wall, if it's a tolerable color, can be a restful and surprisingly interesting part of your house—no wall is utterly without subtle variations in texture, color, light reflection. Some people like to plaster their walls with magazine-clipping pictures, calendars, posters from travel agencies (which you can often get free), outrageous newspaper headlines, stolen placards from the streets, and so on. And certainly it's nice to have a big place for tacking up messages, reminders, unpaid bills, funny or gruesome tidbits. You can easily devote one wall to such purposes—either by putting up a big sheet of wrapping paper to tape things on, or a piece of plywood or corrugated cardboard to tack things to.

You can scrounge or buy cheaply many unusual kinds of coverings for bare floors which can often give a luxurious feel to a run-down apartment. The most sumptuous is outdated carpeting samples from places that specialize in wall-to-wall jobs. They come in squares about eighteen inches on a side, and in many thicknesses, textures, patterns, and colors. You can sew them together in a super-crazy quilt, or you can cut them up into irregular shapes and glue or sew them onto a piece of heavy backing.

Uneven floors, or floors with a lot of cracks in the wood, can be covered with masonite, which is the cheapest possible covering—cheaper even than all but the sleaziest linoleum. But by looking hard you can find rugs and carpeting of passable appearance in thrift shops. If they're small, and not too heavy and stiff, they can be dyed. They can be cut to fit small rooms, or even laid one on top of another to give a softer surface. If you find an especially beautiful rug, it can be tacked onto a wall that's hopelessly cracked or peeling. Burlap, or any other kind of inexpensive cloth, can also be used as a wall covering or hanging.

Japanese tatami mats are the most attractive cheap floor covering, but they wear through easily if you push chairs around on them. They have a good smell, being made of rice straw, and they feel pleasant to the touch when you lie down on them. They are warm to the feet, and absorb dirt less than a rug.

But don't be so sure you need floor coverings. If your place has good wood floors, treasure them! Many old houses have either beautiful patterned hardwood floors or wide, worn softwood board floors. It is worth a lot of work to restore such floors to good condition, for they will be a pleasure to look at and walk on. You can rent powerful floor sanders from equipment rental places, and then varnish or oil the sanded wood. It's hard, dusty work, but satisfying, and cheaper than anything else you could do with your floor.

Never try to remove old linoleum—it's practically impossible. Cover it up with new linoleum or some other surface.

LIVING TOGETHER

Since the 60's, an increasing number of couples have been living together without marrying, either because they are opposed to the institution of marriage as we have known it (which usually meant the inequality of the wife) or just because they don't feel like it, at least not with the person they happen to be involved with. While conservative communities or individuals may still frown on such arrangements, they are now so numerous in most cities that people undertake them with little difficulty, and this is an important contribution to our social and sexual freedoms.

However, if such living arrangements continue very long, problems may result in economic areas, and there is currently a trend toward having an explicit agreement, sometimes on paper, when people move in together. The Lee Marvin case, settled in 1979, indicated that a woman does *not* gain a right to half of her live-in partner's income as she would if she married him, unless there is a written contract to that effect. Equality-minded

couples, therefore, as well as women wishing to be sure they will not be exploited, might well put down on paper what will happen to money and other assets that come in while they are together. There is no need, or course, to make such contracts follow the lines of marriage; they could specify a total separation of resources, down to separate jars of peanut butter in the cupboard, if the partners felt that was the right way to go.

When people start living together, they often feel uncomfortable tendencies to revert to traditional patterns of family life, and a contract can also be a useful way to stave these off. If it is openly and jointly agreed that shopping, housework, and home maintenance work are to be shared equally, old patterns have a harder time reasserting themselves, and can be more easily choked off if they do.

If a couple live together for a long time (seven years in many areas) their relationship may become a "common-law marriage," and the state's rules for the sharing and inheritance of property come into play, along with possible provisions for child support, alimony, etc., in the event of separation. A lawyer's advice should be sought by couples who contemplate or find themselves in a live-in partnership of more than a few years' duration.

See MARRIAGE.

The Living-Together Kit, by Toni Ihara and Ralph Warner (lawyers!). Nolo Press, 1978; Fawcett Books, 1979.

M

MAPS

Maps are both fascinating and useful. But you have to get the hang of reading them—it's a totally different process because it's visual: the map is essentially a picture. Children beginning to use maps have a lot of trouble with this concept—to get the idea of how a map corresponds to its territory is a great leap of imagination. It helps to think that you are a super-tiny ant crawling around over the map, which is a kind of copy of the world. Once you have really grasped that this little inch of wavy line pictures ten miles of wandering river, and that the red line crossing it "is" a highway, you're ready to read maps. After you've read enough of them, you'll be making automatic interpretations, and also having fun.

There are map freaks who can lie on the floor with a big atlas for hours, the way other people do with the Sunday paper. It's incredible what you can find out from a map, even of an area you think you know pretty well: roads or streets you never knew were there, strange poetic names of places, little hidden towns. Besides, if you move around a lot, you'll have to know how to use a map quickly and accurately; if you live nomadically, or if you're in a hurry to get through some strange territory, you've got to be able to read road maps. If you're hiking or camping in the wilderness, you've got to be able to read topographic maps. One useful tip: lay out the map so it's oriented right (so its north is toward the real north)—then you can imagine you are actually walking or driving on it.

Most of the maps around are road maps, put out by oil companies who want you to be able to get from here to there because you'll have to buy gas to do it. These are, as you'll discover if you get into maps, relatively uninteresting maps, because all they show is roads and a few other main features

like cities and big rivers. But they'll do to start with. On them you can learn how to read:

Scale. Somewhere on the map there ought to be a little ruler-like scale that tells you how big things are on the map.

Key. Decent maps include a key to the symbols they use—what mark stands for a big city, how a marshy area is indicated, what kinds of lines are used for freeways, main roads, country roads, dirt roads.

In a library you can check into some real maps. There are several good atlases which contain very carefully prepared and beautifully printed maps; ask the librarian to help you find a good one. Such maps will show, for one thing, the altitude of a place, by a system of different colors for different elevations (there's a key to the colors somewhere on the edge of the map). By using different sizes of type for names, it will tell you how big towns, villages, and cities are. It will show major mountain peaks and tell how high they are. There may be special maps that will show which areas are forested and which are bare. The best atlases around are *The Times Survey Atlas of the World*, the *Rand-McNally World Atlas*, and the *Reader's Digest Great World Atlas*. All these are expensive, but decent libraries will have them. The only highway maps that are really good are those issued by the American Automobile Association (free to members).

A map which provides a good representation of the physical features of your region—its river pattern, mountains and valleys, cities and agricultural areas, will begin to give you an idea of your BIOREGION, and how your life fits into the overall pattern of that region. This can help you to feel truly "at home" where you live.

For the ultimate in maps of the United States, you want the series of super-detailed topographic maps put out by the US Geological Survey. These mostly cover very small sections of territory, only a few miles across, but they will show (in the country) literally every house, what the vegetation is like, how high contours are (essential for hiking), whether streams are intermittent, whether roads are passable in winter, and so on. You can buy these from hiking equipment stores, special map stores, or by mail from the USGS. (They have an index map that shows which maps you need to order.) If the USGS isn't listed under "US Government Offices" in your phone book, write to the USGS Distribution Center, Washington, DC

20242, and ask where their nearest regional map distribution office is.

See VACATIONS for more on maps.

MARRIAGE

Marriage is a contract among three parties: the two spouses and the state. Depending on your financial situation and where you live, marriage may have economic consequences you do not desire or intend. In some cases these can be modified by premarital contracts, which have a long and solid legal history (unlike contracts about sharing household duties and the like—see below). Now that more than half of all marriages are ending in divorce, it is important to be clear about your situation *before* you marry, so that in case you too divorce, the separation can be carried out with as little confusion and likelihood of legal combat as possible. Prospective spouses should expect each other to make full disclosure of their properties and debts, if any, before marriage. If your plan for living together involves one partner going to school and the other working to provide support, and this partner is to be repaid later by a couple of years free (for childrearing, creative projects, or a well-deserved vacation), it is wise to put this agreement in writing.

In Arizona, California, Idaho, Louisiana, Nevada, New Mexico, Texas, and Washington, known as "community property states," everything a couple acquires during a marriage is joint property, no matter how it was paid for or who earned the money. If they split up, this property gets divided equally between them. In the other states, which are called "common law states," the situation is complex. Property and possessions held in the husband's name, no matter where they came from or who earned the money for them (even if they belonged to the wife before marriage) are considered his. In a divorce, the judge has discretion in dividing the property. (See *Sexist Justice*, by Karen DeCrow; Random House, 1979).

In some states it is possible to get married without spending anything and without getting into the clutches of the state apparatus. People over 21 who have been living together can be married by a minister in a ceremony to their taste and then receive from the minister three copies of a document saying he or she has done so. This paper need only be filed with the church, not with the city hall or county. The other two copies are kept by the couple. Thus, if they later wish to dissolve the marriage, this can be done by the simple expedient of getting all three copies together and burning them. No lawyer's fees, court fees, waiting periods, etc. (See, for example, California Civil Code, Section 79.)

This surprisingly unbureaucratic procedure was derived to permit people in the Victorian age to marry without publicity or public knowledge. It costs nothing and it puts into your hands the power of whether you want the government to know you are married. Sometimes this is to your advantage; sometimes not.

Such "people's marriages" are lawful marriages. This means they cannot be dissolved except by the consent of both partners (or by deception — somebody burning up the evidence). They are therefore not a bar to suits for alimony, child support, etc.

Ordinary marriages require a marriage license which costs a couple of dollars (at the city hall or county courthouse), a blood test (to check whether either partner has VD), and sometimes a waiting period of a few days (during which you have a chance to cool off and think it over). In my opinion, it is much too easy to get married and much too hard for childless couples to get divorced. Marriage is a legal contract for the protection of children and spouses in the sharing of income and property. If no children are contemplated, sharing on the economic level can equally well be handled through a private contract—with a time limit, and provisions for renegotiation from time to time.

For some people, getting married signifies an emotional degree of commitment they are unable to maintain for a partner without benefit of marriage; for others, getting married signifies an unacceptable degree of restraint and loss of personal independence. Many compromises and experiments are currently being tried: women choose to retain their name, partners maintain separate bank accounts, or question the importance of monogamy. For the vast majority, however, the act of getting married signifies a willingness to become more like your parents—to pass into the "parental" generation, whether or not you intend to have children. This self-definition, clearly, is not something to rush into lightly, especially as it has, statistically, only a fifty-fifty chance of surviving.

In attempts to make sure that their marriages work the way *they* want, and not the way society or parents suggest, many couples nowadays prepare written marriage contracts. It is often useful to have the help of a trusted but not too close person (a lawyer, clergyman, or marriage counselor), since working out such a contract inevitably raises difficult issues.

Money matters are not only critical, but particularly complex. How income is to be spent has many ramifications in itself. Should the couple attempt to build up savings for some common purpose? Should accounts be separate or joint or a combination of both? How much discretionary spending money should each partner have? How much accounting should the partners expect of each other?

Issues connected with children are also crucial. Some couples specify the number of children they agree to have, and their spacing; others agree not to have any at all. In cases of strong religious differences between spouses, the religious upbringing of the children must be clearly agreed upon. Since the rearing of children will affect the employment availability of the parents, plans to alternate working with staying home should be worked out in advance. How children will be named may also be an issue requiring thought. Many people also attempt to use marriage contracts as a way to establish guidelines for their sexual lives: whether they expect monogamy, and if not, what the ground rules are for sexual contacts with other persons. Other specify in their contracts requirements for the division of domestic duties.

Courts tend to take contracts seriously only when they involve money. Couples should therefore confine their "official" contract to matters that are financially serious (property, income, children) and may therefore become legal issues in case of divorce. A lawyer should help in preparing such a contract. Other more intimate and less "measurable" items should be handled in a second agreement which is intended as a serious personal commitment but not a legal document.

See LIVING TOGETHER.

MASSAGE

Giving a decent massage ought to be as elementary a social grace as the ability to make good coffee or tea. Most people in "advanced" industrial civilizations go around in chronic states of tension and stiffness; we need all the help we can give each other in loosening up. A one-day workshop will teach you the essentials: a series of simple massage strokes, easier to learn than disco steps, which give pleasure and relaxation. You will learn how to soften the knots that form around the base of the

skull, often connected with tension headaches; how to limber up the tight places in shoulders, neck, and back; and effective strokes for arms, trunk, legs, and (most subtle of all) feet. Having mastered the basics, you may then want to go on into more arcane disciplines: shiatsu, polarity, deep pressure massage....

A massage workshop teaches you a good deal about the body's internal structure, which you can explore and refine with your own hands. It will thus give you new understanding of, respect for, and confidence in your own body as well.

Some people arrange massage groups: they share a light supper, quiet talking, the opportunity to work on unfamiliar bodies. (It's also pleasant to have two people massage one, which produces very complicated sensations.) Especially if a hot tub or swimming pool is available, these simple sensual delights can be very invigorating and yet soothing.

Massage can of course be sexual, or the sight of happy naked bodies may simply fill you with mellow feelings and happiness.

The Massage Book, by George Downing, illus. by Anne Kent Rush. Random House, 1972.
Touching: The Human Language of the Skin, by Ashley Montagu. Harper & Row, 1978.

MATERIALS, LIMITATIONS OF

The wise craftsperson does not try to make materials do things that are not within their capacity —but works along with their capabilities, studying their strengths, and designing around their weaknesses. Stone and concrete have great compressive strength; wood has tensile strength and also resists bending. Steel and other metals have great tensile strength (as does glass in fiber form) but do not resist bending unless they are heavy.

The means by which parts can be connected also have their limitations. You should not try to drive screws or nails into the end grain of wood —they will quickly pull out. (If a fillet or other way of attaching is not possible, consider doweling.) You should not drive nails through thin pieces of wood —they will split, especially if the piece is also narrow. Glue can only hold if the joint offers a large enough surface considering the weight or force that may bear on it; otherwise, even if the glue itself holds, it will tear off the surface layer of the wood. Nonporous materials such as glass are hard to glue, even with epoxy or silicone-rubber glue, and even if you clean the surfaces scrupulously. Any joint that is not firm and tight is hard to glue, because slight wiggles during the time the glue is drying will prevent a solid bond. (In gluing a loose chair rung you can wrap a thin piece of glue-soaked cloth around the part that goes into the hole; this will decrease the play.) When clamping a joint isn't feasible, you can probably put a light nail into it, either permanently or just to hold it while it dries. Using glue is usually not only neater but cheaper than screws or bolts.

Nails are best at holding boards together against shearing or twisting stresses; nails driven at an angle have some resistance to pulling (especially in pairs), but if you need to hold two pieces together against forces that try to pull them apart it is better to use screws, and best to use bolts. In soft woods or where large forces are involved, big washers will spread the stress better.

In attaching parts to one another, the principle of triangulation is important: whenever three points are fixed, they create a rigid shape. This is why houses and other heavy structures normally have diagonal frame elements—otherwise they would need very heavy joints to prevent swaying. A flat membrane like a piece of plywood will also stabilize a structure if it is attached at a number of points.

MEAT

Despite the general American fondness for meat, all the food produced on earth is vegetable in origin: it comes from the primary productivity of green plants acted upon by sunlight. We may then feed the resulting grains and grasses to animals, and eat the animals, but we do so at a heavy cost. To produce a kilogram of animal protein requires many kilograms of grain protein (which we could just as well have eaten directly, after all).

People who are seriously concerned about their impact on the food chains of the world (those chains by which grasses produce seeds, mice eat seeds, owls eat mice, foxes eat owls, etc.) try to "eat low on the food chain." The number of people who are VEGETARIANS, either for such reasons or because they believe eating meat is morally or physiologically unhealthy, has been growing rapidly in recent years; and to their number we must add many more people who have simply cut down their consumption of meat, for economic or other motives, and have turned to chicken, turkey, fish, and other protein sources.

It is possible, of course, to have a perfectly healthy diet without eating any meat at all. What seems likely, however, is that American meat consumption will gradually diminish for a combination of reasons. Expense is a major factor.

Even well-to-do people, used to spending about 20% of their income on food (and a quarter of this on meat) are finding it necessary to trim their food outlays; people with modest incomes, who may spend up to half of their money on food, have never been able to spend much on meat. Another factor is worry about meat being contaminated by growth hormones and other chemicals injected into the animals before slaughtering; between 5% and 10% of meat in markets has chemical levels greater than those supposedly allowed for safe consumption. The sodium nitrite preservative used in bacon and many other preserved meats is a possible CARCINOGEN. Moreover, since meat usually contains large quantities of saturated fat that contributes to cholesterol build-up and other disorders of the circulatory system, eating less meat is a way to minimize a number of serious health problems that afflict Americans in large numbers. (There is some evidence, by the way, that heavy exercise somehow reduces cholesterol. If you are a confirmed meat eater, you should adopt a serious program of running or other major aerobic EXERCISE.)

Many widespread ideas about meat are mostly wrong. The cheaper grades (Good instead of Choice) are just as nourishing; surprisingly, tests show that blindfolded people often find they taste better; "lower" grades also have less fat and less waste. Certain cuts—chuck roasts and chuck steaks, for example—are less expensive than others; they are just as tender, however, and the only kind a budgeting cook should use. Rolled roasts have much less waste than rib roasts.

Hamburger is generally the cheapest kind of meat, for its food value, that you can buy. However, as meat prices overall have risen, it is no longer a sure bargain. Moreover, butchers vary in their scrupulousness about what they put into it. Hamburger that is all fat is no good even if it *is* cheap. Try to shop at a market that has several grades of ground meat, so you can choose according to what you plan to do with it. For broiling or pan-frying where the fat can be poured off, you get about the same amount of protein in cheaper, higher-fat hamburger, so you only need lean for meatloafs or casseroles.

Hot dog sales are a barometer of economic conditions; when people buy more of them, times are getting hard. But it is no longer easy to know when hot dogs are really a good cheap source of meat. Actually hot dogs have only about three-quarters as much protein per pound as lean meat; so unless hot dogs cost less than three-quarters as much on a per-pound basis, you're better off buying non-fatty roasts or other cuts. The actual contents of hot dogs are ground up so finely that you can't tell what's in them, but they can have up to 30% fat, and probably do ("All Meat" doesn't exclude fat). They can contain up to 15% chicken and still be called frankfurters. They can have up to 3.5% flour, cereal, or dried milk. Non-fat dried milk is a *good* thing in a hot dog (it's good protein) if the price is low.

There are giant-sized hot dogs called dinner franks, garlic franks, or Polish sausages which have more seasoning than the bland standard dog and usually cost about the same per pound. Regular sausage, however, is so largely fat that it is bad both for your health and your budget.

People sometimes spend more on bacon than they spend on any other kind of meat. This is a big mistake, not only because of the nitrite preservative but because it is very fatty and has very little food value. Try to think of other ways to add flavor to your breakfasts: fry up some hashbrown potatoes with your eggs. Even sausage is better than bacon.

Meat juice is full of vitamins and proteins. Skim off the fat and pour the juice over the meat or other items in the meal, or mix it into gravy, or save it for tomorrow's soup.

The best overall bargain in meats is usually liver. Chicken and turkey are almost always excellent eating at low prices compared to beef or pork or lamb. Kidneys, heart, brains, tongue, and other meats are usually low in price and high in nutritional value; they are especially well adapted to pot pies, scrambled-egg dishes, stews, casseroles, and similar tasty ways of making a little meat go a long way.

Salami, bologna, liverwurst, head cheese, and other special meat products are generally very high in fats, and should not make up a regular part of your diet. Generally they are expensive in terms of their protein content, compared to hamburger. But they come in many novel forms and trying them out can be fun. Dry Italian salami has the virtue that it keeps fairly well without refrigeration, and is therefore good for backpacking and camping purposes.

MEDICAL ABUSES

While much of the medical profession is composed of honest and hardworking doctors and technicians, medicine remains an art rather than a science; its success depends upon judgment. And doctors are prone to fads, to over-prescription, to

certain kinds of systematic misunderstandings, and to trends in "scientific" work which they apply recklessly to human beings. This is especially true in a medical system preoccupied with profits. Besides that, there are also a lot of absolute quacks around: people without proper training, people who act irresponsibly, people who are ignorant or stupid or malicious. It would be remarkable if some such persons did not fasten themselves on to medicine, an area in which human beings usually feel weak, needy, and helpless. The following sections outline some of the worst dangers these people create.

Patent medicines. In the nineteenth century, there were a lot of drugstore remedies which contained opium—so thousands of unwitting people got addicted to So-and-So's Soothing Syrup. The federal Food and Drug Administration has slowly gotten rid of the worst of the patent medicines, but the FDA is chronically understaffed and weak, and the makers of drugs are endlessly ingenious. In general, you should not take any medicines that have not been prescribed by a doctor—and even then, use your own judgment in talking with the doctor about the likely good and bad effects. The human body has evolved to cope with the illnesses and accidents that we are heir to. Scientists who spend their lives studying drugs take as few of them as possible! If you think you need anything more than an occasional aspirin— such as tonics or pep pills or other patent medicines "to keep going"—there is probably something seriously wrong that needs a doctor's attention. If you need cheering up, the only real way is through other people: friends, not medical doctors.

Shock treatment. People with certain kinds of mental illness are sometimes sent, more or less against their will, into electric shock treatment. Hard as it may be to believe, this is still used even though no one understands the effects of electroshock on the delicate mechanisms of the human brain, and despite strong objections to its use by much of the medical and psychiatric profession. Certain doctors seem to like to use shock as a way of "punishing" mentally ill persons for not getting well. If someone proposed that they should undergo shock themselves, so as to know what they were subjecting their patients to, they would turn pale and run. If doctors ever recommend it, for yourself or a relative, ask them if they have ever taken it themselves—and if not, how can they claim it is painless, harmless, and so on? Shock is most used for depressed patients who are often unable to speak up for themselves. You are not doing them any good by helping a doctor talk them into it, or by authorizing it yourself.

Tranquilizers. Pill popping, of both mild and heavy drugs, is unbelievably widespread in America today—reflecting the inability of the medical profession and other social agencies to cope with the stress effects of our society. (Pill manufacturing is also much more profitable than attempts to help people live better so they don't need the pills.)

Reducing diets. Many tantalizing false promises are always made on behalf of the newest "sure-fire" diet craze. But somehow they never work; moreover, some of them are actually dangerous if they involve stringent restrictions of certain kinds of foods. See REDUCING.

Laxatives. If you eat a good diet with plenty of fiber in it (grains, vegetables, fruits) and get enough exercise and sleep, your bowels should move normally and you will seldom or never need a laxative. Some people have a movement every day, some people several times a day, and some only once every other day or so. Any of these natural patterns is OK. But many different types of laxatives advertise to the contrary, hoping to get your dollars.

True constipation is rare except in very old or very sick people. (If you have constant constipation, stop and ask yourself whether bad diet or living habits may be causing it.) But many people get "addicted" to laxatives, and get their bowels used to having them, and then they don't work normally any more.

You can taper off from laxatives, using less and less, by adding lots of fluids (like water, hot tea, or moderate quantities of unsweetened coffee—avoid carbonated and sweet drinks), and by eating laxative foods such as dried prunes, raw fruits and vegetables, and whole-wheat bread. Walking or other exercise helps too.

Mild laxatives are the only ones you should use unless a doctor tells you to: milk of magnesia with several glasses of water, or a three-grain cascara tablet. Camomile and other natural herb teas are more organic.

Never use laxatives when you have abdominal pain, nausea, vomiting, or other appendicitis symptoms.

Sleeping pills. These are both more dangerous and less effective than either patients or doctors realize, but they are the most commonly prescribed medical drugs in the world. Careful research shows that, particularly when used for more than two weeks, the pills don't control insomnia. Moreover, barbiturates are strongly addictive, and are lethal in overdose especially when combined with alcohol; alternatives such as flurazepam (Dalmane) and related drugs such as Valium and Librium are also addictive. Byproducts of Dalmane remain in the body for a long time so you can build up concentrations that dangerously diminish alertness and coordination.

But the most striking research finding about insomnia is that in fact the sleep of most people who complain of insomnia (and seek sleeping pill prescriptions) is barely different from those who think they sleep normally. Sleeping pills are dispensed in hospitals as a matter of routine, and this seems to carry over into doctors' office practice, reinforced by constant sales pitches from the drug companies. The practical lesson is that you should try to live a less stressful life and you will sleep better. Be willing to lose some sleep once in a while; it's not a life-threatening problem, and if your mind keeps racing it is probably telling you to slow down.

MEDICAL CARE

The objectives of our medical services should be to help people stay well, to teach self-help in dealing with minor illnesses and first aid, and to provide competent care in serious illnesses to all people, as a matter of simple humanity and justice. But under the American system of fee-for-service medicine, we get just about the opposite. Most people can only afford to see doctors when they get seriously ill; many poor people can hardly afford it even then. The mass media encourage over-dependence on doctors, and mechanical pill popping as an answer to all medical problems; our educational system fails to teach us even the basics of medical common sense, so that we can rely neither on friends nor strangers when we need help or advice. We spend more on medical care than on any other component of our economy—even the military!—but only about five percent of this is being spent on preventive care, which is what really improves a nation's health.

The results are tragic. America ranks eighteenth among industrial countries in life expectancy for men and eleventh for women. Its middle-aged men have a higher death rate than anywhere in Western Europe. We rank lower than thirteen other countries in infant mortality—a sad comment on how much we prize human life. The medically more advanced countries of the world often spend less on medical care than we do, but since World

War II they have established national health policies that have brought medical information and care to all their citizens—either through medical health insurance, a national health service, or a nationwide system of accessible clinics. Only the United States has left the health of its people to the tender mercies of the medical and insurance industry, allowing doctors, hospitals, and drug companies to operate unhindered, passing on to sick people their skyrocketing salaries, fees, and profits. When we finally adopted the MEDICARE program to help pay the bills of retired and old people, it characteristically turned out to be a gravy train for rate-raising doctors, hospitals, drug manufacturers, and nursing homes; it left many people paying almost the same for their medical services as they had paid a few years before. A sensible comprehensive national medical care plan has been proposed in Congress by Representative Ron Dellums of California. If you have serious concerns in this area, you might work for its passage.

Despite the "medical miracles" of heart transplants and so on, it is extremely difficult for Americans in most regions to secure decent, comprehensive medical care at reasonable cost, whether they are well-to-do or poor. And many of the current trends in medicine—larger hospitals, greater specialization, fancier electronic equipment—will both raise costs further and take medical facilities further away from the people who need them. But they do bring fat profits to equipment companies, contractors, engineers, and make more jobs for administrators.

Most of the problems of our medical system are in fact organizational ones. It's not even so much that we lack doctors—at least, as long as we can rely on foreign-trained interns to staff our hospitals and clinics—but rather that the doctors we have are not being used efficiently.

Doctors often come into cases too late because patients stay away to save money. Doctors' time is often taken up with minor cases which a nurse or first-aid medic could easily handle. (It took twenty years of debate for the American Medical Association to admit that a nurse could be trusted to take temperatures.) Doctors are super-specialized into glamorous fields so that the essential intake and family-care functions of the old general practitioner are done part-time or not at all. Doctors cannot do preventive medicine because well-patient examinations are not routine for spotting trouble before it gets serious. And, because of our class society, the poor are used as teaching cases in the county and medical school hospitals, training doctors so they can go practice in wealthy areas. In short, we have a medical system which is money-oriented rather than medicine-oriented.

To change this will require basic political changes. The power of the AMA, one of the most reactionary forces in American society, must be broken, for its cynically backward-looking ideology is a major roadblock to medical reform. (Already many young doctors have deserted the AMA; less than half of US doctors are now members, even though in many places membership is required in order to send patients to local hospitals.) The insurance companies which have helped doctors plunder Medicare and Medicaid must be put under strict control. The overemphasis on hospitals must be countered: community control of medical facilities, through a network of thousands of neighborhood clinics, is needed to bring medicine to people where they need it—in the places where they live and work. Millions of new para-medical personnel need to be trained in the tasks of nursing, first aid, general medical advice, midwifing, and many other kinds of work which doctors have monopolized—thus both freeing our scarce supply of doctors for more difficult work, and returning some humanity to our treatment of sick people, which has largely been lost in our depersonalized monster super-hospitals. And medical education has to be overhauled from top to bottom, not only to train these para-professional people, but to give doctors competence in many fields now sadly neglected: nutrition, preventive medicine, occupational-hazards treatment, pediatrics (including attention to the special problems of teenagers), and so on.

These needs are urgent, and many wise doctors support them. Federal and state governments pay for about a third of the nation's health budget. It is within the people's power, therefore, to insist that this money is spent on effective medicine, and not on fancy frills or profits that benefit only a few. Though we have spent $5 billion more each year since 1965, we see no objective evidence of improved health care. And the vested interests lined up at the government trough are powerful and menacing: the drug companies with their giant propaganda machines, the AMA with its nineteenth-century profit-seeking mentality, the computer companies who see easy money in government-supported contracts, the insurance industry which wants to skim the cream off of health care, the vastly expanded nursing-home industry, the big-time doctors and medical-school officials who advise both government and private firms for fat consulting fees (and take care of their friends).

If we are to get a decent medical system in this country, it will be over the dead bodies of these fat cats, who truly constitute a "Medical-Industrial Complex."

Meanwhile, what to do when we get sick? We must develop informed health common sense and learn to take care of ourselves and our friends whenever we can. Get hold of a good handbook of medical self-help and study it carefully.

See HEALTH INSURANCE AND HEALTH MAINTENANCE ORGANIZATIONS; HOLISTIC HEALTH; TEETH, DENTAL CARE.

Health-wise Handbook, a Guide to Responsible Health Care, by Toni Roberts, Kathleen McIntosh Tinker, and Donald Kemper. Doubleday, 1979.
Whole Person Health Care, by Mark Tager, M.D., and Charles Jennings. Foreword by Ernest Callenbach. Victoria House, 2218 N.E. 8th Ave., Portland, OR 97212.
The Well Body Book, by Mike Samuels, M.D., and Hal Bennett. Random House, 1973.

MEDICAL DRUGS

Millions of Americans with heart trouble, diabetes, and other diseases depend on drugs for their very lives and millions more need drugs to combat serious illnesses. But Congressional investigations have made it clear that Americans are being literally robbed by the drug companies. They overcharge fantastically on brand-name drugs that do no more than the same drug in a plain package with no fancy name. (Whenever your doctor gives you a prescription, ask whether it is for the cheapest reliable type of the drug—the drug companies spend about $6,000 each year on each doctor to brainwash them into prescribing their drugs rather than cheaper brands.)

The drug companies create a pill-popping society by massive ad campaigns which lead patients to expect drugs and doctors to over-prescribe them, whether or not the drugs are really needed or are likely to help. They fight proper regulation and testing of potentially dangerous drugs, use improper influence on supposedly independent laboratories, sometimes conceal, falsify, or distort experimental tests, and fight the Food and Drug Administration's underfinanced efforts to protect the public. They fix prices at inflated levels. As a result, drug-industry profits are something like twice as high as the average for

US industry. And this just adds to the costs people have to pay for medical care.

What can you do? For one thing, always ask yourself what you can do to get well besides taking pills. But the problem, like many in our medical system, is largely political: the power of the drug companies must somehow be broken. However, in your personal life there are some ways you can save money without jeopardizing your precious health:

Ask your doctor to prescribe by "generic" name and not brand name, and to prescribe organic rather than synthetic drugs wherever possible. The same drug substance with Lilly's name on it may cost three times what it does with another manufacturer's name on it. Your pharmacist is a trained professional; ask for the cheapest satisfactory brand of the drug you need. If your doctor gives you problems about prescribing generically, you may be wise to find another doctor, especially if your health situation requires a lot of medication; it could cut your drug costs in half.

Ask your doctor what actual effects to expect from the drug. Many doctors believe "patients want pills," and will prescribe something or other thinking it will make you feel better. (The more honest ones prescribe a "placebo," which is a pill with no active drug in it at all.) If you are asked to pay a stiff bill for some pills that might or might not make your sniffles go away, you'd probably like to know that's all you can expect—and save the money.

Compare prices. Phone a couple of different pharmacies and read the prescription to them; ask them to tell you how much it will cost. If you are too shy to say you are checking prices, pretend you're not sure you have enough money. Co-op pharmacies and those connected with pre-paid health-plan clinics or unions usually have the lowest costs.

Don't buy non-prescription drugs. People waste a great deal of money on tonics, laxatives, vitamins, iron pills, tranquilizers, sleeping pills, wake-up pills, pep pills, and so on—which are either useless or distract you from taking action to improve your diet, your exercise patterns, or your life style so that you don't need the drugs. If you eat right and get enough exercise and sleep, you should need no drugs except if you actually get sick. Stay out of drugstores except when a doctor sends you there, and spend the money you save on eating better.

Check on the side effects. Laws require pharmacies to remove from certain drug packages the full-information folders placed there by the drug companies. Until these laws can be changed, as they have been in other advanced countries, make a point of asking your doctor whether a drug will cause side effects, or react badly with another drug you are taking. Common side effects can be unpleasant or dangerous: drowsiness, dizziness, jumpiness, addiction, and so on. But some drugs, in some people, have far more drastic effects, both mental and physical. Report to your doctor anything unpleasant or suspicious that happens after you start taking a drug; don't just assume it's another symptom of your disease.

There is a doctor's joke about the patient who comes in with a bad cold. The doctor tells him that if he gets sleep and rest, it will go away, but that there's nothing else that can be done for it. "But what if it turns into pneumonia?" wails the patient. "Ah," says the doctor, "*that* I can fix!"

The reason is that pneumonia is a bacterial disease. If it affects your lungs, the doctor can give you an antibiotic that will kill the bacteria; unless you are old or in an otherwise weakened condition, that will probably cure it without any trouble. A cold, on the other hand, is a virus disease. You can be vaccinated against some virus diseases, like polio and even measles. But once you get them, no pills or shots will help.

Many people go to doctors for colds or flus that are virus diseases, for which your own common sense care is the only remedy, and are surprised when the doctor can't do anything about it; they whine for antibiotics, which may be not only useless but dangerous—causing anemia and other dangerous reactions, killing the useful bacteria that live in your intestines, and leading to the development of resistant strains of bacteria. We are taught that our medical experts are all-powerful, able to transplant hearts (true, not very successfully) and perform other wonders. Why the hell can't they cure colds? The answer is that viruses—and there are many different kinds that cause cold, flu, and similar annoying illnesses—are not sensitive to any antibiotics. They must be fought off by your body's natural defense mechanisms. Viruses, in fact, are very strange things. They are not even quite "alive" in the same way that bacteria are, although they can and do reproduce by the millions within your body cells. The way to help our bodies fight them is to make sure we get plenty of rest and sleep, don't get overtired, and eat well. Remember that habit-forming drugs are also profit-making; BARBITURATES are

probably our single greatest public-health problem after alcoholism.

The Pill Book, by Vito Perillo. Pipeline Books, Box 3711, Seattle, WA 98124. A handy guide (by colors as well as generic and brand names) to hundreds of drugs.

MEDICARE AND MEDICAID

Practically everybody over 65 is eligible for medical benefits under Medicare; apply two or three months before reaching 65. The cost goes up if you delay, and you may miss out on some benefits. Though Medicare has been a help to older people without much money, it only pays a part of their health costs, as there are deductibles and limitations of benefits, and they have to pay for drugs used outside of a hospital. Disabled people under 65 may also be entitled to Medicare.

You apply for a Medicare card at the local Social Security office. Take along something that will prove how old you are. This card enables you either to have your doctor send part of his bill directly to Medicare, or to get back part of the money if you pay the whole bill yourself and then apply for reimbursement to Medicare. In general, it is better to have the doctor bill Medicare directly, since you then don't have to put up the money and wait to be repaid. (You are supposed to get a complete record of the costs in either case, incidentally.) Also, you risk less in case the doctor is overcharging and Medicare refuses to pay its share of the total bill.

Medicare does not pay all of any medical bills. You still have to pay quite a bit yourself. There is always a deductible you have to pay yourself on hospital bills, plus the monthly charge you have to pay (or have deducted from your Social Security) for coverage of doctor bills, plus the first $60 of coverage of doctor bills each year (not each illness). The first three pints of blood in a transfusion aren't covered. And so on. Because of skyrocketing costs, you are therefore likely to be only a little better off than you would have been before Medicare. However, by the same token it's now almost essential for any elderly person to have Medicare, because otherwise medical costs are simply ruinous.

The Social Security office has a booklet on Medicare which explains how it works. Make sure you get one of these when you are approaching 65 so you are familiar with the program.

Medicare coverage extends to most kinds of hospital care (including psychiatric, up to one hundred days' lifetime total), operations, doctors' office calls and house calls (if you can get them), nursing, drugs, laboratory tests, X-rays, nursing-home and physical-therapy treatment, some care at home after being in the hospital, osteopathy, dental surgery (if related to the jaw or facial bones), and some drugs. Ambulance service is only covered if it's a real emergency, and only if you go to the nearest hospital or clinic. Emergency-room treatment, splints and casts, lab tests, and so on are covered, but eye examinations and glasses, hearing examinations and hearing aids, false teeth, orthopedic shoes, and immunizations are not.

Members of group health plans generally do not have to bother with filling out claim forms; the plan applies for repayment directly to Medicare, and you only have to worry about those few services which are not covered by the plan. This is another good reason for joining a pre-paid group practice plan or HEALTH MAINTENANCE ORGANIZATION.

While Medicare is a federal program and operates everywhere on the same basis, Medicaid is administered through the states (except for Arizona). You apply for it at the welfare office, and will generally be eligible only if you are also eligible for welfare, but state rules vary. People over 65 and the blind are also eligible, and some children. Medicaid will sometimes cover expenses that Medicare fails to cover, and it pays for a considerable range of doctor and hospital services; sometimes it pays for dental and eye care.

Both programs are massive. Eleven percent of the population is covered by Medicare, and almost as many by Medicaid programs. If you think you may be eligible, check into it.

MEDITATION, CONTEMPLATION, AND SITTING STILL

Americans are a busy lot, always rushing around doing things. We still have the guilty suspicion that if we aren't engaged in productive activity, we must be doing something wrong. This not only enables us to ignore our own and other people's feelings (because stopping to pay attention to them would interfere with "getting the job done") but it also enables us to get through life practically without ever noticing the fundamental realities of birth, growth, decay, death. We do not pay attention to ourselves in any serious way and we do violence to the natural order and to our fellow animals because they stand in the way of our "work."

Sitting down and doing nothing is, therefore, an intensely purposeful and difficult thing. For many Americans it is literally impossible; they get twitchy if they try it and soon jump up to do something or turn on television. This is why religions prescribe various rites for meditation which help you to focus down on your own being and cut out extraneous distractions: yoga exercises, the lotus position, breathing exercises. There are various special schools of meditation which you can read about or learn about from disciples in Zen groups and other organizations. If organized and ritualized groups do not interest you, however, you can still use meditation or contemplation as a private, personal defense against pressures that throw you off center. Many of our difficulties in confronting modern life arise because our sense of self is dissolved in the roles we must play: employee, students, soldier, customer. Sit down very quietly and become conscious of your biological existence; hear your heart beat, your breath go in and out. Pay attention to your immediate surroundings: the surface you are sitting on, the wall in front of you, the pressure of your clothes upon your skin, but try to empty your head of thoughts. If you can carry this far enough, a great feeling of pure being comes over you—it's not really describable in words, but you feel and at one with your body and the universe. By contrast with such a state, even if you only experience it briefly, the ordinary worries and tensions of daily life seem trivial and petty; when you return to the world of doing, you are likely to find your energies more concentrated and free-flowing.

MENTAL ILLNESS

Unfortunately, the breakdown of our society, which causes a great deal of mental illness, also leads to a lack of medical and psychiatric care for its victims. Our mental hospitals become prisons for the very "crazy," and pill dispensaries for the "crazy-acting." Psychotherapy on an intensive basis is available only to people who can afford expensive sessions. (Some of the cheapest and most effective "psychotherapy" comes from close friends.) Meanwhile, the desperate conditions of modern life continue to create new victims.

Most people who have "nervous breakdowns," "flip out," "go crazy" for a while, or "can't cope anymore" are driven into it by their situations in life—although of course early experiences influence how they deal with those situations. As a neighbor of mine once remarked, "Everybody has the right to be crazy in their own house." Harmless strangeness is a right, not a crime. But what can be done if a person behaves so strangely that family and friends can't take it? If you or someone close to you begins to have serious upsets, the first thing to do is to look at the situation. Serious emotional trouble, as shown by suicide attempts, persistent depression, wild behavior or talk, and so on, is often connected with serious real-life problems—it isn't "all in the head." So help from friends is often what is most needed. People who have breakdowns are seldom dangerous, unless severe depression or rage are obvious; indeed, the difference between "crazy" people and "sane" people is not as great as you might think—we all have some craziness in us. And most of us, if we can get some help from our friends or family, manage to get through our crises somehow.

Here are some basic things to think about. Is there trouble between members of the family, which is bearing down hard on the ill person? (It is partly because our mental anguish is often connected with our families that friends are usually of more help than immediate family members.) Is he or she going through difficult changes with authorities, on the job, or in relationships? Is the economic situation rocky? Is he or she living a solitary life, so that a lot of time is spent brooding alone, without any warm contact with other human beings? Has he or she lost touch with good friends or favorite relatives? (A person who needs friends should change environments, if that's what's needed to find some.)

These things, if they have gone bad, can sometimes be put to rights by concrete actions: a vacation, a change of scene by going to visit people you are fond of, or contact with old friends, ministers, or relatives who are understanding. Most Americans have mental and emotional difficulties at one time or another in life; it's nothing to be ashamed of. Nor is it something to be terrified of: most people, after a time, learn to cope with their problems fairly well, with or without the assistance of professional therapists.

They pretty well have to, because our facilities for dealing with mentally ill people are primitive, scarce, and void of friendly people. Mental hospitals, whose "treatment" consists of a couple of weeks of filling you full of tranquilizing drugs, send you back to "community mental health centers" lacking staff, organization, materials, and resources to help re-integrate you into "normal" life. Private psychotherapists are impossibly expensive for most people. In short, we must learn to do a better job of taking care of each other, sharing the responsibility for helping out in these difficult times—which will hit so many of us at some point or other.

In the past, it has often been possible to get people locked up quite easily—and once you get committed to a state mental hospital, it can be very hard to get out. In most states now, however, it is harder for relatives to put you away. A hearing must be held in a court, psychiatric examinations of a more than routine nature must be held, and you can get a lawyer to defend you rights. Furthermore, mental hospitals are now so overcrowded and understaffed that they are anxious to keep a rapid turnover of patients—so they too have largely resorted to tranquilizers, and after a month on pills they send you home. Mental hospitals probably create more mental illness than they help, but they do scare some people into getting better. In most mental hospitals you seldom see a psychiatrist, and when you do, it'll be only for brief periods. They are basically custodial institutions, and depressing besides. Stay away from them if you can, and if any friends get put away, help them get out and re-establish as normal a life as possible.

Some other smaller places can sometimes help mentally ill people. Medical schools usually have psychiatric departments with low fees. There are Suicide Prevention Bureaus in many major cities. They maintain a twenty-four-hour telephone switchboard which people can call and talk to when they feel at the end of their rope. (You can find them in the phone book.) There are "rap centers" connected with many Free Clinics, which are especially oriented toward drug problems. The Free Clinics are a good first source of help in bad trips; hospitalization should be a last resort.

As legislatures have become conscious of the great expense (and psychiatric futility) of keeping people in mental hospitals, they have tried to put the burden of caring for mental illness on local communities—which are unwilling and incapable of the task, as well as underfinanced. However, in a few cities (including New York) the mental-health departments have neighborhood storefront clinics, serving people where they live. Any community medical center is a good place to ask for information about mental-illness treatment. We will never have really suitable public treatment, however, because in the last analysis social stability and mental health depend on our friends and our values, not on professionals or institutions, however ideal it would be to have small clinics all over our cities, with home-visit nurses and aides available to visit people, help them work out their problems, and follow up when they have returned from the hospital. Local-control health services, like community control of schools and police, seem to be the only way we can ultimately get the kind of medical and mental-illness treatment that would be most acceptable and practical.

Medicare, incidentally, covers up to one hundred days in a mental hospital, on a lifetime basis. Health-insurance policies often have mental-illness coverage. Health maintenance organizations have increasingly extensive psychiatric facilities.

METRIC SYSTEM

There are many undeniable charms to the old system of feet, inches, ounces, pounds, etc., some of them literally feudal (the foot was supposedly the length of the king's foot, the yard his arm-spread). And for many practical purposes, like carpentry, the degree of precision offered by our traditional divisions into quarters or eighths or sixteenths is just about right, whereas the millimeter (less than the width of a saw blade) is too precise and a half-centimeter can seem an alien quantity.

New nomenclature always seems strange for a while, and like any kind of new idea it generally triumphs only after the generation accustomed to the old has died, and the new generation finds the new idea familiar and easy. In the meantime, there's always confusion and noisy arguments. So, no doubt, it will be with metrication in the US and the few other countries which have remained on other systems. In abstract principle, a measuring and arithmetic system based upon the root 12 instead of 10 would have many handy advantages, but we don't really have that option—just as in the economic world we really don't have the option of isolationism within our own borders, where we could use measurements based on the length of the president's nose if we felt like it.

The great virtues of the metric system (though various complicating refinements have been developed in the scientific community) lie in its simplicity. In metric, you never face problems of how many tablespoons make a cup, or how many cups in a pint, or how many feet or yards to the mile. Everything is in neat units of tens or hundreds or thousands. They convert and interrelate with magical ease.

But of course you have to get used to knowing instinctively roughly how much a liter is, or a kilo, or a meter. This task has been successfully carried out by about four billion other human beings, including a billion or so children, so you shouldn't be too intimidated. In my experience it's a waste of time to try to work out exact metric equivalents mathematically. (A nice chart of them, however, is available from T & E Enterprises, Santa Monica, CA 90405.) If you go abroad, of course, you *will* have to learn metric, and quickly. But around home you can work into it gradually. Get yourself a meter stick (which is just a bit longer than a yardstick) and start using it for carpentry or sewing measurements; you can find one at a good hardware store. If you buy a household or kitchen scale, make sure it has metric figures, and the same for a thermometer. Then after a bit you can put tape over the avoirdupois and Fahrenheit numbers, which will force you to get the "feel" of the metric quantities. In time you might even want to switch to a cookbook with metric recipes and get metric measuring utensils.

And, for your children's benefit, make sure they know how to use metric terms or at least know what they mean. Then, even if the more picturesque English measures persist in some areas of life, they'll have the "vocabulary" to deal with manufactured items—made to metric measurements in the rest of the world—and the metric familiarity increasingly required by jobs, travel, or scientific work.

MICROWAVE OVENS

There are some appealing aspects to microwave ovens: they cook or warm things rapidly and with some energy savings. But many of them leak microwave radiation into their surroundings, and the dangers connected with them have not yet been satisfactorily measured. Microwaves cook flesh (the eyeballs are particularly sensitive, and people working at radar stations have sometimes developed cataracts) and they may well have other, subtler effects; scientists in Eastern Europe have set safety standards 10,000 time more stringent than ours, and they may know something we don't—perhaps about the effects of microwaves on the delicate electronic patterns of the brain.

The wisest personal strategy is to avoid microwaves whenever you can. Keep your children (who love to peer into oven windows) away from any microwave ovens in your friends' houses. Be aware that certain kinds of ceramics are unsafe in microwave ovens because dangerous substances leak out of their glazes into your food. Don't sit near the microwave oven in restaurants; don't have one in your house; if your apartment neighbor has one next to a shared wall, try to cut down your use of the area near it. (Microwaves pass through ordinary wall construction; metal screens or even aluminum foil will obstruct them.) Commercial and military radar installations, along with television stations, are other major sources of microwaves in our environment; try never to live close to one, especially in their "line of fire." In time, television should be reduced to a cable-only system, which will not only enable it to become a two-way communications system with greatly increased channel capacity, but cut down on microwave emanations.

MIGRATION

Most people move to another city or region chiefly in hopes that finding a job will be easier there—and they tend to go to places where they have relatives or friends to whom they can turn for help in learning the ropes. Unfortunately, many of the rumors you hear about plentiful jobs in other places turn out to be false; the country as a whole has a surprisingly inefficient distribution of jobs—there are whole regions which have serious unemployment problems (such as California and Oregon) but keep attracting new people anyway. If you are contemplating a move, try to get really specific advice from your contacts, and try to get some reliable information on jobs by visiting your library and asking the reference librarian for help; also, write to the department of employment of the state you are considering, and ask what the situation is there. They will probably be glad to reply, for states are anxious not to add to their unemployed. Alaska goes so far as to maintain a special warning office in the Seattle airport to steer hopeful job seekers away.

Another good way to find out about both jobs and other aspects of life in a city you might move to is to subscribe by mail to their local newspaper. Besides studying the want ads on jobs, houses, and so on, you can get some feel of whether the style of the city might suit you.

A recent Supreme Court decision makes one eligible for welfare in a new state without waiting out the former residence requirement period, so the risks of migrating are now a bit less severe; but remember that a welfare department can often find some other reason to disqualify you, and in the

difficult financial situation of the 80's is almost certain to try to do so.

MILK

The food value of milk is so high that, if necessary, you could subsist for days on practically nothing else. It has recently been discovered, however, that this is true only for people who, like Western Europeans, have a strong dairying tradition and whose digestive systems preserve the enzyme lactase into adulthood—adults in some other cultures can't digest milk well and develop stomach upsets if they consume much of it. In addition, cow's milk (which after all is presumably adapted to consumption by calves) causes allergic reactions in considerable number of children, and sometimes in adults.

If your diet is going to be lean or deficient for a while because you can't afford anything but beans and rice and a few vegetables, try to get together enough money to buy a twenty-five-pound bag of non-fat dried-milk—which will last you a long, long time, even if you drink several quarts a day.

Buying milk can use up a big chunk of the food bill. It's money well spent, no doubt of that—especially for families with children. However obnoxious you may find the "Drink More Milk" propaganda of the dairy industry, it's not a bad idea to drink plenty of non-fat milk.

There are two kinds of milk, wet and dry. Each one has special characteristics and ideal uses. Whole wet milk is fatty or creamy. It must be refrigerated or it spoils. It has to be brought home in heavy containers. It costs about three times what dry milk costs, and low-fat or non-fat ("skim") wet milk is only slightly cheaper. Do not burn wet-milk cartons, incidentally; their inside plastic coating will give off a poisonous gas.

Dry milk is almost always "non-fat." When you mix it up, therefore, it has a distinctly different taste. Besides being much cheaper, it is more compact to store, as it doesn't need refrigeration until it's mixed; just keep it in a cool cupboard with the container tightly closed to prevent staleness.

Dry milk needs to be colder when you drink it than does whole milk. Its protein or body-building power is equal to whole milk; it lacks only vitamins A and D. (Sometimes it is, however, fortified with these vitamins. Check the label. Unless you get a lot of vitamin D from other foods, you may want to take vitamin D capsules.) From a health standpoint, it is much superior to whole milk because of its small amount of fat.

In general, dried milk is a much better deal and it's wise to use as much of it as possible. If you do drink wet milk, get used to the non-fat type—you can switch to it gently by using "low-fat" milk for a week or two, and then gradually mixing non-fat with it. If you or your family are heavy milk drinkers, this can make an enormous difference in your fat and cholesterol intake.

Most people who have not been brought up on dried milk don't know how to mix and use it. The directions on the package are not always very good. Here's how: Use a *big* jar, preferably a two-quart pickle jar or something, the bigger the better, so long as it will fit in your refirgerator. Dried milk is like beer: it improves with age, over a day or so, so you want to mix as much up at once as you can. You use about one-third as much power as water. The best way to get the powder dissolved is to put it in with about half a jar full of water, and then shake vigorously; this is much better than stirring, and also more fun. (Put some music on the record player!) Set it down—in the refrigerator if the house is warm—until the foam settles. Then fill the jar with cold water.

Try to mix up your supply of milk well in advance of when you'll drink it. It takes several hours for the flavor to develop, and it also takes time for the refrigerator to cool it down. I have found that a good time to mix it is after supper, during the clean-up period; then the next day's supply is ready in the morning

Cooking with dried milk presents no problems. Where a recipe calls for a cup of milk, put about five tablespoons of dried milk and three-quarters of a cup of water. You can use it this way in soups and chowders, baked foods, stews, omelets, puddings, and so on. To increase the protein in baked foods, you can also replace up to a quarter of the flour in recipes with dried milk powder. (This makes them get a little browner.) You can also strengthen the protein in meatloaf, mashed potatoes, sauces, and hot cereals by adding a little milk powder.

There are even some recipes that *require* dry milk rather than wet. You can get these from the American Dry Milk Institute, 130 North Franklin Street, Chicago, IL 60606.

Further tips about milk: you can put added protein in regular milk by stirring some dried milk into it. (This is especially good for pregnant or nursing mothers, or growing children.) Yogurt and buttermilk are not particularly cheap, but they are tasty and provide about the same nourishment as regular non-fat wet milk. Evaporated milk, in cans, is also cheaper than wet milk, but it tends to spoil if kept in the can. (Avoid sweetened "condensed" milk, which has a huge sugar content.) Milk keeps almost a week in the refrigerator. Don't let milk stand in the sunlight—that destroys its riboflavin and changes the taste.

In heating milk for drinks, puddings, and so on, use a low heat. At high temperatures milk forms a film and may scorch, giving it a funny flavor. Acids, such as lemon or tomato juice, may cause milk to curdle.

You can whip canned evaporated milk as well as cream. The secret is to get the bowl, mixer, and liquid very cold (evaporated milk should go into the freezer compartment to chill until ice crystals form around the edges). Never buy pressure-can whipped cream or pseudo whipped cream. It costs a fortune and doesn't taste nearly as good as ordinary whipped cream. You can make whipped cream with a whisk; you don't really need a mixer, hand-operated *or* electric.

Keep milk and milk products tightly covered, since they tend to pick up odors from other foods.

In some places, through the connivance of local or state governments, vitamin D reinforced milk is allowed to cost more than plain milk, though the actual cost of adding it is virtually nothing. Lack of vitamin D causes rickets—a disease which was supposedly wiped out many years ago, but which is still found among people with poor diets. Buy vitamin D milk if it's available; even if it costs a little more, it's cheaper than buying vitamin pills. And protest to your representatives about the unfair penalty to health if reinforced milk costs more in your region.

It is also desirable to pressure milk suppliers and local authorities to provide milk that is not homogenized. There is some evidence that homogenization, especially of whole milk, results in fat particles so tiny that they can pass through cell walls into the blood without going through the digestion process. But non-homogenized milk is so far available only in a few places, usually in the form of "raw" (unpasteurized) whole milk. What we need is non-homogenized non-fat milk.

MIRRORS

Every house needs a more or less full-length mirror—women and men both like them, and it's also important for young children to get some idea of what they look like. New mirrors are expensive, but secondhand stores sell mirrors at reasonable cost, especially when they have a cracked corner or a little patch of the silvery backing flaking off. But check that the mirror is really flat—stand back at least ten feet from it and see if it gives a true reflection. A wavy mirror is madness-making. It's best to have a good flat mirror, even if it has small defects or an unaesthetic frame (you can always take a frame off or replace it).

MOBILE HOMES

In the Ecotopian future, with an abundant supply of timber reestablished through an active reforestation and forest management program, most permanent dwellings will be constructed of wood, which is the most satisfying material for human beings to spend a lot of time around in all but very hot climates. However, we will always have a need for light, movable, and inexpensive dwelling space—a need which we presently meet with "mobile homes," most of which never move, but possess wheels in order to escape the requirements of the housing code. Someday we will have extruded houses, or molded houses, made from biosource and biodegradable plastics or other factory-built dwellings produced on a truly continuous-process basis, which will make them very cheap.

At present, however, few families of average income can afford to buy a house of any kind, and they are therefore turning to mobile homes. In 1977, 67% of all new dwelling selling for under $35,000 were mobile homes. There are something like 24,000 mobile home communities in the country, containing more than 1,800,000 homes; an equal number of mobile homes exist on individual sites, most of them in rural areas. (Some counties allow separate mobile homes, some do not.) In the 1970 census, 8 million people were living in mobile homes. The number will probably rise steadily in the future, and "stacked" developments, in which mobile homes are parked on "shelves" in high rises, seem likely for urban areas. Many towns which formerly turned up their noses at mobile homes are now beginning to allow them on ordinary town lots.

Financing for mobile homes has increasingly come to resemble that for conventional houses, with VA and FHA loans available for 12- to 20-year terms. Construction and fire safety requirements have been formalized, so that the structures increasingly resemble a cheapened standard house. Unfortunately, no significant amount of architectural taste or creativity has ever been devoted to mobile home designs; they are almost universally graceless. Generally mobile homes are sold complete with appliances and furniture; their deficient insulation often makes an air conditioner standard equipment. Their average square feet of interior space has steadily risen, from 732 square feet in 1970 to 1,105 in 1977.

People planning to build a house themselves in the country often find it a good idea to live in a mobile home while they're doing it, and in town, if you plan to do a serious remodeling job, you might want to park a trailer in the driveway and live in it for the period when the house is totally torn up. Generally urban trailer "parks" are depressing places, though some of the new ones (which usually have only around 150-175 sites) have trees, green areas, and a spacious feel. Since many parks provide a central recreation area where laundry, playgrounds, and other common facilities are located, they often generate quite a feeling of community. Traffic inside generally moves slowly (if road bumps aren't installed, they should be) and children are safer than on ordinary streets. Check out a possible park on a hot day, however; the expanses of asphalt and close proximity to other people's windows (and radios) can be hopeless disadvantages.

Some parks are mainly inhabited by older people, or by very conservative folks. It is time for parks to be established to cater to other tastes as well: students, or professional couples, for example. Such parks would generate a market for mobile homes with higher design standards.

While most mobile homes are owner-occupied, there are usually some for rent. There is a brisk market in used mobile homes which are available for far below the cost of any kind of fixed house. Lot rentals for space to park them on often cost more than the monthly mortgage on the mobile home itself, but vary widely.

If you are actually interested in mobility, you may want to consider living in a camper, recreational vehicle, or converted potato-chip truck. As gas prices have risen, RV's have become quite inexpensive. (Some of them only get a half-dozen miles per gallon, and desperate owners have taken to torching them and trying to collect on the insurance.) But if you don't drive it much, an RV can be a fine way to live.

MOPS

One of the jolly little swindles that keep American businesses going is in mops. The old string-type mops are a mess to handle, and you really need a bucket with a wringer to dry them between swabs at the floor. Hence someone invented the mop with a sponge and a little lever to squash the sponge and get the water out. This was so clever, in fact, that many mop companies started making them. But each mop company shaped its device a little differently, and each company designed a slightly different replacement sponge, with a different method of attaching it to the handle. This ensured that nobody could replace a Brand X sponge with a Brand Y sponge, and since Brand X ones are likely to be out of stock at any given time, this means that you can chase around a long time before finding one that matches. Worse still, you may try to make the Brand Y sponge fit. But it won't.

Since the objective of the mop companies is to make all replacement sponges practically useless so that the harried mopper will buy a new mop each time and maybe waste some replacement sponges besides, they keep changing even their own designs. Thus, if you buy a Brand X mop this year and go back for a replacement sponge next year, you will have a surprise. By drilling new holes, you may be able to use the new type. But then again you may not.

Your only possible recourse is to march into the store with your mop and ask the clerk to put a new sponge on it. The chances are about 99 to 1 that clerks won't be able to do it, even if they are willing to unwrap the sacred cellophane packages. You then ask to see the manager, pointing out that you bought the mop less than a year ago, paying a hefty price for it, and how come its sponge can't be replaced? (You talk in a loud voice in scenes like this and wave the old mop handle around, and complain about stores not standing behind their merchandise.) If you're lucky they will simply give you a new mop to stop you from discouraging sales to other customers.

When you come back for a replacement sponge the next year, of course, you'll find that there is another crop, and that none of the new sponges fit either. This is known as progress. Maybe it explains why American Indians got along with dirt floors.

Mop sponges may be a fertile area in which to try STOCKING UP.

MOTORCYCLES, MOTORBIKES, MOPEDS AND SCOOTERS

Some people ride motorcycles for economy and convenience, but many get hooked on the sheer excitement of it: you're in direct contact with the rushing air, so that it seems more like flying than driving; you're in direct physical command of the machine, which won't even stand up without you. (You're also, of course, in more direct peril of your life, and have something like a four times greater chance of accidents than in driving a car, which is the most dangerous activity that most people engage in.) You can ride on dirt tracks, over hills, through trees, even through creeks—where only a four-wheel-drive car could go. You can park between buildings, between cars, under stairways or porches, usually (though not always legally) on the edge of sidewalks. And, unlike riding a bicycle, you can carry a passenger with you.

You can now buy a light motorcycle new for only a few hundred dollars; it's by far the cheapest motorized transportation around. Used cycle prices, however, may not be as low as you'd hope— you can rarely get a cycle that's in safe operating condition for the amount that will sometimes get you a working car. Gas expenses, on the other hand, are far less; and as gas prices rise, more people will certainly turn to two-wheeled vehicles for their basic transportation needs.

Hundreds of thousands of people even now ride small Japanese cycles, for pleasure, to work, and around town. A light machine with an engine displacement of 125 cubic centimeters or less will easily keep up with town traffic. A slightly larger machine will handle anything you'll encounter on the highways. (In learning to ride, make sure you have an experienced teacher, and develop a healthy respect for the power in even a small engine, or you may quite literally flip out.)

In the past, motorcyclists tended to be mostly mechanic types who loved to putter with their cycles. Nowadays repair service is widespread enough that you don't really have to do your own work—though it will give you a sense of security in remote places if you learn how to handle basic repairs. (Although cycle repairs are generally cheaper than auto repairs, doing your own work can still save you a good deal of money.) The engine and transmission of a heavy cycle are as complex as those in cars. One great advantage of the light new machines is that they have two-cycle engines: removal of cylinder heads is simplified, and so is transmission work. However, this simplicity of construction is paid for by faster wear, since their moving parts move faster. They are also noisier and smellier.

People who entrust their lives to a cycle should learn how to check it over carefully for worn parts.

A frayed cable or loose nut could cause you to lose control at a fatal moment. Check your tire pressures often: low pressure can allow a tire to rotate on the rim and cause trouble just when you least need it—in fast acceleration or braking. Make sure your brakes and lights are always in perfect working order; a motorcycle is a small, light, and difficult-to-see object in heavy traffic.

Riders of really big bikes, whose engines have more than a thousand cubic centimeters and may develop more horsepower than a light car, say there is nothing like them for speed, comfort, and the pure joy of movement. But a tiny Yamaha or Honda 50 will get you around, and at far less cost than a car. Mopeds, which can usually be pedalled to start them up or if the motor fails for some reason, get fantastic mileage. They require no driver's license, can be parked in bicycle racks or on the sidewalk, and will keep up with street traffic. They are generally user-repairable. Their operating costs are around a penny a mile. Such light bikes are safer than scooters, which were developed in Italy for dodging through foot traffic—they're very maneuverable but have small wheels and high motors and are thus not so stable.

Once you are an experienced rider, you can not only borrow cycles but also rent them, if you need transportation briefly or in a distant city.

Being a good passenger. The rider of a motorcycle steers and controls it by small movements that redistribute the weight slightly. As a passenger, you should not try to anticipate the movements or "help" steer. Keep your feet on the pegs and keep your body like a rigid part of the bike, your weight squarely on the saddle, with as little wiggling around as possible. Hang on tight to the rider or the hand grip; a hunched-over posture may be the most comfortable on long rides. (Frequent rest stops are a good idea in cars, and even better on bikes.) Wear shoes and heavy clothing for protection against the wind and in case of a spill. Women should not let long hair loose—it will fly up around their faces and may flick dangerously across the driver's face as well. For safety, passenger as well as rider should wear good crash helmets. It's hard and distracting to talk on a bike, so develop signals for stopping, warning of cops, giving road directions, and so on.

NEW FAMILY CONCERNS

Adoption and foster-parenting. Children available for adoption are no longer in over-supply, and indeed a sort of black market has developed, in which babies are sometimes "sold" even before they are born. Normal adoption, however, is a legal process, and one in which the state takes a proper interest on behalf of the child's welfare. A court must approve adoptions, usually on the recommendations of social workers who have interviewed the prospective parent(s) and checked on the home situation. Retaining the services of a lawyer is usually a good idea, and you will certainly need one if you are single, over 45, of a different race than the child, and so on. The tendency in recent years has been toward evaluating the actual psychological and social characteristics of the people wishing to adopt, rather than relying on traditional notions of "normalcy." In some areas, even single men (including gay men) able to provide a good environment for a child have been able to adopt.

Many older children are in need of foster homes —whether because of deaths in or dissolutions of their biological families, incompatibility with parents or step-parents, or emotional difficulties. Our society includes an astonishing number of people—some but not all with strong religious orientations—who undertake to provide good homes for these young people. Such relationships obviously make demands on both parties that go beyond the usual stresses of parenthood, but they sometimes offer unusual rewards as well. In addition, foster children placed through government agencies bring with them substantial child-support funds, and foster-parenting thus makes economic sense for some parents. It is certainly not, of course, anything to enter into lightly, or just for the money.

Childbirth. For certain knowledgable parts of our population, there has been a notable improvement in birth conditions. Hospital delivery rooms and labor rooms have been revamped as tolerable human environments; medical attendants have grown in understanding of the birth and nursing processes; the dangers of drugging mothers during delivery are known; the possibility of rooming-in arrangements facilitates rather than obstructs satisfactory beginning of nursing. In a few hospitals, quiet, low-lit surroundings are provided to give the baby a relatively comfortable first experience of life in the outside world. Sometimes the Leboyer warm bath immediately after birth is available, with dim lights and little noise or commotion. And in some areas midwives are available for home deliveries—who, in Britain and Holland, have a better medical record than our hospital deliveries.

Unfortunately, however, these advances are extremely spotty, and even parents living in relatively enlightened communities may have to work hard to find and be able to utilize facilities that seem decent to them. One strategy is, of course, simply to leave the hospital as soon as practicable after birth. For an easy, and especially a non-first birth, this may be in a few hours. For most women with no complications, it should be early the next day.

Many obstetricians are still obstinately non-cooperative with women who wish to give birth without anesthetic, in one of a number of "natural childbirth" methods. Some will promise to cooperate and then renege—which the father's presence in the delivery room may be able to prevent. (His presence is of course highly desirable for other reasons! This is especially true of the Lamaze method, where it is generally the father's role to lend support, time contractions, and generally monitor and facilitate the labor process.) Contrary to common belief, the number of drugs being given to women in gestation, labor and delivery is rising. Episiotomies, though not required in many deliveries, are done as a matter of routine. Caesarian deliveries have been rising sharply in frequency, even though research has shown they are often not necessary. As in the case of episiotomy, the motive seems to be legal prudence—protection against possible malpractice suits rather than medical prudence.

The drugging of mothers during delivery often may affect infants during the first years of life, causing losses in IQ and motor development. (Characteristically, the NIH research study establishing this was withheld and only obtained for public dissemination through a Freedom of Information Act suit.) In some cases, of course, an anesthetic is truly needed for delivery, and may well be the only reasonable procedure. But medical and public policy should attempt to minimize it. It is scandalous that many doctors and hospitals still regard parents' desires to have drug-free births as bizarre. Do your best to find an obstetrician and hospital with whom you can be comfortable.

Moreover, though no one quite knows why, babies who have protracted close contact with their mothers in their first hours after birth (rather than being snatched away by nurses) turn out to have significantly higher IQ's at age 5. Attention from fathers also leads to calmer, happier babies.

Actually, hospitals are unpleasant places to be in under any circumstances, and especially for a joyous event like a birth. They are also extremely expensive. Home births allow the entire family to participate in the birth. This is one of the strangest, strongest experiences a human being can have—reminding us where we have all come from, and putting us in touch again with the biological basis of our being. A birth ought to be a happy human occasion, and not treated as a medical "problem" or emergency. An expectant mother should have the right to have her baby where she pleases, providing that she makes proper arrangements.

There are people who deliver their own babies, and some will tell you that the risks are small. In reality, childbirth risks are sometimes large, both for mother and baby. This is why home delivery should only be considered under carefully arranged conditions: (1) proper prenatal care and examinations by an obstetrician or trained and experienced midwife who can tell whether the baby is in position for normal delivery; (2) a normal labor (not over twenty-four hours, no bleeding, fever, or other unusual factors); (3) supervision of the birth by a doctor, ideally the same one who has supervised the pregnancy; (4) definite arrangements with friends for immediate and rapid transportation to a nearby hospital in the event of complications; (5) faithful participation by the mother and father in natural-childbirth training procedures. Generally speaking, these conditions can only be met in cities where there are sympathetic, sophisticated doctors and easily reachable hospitals. They are especially necessary for mothers having their first baby, who may panic in a hard labor, even with the best preparation and greatest devotion. It is also desirable to have the support and advice of experienced friends, who can help you prepare for the birth. Since two lives may be at stake, childbirth is not a matter where heroism is to be considered more of a virtue than caution. If you have trouble, head for a hospital.

Generally the mother should take it easy for the first twenty-four hours after a home delivery, only getting out of bed to go to the bathroom. On the second day she can take a shower and begin to resume her activity gradually. It helps to have a woman friend around who has had a couple of children and whom you trust to have both good instincts and accurate information.

Many mothers find it difficult to begin breastfeeding a first child in a hospital, where the atmosphere may be discouraging and where some nurses disapprove of breastfeeding. Here again, the help of reliable friends is your best defense.

The next best thing to having your baby at home is to have it in the hospital, but go home twenty-four hours later. Some doctors actually encourage this practice. Even if yours doesn't, there's not much he or she can do about it, as you are free to leave at will.

Babies born at home need to be examined (by a pediatrician if possible) within twenty-four hours at the most.

Since 1978, childbirth has been legally classified as a "disability," along with certian complications during pregnancy. This means that (if you work in a company with 15 or more employees) your health plan must cover pregnancy and delivery like any other medical situation. The actual birth period qualifies as sick leave, as would absences caused by nausea or varicose veins during pregnancy.

The Birth Primer, by Rebecca Row Parfitt. Running Press, 38 South 19th St., Philadelphia, PA 19103.

Immaculate Deception: A New Look at Women & Childbirth in America, by Suzanne Arms. Bantam Books, 1975.

Birth Without Violence, by Frederick Leboyer. Knopf, 1975.

Infant care. There seems to be some primordial urge to wash off a newborn baby, but this should not be done for at least a week; the baby is born with a coating of grease on its skin, which is necessary to its protection. After a week, sponge baths are OK, but all-over wetting should wait until the belly button is healed.

Newborn babies are often covered up too heavily by worried parents. So long as the room is reasonably warm, they need only light covering. (Too much may give them heat rashes.) A diaper and a lightweight blanket is all the "clothes" a new baby needs; after a couple of days you can add an undershirt. If the weather is warm, new babies can be taken outdoors—a little sunlight does them good, but don't overdo it.

Mothers and fathers used to feel tied down to the house with a new baby, but in fact young babies are more "portable" than older ones. You can carry them easily; they sleep a great deal of the time; and as long as the breast or bottle is handy they will be happy.

There are important biological and psychological advantages to breastfeeding, though bottle-fed babies also develop well. Breast milk contains substances that cut down the risk of infections. Moreover, breastfeeding frees the mother from all the paraphernalia of bottles and sterilizing; besides being the natural way to feed babies, with the best milk they could get, it is handy. But propaganda for bottles as a "modern" method prevailed in this country for several decades, so many women have not learned from their mothers or friends how breastfeeding is done. The better hospitals are helpful to new mothers about it; and pediatricians (baby doctors) are too; if yours isn't, you should change to one who is. A new mother's greatest worries about her baby usually center on feeding. There is nothing more terrifying than the thought your baby may not be getting enough to eat—and it's your fault. Luckily, however, few mothers are truly unable to breastfeed; the human breast and the baby it feeds are ideally adapted to each other, or the race would have died out long ago. The only other thing a young baby needs is an occasional few drops of vitamin D.

It takes a couple of days to get the nursing going well. If you encounter problems your experienced friends can't help you with, or your doctor can't help you as you think he or she should, get in touch with the local LaLeche League—an organization of experienced nursing mothers, who help each other with any problems. Don't be afraid to ask for help. It's too important a thing to give up on easily. And then you'll be able to show friends or your daughters how it's done. (As an added bonus, it is a great and surprising advantage of breastfeeding that the feces of breast-fed babies smell sweet until they begin to eat solid foods.)

See CHILDREN.

The Well Baby Book, by Mike Samuels, M.D. and Nancy Samuels. Summit Books, 1979.
Nursing Your Baby, by Karen Pryor. Pocket Books, 1973.

Pets. In Ecotopian conditions, pets are rare—people obtain emotional consolation from other human beings, and lavish emotion upon each other rather than dependent animals; when they keep small animals, it is generally to serve as practical helpers—sheepdogs or mouse-catchers. We are not so lucky in our emotional support systems as the Ecotopians, and amid the alienation, loneliness and despair prevalent in our society, many a dog is its owner's literal best friend, and many a cat is the chief source of grace and calm in a harried life.

A relationship with a dog can be as complex and intense as one with a child; moreover, dogs often serve as an emotional lightning rod through which families discharge emotions just as well not discharged on each other. People also get dogs for protection; remember, though, that training a big dog to be under your control can be almost as demanding for several months as bringing up a child. But above all, having a dog gives you a window into the life of another species; if you let your dog have a natural social life (which many cities prohibit through leash laws) you can observe the clear territorial rules, the established dominance-submission patterns, and the sexual rites which make canine life, if freely led, so much better than the "dog's life" it is often imagined to be.

Through our dogs we may also get in touch with a neglected—in fact largely taboo—aspect of our own emotional lives. Sexual attraction in humans, as in other animals, is directly connected to the sense of smell. Hygiene handbooks never mention it, much less cosmetic ads, but the fact is that some people's smells make us feel good and some make us uneasy. Smell, though no one lists it as a factor in marital compatibility, may indeed be more important in how people get along than physical appearance, religious beliefs or politics. We never get used to smells that don't please and reassure us.

Usually the sense of sight is thought to be our dominant sense. But sight is rather impersonal and neutral, and it is connected to our brains through an intermediate sifting-out circuit. The nose, however, is plugged in directly; its signals affect us, directly and overwhelmingly, though not so subtly as a dog's. Sooner or later, wise people realize that they have to relax and trust their sense of smell.

But such sensibilities can, of course, be cultivated without the presence of a dog; and we can't avoid the ethical questions involved in keeping pets. Relations between humans and other animals pose serious moral dilemmas and it is no longer only vegetarians who are conscious of them. Humans used to tell themselves, in the name of the Jehovah they invented in their own image, that they had been given dominion over the fish, fowl, and other animals of the earth. This anthropocentric notion has led us to imprison and kill other animals without a thought, whenever it suited our convenience. But if we are serious about extending to other species the kind of consideration we would like to have for ourselves, we must question whether we wish to kill and eat them; whether we wish to shape them genetically and keep them in limited artificial habitats like feedlots and smelly cramped cages; and finally, whether we wish to subject them to emotional and practical dependence on human households.

This is not the same question as whether pets are "happy"; like humans, dogs and cats are adaptable to many conditions, though it is surely unkind to keep large dogs, whose biology equips them for pack life and running fast over long distances, cooped up alone most of the time in city apartments or even backyards. Real love for animals, in my opinion, means trying to help them live in conditions their evolutionary history has suited them for; and such conditions are rarely available in cities.

In any case, if you decide to keep a pet, you should understand that it is a serious and lasting responsibility, both psychologically and financially. Inoculations for rabies and other diseases are essential; vet bills can run high. Spaying, which is the only way to prevent your pet adding to an already bulging population of unwanted puppies and kittens, is expensive. And food for a pet, even if you feed it mostly table scraps, will cost a surprising amount. Dry foods tend to be cheaper than canned ones. Accustom your pet to them from the beginning.

Humane societies and animal shelters are full of healthy, well-trained animals available for adoption; check your phone book.

Single parenting. The supposedly "normal" nuclear family of the past (father works, mother stays home with two children) is now a small minority of American households—less than one-sixth, in fact. "Blended families," including step-parents and step-siblings, are increasingly common—since most divorced people remarry, often with other divorced persons who may also have children. At current rates, two out of five children will spend at least part of their childhood or adolescence in single-parent homes; in 1975, 11 million children lived with their mothers and 1 million with their fathers.

Single parenting, thus, is an overwhelming reality of American life, but we have not, as a society, developed satisfactory ways of dealing with it. In many communities, some stigma still attaches to divorce, especially if children are involved, and divorcing parents' friends may express unwarranted and counterproductive pity in such cases. In fact, as various careful studies have established, children after divorce do at least as well emotionally as children whose unhappy homes have remained "intact." Nor do children of divorced parents have higher rates of juvenile delinquency, school problems, or sexual identity problems; it is at least as possible to become warped by two unsatisfactory parents as it is by one! Most children and adolescents recover from the pain and confusion of divorce fairly readily, unless one or both parents configure it as a matter of lasting and earth-shaking trauma. If the parents establish satisfying lives for themselves, and do not fall into patterns of conflict over the children, the children may even experience positive benefits from the divorce—for example, in receiving more and higher-quality attention, especially from the father. Single-parent children may have higher verbal skills, and they may be more socially mature, doubtless because of greater closeness to the parent. If you are a single parent and your child is having some kind of emotional difficulty, don't leap to the conclusion that it is due to your status as single parent. All children go through developmental stages that give them some trouble. Read a child-development book, or check with other parents, before you convince yourself that something is terribly wrong. (In this and other situations, watch out for unconscious—and unjustified—feelings of guilt.)

It is obviously critical for ex-spouses to transcend their grievances and establish fair and healthy visitation schedules or child residence-sharing. In recent years, many couples who parted on relatively good terms have found joint legal custody an attractive arrangement (though many older judges still view it with distaste). It establishes shared responsibility for the child; it symbolizes that both parents still love and will care for the child. Instead of opting for the child to live entirely with one or the other parent, it encourages more extended living (summers, or alternate months when ex-spouses live nearby) with both parents. Contrary to earlier fears, many parents who got along acrimoniously while living together turn out to be able to cooperate quite decently toward their children's welfare once they are separated. Custody is also given to fathers much more frequently today, and _ is sometimes the best solution. A court fight over custody is expensive and almost certain to be harmful to both children and parents. (Most children of divorced parents who *do* have serious emotional disturbances have parents unable to agree how the children should be raised, with consequent inconsistency and quarrels.)

The greatest hazards of the single parent are isolation and poverty. Single mothers, especially, sometimes find themselves isolated from their friends or other steady adult contact—and prolonged exposure to nobody but children can drive you off the deep end. Some newly divorced parents embark on a sexually open lifestyle, as if to make up for the time they lost while unhappily married. They may segregate their sexual lives from their home lives, so that their sexual partners are not real participants in their or their children's lives. This is unwise both from your standpoint (since it doesn't help your general isolation) and your children's (since it gives them no adult life to learn from). Your reality is that you are both a parent and a sexual person. This is a reality that children can accept, and accept better than they tolerate concealment or deception.

But no matter how you manage them, sexual relationships alone cannot constitute a healthy social life. You need to pay conscious attention to building up a solid, sustaining friendship network. You can start with other single parents, for which churches and other organizations have special groups. But make sure that you pursue genuine interests of your own, as well as seeking company; you are most appealing to other people when you are following up things that really mean something to you.

And you may wish to consider joining forces with one or more other single parents, and living together in one household, or in adjacent apartments or houses. In this way you can provide each other regular moral support, exchange child care, cut down on everybody's cooking and laundry chores, and generally make your home life more interesting. It's important, of course, to explore beforehand your basic ground rules about rent-sharing, overnight visitors, housekeeping responsibilities, and so on, to avoid surprises later.

Since most single parents are women, they are generally economically disadvantaged. (The average single father makes twice what the average single mother makes.) Only about 20% of all divorced and separated mothers receive child support regularly; another 7% receive it occasionally. Only 8% of all divorced or separated women receive any alimony at all. Many mothers who work fulltime may have incomes so low that they qualify for welfare; don't be ashamed to look into it! Extensive training programs exist for single mothers; inquire about them at the state employment office. There are also "earned income credits" for women who earn below a certain amount. And of course AFDC welfare programs apply to divorced, abandoned, or never-married mothers.

NOISE POLLUTION

Our organisms evolved to be very sensitive to noises, since we needed to hear the approach of predators or other dangers to survive. If you manage to spend any time in a wilderness area that is not overflown by airplanes or helicopters, you will probably be astonished (and perhaps alarmed) at your ability to hear tiny cracklings of twigs or rustling noises, which your mind may transform into rattlesnakes or marauding bears.

This delicate sensing mechanism is overwhelmed by the intensity of sound to which we customarily subject it, especially in cities. Transmission of sound in the inner ear involves microscopic hair cells which in many people are damaged by loud noises. This is the mechanism by which truck drivers, rock musicians, and heavy industry workers habitually exposed to loud noise become deaf. But this damage begins at sound intensities around 85 decibels—a level often achieved by a vacuum cleaner, power saw, lawnmower, or motorcycle. Noise pollution is thought to be a substantial contributor to deafness rates and to hearing losses in the high-frequency ranges.

But noise pollution probably has far worse effects on our general health and well-being. Evolution has also given us a superb "startle response" to loud noises: hearing the saber-tooth tiger's growl, our ancestors leaped out of the way, insulin charging their muscles instantly, heart rate surging, breathing rate shooting up. When you are lying in bed asleep and a semi-trailer truck goes by at a sudden 100 decibels, your body (which is never entirely asleep) reacts as if the truck were a tiger. Once a night or so, this might not be so bad; but if you live on a busy street, it may happen hundreds of times a night. Your sleep is disturbed; your vital organs and systems are stressed; your irritability increases.

Loud or irritating noises are so prevalent in our cities that we learn in self-defense not to be conscious of them, though they enter our systems nevertheless. A very large part of this noise pollution is due to automobiles and trucks—adding a substantial social cost to their other drawbacks. Even vehicles with relatively quiet engines and mufflers emit loud tire noise; in high-speed areas they create wind hiss and roar. These sounds easily penetrate walls and windows, and are especially bothersome in summer when windows tend to be open. Trucks and buses literally shake our dwellings through their foundations. (In Europe, ancient monuments are being eaten away by corrosive industry- and auto-polluted rain, and auto traffic vibration is shaking them down.)

It behooves us, then, to cut down when we can on this onslaught. Make sure your own muffler is in good shape; at this point, driving with a noisy muffler is like wearing a big sign on your forehead labeled "ASSHOLE". If you have neighbors with noisy mufflers, tell them politely that they're waking you up with them, and point out that a new one can be installed for surprisingly little at a muffler shop. If you are outraged by a noisy (or smoke-emitting) vehicle, turn in its license number and description to your local cops, though it's doubtful they will do anything about it.

Air conditioning and other mechanical systems in buildings often contribute low, unnerving humming noises that cause tension and distress. Many household appliances contribute annoying and erratic noises, though under EPA's new noisiness-rating labels their levels should decline. And of course air traffic, with its deafening jet roar, is not only unpleasant but demonstrably dangerous:

people living under airport approach patterns enter mental hospitals far more often than similar people living elsewhere. (Aside from its enormous levels of fuel consumption, and its damage to the upper atmosphere, the Concorde supersonic airliner is also very noisy; it should not be allowed to land at any American airports.)

How can you defend yourself against noise? First, of course, attempt to avoid noisy environments in your daily activities—try not to live on heavy-traffic streets; try to work in buildings with natural ventilation (and with silent incandescent lights, to avoid the hum of FLUORESCENTS). When possible, drive with windows closed, using air vents for fresh air and cooling. You may, in particularly noisy but otherwise desirable situations, want to try blocking out sound. Double windows, especially of heavy plate glass, will cut down sound from outside substantially. Double doors, if sealed around the edges and sills with weatherstripping, can reduce noise from hallways or between rooms. Using sealant to provide a tight gasket around metal-frame windows can stop the surprising amount of noise that can enter through very small cracks. (Use waxed paper, to which it won't stick, if you want to keep the window openable.)

Some people also use white noise generators—devices that produce a kind of neutral hiss, made up of all the frequencies in the sound spectrum—in hopes of masking undesired noise. A small recirculating water fountain (using an aquarium pump that's submersible) produces white noise and also helps humidify your air. It is also possible to play records of surf noise, rainstorms, and so on—though generally these are best played at very low volumes, and therefore don't have much masking effect.

And you can, of course, resort to ear plugs. Waxy types fit themselves to your ear passages and are quite comfortable. Hearing protectors, which look like high-fi headphones, are also being rated by EPA, and are advisable for anyone who works in an industrial environment which is uncomfortably noisy.

OYSTERS

The rich consider oysters a gourmet delight. There are elegant dishes with names like oysters Florentine and oysters Rockefeller—delicately seasoned oysters baked in half shells on a layer of rock salt. But some people, unfortunately, think oysters are repulsive. Too bad for them! Actually, oysters and their shellfish relatives—clams, mussels, and limpets, along with some other near-shore species like crabs and shrimp—were important in human evolution: they were a reliable high-protein food supply to our ancestors, who lived along the shores of oceans and lakes. Not only were they very tasty, they were also not nearly so dangerous to catch as larger creatures, who tend to be fleet of foot or equipped with fang and claw.

Oysters contain twice the protein of soy beans and about half that of deboned chicken. They also have half the calories of chicken and about two-thirds the cholesterol. Moreover, since oysters are grown in bays—sometimes unaided by nature and sometimes on wires—they don't require gas-guzzling farm machinery to produce, and thus tend to be cheaper than most other animal proteins. It is not only an ecological disgrace but an economic disaster when human beings poison oyster-rich estuaries like the Chesapeake Bay with chemicals like kepone.

All in all, thus, the lowly oyster should not be neglected. You can buy oysters in jars all year round, and raw oysters in their shells during the season (they're more expensive). Cookbooks are full of delicious oyster dishes. My favorites are oyster stew (with lots of milk and pepper), oysters lightly fried with ginger slices, and most of all oysters baked in the shell on a fire at the beach, with lots of friends gathered round dipping them into butter-lemon sauce, drinking wine to wash them down, and munching on good crunchy French bread. (Remember to take along a stout knife to pry open the shells!)

A worthy bivalve relative of the oyster is the mussel, which you can often gather at low tides. Mussels grow in vast quantities just offshore on cool, rocky coasts, and have been called our single greatest unexploited food resource.

Avoid mussels, clams, or other shellfish you catch yourself during the summer months or times when public health authorities issue temporary quarantines because local waters are full of certain unhealthy microorganisms. (A phone call will relieve your anxiety if you can't remember whether to favor or avoid "months that contain the letter R.")

P

PACKAGING

Packaging is a major weapon in the manufacturer's constant campaign to cheat the customer. And despite successful political pressure to simplify packaging sizes so there are not quite so many odd ones, the companies managed to stave off legislation that would finally have made it possible to tell how much you're buying. So you still find packages that contain 5¾ or 17½ ounces. And, though in most countries adoption of the metric system has meant simplification of packaging sizes, American corporations will probably continue producing confusing sizes as long as they are not forced into more rational practices.

It is important to realize that the companies are absolutely shameless in their attempts to deceive you—and that most of the time they get away with it. Breck, for instance, simply changed the size of its shampoo bottles. They used to be simple and round and contained 16 ounces (an even pint). The new bottles are higher, thinner, and shaped funny. They only hold 15 ounces. But lo and behold, the price has gone up! Presumably Breck has discovered that buyers are so stupid that they think a taller bottle always holds more than a shorter bottle, no matter what its shape. They also know that most consumers have no real way of making comparisons since few supermarkets have "unit pricing," that is, shelf labels telling you how much the different package sizes cost you per pint, or per ounce, or whatever.

A great deal of noise has been made about deceptive packaging by consumer groups. There are really only two things to be done. One is to buy as little junk in tubes and funny bottles as you can—the less you can buy, the less you'll be shafted.

The other thing is to support legislative campaigns to enforce rigid governmental packaging standards. This is the only remedy, short of nationalizing industries, that will persuade manufacturers to put their products in honest packages so you can tell how much you're getting and how much it's costing you. There is no reason why a buyer should have to use a calculator to tell what something costs.

Packaging is not only deceptive, it's wasteful; in some cases the fancy printing, special shapes, and plastic wrappers actually cost as much as the product. Generally, you are better off buying things in simple packages if their prices are similar to prices on fancy-packaged items of equal contents. What the fancy packers spend on the wrappings, they often take out in lower quality of the goods inside.

Incidentally, even simple packages are often used deceptively to make things look better: thus carrots are packed in plastic which has thin orange strips printed on it to make the carrots look more orange; green vegetables get the green-ink treatment, apples get the red-ink treatment. Tell your supermarket manager that you think this is cheap deception and request that the store buy from other suppliers. Similar deceptions prevail in meat departments where pink light shines on the meat to make it look redder. Try to shop in a co-op grocery where such practices do not prevail—and you may even be able to buy many foods "in bulk," with no packaging at all.

PAINTBRUSHES

Professional painters buy very good brushes and use them for years. But they have gallons of solvent, paint thinner, or other cleaning agents handy. For the person doing an occasional small paint job such as a chair or table, it is cheaper to buy a "throwaway" paint brush, since you would spend at least as much buying the cleaning stuff. (For very small jobs, you can make a temporary "brush" by rolling a little piece of thin rag around the end of a stick and tying it on; it isn't elegant, but it works.) But if you like to do painting, it is a pleasure to have two or three really good brushes; they put the paint on much easier than a cheap brush. A good brush has soft, dense bristles. To take care of such brushes, clean them immediately after use by working them in a container of thinner and hanging them up to dry (drill holes in the handles if they don't have them already) so the bristles don't get deformed. Don't rub a good brush on the lip of the can when you load it; tap it against

179

the inside of the can. Don't use a natural-bristle brush in latex paint.

You can clean a brush on which paint has hardened, but it isn't easy and is hard on the brush: first scrape off all the paint you can with a putty knife or other dull scraper, then soak the bristles several hours in diesel oil. You can also use paint remover, but it's so expensive that this is only worth it if you happen to inherit a really superb brush and want to restore it to good shape. For work you're doing to continue next day, you can make a little rig to suspend the uncleaned brush in a can or bottle containing linseed oil (so the bristles don't lie on the bottom and get bent). If you're putting away a brush for a long time, soaking it with linseed oil beforehand will help it stay supple.

Latex (water-base) paints give the least trouble in the cleaning of brushes and rollers. Wash them in rapidly running plain water as soon as you're finished with them. If you stop work for a while, wrap them in waxed paper or plastic film to keep them damp and flexible.

PAINTING AND VARNISHING

Don't be too eager to paint things, especially wood things. There is a terrible compulsion in America to keep things freshly painted—whereas in fact houses, furniture, shelves, utensils, and many other things can often look more interesting with a certain patina of age upon them. Wooden shelves, chairs, tables, cabinets, and so on are often best left uncoated; leave the wood to face the world and it will take on a soft luster, a pleasant variation in surface tone; it will feel good to the touch. Even houses are a doubtful object for painting; paint may protect the wood somewhat, but probably the cost of the paint is not balanced by longer life of the wood. And weathered wood has a special soft beauty of its own.

If you do decide to paint, remember that a good painter almost always spends more time preparing the surface than in actually painting it. You need to scrape off the old paint where it's loose, fill the holes with putty or spackle, use a piece of sandpaper wrapped around a block of wood to sand off the irregularities, and generally make the surface clean and free of grease (which keeps paint from sticking). Then give it two coats. The ad on the can probably says "covers in one coat." There are rare cases where this really works, but don't kid yourself; look at the dry first coat in the light of day. For light colors over dark, especially, you can't do a decent job with one coat.

Varnishing needs even more careful preparation, because there the wood itself will show through. Hard woods will stand an incredible amount of scuffing, chopping, cutting, scouring, dripping, and general abuse, and will often get more beautiful in the process. You can give them some protection by soaking linseed oil or sealer into them, which won't make them shiny. But if you want to give them a tough coating, either spar varnish or one of the plastic varnishes like Varathane is best; they can be gotten in dull as well as shiny finishes. Try to do varnishing in a dust-free room—varnish picks up dust as if it was flypaper.

There are basically three kinds of paint: water-based ("latex"—rubber paint), oil-based, and plastic-based (acrylic). Water-based paint is the easiest to use because it can be washed off fingers, brushes, rollers, and floors with plain water (if cleaned off before it dries). White latex wall paint is the easiest overall for hiding your predecessors' peculiar choices in wall colors. Oil-based paints are usually the most feasible for outdoors, where sun and water give surfaces a tremendous drubbing. Acrylic paints, which are quite expensive, have intense, long-lasting colors which endear them to artists; and they are resistant to weather. Most modern paints contain chemicals which are injurious to health. Keep as many windows as possible open while you paint, and for several days thereafter; try to sleep somewhere else for a few days if you can. (It is a good general rule that if something has a penetrating "chemical" smell, it will not do you any good. Trust your nose!)

Any kind of paint can be put on with a brush or roller, but rollers are only useful when you're covering large flat areas. Even if you use a roller, you must have a brush too to do the corners, moldings, and edges. Some people claim good results with foam painting pads; they don't speckle you with paint the way a roller does.

A gallon of paint covers about five-hundred square feet—which is the ceiling and wall area of a room ten feet square and ten feet high. Thus, painting a whole apartment can get expensive. If you're not too fussy about exact matching of shades you can find paint in surplus stores and other low-cost sources. However, it won't last as well as better paint, and it may not cover up the underlayer quite so well. A discount paint store is your ideal source.

It is also possible to use whitewash, the ancient covering for country fences, barns, and whatnot. It washes away very slowly and irregularly, leaving an extremely nice weathered effect. To make it, buy from a paint store some lime, fine-ground casein (the main ingredient in white glue), ground kaolin (white clay), and sodium carbonate (if you intend to use it outdoors). Approximate ratios for outdoors use: 32 ounces lime, 8 ounces casein, 6 ounces kaolin, and 1 ounce sodium carbonate. For indoors: 30 ounces lime, 20 ounces kaolin, and 3 ounces casein. Precise measurements are not essential. You mix all the ingredients dry, very thoroughly, then add about half their volume of water. Stir until dissolved, and let stand a half hour before application.

There are other alternatives to paints and varnishes. Pre-technological societies found other ways of giving wood a finish, and you can sometimes find ways of doing similar things. The soft, lustrous surface of the veranda planks in traditional Japanese houses comes from their being wiped down by hand over the years so that a mixture of sweat oils gradually protects them; linseed oil, rubbed in, will give wood a similar beautiful soft glow. Sculptures in some New Guinea areas were polished with animal fats rubbed thoroughly into the wood, and in fact practically any kind of fat or oil will tend to give wood a protective gloss. Actually any kind of hard rubbing down tends to close the surface pores of wood slightly, making it a little less water-absorbent. If you don't like the raw look of newly sawed wood you can "paint" it with a mixture of earth and water; this darkens it and makes it look a bit weathered. Painting new redwood with water with baking soda mixed in it will give the raw wood a pleasant old look.

PARTIES AND CELEBRATIONS

The best parties are focused around some activity (other than drinking), but they do need some kind of focus, and this seldom comes about automatically. If you happen to know musicians, live music gives a beautiful center for a large party; dancing to a band is always more exciting than using records. Providing food gives people a chance to relate to each other by relating to something real, especially if you either arrange a big potluck with lots of surprises or have some special treat like a big fish to cook. Even work parties tend to be better than unformed parties: it's pleasant to get together with friends to paint an apartment, assemble a newsletter, or do some other chore that's time-consuming

but doesn't interfere with socializing. It's true, of course, that sometimes a very good party happens spontaneously—a combination of people drop by who relate well to each other, good things come up to do, and everybody ends up feeling warm and loving.

You can also organize parties around celebrating something: a birth or birthday, a marriage, a new apartment, a discovery, a departure or return, a success of some kind. At any such gathering, good music is important, because dancing is a basic human way of celebrating and marking important occasions, and because it does away with a lot of needless talk. The cocktail party was basically an opportunity for trying to impress others, but we hardly need more of that in the contemporary world. What we need to create are opportunities for touching each other, for responding to and expressing basic feelings, and for taking our lives and friends seriously. A good party is an occasion for celebrating and enjoying collectively these important needs.

See HOLIDAYS.

PASTA

Every diet needs to include carbohydrate energy foods, and much of this should be starches rather than sugars. So foods like POTATO, RICE, and pasta are important and you should not shun them; many Americans in fact eat more protein than they need anyway. If your weight is your main concern, it's better to cut down on FATS and SUGARS.

Unfortunately, most available pasta (spaghetti, noodles, and the dozens of little round, curly, or shell-like shapes devised in Italy) is made with heavily refined and sometimes unenriched flour. But whole-wheat pasta is slowly becoming available, and noodles are made in green types, with vegetable components—they are both interesting to try and slightly more nutritious. The Chinese transparent noodles called "bean threads," which you can buy in any Chinese market (Japanese stores have a similar product) are made from soy beans and contain some protein. There is no reason why ordinary pasta could not be produced in forms reinforced with soy protein, which would be a dietary help for people living on very low budgets, but the US Department of Agriculture has been chewing over this idea for many years and has never allowed it. If both plain and reinforced types were available, we would clearly be better off.

The first "New Earth Exposition," in San Francisco.

PATCHWORK

The patch is an ancient and honorable device and by no means a sign of disgrace. An honest, forthright patch is not a disfigurement, and it can be a decorative addition. Keep bright-colored pieces of cloth around, even if they're small; you never know when a shirt or skirt or pair of pants may wear through. Don't forget that patches can be laid over patches, too—and patches can be round or square or oval or oblong or star-shaped . . . .

"Iron on" patches don't stay ironed on forever, and they're dull and standardized besides. Use strong, honest cloth and sew it on carefully. Sew around the outer edge of the patch (turning it under neatly) and then also around the edge of the hole or rip, so the fabric is firmly attached to the patch.

You can adopt the principles of our grandparents' patchwork quilts and make large pieces of cloth out of patches—big enough for curtains, quilts, furniture covers, car seats, tents, who knows what. You can often find beautiful fragments of cloth in the rag bins of secondhand stores. Let your imagination have free rein. The best patches are the boldest patches.

PEANUT BUTTER

This would be one of the foods hardest for many Americans to be deprived of. It's tasty, and it's full of protein—altogether an excellent kind of food. You can do other things besides make sandwiches with it, too: spread it on celery, use it to make cookies, or just eat it out of the jar. Four tablespoons plus a cup of milk give you almost as much protein as a quarter pound of meat. (It also, of course, gives you a sizable amount of vegetable fat—which in many brands sold today is added saturated fat and bad for your health.)

Unfortunately, in recent years real peanut butter has become hard to find. Proper peanut butter is crunchy (the nuts aren't all squashed up, which makes it stick to your mouth less) and oily on the top (it hasn't been homogenized). Most of what is sold as peanut butter these days is only partly from peanuts; the rest is hardened vegetable oil and a form of sugar. But co-op groceries and good supermarkets sell "crunchy old-fashioned" peanut butter; it's worth looking for. Buy it in the large-size (three-pound) jars, since you'll use a lot of it and the jars are excellent for storing flour, beans, rice, sugar, etc. However, if you ordinarily don't consume this much in three months, buy a smaller

size. If the label is vague, check the ingredients. Real peanut butter is simply ground-up peanuts with salt added. Anything else on the label should make you suspicious. The fat in real peanut butter may give you unwanted calories, but it is otherwise harmless.

If the separation of oil annoys you and you don't want to stir it occasionally, turn the jar upside down on the shelf part of the time, especially when it's new. Then one good stir when you open it will give a satisfying consistency.

You can make your own peanut butter if you have a grinder or heavy-duty blender, and you can also make other nut butters. (Walnut butter is actually better nutritionally than peanut butter because it has very little saturated fat; it has an interestingly different taste.) Put in modest quantities of shelled nuts at a time. You may have to add a little oil to get a smooth consistency—use peanut oil or a polyunsaturated, nonhydrogenated oil like safflower oil. And go easy on the salt—it only takes a little.

Some alarm has been expressed in recent years about aflatoxin, a carcinogenic substance that is produced when moldy peanuts have been made into peanut butter. The extent of this hazard has not yet been firmly established. Keeping your peanut butter in the refrigerator may help. (Of course you should avoid eating moldy peanuts.)

PERIODICALS AND NEWSPAPERS

A taste for reading magazines quickly gets expensive. You can, of course, simply stand at magazine racks reading them for hours at a time until you get ousted, and this is a great and cheap pleasure. But you should also find out about the periodicals room of your library, where recent issues of many well-known and also more obscure magazines are available—often with comfortable chairs to read them in. (Sometimes they can't be checked out of the library, at least not the brand-new issues.) You may not realize it, but there is probably a magazine devoted to any subject you care about, from films to fortune-telling. Some are popular, with information ranging from the intensely useful to the purely commercial (never trust a magazine that carries a lot of big ads from manufacturers in its field). A visit to a big university library periodicals room is an exhilarating experience: row upon row of magazines, newsletters, journals, in many languages.

Since it takes about a year to publish a book, new information, especially of a technical or political nature, usually first appears in magazines. The way to locate it is through the *Reader's Guide to Periodical Literature*, which indexes most of the major magazines, and can tell you which ones have printed articles in the last year on jet engines, capital punishment, food adulteration, Albert Einstein, or Susan B. Anthony. A reference librarian always has the *Reader's Guide* handy, and can show you how to use it, along with more specialized similar guides in the arts, social sciences, and other fields.

Some people love newspapers and couldn't get up in the morning if they knew the paper wouldn't be there; others find newspapers unbearably depressing and read them once a month if at all. American newspapers are certainly not getting any better; in most cities, the biggest paper has managed to wipe out its competitors and is getting fat from having all the advertising to itself. Naturally, its owners are friends and relatives of the establishment of the city, and generally take care that nothing gets printed which might upset political and business bigwigs. Often the same people who own the paper also own at least one television and radio station—so they control much of the "media" in town, and it's no wonder that important stories get suppressed. The natural result has been the growth of small, independently-owned community papers, sometimes evolved from shopping guides and oriented toward cultural events and political issues the big papers wouldn't consider, and often printing new writers with something trenchant and original to say. (They also tend to have useful classified ads.) Besides printing news from a generally radical viewpoint, they also have interesting features about local happenings, plus advice columns on health and other practical matters that wouldn't be touched by the big papers. It has also become much easier to obtain the *New York Times* in remote parts of the country, which (despite the *Times*'s own failings) gives you some check on the performance of your local trivia purveyors.

Newspaper coverage may not be unbiased, politically reliable, or complete, but it is immensely more complete than television news: the material presented on the television news could fit into a couple of columns of a newspaper. Oddly enough, however, the television networks do produce some special documentary programs which are more politically informative and critical than anything you will read in newspapers. Unfortunately, there is no practical way to find out about them in advance, though newspapers sometimes mention them the day before.

See INFORMATION, HOW TO FIND and LIBRARIES.

PESTICIDES AND HERBICIDES

Late in the 70's it finally became clear to large numbers of people, and after that to the Environmental Protection Agency, that the indiscriminate spraying of pesticides (insect-killers) and herbicides ("weed"-killers) was making a lot of people sick, and causing miscarriages, birth defects, and other types of serious health problems. These problems were, of course, suspected for a long time, ever since large-scale spraying was used militarily in Vietnam. They first became indubitably clear in forested regions of the Northwest where small towns were surrounded by heavily sprayed areas, and their water supplies as well as air probably became contaminated. It is crucial to remember that the government took no action until the citizens of these areas (and some of their doctors) became so alarmed that they organized a political campaign on the issue. The reason is not necessarily that the government offices are heartless, incompetent, and overworked; they were also subject to heavy pressure from lumbering interests, who would have to spend a little more money to manage their forests if they could not use herbicides.

As it happens, using human labor rather than helicopter sprays in forest management has many ecological advantages as well as social ones. Cutting back broadleaf tree seedlings to "release" the conifers among them to grow better—which is what the herbicides were being used for—can be done by hand, and in the process other kinds of attention can be given to the forest floor, to prevent erosion, recover usable lumbering residues, and so on. This also avoids the drifting of spray onto residences and schools, which was formerly common.

Moreover, through programs of integrated pest management, the amount of pesticides used in agricultural production could be cut in half, reducing health hazards to field workers and to consumers, and also cutting food prices. To accomplish this, the power of the chemical-oil industry over the farm advisor system must be broken.

Pesticides and herbicides are mostly artificially created chemical substances, and are thus automatically suspect as both carcinogenic (cancer-producing) and teratogenic (mutation-producing). One impurity that usually occurs in minute quantities

The Hoedads of Oregon doing forest maintenance. Though more labor intensive, the tree yield is higher, with no use of chemicals.

in compounds called 2,4,5T and 2,4D is "dioxin." Dioxin is the most toxic substance know, even more lethal in tiny amounts than plutonium; it is the only substance that could indeed literally wipe out all life if a modest amount of it were distributed around the globe. Regulators have belatedly begun to realize how important it is to minimize exposure to dioxin and to prevent chemical plant accidents such as occurred in Seveso, Italy, which rendered a whole town uninhabitable through the widespread dispersion of dioxin.

In your personal life, you should minimize exposure to all pesticides and herbicides, as well as to other suspicious chemical compounds. Natural pesticides (rotenones, pyrethrins, etc.) are available for your garden. Take proper precautions when using anything in spray or dust form, of course—a paper mask, or at least a dampened handkerchief over nose and mouth. A few bugs should be tolerable; they take a kind of natural "tax bite" out of your produce, and most of them have predators (lady bugs, birds) which keep their populations reasonable.

Herbicides have no acceptable place in home gardening or indeed in any urban land maintenance. Manual mowing or removal of undesired plants is always preferable. One enterprising Ecotopian has also set up a business of clearing overgrown lots using two nanny goats, who eat anything and produce fertilizer besides!

One paradoxical reason to buy furniture and rugs secondhand is that new ones are now impregnated with insecticides (as are many building materials). These smell peculiar and may be carcinogenic. Let somebody else live with them until the chemicals have dispersed.

PILLOWS

A supply of large pillows and cushions can substitute for bulky chairs, and make couches or sofa areas more comfortable, colorful, and appealing. Elegant Japanese-made flat cushions are available in more and more stores now. You can also make cushions or pillows yourself from pieces of surplus-store foam rubber, pillow stuffing bought in sewing stores, old rags, or whatnot.

Some people sleep without pillows, but most of us sleep better with a pillow that suits us. It is, in my opinion, a necessary luxury to buy a pillow you really like. The best seems to be feather-filled pillows of a moderate firmness; foam tends to be too bouncy, and other stuffings tend to sag down into heavy, lumpy layers.

PLANTINGS

Traditionally, people have been reluctant to mix decorative with edible plants. This prejudice is now luckily being overcome. Asparagus, for instance, makes an attractive shrub after you have your fill of its springtime shoots. Artichokes and rhubarb are dramatic garden accents. Beans, peas, and some squash can be trained on trellises to give privacy or shade. Strawberries and New Zealand spinach provide ground cover plus edibility. Nasturtium leaves give a tangy taste to salads (as, of course, do dandelion leaves when young). A row of bush beans will make an attractive backing for low-growing flowering plants. Alfalfa is a hardy, pleasant-looking plant which you can use in planting strips and also feed to your rabbits—not to mention sprouting its seeds for yourself.

See COMMUNITY GARDENS and GARDENING.

PLANTS, INDOOR

Even the drabbest apartment looks better with flowerpots on the windowstill, and green plants will make any space more livable. There is something about living plants that makes people feel good: my theory is that it reminds us of our ancestral origins. Plants also give off oxygen during the day, which can't hurt either.

It's not hard to grow most indoor plants. Ask advice at a garden-supplies place (some dime stores have garden departments), and start with the easiest, cheapest types. Avoid the conventional rubber plants and philodendrons—try ferns, ivy, or others. If you have kids around and worry that they'll knock the plants over, hang the plants on wires or brackets (you can put them in hanging baskets); you can also improvise containers from large painted tin cans or wooden boxes. Most plants need to be near windows but not in hot sun. (If they need more light, paint the wall behind them white, or put a mirror there.) Backyard dirt in many cities is utterly worn-out soil and has to be fertilized and composted to be fit to grow anything in. Look around your neighborhood for a construction site where you might find a couple of bucketfuls of good earth. Or at worst you can buy potting soil from the garden-supplies place.

In a heated apartment or house, plants need a surprising amount of water. Some that most willingly grow in damp places, like the beautiful ferns, need daily watering. Start with only a few plants so you can study how they behave and you'll learn what they need.

Most vegetables won't grow in a heated place in winter, but you can grow hardy things like peas in a window box during the summer; they have beautiful, delicate flowers and fresh peas taste much better than frozen or canned ones.

You can even plant small trees indoors if you pick the right kind of tree, and trees are surprisingly cheap—sometimes less than a big potted flower plant. They will need quite a lot of water and do best if you don't keep the temperature terribly high. Ask at a garden-supplies place or nursery. Some nursery salespeople refuse to believe trees can survive indoors. Keep looking around

until you find one who has tried it and knows what he or she is talking about. *Ficus benjamina* is one species that grows well indoors.

Nowadays many people are buying small live evergreens at Christmas instead of chopped-off trees. That way you aren't encouraging the killing of trees, and you get to plant your tree after New Year's in your yard or in a park or along the street somewhere. Evergreens can stand a week in a moderately heated house if you put them in the coolest spot—usually next to a big window—and if you are careful to keep their roots thoroughly moist at all times. (Even a three-foot-high tree can give off a quart or more of moisture a day, and this must be replaced through the roots.) A live Christmas tree smells nice, and it is in accord with the reverence for life we like to think we are expressing at Christmastime. Nurseries can give you detailed advice about planting the tree. The essentials are to dig a big hole and provide some soft earth in it for the tree's roots to penetrate—and to make sure the tree gets enough water in its early months in its new home. Remember that a small tree will someday be enormous, with powerful roots; don't plant it right next to your house. See TREES.

Grow It Indoors, by Richard W. Langer. Warner Books, 1975. For the truly dedicated.

House Plants: A Primer for a Dumb Thumb, by Nancy Roca Laden. Apple Pie/Ten Speed Press, Box 4310, Berkeley, CA 94707.

PLANTS, WILD

Foraging for wild plants is a hobby which can provide you with a great deal of tasty food; wild plants abound in cities as well as the country. Wild plants are sometimes studied by people who worry about how they would eat if atomic war struck and they happened to survive. But even if you have less apocalyptic reasons for being interested, it is nice to know which plants that grow in your region are edible. Immigrant peoples are often well informed about such things; I remember seeing old Polish women in Chicago wandering about in the rain in the parks—picking mushrooms. Here are some of the most common and easy to recognize:

Dandelions. This often despised "weed" (a weed is only definable as a plant growing where humans don't want it) can be eaten in salads or boiled like spinach. It's full of vitamins. The new small leaves are the tenderest. Dandelion roots in the spring can be dug up and sliced and boiled. The embryonic flowers, before they rise up from

the crown of the plant, are also edible. And the roots can be dried, ground up, and brewed to make a drink that tastes rather like Postum.

Mustard. A widely distributed plant that is also grown commercially. Good boiled when young (use the big leaves, not top ones; boil thirty minutes.)

Wild aparagus. Steam like the commercial type.

Cattails. Although gathering cattails can be a tricky and chilly job, this plant offers several edible parts: you can boil the new heads (just before they come through the sheath); you can pare new stalks and boil them; you can pull up the root tubers and mash them in water (giving them several washings) for a starchy mush; you can fry the small top knobs on the tubers; and you can use the pollen as flour.

Acorns. A staple of Native Americans, acorns must be leached before they become edible; you do this by boiling them, whole, for two hours, and then either running water through them for some time or soaking and rinsing them with several changes of water. You can eat them as a meal or mush; you can even candy them. To make a flour that will keep for a little while, you can grind up the fresh acorns, mix with boiling water (to leach), and press out through a cloth; repeat this several times, then spread thinly in a pan to dry, in the oven or in hot sunlight.

Berries. Blackberries are probably the most widely available wild berry; once established, a blackberry patch is practically impossible to exterminate. Blueberries grow wild in many areas; so do huckleberries (which are red, not blue). There are also wild strawberries and cherries. As in eating any wild plants, you need to study identification guides with an expert outdoor person before you eat berries: some are poisonous.

Mushrooms. Many people have an unreasonable fear of mushrooms. With a good identification guide and some human guidance to alert you to the dangerous types, however, you can make a very good thing out of mushrooms: some of them are absolutely delectable, and mushroom hunting is one of the nicest ways to spend an otherwise dreary wettish day.

Nuts. Walnuts, hickory nuts, hazelnuts are all tasty and good sources of protein for the diet; so are sunflower seeds, which grow wild in some areas. (See TREES.)

There are many other plants which can be eaten. Watercress grows wild by many spring-fed streams; it is related to nasturtiums, whose leaves are also a delicacy in salads. Wild onions can flavor your dishes. Chicory can give you a kind of coffee. Clover blossoms and mint leaves make good tea (dry them away from heat or sunlight), and catnip tea is reputed to be a good sedative. There is an elaborate international folklore based on the use of plants—both nutritional and medicinal uses, far too extensive even to summarize here—and only now beginning to be explored by science.

PLASTICS

The very term "plastic" has become an adjective of abuse, connoting ugliness and artificiality; to which, in recent years, has been added physiological hazardousness, since the vapors from polyvinyl chloride (very widely used as a packaging material and in water pipes) are known to be carcinogenic.

It is essential to recognize that plastics come in two types. *Biosource* plastics are derived from trees, cotton, and other renewable biological sources. Thus cellulose plastics are the basis for camera film, celluloid and cellophane, and acetate fabric fibers including rayon. (Cellulose from trees is, of course, the basic raw material for paper and cardboard.) Plastics like bakelite (used for insulators) are made with lignin fibers from trees. Men's shiny opalescent shirt buttons are casein plastics, derived from milk—as are certain white casein glues. The ingenuity of plastics chemists can doubtless produce many more such products. Moreover, the basic materials for many *petroleum-based* plastics can be derived, if desired, from biological sources through the processes of fermentation and distillation. Plastics are comprised of long-chain "polymer" molecules, hooked together from smaller, simpler molecules. These molecule building blocks can be biosource, but at present to make 2,000 pounds of plastic requires something like 72 gallons of oil and 340 gallons of liquids derived from natural gas (plus energy equal to about the same amount of these materials again.) In time, we will need a plastics industry that relies mainly on biosource materials, and that produces materials which are biodegradable so that they can be recycled back onto the land—to produce more plant material to make more plastics, and so on *ad infinitum* in a stable state system.

The commonest existing petroleum plastics fall into three groups: polyethylenes, which are soft, colorless, and translucent (often used for water or milk containers); polystyrenes, which are stiffer and white, and can be fairly strong even though

thin (often used for margarine, yogurt, or sour cream containers); and polyvinyl chlorides, which are normally clear and quite strong and hard (used in phonograph records, water pipes, and shampoo bottles; they're also made in thin plastic film form).

Polyvinyl chloride is such a widely used product that no serious attempts have been made to restrict it, despite the fact that it gives off small amounts of the carcinogenic gas from which it is manufactured. When possible, you should avoid food products that come in "blister packs" or other thin plastic films, since these may be "PVC" as it's called. And don't store food or beverages in plastic containers or wrappings; use glass or ceramic containers, or waxed paper.

PLUMBING

Plumbers don't actually make the stupendous wages people imagine (much of their bills are for the same kind of overhead every business charges you for), but calling a plumber is bound to cost quite a lot. And most plumbing troubles are essentially simple and can be fixed without spending more than a few cents.

Clogged sinks. Sinks and washbasins have a "trap" underneath in which a little water is retained to keep sewer gases from backing up through the drain into your house. But these S- or P-shaped traps also trap grease from dishwater or hot fat which gets poured down the sink. When the grease hits the cold pipes, it tends to solidify and then pick up small pieces of food, etc. When it does get clogged—and every sink will, sooner or later—you'll need to borrow (if you don't have one) a "plumber's helper": a rubber bell-shaped thing on the end of a wooden stick. Put it over the drain, making sure it seals well, and work it up and down briskly. You will hear gurgling noises in the drain; that means it's working. Stop and see if the water is doing down. If it isn't, or is going down very slowly, do some more "plunging." When it does get running better, turn on the hot water very hot, and run that for a while.

This is almost sure to work. If it doesn't, there are two possibilities: either the trap is so clogged with old material that the sucking-and-pressure of the plumber's helper won't loosen it (this might be the case if your sink has drained slowly for a long while) or the obstruction is somewhere below the trap. (In that case you or your downstairs neighbors may have noticed leakage elsewhere in the house drains.) The trap may have a clean-out opening which comes out by turning it with a wrench, but chances are you will have to remove the trap. This requires a large pipe wrench, some rags or tape to wrap around the nuts to prevent scratching them, and two replacement rubber gaskets to keep the trap from leaking when you put it back again. (Measure the diameter of the drainpipe and go out and buy these gaskets before you start the job. Most hardware stores carry them. On old traps that have been scratched or bent, these gaskets may not seal, so it is wise to have some silicone cement handy, or at least some pipe compound, as back-up.) Rings or silverware that fall down the sink can also be retrieved by removing the trap.

Backed-up toilets. There are few things as depressing as sewage floating around in your bathroom. Unfortunately, toilets easily get clogged by tampons, sanitary napkins, pencils, paper diapers, pieces of cardboard or plastic, and other things that children like to flush. On a fishing boat I once saw a sign that read "Don't Flush Anything Down This Toilet You Haven't Swallowed First," and although this rule reflects the stringency needed to keep a boat toilet in working order, it's a good reminder that the toilet drainpipe is only about three inches across, and the pipe through which sewage flows has many joints that are not perfectly smooth inside. In short, a toilet will only satisfactorily carry away things that dissolve quickly in water.

When your toilet backs up, the first thing to try is the plumber's helper. Get it well set in the neck of the toilet bowl before you start plunging up and down with it. Most often the obstruction is within the toilet itself, not down in the drainpipes, so you have a good chance of dislodging it. More stubborn obstacles can be removed with a "snake," or long thin flexible cable, which you gently twist and wangle down through the toilet. This must be lightweight or you will damage the toilet, which is actually a huge piece of crockery and quite crackable as well as scratchable.

Running toilets. Toilet tanks contain a valve which is operated by a float. Theoretically, when the tank has filled up, the valve shuts off the water. If it doesn't, look inside the tank. The most likely trouble is that the rubber tank stopper (way down at the bottom, where the water runs out to go into the toilet bowl) isn't fitting into its seal properly; it's allowing a little leak, and thus the water level never gets quite high enough to shut off the valve. These ball-shaped stoppers get tired, flabby, and don't fit tightly anymore; new ones are cheap and

screw onto the end of the wire that holds them. (Don't be finicky about working inside the toilet tank with your hands; the brown deposits you may see are deposits from the clean incoming tank water.) Once you have put on a new ball, the thing should work OK. If it doesn't, the wire holding the stopper may be bent so it doesn't slide easily through its holder. Float balls may be waterlogged (replacement balls are easily obtainable) or their support rods may be bent. A little oil can't hurt, where the valve-action levers are supported. The valve itself is seldom at fault.

Clogged shower heads. All water supplies contain minute quantities of minerals and other substances, and as the water runs through fine holes some of these get deposited. Take off the shower head and poke the holes open with a needle. (While you're at it, install a flow restrictor disc, which will save you a surprising amount on your water-heating bill.)

Leaking pipes. If you spot a leak that is not at a faucet or other fitting, repairing it is probably a job for a plumber. The water in pipes (except drainpipes) is under high pressure and will probably push away any patching or tape you apply. However, I have sometimes, rather to my surprise, managed to get small leaks stopped at joints. There are compounds at plumbing supply stores intended for such use: you slop them on and then tightly wrap the leak with wire or something else that will retain the water pressure. Ordinary friction tape may slow a leak but can never stop it. Naturally, any attempt to stop a leak has more chance of success if you can relieve the water pressure first by turning off the main house valve and draining the water from the house pipes by opening a faucet below the leak.

Leaky faucets. Faucets contain little rubber disks called washers which press against a round seat to stop the water from flowing. These washers slowly wear out, causing the faucet to drip, and must be replaced. But before unscrewing the packing nut at the top of the faucet, be sure you have turned off the water—either at the shut-off valve under the sink or basin, or at the main house water supply valve. Chances are that you will not be able to tell what kind of washer is needed until you get the faucet apart. Hardware and plumbing-supply stores sell little bags of assorted washers. When you replace the packing nut, be careful to get the handle part screwed in right, and don't tighten the nut more than is needed to stop seepage around the faucet stem.

When a faucet starts to leak, don't take to twisting it shut with force and violence. That will just wreck the poor washer and possibly its seat as well, which means real trouble. Fix it—and any others around the house that are dripping—because even a slow drip can waste an astounding amount of water.

Banging noises in the plumbing. Hammering noises signify that something is seriously wrong which will tear the plumbing apart in time. Tell the owner about it and metion that real plumbing trouble is likely if it isn't fixed. Chattering in the pipes may be caused by worn or loose washers.

Incidentally, the single-handle faucet is a fine example of the kind of technological "progress" we get from our housing industry: it looks fancy and streamlined, and is expensive—but it's very hard to adjust to give the temperature and amount of water you want, and if anything goes wrong with it, you may have to call in a plumber.

The Toilet Book: Knowing Your Toilet and How To Fix It, by Helen McKenna. Bookpeople, 2940 7th St., Berkeley, CA 94710.

POISONS AND CHILDREN

Children seem to be more foolhardy than animals—at any rate they gobble up poisonous (and often foul-tasting) stuff surprisingly often. (The manufacturers are partly to blame, because they make poisonous stuff look like milk, strawberry soda, or other goodies.) The commonest causes of child poisoning are cosmetics (permanent-wave neutralizer and polish remover are especially bad), pesticides, petroleum products such as kerosene, soaps and cleaners, disinfectants and deodorizers, polishes and waxes, and lye or other corrosives (such as Drano). Most of these substances should not be accessible to children in a sensibly run house.

Never leave medicines on a bedside table or bathroom sink where children may find them and imitate you by taking them.

For the rest: inflammable, corrosive, or poisonous substances should be stored in tight-closing containers on shelves or in cabinets far above the reach of small children. Teach children by your example that foul-smelling liquids are to be shunned: if you use ammonia for cleaning, make a face when you pour it out.

There are antidotes for many poisons, but stomach pumping is also sometimes necessary. If you think your child has eaten or drunk something poisonous, immediately call a doctor or hospital and explain what it was. In some areas, "Poison Hot Lines" have been set up. (Take the container to the phone with you, so you can read to the doctor from the label if asked to do so.) Then get the child rapidly to the hospital or clinic.

POLITICS AND POLITICAL ACTION

Whether you pay conscious attention to it or not, your politics largely determine your life style, and you cannot think about one without also thinking about the other. Politics—in the large sense of our attitudes and our actions in regard to the way our society is organized and run—comprises a central fact of our lives, even when we try to pretend we can ignore it. In fact, ignoring it is about the worst thing you can do, because of course the political structure does not ignore *you:* it just rejoices that you are willing to be an unthinking victim.

Though much of this Encyclopedia concerns things you can do to live a more satisfying and productive life on a purely personal level, in reality there is no problem of life that can be solved by individual action alone. Little by little, we can build up new patterns of helping each other live better in our daily lives, and these will slowly replace the old. But we cannot escape the political struggle. It is government action or inaction that makes people poor or keeps them that way. Government destroys houses and prevents the building of new ones; it allows the adulteration of our food; it maintains a giant military machine with its tentacles into every aspect of national life. It is government and not blind fate that gives us deadly cars, decrepit trains, ugly cities, unemployment, scarce doctors, expensive drugs, a scandalously regressive tax system.

Government agencies intended to protect people turn out to be in bed with the very interests they are supposed to guard against. None of these dangers to life and health and happiness can be removed except by organized political action.

It is perhaps surprising, in view of how much we now know of the corruption of our government and its incompetence in ensuring our welfare, that many people still believe it can be reformed. The government, as radicals say, is the executive committee of the ruling class. But the people are many, and the rulers are few; in times of crisis, their administrators and police and armies become unreliable. And so, taking the long view, if the rulers will not or cannot quicken the pace of change so that a decent life is possible for all citizens, sooner or later the people will rise against them. First comes protest, then sabotage, then guerrilla war, and finally the seizure of the centers of power. As Thomas Jefferson reminded us, revolution is a permanent right, and a possibility that every people may have to face as the only way to obtain "the blessings of liberty."

Political action that comes down from above includes taxation, wars, control of mass media, police, jails, and so on—in short, the means by which the ruling class exercises its rule. Indeed, as William Domhoff demonstrates in *Who Rules America?*, the only American institution not under the firm control of the ruling class is Congress; the universities, the judiciary, the federal administration, the military and the federal police, and of course the economy itself are tightly controlled by a small group of families. To restructure society so that it primarily nurtures and sustains everyone rather than just the ruling class, we must not only combat these top-down pressures but must also exert our own political pressures from below, on a human and direct basis. This means working in small political groups; it may mean developing a national revolutionary party in time; it certainly means transforming the ways we live. For political action cannot liberate society if its own forms are non-liberating and bureaucratic, such as those of earlier left-wing parties. The particular challenge of contemporary American politics is that if we wish to escape the repressive forces of the existing system, we must act in ways that will not just replace it with a new repressive system. We know that we must seek, instead, a non-system, a biological community. And hence we must ask whether the ends and means of any political action preserve or harm our bodies and the ecological web around us. Is it a vital and pleasurable activity or does it produce tension and physical or mental pollution?

It is only through our own personal acts, one by one, day by day, that we can truly produce a new society. Thus, every time you do something for your friends so they don't have to have it done by a business or turn for help to an institution, you help produce a decent future. Every time you refuse to participate in a demeaning bureaucratic process, every time you decide something with your friends and do it rather than depending on decisions made on high, you lay the foundation for better living for all.

But it is also necessary to carry the struggle into the public arena—by maintaining large and powerful groupings. As we confront the harsh issues of the 80's, all of us need to understand the mechanics of political work—demonstrations,

One of hundreds of demonstrations against nuclear power in the 70's.

leafletting, dealing with the mass media and the police, mobilizing public opinion to spotlight abuses and compel the government to redress grievances.

The variety of tactics and purposes in mass actions are limited only by the ingenuity and daring of the groups involved. Fundamentally, a mass action aims to show that a large number of people have an important complaint and "aren't going to take it any more." They are usually doing what the Constitution refers to as "petition(ing) the Government for a redress of grievances," although mass actions are sometimes mounted against corporations or universities, especially those participating in unjust or oppressive activities.

Usually the presence of the protesters itself becomes the immediate issue, and a free-speech issue is thus added to the original point of the protest. The police refuse a permit or order people to disperse; in the name of their cause and their democratic right to be heard, the protesters refuse. Depending on circumstances, the police then beat up, arrest, fire upon, gas, or otherwise attack the group. In times of especially acute political crisis, fighting breaks out and people are shot and sometimes killed. In planning and publicity for a mass action, it is important to make careful plans to keep your demonstration nonviolent, so that if trouble occurs, it will obviously be the fault of the police. For a large demonstration, this means a well organized corps of monitors, equipped with walkie-talkies, and if possible some training beforehand in nonviolent methods of resisting arrest or other police actions.

A good way to bring media attention to a protest is by setting up a picket line. Massive picketing can so interfere with business that great economic pressure is put on the businesses, though the picketing is perfectly legal. Even a small picket line is an effective way of attracting attention to your position. Make sure the news media are informed *beforehand:* they may not consider the action newsworthy, but if they do they will need some time to get to the scene.

To make your picket effective you need signs to set forth the basis of the protest in slogan form. But you also need leaflets to hand to passersby (and participants too so they can use them in talking to other people) which set out clearly and strongly what is going on. Many Americans are basically sympathetic to picketing because of its long history in the labor movement, but just a couple of signs won't convince them you're right.

In a large picket action, as in a mass demonstration, your group needs to organize for communications, dealing with the police, monitoring disturbances by hoodlums, and so on.

In planning actions to help bring about change, you will sooner or later need to try to secure favorable media coverage for your organization and its events. Make sure you talk in advance to reporters and find out how to work with them. It is important, if you are looking for television coverage, to schedule events so that if they are filmed, the film can be ready for a suitable news slot; otherwise, no matter how exciting the material is, it won't get on. (TV never saves a story for another day.) Similar deadlines apply to newspaper writers. If you contact city editors about a coming demonstration, explain that it is a serious political event and suggest that, even though arrests are always possible, a crime reporter is not an appropriate kind of person to cover it; offer the opportunity for advance interviews. Leaders interviewed by the media of course need to come up with quotable material. But they and

their organizations need to beware of the tendency for leaders to turn into media "stars" and consequently lose touch with the constituency.

Political Ecology: An Activist's Reader, ed. by Alexander Cockburn and James Ridgeway. Times Books, 1979.

POPULATION

The US has never had a coherent population policy; indeed it has only with difficulty gotten to a position where contraception and abortion are legal. But, as Americans have increasingly come to live in cities, most of us have felt population pressure as a definite sense of crowding and congestion; a certain amount of alarm over the world's total population has also helped to convince people that there are simply too many of us. However, our devotion to the idea of growth and progress has kept us from looking squarely at the question of how many of us there really ought to be. Unlike the populations of many other nations, ours is not pressing on the limits set by famine and disease; still, by public policy we could influence it downward if we wished.

In one sense we *have* had a de facto population policy: government procurement programs have acted as a gigantic money pump, sucking taxes out of the industrial Northeast and spewing them out over the South and West; where money goes, people soon follow. Since the people have votes, they then demand water, energy, highways; and, as in Los Angeles, they may come in their millions to occupy a territory with a natural carrying capacity that could barely support thousands.

It is doubtful whether, in a democratic society, a great deal can be done about this, except to direct the money pump at parts of the country capable of supporting more people in an ecologically sane fashion. In any case we seem to be developing a kind of informal population policy by default. Changing family patterns and life styles are making childbearing more a rational choice; it's no longer inevitable that people will get married and have children. Our birth rate has fallen, and seems likely to stay fairly low, though not low enough to make the population total actually begin to decline. Childless people outnumber parents for the first time in our history, and the electorate is reluctant to approve expenditures for education—though it is obviously essential for the future of the whole society that our children be well educated (even if only to be able to provide the Social Security funds to support their elders!). And parents are spacing out their children, which can sometimes mean they don't get around to having some they had planned, because of divorce or other changing circumstances.

How all this will work out in the end, no one can foresee, because birth rates are quite sensitive to economic conditions. However, because an unusually large crop of babies was produced during the years 1946-64, we can make several predictions for the 80's. Crime rates should drop, since these people will be moving out of the ages when arrests are highest. There may be some rise in birth rate as the women of this group go through their childbearing years—with a resulting increase in demand for day-care facilities and, after about 1985, for primary school facilities (which have been declining for some years). The total available work force will grow from 83 million (1970) to 119 million (1990)—a factor which may produce chronic tendencies to massive unemployment. And there will be a slow rise in the number and proportion of older people in the population.

POSTURE, BODY ALIGNMENT

The eyes may be "the windows of the soul," but we have learned from the work of bioenergetics therapists that posture *is* character. Actors have always known this: attitudes and feelings are literally "bodied forth." But so are deep-laid childhood patterns, including neurotic behaviors, which constitute our fundamental orientations toward the world.

Nonetheless, this doesn't mean there is nothing we can do about it. Posture is a matter of daily habit; by retraining, ideally with the help of a bioenergetics mentor, we can reshape our bodies, unlocking our "body armor" so our energy flows more freely, allowing better connections through the common blockages at neck and shoulders or pelvis. Many practical and pleasant postural improvements can be done in your daily routine. Avoid locking your knees into a rigid vertical stick when you are standing in line, for example; this keeps the whole body more flexible and energized. (See WAITING.) Keeping shoulders and neck muscles loose (friends can help here with massages) helps your breathing to become unrestricted and deeper. Avoiding the TV slump (remember your body is built both to sit up and to lie down, but not to do both at once) avoids deleterious pressures on internal organs and minimizes the passivity of body and mind that TV induces.

Yoga, dance, and various other disciplines are also helpful in paying decent attention to your body's needs and capacities. Exercise alone is necessary, but not sufficient; to achieve the grace and comfort your body is capable of, you need to understand its muscular workings in some detail. Your body's welfare is just as important as your mind's, and indeed the two are intimately connected. It is a sad thing in our society that so many people do not make any serious effort to know their bodies, and hence cannot appreciate their extraordinary capacities for pleasure, agility, strength, endurance, and beauty.

POTATOES

These provide more than starch, and possess more protein and other nutrients than most people realize. (There are peoples in the Pacific who subsist almost entirely on yams, which are in my opinion moister and more tasty than sweet potatoes.) Potatoes themselves are not fattening; it is the butter, sour cream, frying fat, gravies, and sauces we add to them which carry the calories.

You will be happiest with potatoes if you do not treat them just as fillers. There are many delectable potato dishes such as potato pancakes; fried potatoes can make the difference between an ordinary breakfast and a real, solid breakfast; sweet-potato pies are superb eating. Baked potato skins are nutritious, and delicious with a little butter or margarine.

Potatoes will bake much faster if you stick a big nail through them, to conduct heat into the center. Poke the skins of potatoes with a fork or knife before baking, lest they explode—this is especially necessary when baking them in a campfire.

Although potatoes keep well in a cool, dark, well-ventilated place, they only keep about a week at normal room temperatures, so don't buy too many.

POTLUCKS AND COMMUNAL COOKING

Sharing regular potlucks with people you like is a good way to escape the grind of your own solitary food preparation even if you don't want to consider some regular kind of communal living arragement. It's also great fun to give an occasional big eating party. Eating together is a much better way of cementing basic human contact than drinking together.

Neighbors who are friends sometimes set up arrangements to share cooking. If five families participate, each one has to prepare the meal for all just one evening a week. This makes possible putting some extra effort into the planning and cooking, and usually makes the meals into more festive occasions with gourmet aspects you might not undertake just for yourself. It also tends to save money as well as time, and gives you the feeling of eating out without having to depend on restaurants.

POTS AND PANS

There's almost no reason to buy pans new. Secondhand stores have a good supply of heavy old frying pans and pots of many sizes, discarded by people who have gone in for Teflon-lined pans, electric pans, and other "gourmet" ware. (Teflon, when it gets overheated, gives off a poisonous gas; don't let it in the house.) In a general way, the heavier a pan is, the better, because it will conduct heat more evenly. Thin aluminum pans conduct heat all right, but they dent easily and have a tinny feel. There is some evidence that constant cooking with aluminum pans introduces small but unhealthy amounts of aluminum into your syustem. In any case, stainless steel pots are the easiest to keep clean and are very durable. The best contain aluminum bottoms, which aid heat distribution. Try to get pots with tight-fitting lids, because they save a lot of heat and also help in cooking vegetables quickly. It may be worth it to buy a brand-new lid to go with a cheap secondhand pot, even though you spent more on the lid.

Many professional cooks, and others who appreciate antique or peasant goods, cook with copper pots coated inside with tin. These are now expensive in the United States, but they're very beautiful, last forever (though they need an occasional re-tinning), and make soft sounds when stirred in or knocked against.

You don't need an expensive pot rack to hang pots from. Use nails or dowels in an attractive board (or the wall) or wire hooks made from coat hangers.

The truly free person, like a Gypsy or a backpacker, carries all the essentials wherever he or she goes. Most people can't achieve this supreme simplicity and concentration, but it's still a criterion to keep in mind when you try to evaluate your wordly objects and the prospect of adding to them. The less you diffuse your consciousness into goods, the more of it there will be for yourself.

POULTRY

Chicken, turkey, duck, and goose are excellent and relatively inexpensive protein sources —especially chicken—and they contain other important nutrients as well. You can buy them either fresh or frozen; ducks and geese are usually *only* available frozen, except on special order. If you don't intend to use it by the next day, frozen is best, because fresh poultry only keeps under refrigeration a day or two. Avoid pre-stuffed, frozen forms—they cost more, and the stuffing is a food poisoning hazard.

You can buy chicken parts rather than whole chickens, and for some recipes this is a good idea. It also makes it possible to buy cheap parts such as backs, which are fine for soups, or delicacies such as chicken livers.

The low price of chicken has come about because chickens are now raised in what amount to factories: huge, automated places with cage after cage of chickens, mounting up into the tens or even hundreds of thousands, and artificaly lighted (especially for egg production). A contemporary chicken may never see the sun, and her feet are almost sure never to touch the ground. Laying hens are kept in tiny cages where they can hardly turn around. Feed and water come on automatic conveyors, and the eggs are taken away by the same process. You may not have much fellow feeling for chickens, but consider: these chicken high-rises are the counterparts of our own; our productivity is watched over as carefully as that of poultry; we too may seldom see the sky or feel the earth under foot; and our nourishment soon may come in tubes or pipes from central dispensaries. If some chicken tells you the sky is falling, it might not be a bad idea to think about it.

PREMARITAL CONTRACTS. See MARRIAGE.

PRESENTS

In our society many people think that gift giving is an obligation—something you have to do at Christmastime. And secondarily, they feel, gift giving also helps keep the economy from going bust.

We should stop all that and begin giving each other presents just for fun—our own fun as well as our friends'. A beginning is simply to abandon Christmas giving to adults (it would be too hard to take our children off presents, cold turkey) and send letters or cards instead. Then, at other times of the year, we could give little surprises. Things we have collected or made or found. Surprise small luxuries of food, clothes, or other items. Unnecessary long-distance phone calls. Mysterious messages or poems. Posters. Tickets. Maps. Used books. Beautiful dry leaves.

See HOLIDAYS.

PRICES

Is there any way of knowing what is a "fair price?" Not really, because prices in our economic system (monopoly capitalism) are set by the largest corporations, which have circumvented price competition and thus destroyed the traditional economic meaning of "price" —a charge arrived at by a balance between supply and demand. Today only agriculture and the grocery industry retain any significant degree of price competition. Prices are what US Steel, Exxon, General Motors, General Electric, and the other giant companies say they are. "List prices" are not often real prices, by the way—they are imaginary prices set somewhat higher, so you can be conned into thinking you're getting a bargain.

Beware of items that have labels reading "15¢ OFF REGULAR PRICE!" or something like that. Such labels are often deceiving: check the quantity in the package, compared to other brands—the contents may have been cut down.

There are, however, some ways to tell whether or not you are being fleeced. Fairly standard prices can be found in the catalogs of Sears and Montgomery Ward. If your neighborhood store is offering "bargain" towels and you see good towels in the catalogs for only half the "bargain" price, you can be pretty sure you're being swindled. These days, to get a mail-order catalog of your own, you have to be a regular customer—but you can find them in the Sears or Ward stores. There's practically nothing, except cars, that the catalogs don't list and describe.

Your library also has (probably in the reference room) the *Consumer Reports Buying Guide*, which rates products on performance, safety, and durability and lists "suggested" (often fake) list prices. Unfortunately, neither *Consumer Reports* magazine nor the *Buying Guide* make much effort to suggest whether something is worth buying at any price.

Another way to check prices is to shop around in middle-class stores. Careful surveys have proved that stores in poor neighborhoods charge more and stock poorer goods, on the average, than stores in middle-class neighborhoods. Therefore, when you are interested in finding something, look there, note the different prices and different qualities— and then find what you're after secondhand. If you have a car, you should certainly do your main grocery shopping each week in a big middle-class supermarket. Avoid sleazy "bargain" or "close-out" stores unless you are really an expert on what they're peddling; usually their sales are frauds.

PRIMARY PRODUCTIVITY

In ecological terms, primary productivity is the photosynthetic activity which, in algae, grasses, plants, and trees captures the energy of the sun and makes life possible on earth. All other forms of life depend on the primary productivity of green plants, both as oxygen-producers and as sources of nourishment. We survive only because of the intense biological activity that takes place at the interface of water or wet top-soil and the air. High primary productivity is not always a good thing; in a polluted lake, for example, plant organisms multiply rapidly to use up the nutrient materials flushed into the lake by sewers, run-off water containing fertilizers, etc.; the result can be algae scum. But when the primary productivity of food crops or natural forest cover is diminished by human activities, we endanger the very foundation of our society.

A society also possesses a kind of primary productivity: the work by which its essentials are produced. Food, shelter, clothing, transportation and medical facilities, devices required for communication and education: these must be produced and reproduced if a society is to continue, and they provide the foundation for the usually much more dramatic edifice of culture, government, and service occupations.

We all need to know, from an early age, how these basic necessities are produced, how to scrounge and improvise them in case of emergency, and what the requirements are to keep them in production on a healthy, reliable basis. Without this "tending to business," we citizens remain at the mercy of the corporations that presently control these things, and our prospects for long-term survival are slight.

PRODUCT DIFFERENTIATION

In an economic system dominated by huge advertising programs which often cost more than the product being advertised, you have to be constantly on guard against phony "refinements" to a

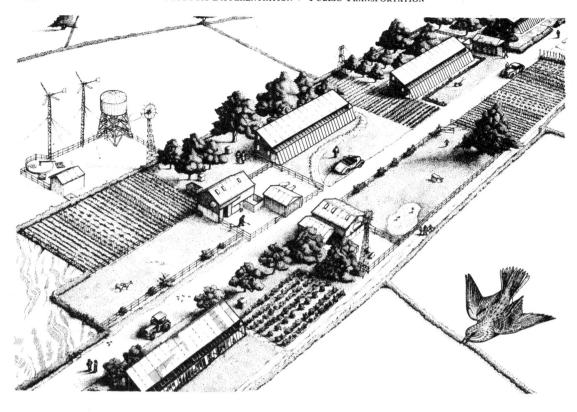

product which are used to justify higher prices. To add perfume and pink coloring to a detergent may not really increase its manufacturing cost at all; but its retail price will certainly be higher than if the detergent were unadorned. Soap with a fancy label and a special smell doesn't wash you any cleaner than the cheapest soap you can buy which comes wrapped in plain tissue paper. (It's so cheap that most stores except co-ops won't stock it. There are, unfortunately, many stores in which practically all the merchandise is of the fancy, inflated-price variety.)

The industries in which this sort of advertising distortion is most extreme are precisely those which advertise the most: cars, tobacco, soap, detergents, cosmetics, beer, breakfast foods, and so on. You can, in other words, be reasonably sure that more effort has been spent in advertising the products than in trying to increase their quality; the differences from one brand to another are minimal, so a lot of money has to be spent to convince you that those differences exist at all.

The basic ploy of the advertisers is to try to make you feel that by buying their product you will somehow feel better: sexier, wiser, handsomer, cleaner, less worried, and so on. But, of course, no product can really change how you feel —even if it did what it's supposed to do.

PUBLIC TRANSPORTATION

Under the impact of high gas prices, many people are switching to public transit, at least for commuting. They are finding, of course, that public facilities, which were starved for money during the era when the private auto reigned supreme, are having a hard time catching up with our new needs. Our once excellent streetcar network was scrapped; local transit companies were bought and killed deliberately to make people dependent on cars. Valuable rights-of-way were allowed to lapse. The frequency of remaining service declined so that using it became inconvenient. But now that it is no longer only the poor and disadvantaged who want to use public transportation, its quality will rise sharply. Suddenly new, imported technology is producing articulated buses. Social ingenuity is applied, resulting in reserved bus lanes. Shelters are built so that middle-class passengers can wait protected from wind and rain. Schedules are constructed with new intelligence, making connections easier; routes are extended; special runs are laid on for groups of passengers with common destinations. Where safety problems exist in stations or on late-night runs, guards are provided, and operators given radios. And so, ever so slowly, we are upgrading our public facilities to the standard of European countries 20 years ago. In doing so, we will save large amounts of energy and money, since the private automobile is the most wasteful means of moving about ever developed in human history. With sufficient public pressure, we may some day achieve a truly satisfactory urban transit system.

The degree to which you can utilize public transit, and either use your car less or get by without one entirely, varies with your location; but many people who actually live quite near frequent bus service don't realize it is there. You may just be in one of those well served spots which has frequent, rapid service in all the directions you usually go. If you are a sociable sort, you may find riding the bus rather more interesting than sitting all by yourself in your car, listening to some idiot on the radio. So call up the main office of your transit system and ask them to send you a free map of their lines, plus schedules for those lines you plan to use, if you know their numbers. Once you have the map, lay it out and study it awhile. Mark on it the location of your house, your job, and wherever else you go a lot—clinic, school, supermarket, downtown—or would like to go. Now try to figure out from the map whether there are direct lines that run from near where you are to near where you want to go. (With parking the way

it is these days, a comparison with car travel makes "near" anything within about six blocks.) If there's no direct line, what's the next best way to go—the one that involves the least changing? In the central areas of most cities, you should be able to get to most other places with one or two changes. If the best way to go is still not clear, sit down at the phone with the map in front of you and call the information office of the transit system. The line will probably be busy; keep trying. Tell them where you are and where you want to go, and be ready to write down what they say.

In most cities, bus or streetcar service is so infrequent that you need a schedule if you want to avoid standing on the corners waiting. Drivers carry schedules, or if there is no printed schedule, they know how often their lines run at different times of the day. Systems that have printed schedules will usually send them out if you ask by phone.

Don't get the feeling that you can't get around if you don't have a car. One of the secrets of living an interesting, vital life is to not let yourself get restricted to your own neighborhood. Get out and circulate. Don't be ashamed to carry large objects onto the bus. Parents wear papoose-type baby carriers or take on baby strollers; shoppers carry on big bags or little two-wheel carts; hikers wear knapsacks; travelers carry on luggage. It's a public service, and you're the public. Also, if drivers give you any difficulties, or are unpleasant, note down exactly what time it is and what bus line you're on; then write a tough letter to the transit company, giving this information and describing the incident. Bus driving isn't exactly a joy to the soul, but drivers owe it to the public to be civil.

And even if you do have an occasional bit of discomfort in using public transit, remember parking meter and parking lot fees alone would cost you more than what you're paying.

R

RAZORS

You like the idea of an electric razor? Well, don't be so sure. For what you pay for one you can buy about fifteen years' worth of safety-razor blades; and long before that time you'll have to lay out more money in repairs and replacement cutters on the electric job as well. But the worst thing about electric razors is that they make an obnoxious noise which shouldn't be allowed in any peaceful house.

Besides, you should really consider the question of whether to shave at all. The great trend towards beards and moustaches in recent years is not entirely a fad, but also a sign of new respect for our biological constitutions. (This is also true among women, who are discovering that, like most European women, they don't really have to shave their legs or underarms; leaving the hair alone also usually leaves it lighter and softer.)

Lots of people spend money on shaving soap or cream, which now exist in many tantalizing, perfumed forms. Actually any kind of soap will produce a decent lather if you have reasonably soft water in your area. If you want style in your shaving, it's better to get a really luxurious shaving brush. Incidentally, there's no need to wash the soap out of your brush every time you use it; just leave it lathery in a cup, or standing upright—saves soap and trouble.

Unless you have a super-tough beard that finishes off any blade in one shave, stainless steel blades are the best buy. (Some people can use the same stainless blade for weeks.) The story of these stainless blades is interesting. They existed in England and Sweden for many years before the American companies deigned to put them on the American market. (In fact the patent on one major "British" make, Wilkinson Sword Blades, reportedly was held by Gillette; later, Gillette bought the British company up.) The sole reason for the delay was that the companies could make more profit from the old blades. Keep this in mind when you read ads about "progress" in manufactured goods.

The ultimate style and the ultimate economy as well, is the old-fashioned straight razor. These have elegant bone or mother-of-pearl handles, cost only a couple of dollars, and literally last for a lifetime. All they require is a leather strop for sharpening—and a steady hand. Get somebody who knows how to teach you the special loose wrist motion that's required.

READING

When television came in, and Americans began spending huge portions of their waking time staring at it, technology mongers told us that the book would soon become extinct—or at least that we would begin to read even less than we had in the past. For reasons nobody really understands, this has not happened. Although some Americans still read nothing but newspapers and popular magazines, as a whole we are reading far more books (both in total and per capita) than ever before. One cause may be that more people have now had at least a year or two of college. Another may be the stupefying boredom of most television programs. At any rate, many people have discovered that nothing is as endlessly entertaining, mentally stimulating, hassle-free, and inexpensive as just plain reading.

Indeed, as our mass-media culture (including mass-market paperbacks) is increasingly controlled by giant multinational corporations, it will probably become ever more stuporous—which will make even more intriguing the crazies and geniuses who persist in writing personal, passionate books. A real writer is not the paid employee of some network, but an individual—probably a rather crotchety individual, with something pressing to say—and not just filling in time until the next commercial. Nobody bleeps writers out. When you read, you are getting what truths the writer may have to utter, as straight and unconstrained as possible—especially if you seek out works published by small firms and university presses, which are still run by people who have eyes for more than "the bottom line."

Thus no matter where in the world you live, if you have access to a library or a bookstore you can put yourself in contact with the finest minds humanity has produced—people seldom seen on the tube. You can match your wits against truly original persons whose thoughts put the "information" we are barraged with into a much clearer perspective. And you can escape the dead hand of network-approved "controversy"—it is in print that you have to look for really dissident, really critical opinions. We read to survive, we read to find out what is really going on, we read for pure pleasure. In fact, with new millions of people now literate, the world is going through an explosion of reading.

See LIBRARIES.

RECYCLING

Recycling is a fundamental Ecotopian philosophical notion. In any naturally operating ecosystem, all materials recycle, though not all at the same speed; this is the main reason why living systems have been able to persist on the earth's surface, in the face of great obstacles. Recyclability is not identical with survivability, of course, but it is intimately connected with it. Organisms that, like human beings, manage to exploit their environments on a large scale without recycling the nutrients they utilize will inevitably produce large-scale perturbations in the life systems that support them. The recycling of nutrients back into the agricultural system is, in the long-range view, about the most critical task any civilization must perform if it aspires to stable and long-term survival. We are performing it today with truly perverse incompetence in vast areas of the United States.

The recycling of metals and other structural materials is desirable for other reasons. Given relatively pure sources of scrap materials, it is much cheaper in energy and money to manufacture objects from recycled materials than from "virgin" ones. This is especially true for certain materials such as aluminum, whose original production entails vast electric power consumption. Moreover, mining in general is a process that is highly destructive to the earth's productive surface. It destroys surface agricultural or forest PRIMARY PRODUCTIVITY. It often pollutes water on or near the surface with acidity or particulate matter, and sometimes requires water supplies so vast as to deplete an entire region's water table or streams. While some mining will doubtless always be necessary (it goes back to neolithic times) we should attempt to minimize it, whether for metals or for coal. In a stable-state, non-expanding economy that possessed recycling mechanisms for steel, aluminum, copper, and a

The legal Clivus Multrum at Earth Cycle Warehouse. Kitchen garbage is brought out and added. Jar attached to the side of the fiber-glass tank catches flies. Finished humus is removed through hatch at lower left. Note insulated vent stack.

few other metals that were truly effective, our needs for newly mined metals would be small.

Such recycling, however, will depend upon what is called "source separation." It is difficult and expensive to separate out the different components of a "waste stream," as our production of garbage and industrial waste products is called, once everything has been thrown in together. Thus, in both households and businesses, we need to begin separation—mainly of glass and metals from burnable materials (which will increasingly be used in municipal generating plants) and from compostable materials. Gradually a network of recycling centers and buy-back centers will be set up; by 1985, the EPA estimates, these could be handling 50 million tons of our total 140 million tons of waste. (At the outset of the 80's, they handled about 10%.)

At present, use of virgin materials is subsidized by lower freight rates, and by hiding of the environmental costs of producing them. Recycling efforts should be subsidized to counteract these factors. In early stages recycling efforts will depend to some extent on the devotion of environmentalists. If costs can be accurately introduced into the pricing system, however, there will be strong economic incentives for recycling. These already exist in some industries, as for example in glass bottles; but recycling has been resisted by the corporations for other reasons.

REDUCING

Some three-quarters of all Americans are overweight, and at least a third of us seriously so. Obesity is not the only cause of our high rate of heart disease (cigarettes are another major cause), but it certainly doesn't do anybody any good to be overweight.

Being fat is ordinarily a long-range problem; it comes from a group of eating and living habits, and it can only be overcome by a great and serious effort—just like smoking. The first thing you must be clear on, therefore, is whether you care enough about it to make a real campaign to be thinner. Formerly heaviness was looked down upon less than now—it was a rare person who could get enough food to grow fat. We still sometimes hear it said that a fat child is a healthy child but this just isn't true—in fact, fat cells developed during childhood can never be got rid of. Children and teenagers can be obese just like adults. In general, of course, fat people suffer a great deal, especially from being unattractive sexually. But if you really don't care about how you look, relax and enjoy it; be fat with style like Falstaff, although of course your health will suffer.

The great fact about reducing diets is that most people can't stick to them, however mild they may be. This is why fortunes have been made with "magic" reducing aids (few people can stick to them, either). You can, surely, try to keep your caloric intake down; it can't hurt you. But there is really only one way to reduce. *To remove fat, you must burn it up through exercise.* Trick diets, shimmying machines, and other panaceas have no lasting effect whatsoever. (Amphetamines—reducing or appetite-depressing pills—are "speed" and fairly addictive and it's probably better to be fat than a speed freak.)

The only reliable and healthy way to get thinner is to be more active, regularly, every day. This doesn't mean that a body-building course or taking up a sport is necessary, unless you happen to go for that sort of thing. (See EXERCISE.) It just means *using* your body—for something other than a bag to store your guts in. You can burn up stored fat by making love (or masturbating, for that matter), by driving nails, by running, by doing sitting-up exercises, by scrubbing floors, by chasing children, by riding a bicycle, by walking around your office, by shopping. In the end, it usually comes down to walking. Walking briskly one-half hour every day is better for your health and your weight than occasional frantic exercise (which may actually do you harm if you're not in shape for it). So try to find some way of getting this into your daily routine. Can you walk to the store instead of driving? Can you pick up your children on foot instead of by car? Can you walk up and down stairs instead of taking the elevator? A daily half-hour of active walking (not just strolling) means, for most people, that you have turned the tables and will begin getting slowly thinner instead of slowly fatter. Don't be in a hurry; just keep at it.

Of course it's lovely if you happen to be interested in dancing, or hiking, or swimming, or table tennis, or tennis, or some other activity that involves bodily action. Home carpentry, scavenging, and many other activities involve the expenditure of considerable energy. So do manual jobs and many semi-manual jobs, of course: I was never as fit as when I was a book runner in a library.

You may worry that exercising more will also cause your appetite to grow—to the point where it cancels your hoped-for weight loss. Luckily, this doesn't happen. As a moment's calculation will show, if it did, anybody who was physically active would grow infinitely fat. In reality, your eating can never catch up with your exercising if you are active. It only catches up when you are sedentary, spending most of your waking hours at a desk or in front of a television. It has recently been shown that sedentary men average about 20% heavier than active men, though the active men eat 600 calories a day more. Sedentary women are 30% heavier, although active women eat 570 calories more. The moral is plain: if you are really active, you will be able to eat more and still weigh less!

Incidentally, people sometimes forget that alcohol is a drug that has considerable calories in it, as do the dips, chips, and nuts that often come with it. Cutting out booze may in itself cut down your calorie intake enough to send your weight down.

There is a persistent and sad delusion in American thinking about reducing—that somehow, by the invention of some new sweetener, or some pill that will magically circumvent the body's natural processes, we will be able to eat sweet stuff, do no exercise, and still not get fat. In the pursuit of this dream, we once turned to cyclamates in our soft drinks; they turned out to be carcinogenic, as even saccharin may be. Now we are chasing hopes that some chemical can be found which will help our bodies unload the vast amounts of fat and sugar we pour into them. In the end, we will have to accept our bodies as the wonderfully resourceful organisms evolution has bequeathed to us, and recognize that we can learn to treat them right, and count on them coming through for us if we do.,

Besides, a nutritionist named Timothy Lohman has calculated that if Americans reduced their intake of animal FATS enough to get down to their ideal weights, it would save more energy (in food production, transportation, processing, marketing, storage, and cooking) than the combined residential electrical requirements of Boston, Chicago, San Francisco, and Washington!

REDUNDANCY AND REPAIRABILITY

It was the failure of San Francisco's BART engineers to provide redundancy (parallel and "duplicated" capacity) in the control circuits that led one of its trains to go when the computer said stop—so that it ran off the end of the tracks. Luckily, in this case, no one was badly hurt; but wherever important things like human life are at stake, designers ignore redundancy at great peril. In the DC-10 case, for example, McConnell-Douglas's failure to provide alternate means of controlling wing flaps in case an engine pylon was damaged seems to have been the immediate cause of the terrible 1979 Chicago air crash.

What is striking is that in nature both organisms and systems generally possess great redundancy. Nerve circuits and particularly brain interconnections have alternative pathways. If messages do not get through one channel, alternatives

are often available. If nature were designing a nuclear power station, it would be arranged so that no fire in the control wires could totally disable the safety mechanisms. It is perhaps because nature has no mathematics that she relies on such double safety provisions while we, proud of our statistical probability theory, comfort ourselves with the belief that fatal accidents can be predicted with sufficient exactitude to make lethal risks acceptable. Generally, in such calculations, it turns out that something has been neglected, with the result that risks are much greater than we thought. It was probably a farmer, at any rate certainly not an electronics engineer, who invented the old proverb, "Better safe than sorry."

Natural systems, both organism ones such as mammalian bodies and ones such as a meadow or a forest, also possess the capacity to repair themselves when damaged: scars heal, bones mend, grass re-covers fire-burned areas, populations scourged by disease rebuild themselves. Most simple technology was also repairable, and by its untutored user, generally without specialized tools. Now, even "simple" appliances such as a refrigerator have many complex circuits, are constructed so access to parts is difficult or impossible, have many more components subject to more kinds of failure, and must be repaired by specialized persons if they can be repaired at all. This tendency, especially when added to a lack of redundancy, makes our technology inflexible and relatively vulnerable to massive dislocation in emergency conditions. It is, indeed, a special technological kind of decadence.

REFRIGERATORS

According to the research chief at *Consumer Reports*, it is not true that everything is of inferior quality today. Refrigerators and wringer washers, he says, are definitely better today than in years past.

Actually any refrigerator that is less than five years old can be expected to give many years of service, and many older machines still have plenty of life in them. So simple and sturdy are the compressor-pump units which do the actual work that they outlast the springiness of the rubber gasket around the door.

There is no real reason to buy a refrigerator new, in spite of the "Look, no defrosting" advertisements. (Frost-free models cost 40 to 100 percent more to run, besides costing more to start with. They also have complex circuitry, fans, heaters, and so on that break down.) Defrosting a refrigerator merely requires turning a switch and removing the water as the ice melts; why so many people regard it as a fearsome chore is beyond me. (If you don't like to lift out the tray full of water, use a little piece of plastic tube to siphon it into a pan or bucket.) But make sure you turn on a secondhand refrigerator for a while before buying it to see if it also freezes ice; and listen to the motor to see if it labors, especially when starting up.

There are three main ways to save energy and money on your refrigerator. One is to keep it at a temperature no colder that 40°F (5°C). (Put an ordinary household thermometer in the middle of the box for ten or 15 minutes.) Another is to buy a new door gasket for it, so the cold stops leaking out. (Check the gasket's tightness by putting a sheet of paper against it and shutting the door; if the paper slips out without friction, the gasket is probably shot. Try this at several places around the door.) Third, make sure your refrigerator is no bigger than you really need. A big box loses more cold than a small one; it also may waste food that gets hidden in the back. In recent years small "apartment-size" boxes have come on the market. They stand counter-high so you can prepare food on the top, and they have a freezer compartment for temporarily keeping frozen foods.

Frozen foods should not be kept more than a few months, even in a separate freezer at zero degrees; they lose their nutritive power. Only if you freeze home-grown food are you likely to save on a separate freezer as much as it costs to buy and run it.

RENT STRIKES

The law works slowly and sometimes it does not work at all. In the case of real estate, moreover, the law gives owners winning cards which have enabled them, in serious disputes, to throw tenants out in the street almost immediately. In New York and other cities, through rent strikes and the work of tenants' unions, the law has been adjusted slightly more in the tenants' favor. However, the tenant is still in a very weak position. It is desirable, therefore, to maintain a friendly relationship with your landlord whenever possible. By making an appeal on a friendly basis (see APARTMENT REPAIRS) you may be able to get some of the worst things about your building fixed.

If you complain to the city and the owner still refuses to make legally required repairs, the city authorities may let him or her get away with it. In some states, you can withhold a month's rent in such cases and apply the money to a fund for doing the repairs. But your lease probably waives this right, and anyway it is a tricky legal procedure; you'll need the help of Neighborhood Legal Service, Legal Aid, or a tenants' union lawyer.

Rent strikes, where tenants withhold rent in hopes of forcing a landlord or group of landlords to improve conditions or lower rents, have not proved widely successful in the United States so far, either practically or legally. However, recent court decisions have begun to hold that when tenants have requested a landlord to make repairs required under the local housing code and the repairs have not been done, they may legally withhold a part of their rent—how much depends on the extent of the needed repairs. The tenants must get together, work with the Neighborhood Legal Service office, and sue the landlord in court. If this trend spreads throughout the country, it will help enormously to improve our substandard housing.

However, in many situations it may be possible to force owners to improve conditions in their buildings through militant campaigns to expose them: picketing of their downtown offices or homes in fancy suburbs, well-publicized complaints through housing authorities, suits in small claims or other courts, and so on. Many slum landlords are outwardly respectable doctors, lawyers, universities, and others, who dislike being held up in the public eye as malefactors. If you can figure out ways of getting to them where *they* live, you may force them to fix up where *you* live.

Sometimes a determined rent strike will cause a landlord to abandon a building. Tenants' unions in some cities have seized such situations as opportunities: they have used their political pressure to get the city to condemn and purchase the buildings; then the city may either rehabilitate them or sell them to the tenants, who set themselves up as a co-operative to own the building, install solar energy equipment for heating water and other purposes, and generally improve the property through their own work—"sweat equity." This pattern, if it becomes widespread enough, could lead to important changes in housing, giving people a real stake in improving their environment. So tenants' unions should be aware of the possibilities and plan to take advantage of the opportunity if it arises.

REPAIRS, HOME

Every home needs to have a drawer or box or cabinet which is its toolbox. There you should keep a small but basic supply of fix-it materials. You'll have a certain amount of money tied up in these things, so you'll want to accumulate them slowly. But every item you can make last a little longer saves you the cost of replacing it. Often a minor repair, which costs nothing except the use of a pliers or some glue, will extend the life of an object for years. Some people, of course, make it a mark of pride never to have any repairs done outside the house; they allow into the house only things they know they can take care of. Most of us, though we admire such firmness of character, like to have at least some things around (such as a stereo) that we know we can't deal with entirely. But we can cope with many of the minor problems that arise.

Here are the basic household tools: hammer (a full-sized one, not a tack hammer); screwdriver; pliers; wood saw; pipe wrench; crescent wrench; a small wood plane; medium-sized file; hacksaw (for metal); wood chisel; putty knife; paintbrush; oilcan.

The basic household repair materials should include: electrical tape; some jars of assorted-sized nails; a jar full of assorted screws; another jar full of assorted nuts and bolts and washers; a box of spackle to patch holes in walls; paint thinner, diesel oil, or linseed oil to clean brushes. Also you'll find a collection of several kinds of glue useful: epoxy glue (for difficult gluing jobs, even glass, and where moisture may be a problem); Duco cement (for small objects—quick drying); white glue (Elmer's , etc.—for wood, paper, and similar materials); Barge Glue (a flexible, strong, waterproof glue for practically anything—hard to find, but worth the hunt). There are several other useful kinds of glue to have around, such as contact cement (for things you can't hold or clamp while they dry), silicone-rubber cement (for joints that must flex), plastic-mending cement, and waterproof resorcinol glue (for use on furniture that may get wet or steamy).

You should also have a can of lightweight oil to lubricate small motors or hinges; a spray can of silicone lubricant for sliding doors and drawers; and a penetrating oil for freeing frozen nuts, locks, and hinges.

Once you have a set place where you keep working materials, you will slowly accumulate more—leftover pieces of wire, steel, hunks of rubber tire or inner tube, bits of leather, partly used cans of paint (hammer the top back on tightly, or the paint won't keep), and lots of other fascinating things. Don't let anybody shame you into throwing any of this stuff away; you'll need it the next day! (If necessary, store it in boxes to save space.)

Beginning do-it-yourself repairers often get discouraged because they manage to get something apart, find nothing wrong with it, and then can't get it back together. There are two tricks you can use to make sure this doesn't happen. But you should also take comfort from the fact that often merely disassembling, oiling and cleaning, and reassembling a device or appliance will make it work again—you may not have noticed it, but in taking it apart you removed some dirt that was fouling a contact, or loosened a shaft that was binding.

The first trick is to provide near your working place a big surface on which you can lay parts out strictly in the order you remove them, and so far as possible in the relative positions they occupied. That way, even if you get confused as to what does what, you can always just blindly put everything back in order, if necessary. Be especially careful about washers, spacers, and other small and apparently trivial parts: they may have to be in just the proper order for parts to move properly, or even stay together at all. As you remove each part, notice if it has grooves or keyways or special-shaped holes or pins, and how they fit.

Secondly, you can code parts by marking them. This is essential in many gear mechanisms, for instance, where worn teeth must run just as before or they will bind; you mark them by putting small punch marks on two teeth of one gear and on the tooth they meet on the opposing gear. With wires, you can attach little bits of colored yarn, or small tags, or pieces of masking tape with colored markings. With wooden objects, you can write corresponding key letters or numbers on the part of each piece where it meets another piece, so that in reassembling you bolt A back onto the other A, and B onto B.

Most mechanical devices turn out to be full of old, gummed-up oil and dust which needs to be removed by soaking or wiping and dabbing with alcohol, paint thinner, or some other solvent. Avoid over-oiling when you reassemble. And in devices with small, delicate parts, such as clocks, you need special very light instrument oil or sewing-machine oil, used sparingly. Sometimes you can clean such devices without disassembling by using a straw and blowing hard, and then dabbing solvent on the end of a toothpick or a piece of heavy string.

Around every house there are things that drive you crazy because they won't work right. In many cases, this is a sign that you should get rid of them. But there will be times when you don't want to, or can't.

Cabinets that won't shut or stay shut. Scrape off the bumps of paint that have accumulated around the edges of doors and around hinges and latch. Unscrew the catch and soak it in paint remover or at least scrape it and squirt some penetrating oil into it. Better yet, throw it away and replace it with a cheap magnetic catch (one of the few modern household inventions that is a real improvement over what it replaced). If the cabinet is no longer square, you may have to unscrew the hinges and plane the edges of the door (or the door hole).

Can openers that won't cut or turn the can. Soak in hot soapy water, then clean the working parts with an old toothbrush, toothpick, etc. If the handle doesn't turn easily, put a drop of oil where the handle or shaft passes through the frame.

Handle loose on knife. If the blade is simply extended down into the handle, pull it out, fill the hole with epoxy glue, and force the blade back into place. Let it dry for two days to cure the epoxy fully, or wetness will loosen it again. Big knives usually have riveted handles that can be pounded to tighten.

Bed squeaks. Get rid of the springs (better for your body anyway). Lay a panel of plywood over the slats and sleep on that. If the frame of the bed squeaks, try gluing the loose joints. Or maybe now is the time to think about doing away with your bed entirely (see BEDS).

Electric fan doesn't go back and forth. Clean the oscillating mechanism under the back of the fan with alcohol, paint thinner, or even a small rag with soap and water. Put a little oil on the moving parts. Oil the fan motor—just a few drops—if you can find an oil hole.

Electric iron sticks. Irons get fouled from starch, soap residues, etc. Washing when cool (and unplugged) with soap and warm water will usually remove the stuff, or use very fine emery cloth or steel wool. Then coat the iron with candle wax, beeswax, etc., and wipe off the excess.

Stove pilot light won't stay on, or burners won't light. Since grease is probably the culprit, clean the whole thing thoroughly first or you don't have a chance. Warm water and ammonia works. Poke a needle through all the gas passages. Adjust pilot gas at the little screw where the tube begins that goes to it. Remove tubes to burners and make sure they are clear. They also need to be level. Sometimes blowing on it will light a stubborn burner. You will save energy and money by installing an electric ignition system (or by using a laboratory-type lighter and turning the pilot off for good).

Screen door bangs. Tack several layers of inner-tube strips along the doorframe to cushion bang. Or buy a door closer (tubular gadget) or a snap-shut device that flips over as the door closes.

Window blind snaps up, or won't stay down, or won't go up. On the whole, shades aren't very attractive. But the lightproof kind are the best way to make a room dark during the daylight hours. If you have them, you should understand the clever little ratchet mechanism inside one end of the roller. A shade that won't stay down can usually be fixed by oiling that little ratchet. It has a spring which enables it to rewind the roller just as much as it's pulled down, but no more and no less. If the shade is dropping loosely, you wind the spring up by pulling the shade down and then taking it out of the brackets and rolling it up to the top by hand. If it's snapping up too fast, reverse this: take it off the brackets and unroll it by hand. A shade that rubs against one of its brackets all the time may not be mounted level, or you may be pulling it sideways as you reach for it. If the edges get frayed, trim them with a scissors.

Electric plug won't stay in receptacle firmly. Sometimes you can get it to stay by bending the prongs of the plug outward slightly, and then re-inserting it. In very old receptacles, however, you may need to turn off the house current, remove the receptacle from its box, and put in a new one.

Bathtub and shower drains. These usually get clogged with long hair, which catches on the little crisscross just below the drain opening. With a long-nosed pliers or a big hairpin bent into a hook you can usually fish out most of it.

See also PLUMBING.

Electrical trouble. When you move into a new place, make sure you find out where the fuses are. The most common trouble with electricity is that a fuse blows out because too many electric appliances are turned on at once. If that happens, all the lights on that fuse's circuit will go out. Turn off most of the light switches and all the appliance switches and go with a flashlight or candle to replace the fuse (it screws in just like a small light bulb) with another of the same amperage rating (usually 10, 15, or 20 amps). Keep a box of fuses on hand, since fuses almost always blow at night when the stores are closed. A blown fuse has its little window blackened by the melted fuse metal inside. If the replacement fuse also blows, you've got real trouble, and an electrician is needed. Never put a penny into a fuse hole; if there is a short circuit in the walls, you may burn down the house. Replacing a low-amperage fuse with a higher amperage one enables you to operate more lights or appliances, but decreases the safety factor in your wiring, especially in old houses with their original wiring. If your trouble, however, is sudden surges of current from the starting up of a furnace or refrigerator motor, "delay" fuses will tolerate these surges without blowing.

Old houses tend to have too few electrical outlets, so people get multi-receptacle plugs to stick into them, and run extension cords all over the place. There is nothing wrong with extension cords, but most of those sold in ordinary stores are too light; they get frayed or worn and short out, or pets or children chew through them. The best thing is to build your own extension; measure to where you want it to go, and buy heavy-duty wire, a good solid plug, and a multi-receptacle outlet for the other end. It's also a good practice to staple the wire to the baseboard as it goes around the room to keep it from getting mashed by furniture, vacuum cleaners, etc. Be sure to use the "padded" staples for this and don't puncture the wire.

Keep electrical cords and devices away from sinks, bathtubs, and pipes, since water conducts current and you might get a nasty or even fatal shock.

If you are really short of outlets (or blow fuses often), consider whether you have too many electrical devices in the house. For ideas on how to cut down, see APPLIANCES, and also individual appliance names.

Complete Manual of Home Repairs, by Bernard Gladstone. Times Books, 1978.

RICE

Of all the world's basic foods, rice sustains the most people: it is the fundamental food in most of Asia and is widely eaten elsewhere. But many Americans eat it rarely. This is a pity, because rice lends itself to a great variety of tasty dishes which are easier to prepare than many dishes based on potatoes or even pasta.

Americans' lack of experience with rice may partly be due to the fact that we are not taught how to cook it properly, so a lot of people think rice is sticky. There is a surprisingly simple way to cook rice so it is fluffy and the grains separate properly; it doesn't even require any measuring. Pour enough rice into the pot. Do not rinse it unless the original container told you to—that washes away vitamins. Shake it level, and stick your finger down through it to the bottom. Put your thumb against your finger at the level of the rice.

Carry the pot to the sink, and slowly run in enough water so that when your finger tip just touches the rice, the water comes up to where your thumb is. Now put it on the stove and bring to a boil. Then turn the heat down low and cover. Brown rice, which is the best and most nourishing, takes about forty-five minutes; enriched white rice takes about twenty minutes. (Some people don't mind "instant rice," but I find it has no taste; but if it is enriched, it isn't actually bad for you.) Stir the rice every ten minutes or so to spread the water through it and break up lumps. When it's cooked, all the water will have been absorbed. If you like your rice dry, take off the pot cover toward the end and stir the rice; this will let the remaining moisture escape. (You can cook bulgar wheat, which is equally nutritious and can be used in place of brown rice in many recipes, in the same way.)

This method, besides being easy, conserves all the nutrients in the rice. While the rice is cooking, you can be preparing the other materials of your main rice dish. Fundamentally, rice dishes (except for those baked in the oven) are just rice-with-a-tasty-sauce-containing-protein-foods-and-vegetables. Within this general formula you can improvise wildly and still provide excellent nutrition at low cost.

S

SALADS

Like a big soup, salads are delicious and inexpensively nourishing, and are an especially good idea if your diet tends to be heavy and starchy—a vinegary salad dressing will cut through soggy aftertastes, and the green vegetables of a salad are full of vitamins and good for your digestion. (Most vegetables are healthier eaten raw than cooked).

The American notion of a salad—a layer of soggy, pale iceberg lettuce with a thin slice of half-ripe tomato laid on it and some kind of gooey dressing—should be forgotten. A proper salad is mixed in a very large bowl; if you have a wooden bowl you can rub it with garlic first. The lettuce should be dark green and crisp, and it is interesting to use several types. Many other vegetables are good in salads: shredded raw cabbage, cucumbers, carrots sliced very thin, green peppers, green beans, peas, small pieces of raw cauliflower, and so on. (Canned or frozen things are fine too.) Then, when you can afford it, you can add piquant touches with pickles or Italian pickled vegetables, anchovies, avocados, small bits of cheese or chicken, and so on.

Like coffee, salad dressings are an intensely individual question. You should get some good ingredients (olive oil, wine vinegar, pepper and other spices) and experiment with different proportions and flavorings until you find what suits you best. Recipes, in my opinion, generally call for a dressing that is too oily and not sharp enough, but they will give you ideas. A little dry mustard and a dash of lemon juice, soy sauce, or tabasco sauce also serves to liven up a dressing. If you don't particularly enjoy mixing salad dressings, make a whole jarful at once and keep it in the refrigerator. Even with the finest ingredients, making your own is far cheaper than buying ready-made dressings.

There are, of course, many other types of salads that offer tasty possibilities: tuna and chicken salads, salads with gelatin rings, and so on.

SALT

You might think that salt is just salt, and that there couldn't be anything to worry about in grabbing for the nearest package. Wrong! Large numbers of people in this country suffer needlessly from goiter (enlargement of the thyroid gland in the neck) because they use non-iodized salt rather than iodized salt—which costs exactly the same, but which many stores don't bother to stock. Unless your diet contains a lot of fish (which are rich in iodine) or unless you're allergic to iodine (which is exceedingly rare), buy iodized salt. Unfortunately, only about a third of the table salt sold in this country is iodized. If your grocer doesn't handle it, explain why it's a good thing to stock.

Many people eat too much salt, which tends to increase blood pressure and may, especially in pregnancy, contribute to needless weight gain. Never salt food before tasting it, and try to develop your palate's sensitivity to other than salty tastes—you might be surprised at the delightful delicacies you've been missing by oversalting things.

Prepared or processed foods tend to contain surprisingly large amounts of salt (as well as sugar), which is another reason to minimize your use of them. Bouillon cubes and dried soup mixes are usually very salty. Some things you think of as salty, like potato chips, may actually contain less salt than corn flakes. In general, anything that is pickled, smoked, canned, or frozen will have much more salt than its natural counterpart. Restaurant and fast foods are also usually very high in salt—yet another reason to eat at home.

Killer Salt, by Marietta Whittelsey. Avon Books, 1978.

SAUNAS, HOT SPRINGS

Contact with hot water has been regarded as a delicious and even holy experience for thousands of years, and hot springs are widely believed to have health-giving properties. But natural hot springs are rare, so various ways of providing similar experiences have been devised.

Like the hot springs, a sauna is a purifying experience. The Swedes, Finns, Danes, and Norwegians regard saunas as more essential to life than refrigerators. You may not like them, but it's worth trying. The sauna is a steam room (not the little steam cabinets found in some gyms or reducing salons). You can make the temperature in a sauna incredibly hot (like 160 to 195 degrees) and the sweat will begin to pour out soon after you go in—a strange but pleasant sensation. There's usually a shower in commercial sauna establishments, so you can cool off when you get too hot and when you're ready to leave. The sauna is a severe test of your circulatory system; if you have heart trouble, check with a doctor before you try one. In any case, don't stay in too long on your first try—ten or fifteen minutes will probably be plenty. And if you feel faint earlier, leave.

Saunas exist in many fashionable and expensive hotels, ski resorts, and so on; but homey and inexpensive ones can now be found in many city neighborhoods (look in the Yellow Pages under Steam Baths). Generally you get access to a sauna or hot tub, a shower, and a small changing room with bed, plus towels.

It is possible to build a sauna chamber into your house or apartment, though careful design is needed to avoid moisture damage to the structure. It is easier to construct (though more energy-consuming to operate) a hot tub, if you have a yard or a porch that can be strengthened to support one. See BATHS.

The Scandinavians have a custom of slapping themselves or each other with birch branches in the sauna; there's something about the sauna experience that sensitizes the skin and makes it receptive to the scratchy, sharp impact of the branches.

Incidentally, steam baths have no effect on weight reduction in the sense of removing fat; any drop in weight is just loss of water through sweat and will soon be restored.

Hot springs. These remarkable institutions are common in Japan where comfortable, inexpensive resort facilities are available near the hot springs. They were very popular in this country too in the early years of the century, then lost favor for a while, and now have found a new public among people who practice massage disciplines, try to take better care of their bodies, or simply enjoy the soothing, revivifying effect of soaking in hot and naturally mineralized water. Esalen Institute's site is a traditional hot springs resort; the spring was used, as most were, by the Indians. (The West is much richer in hot springs, which tend to occur in volcanic country, than the East.) Some people also believe that hot springs have curative powers; spas were common in Europe, and some hot springs resorts in California still have this kind of health orientation, occa-

sionally with mud baths. Most, however, are now for pleasure use, like the hot tubs which have become a derided but delightful feature of so many California back yards.

In a good hot springs the water is run into tubs in pleasant, simple buildings where there are facilities for changing clothes and for lying down when you come out—after ten or fifteen minutes in a 103-degree bath you will sweat for about a half hour and end up feeling high and purified, as if nothing can touch you.

SCAVENGING

The fact that American society produces immense quantities of garbage and junk is bemoaned by people who understand ecology. A city of 100,000 people produces enough solid wastes *each day* to cover two football fields a yard deep. Some of this material should never be produced in the first place (such as most packaging); some of it can be recycled, or burned to produce energy. But some of it is perfectly usable stuff that has simply been discarded by people who were tired of it; we need better ways of putting this component of the "waste stream" to use.

There is a particular kind of enjoyment gained in salvaging from a junk pile something whose beauty or usefulness only you can appreciate. There is always a sense of mystery and adventure connected with scavenging expeditions: you never know what you may turn up. Sometimes you may even turn up useful objects which you can really never identify—like the four crates made of expanded metal which I once found at the Berkeley dump, and which I've used for years to support bookshelves or plants.

In times past, anybody could scavenge at the town dump, and you still can in some towns. Both households and industries throw out an astounding quantity of perfectly usable pans, paper, clothes, appliances, boards, springs, tools, metal, cloth, glass. People are evidently dismayingly incompetent at simple repairs, leading them to throw out valuable motors, fishing equipment, tires, garden equipment, chairs whose only fault is a missing rung that you can replace with a dowel in ten minutes. Some of the most interesting objects are discarded merely because they are old: old metal washtubs, old car jacks, old window frames. Frequently these are much better quality than comparable new ones.

Even if going to the dump is not your idea of a pleasant outing, you can still be a scavenger. Every

This house was built almost entirely of scavenged materials—something quite common in these inflated times.

industrial establishment has some kind of private dump where it throws things that are later to be hauled away to the main dump, and you can go through it if you make sure the security guards know what you're doing (i.e., not stealing things the company wants). Companies throw away defective products, clippings and leftovers, old machine parts, office furniture, outdated paper forms, old reference books, a huge miscellaneous collection of stuff. Wander around the industrial section of your town and get to know what goes on there. Sometimes you will also find vacant lots where companies have dumped stuff in the past. Shipping companies stack crates and dunnage lumber for people to haul away free. Lumber mills sell slab ends (rough but usable slices off the logs) for practically nothing.

It is also possible to scavenge free food. Every day every supermarket throws out a considerable quantity of wilted vegetables and banged-up fruits.

Most of these are perfectly edible—they're just not pretty enough to sell at the prevailing high prices. Rather than let this produce rot and be hauled away, supermarkets will tolerate people dropping by to see what they can use. You'll also find dented cans, leaking detergent boxes, etc. Usually boxes or crates are lying around in which you can put the stuff you want. There are families in this country whose entire selection of fruits and vegetables comes from this source; they use their food stamps or small cash incomes for other foods.

The catering services which provide foods for hospitals, nursing homes, industrial cafeterias, schools, and so on are another source of free food: specifically, the daily leftovers of such institutions. Theoretically, they are obliged not to give excess meals away; in practice, by hanging around the kitchens you'll probably meet someone who can't bear to waste perfectly good food and who will pass some on to you. On such expeditions, carry along an innocuous cardboard box to conceal your haul and avoid getting your friendly supplier into trouble.

The extent to which you can make use of "waste" material is limited only by your own ingenuity. Given enough of it, you could theoretically construct a whole house, furnish it comfortably and cozily, and manage to supplement your diet wholesomely without spending any money. The key is to learn to look at things without preconceptions. Maybe that funny-looking metal bracket would make a clothes rack. That nice broad piece of wood? How nice it would look as a shelf. And isn't it possible to remove that pair of wheels, which would be fine for a little garden cart or a kid's pushcart?

Schools, Improving

Our school system is a very large bureaucratic machine, and it traps both pupils and teachers. Moreover, it is inhabited by large numbers of young people who would rather not be there; so its administration and operation take on many of the characteristics of penal institutions, which bear even on the students who *do* want to be there. It is doubtful whether the overriding problems of our schools can be solved except by drastic overhauls that address this central fact—which is, of course, connected with all the other problems: segregation and ensuing budgetary imbalance, racist and sexist (and just plain incompetent) approved textbooks, rigid seniority rules, and so on.

Despite the fact that their taxes pay for the schools, most parents are in awe of the school with its administrators, teachers, bells, and rules. They tend not to complain when their kids are getting a bum deal, or to complain too meekly, and get no results. In the end, schools must be cut down to manageable size and somehow returned to the control of the community; but what can you do in the meantime?

First of all, the basic law of bureaucratic life applies in schools just as in all organizations: the squeaky wheel gets the grease. Whatever your complaint, unless you make noise about it, it will never receive attention. And, unless you run up against either a firm rule of school policy or some really stubborn administrator, the louder your noise, the greater your chance of success.

The second rule is, find out who is who at the school. You'll generally be told the principal's name, but everybody else in the school bureaucracy tends to be shadowy. Be friendly and find out the names and duties of the people in the school offices; find out about the assitant principal and the other school officials. When you get put off, it helps to know whether the person doing it just doesn't want to be bothered, or whether you are getting an official No. Like all bureaucrats, school administrators hope you will take a vague difficulty as an official No, and go away: so your strategy is not to go away.

Third, spend time at the school. Officially schools are supposed to be open to public visits and inspection (usually you have to get a pass from the office to visit classrooms). But informally, many schools discourage active parent participation in the life of the school; you are supposed to go join the PTA, which meets in the evenings when the school is closed. Don't let them discourage you. Hang around sometimes and see for yourself. Most of all, let your child know that you care about what happens at school, and that you will go to bat about it if necessary. The school may be a separate world, but it should not be insulated from parental input.

Schools must somehow be provided which address the real needs of their students, in ways they consider appropriate. Whatever these ways turn out to be it seems certain they will not be invented by the present monolithic educational apparatus, which does everything in lockstep and on fundamentally white middle-class assumptions.

Some people have begun to argue that competition should be introduced and an educational "market" created, in which children and their parents could choose among different types of schools. Some schools would spring up that strongly stressed the three R's, while others emphasized artistic creativity or social development. Some schools would control students' every move and utilize harsh discipline, while others would expect students to police themselves. Some schools would emphasize intellectual attainments, while others would be oriented toward practical skills and perhaps production of goods and garden produce or services, relying on these activities to stimulate intellectual growth. Schools and teachers that, by some means or other, convinced students and parents they were doing them good, would get enrollments and prosper; those that didn't would go out of business.

Generally such schemes are connected with a "voucher" plan, which would in effect give parents a check, good for about what the existing monolithic system spends per child, which could be used at any school of their choice. (Indeed, proponents argue, the present system of assignment violates constitutional rights by its purely arbitrary nature.) Such plans will probably appear on the public agenda throughout the 80's. They are violently opposed by school administrators, teachers' unions, and just about everybody presently connected with the school system—which may of course be a sign they are on the right track. One critical consideration is whether schools would then divide into "good," academically top-notch ones and "bad," academically inferior ones (inhabited mainly by low-achieving black and Hispanic children). This is what has in effect happened in New York, where the middle-class sends its children to private schools, abandoning the public schools to minority children. If this model prevailed, it would obviously be tragic. However, the New York situation gives minority families and children no choice: they are simply stuck with their public school assignment. If they had a real choice, they might not be so unskillful in using it as critics of the voucher program seem to fear. Indeed, the real promise of the voucher scheme is that it would give such parents concrete economic power to influence the schools in ways the present system denies them. With all that money at stake, it seems improbable that nobody would be able to create schools that served genuine needs.

Even aside from such revolutionary changes, some steps could be taken to improve our schools within the ground rules of the existing bureaucracy.

All *big* organizations become rigid, rule-bound, and impersonal, whether they are companies, governments, or schools. The rulebook grows fat and replaces personal judgment; the individual child (and the individual teacher) become mere disposable units in a huge machine. This not only makes everybody tense, unhappy, and rebellious, it stands in the way of real learning, and encourages a reliance on meaningless standards of performance which are not related to a child's real life. As Paul Goodman has pointed out, the entire curriculum of the first eight grades can be learned by a twelve-year-old child of average intelligence in about four months; but schools insist on spreading this "achievement" thin, like prison busywork.

There is such a thing as a too small school. Children need the stimulation of a varied group of children, and a large enough group to find friends in. The ideal size seems to be somewhere between 60 and 120 children; a school of this size needs very little "administration." Indeed, a school of forty

children and four teachers should need none at all—the teachers could easily attend to the necessary "business" themselves. This means that the amount of tax money presently spent on schools could just as well support small schools operated in large old houses, warehouses, former stores, and so on.

It is also possible, of course, to take one huge existing factory-style school and simply divide it up into small, independent schools: instead of one school with eight hundred kids, you would have ten schools with eighty kids and six teachers each. But it is important to do this with real walls, and not just administrative ones; each school needs to become its own small world.

Each of these "mini-schools" would have its own ideas about how to do things, its own way of setting up classes. Although the rigid state requirements (one of the curses of a teacher's life) would still be there, they would hardly be enforced to a great extent in such a decentralized system.

Most of the teachers now working are well-meaning people who believe they have the welfare of children at heart. But the older ones were, for the most part, trained for a repressive system; the younger ones, who were looking for something better, have mostly settled into the patterns of the repressive system—they have had, after all, no real alternative in the public schools. Battered by administrative rigamarole on one hand and by hordes of desperate children on the other, they soon find they are really guards, not teachers. And because of this they demand higher salaries; their union adds its own rules to those of the administration; and the institution as a whole becomes still more rigid.

Many of the existing teachers have been selected by the system because they fit into it; they would not fit into small schools, with free atmospheres where the one-to-one relationship between teacher and child was direct, open, and challenging—in short, where children were treated as human beings. On the other hand, many intelligent and sensitive people who will now not consider going into teaching would be drawn to it once schools were smaller and more flexible.

Meanwhile, parents can sometimes find situations where a really good teacher is operating, and get their children into these classes. A good teacher is able to deal directly with children, without putting on a special face or talking in some special way. He or she knows that an adult has some natural authority, and uses this rather than trying to overpower children. Such teachers don't fear children's liveliness, and they deal with mischievousness and meanness frankly. Above all, they notice how children's minds work, and help them to apply their intelligence to the things that really matter to them. It is this, and not rote learning, that will help a child to become aware of what is really essential in education: how to learn.

SCHOOLS, STARTING

Oddly enough, it seems to be fairly easy to run an independent school if your children's parents have the money to pay tuition. In theory you have to conform to state school regulations about curriculum, but since these are so minimal they can be attended to in a few weeks' time. You do usually need at least one teacher with an official certificate, meaning he or she has gone through the education courses at a college or university. You also have to keep, or make up, some kind of attendance records. The real problem, as so often in America, turns out to be a purely mechanical matter: building inspection. In order to house a school, a building must conform to a large number of city regulations. Some of these, having to do with structural safety, number of exits, type of exit hardware, fire escapes, and so on, are excellent and any responsible person should attend to them anyway. Others, having to do with toilets and such things, carry very unreasonable requirements from the standpoint of a small school. You have two alternatives. One is to try to find a church, meeting hall, or other rentable structure that is already city-approved for group gatherings. (Some churches have Sunday-school classrooms they are glad to rent out during the week.) The other is to rent a big house, store, or other building and convert it to what you need. However, this means investing money, and also going through the city building department, which will require architects' plans, inspections, revisions, and endless hassle—and at the end of it all, you have no guarantee that an unfriendly inspector won't come up with some new problem you don't have the money to solve. If you do plan to take this route, make sure your lease contains a clause which releases you from it if you cannot come to satisfactory terms with the city.

SELF-DEFENSE

Opinions vary as to whether it is wise to resist attempted assaults (or rapes). Police often believe that resistance is likely to increase the danger of mutilation or death. But people (especially women), angry at being thought of as easy victims, have been practicing karate and learning other defense techniques: fingers in the eye, palm-heel against nose, knee-in-groin, instep stomp, and others. These may be effective if brought into play quickly by people who have been trained in them thoroughly, and are especially effective if the assailant is unarmed. The best defense, however, is to avoid situations where assault is likely to occur, and to be ready to run away screaming from anyone who threatens you.

In Defense of Ourselves, by Linda Tschirhart Sanford and Ann Fetter. Doubleday, 1979.

SENDING MONEY

Suppose you want to send money to relatives or friends in another city. If you have a checking account you can simply send a check, but the person receiving it will have to have an account at a bank and go there during banking hours to cash it; and even then it may not be easy. If it is important that the receiver gets the cash in hand quickly, it is better to buy a money order at a post office or bank; it costs about the same as or a little more than a check and can be cashed in at any post office or bank. Sending money to another country is usually quickest by bank money order or "bank draft," which you buy at a special counter in the bank. If you order something from abroad, or have to pay fees to a foreign government, a money order may not be acceptable and a bank draft may thus be necessary.

Money can also be transmitted by Western Union; see TELEGRAMS.

SEWAGE

Properly understood, sewage is an inspiring rather than dismal subject. In fact, it was out of meditation upon the sad state of our current sewage system that I first began to contemplate the possibility of imagining an Ecotopian society that would do such things *right*, from a biological point of view. Our present sewer system, with a few exceptions such as Milwaukee, is a waste system; it attempts to "dispose" of sewage. But, if we could rid it of toxic metals that industries dump into it, our sewage would become a prime fertilizer material; we could return it to the land, to grow more food, which would in turn become sewage again, etc., etc., etc., in the stable-state cycle so dear to Ecotopian hearts and minds. (See RECYCLING.) Properly run urban sewage plants have another appealing property:

sewage processing gives off methane gas, which can be captured and used to run the dryers necessary for fertilizer production, and also to generate electricity for pumps and lights; such a plant needs no energy from outside sources.

In time, however, we will adopt more direct and efficient methods of returning our excrement to the earth, in both a large number of urban households and most rural ones. Rapid progress is being made in composting toilets of various types, some of which also accept kitchen wastes, and which require no water (see WATER CONSERVATION). They provide fertilizer that can be returned to gardens or fields, and make our elaborate system of sewer lines superfluous.

The Toilet Papers, by Sim Van der Ryn. Capra Press, 631 State St., Santa Barbara, CA 93101.

SEWING

All you really need for sewing, of course, is a needle and thread and some scissors. But an old straight-sewing machine can be picked up cheaply, and it should last forever. The fancy zigzag models cost a great deal more and are essentially designed for virtuosos. They also have extremely complex works, and if not used and oiled just right may give trouble. So get a workhorse type, then relax and enjoy it. Unless you like to make salespeople squirm (and don't mind coming away empty-handed anyway) stay out of the shops that advertise "fantastic repossession bargains": these are bait-and-switch ads, and the advertised machines somehow never are there.

You'll also need a tape measure, a piece of chalk (for marking cloth), a good supply of straight pins, an assortment of different colored threads. It helps to have a sewing box or basket with compartments to keep things in, as you will begin to accumulate buttons, zippers, snaps, hooks, and other little objects. Also thread comes in so many lovely colors that it's a pleasure to collect them.

It's unwise to try anything fancy at first—stay away from items with turned-down collars, pockets, and other complications. Go to a fabric store and look for patterns marked "easy to sew," which have very complete and precise directions. Follow them slowly and don't cut any corners, literally or figuratively; there really *is* a reason for everything!

You can learn to work up your own designs by moving from the very simplest designs to more complex ones. You can start with the cloak, poncho, or serape, basically just a big piece of fabric with a hole for your head.

The next simplest item is a kimono or robe, which fits a bit more closely, but also requires no cutting except chopping pieces off a length of cloth. Sew the sleeves onto the main part, and then sew the sides together, and you have a pullover kimona; to make it a wraparound type, split down the front and hem the edges.

Full skirts that pull in around the waist with elastic can also be made in a few minutes. Make a large cylinder of cloth, run a wide hem around the top, and put a piece of elastic through it. Try it on, hem the bottom at the length you want, and that's it.

Shirts are complicated if you do tailored collars, so stay away from them. A super-simple blouse can be made just from one piece of cloth folded over, like the top part of a kimono. Sew the sides together from the armpit down to the bottom, Cut a slit for the neck hole and hem its edges. In cold weather such a garment may not keep you warm by itself, but it can be worn over some kind of turtleneck or other close-sleeved shirt.

All conventional clothes can be thought of as sets of tubes attached to each other. The body has a tube, the arms have tubes, the legs (in pants) have tubes. Since you can make a tube shape simply by sewing a piece of cloth up both sides, everything else is refinements: tucks, gores, linings, bindings, buttons, pleats, and so on. As long as you stick to clothes that drape rather than hug the body, you can exercise your ingenuity freely. Best of all, you can wear fabrics that may not be widely used in ready-made clothes.

One of the nice things about draped clothes, incidentally, is that they lend themselves to decoration: fringes, laces, rick-rack, frogs (fasteners you sew on, without buttonhole making). Sewing stores and secondhand stores are sources for thousands of such curious additions.

SHOES AND SANDALS

Like all clothes, shoes are a highly emotional subject. Some people enjoy shiny shoes and take a great deal of pain to preserve their leather. Others wear suedes, which can go for years with only an occasional brushing (you never polish them).

But there are some things to look out for in shoes. The worst is a tendency to produce deformed feet. In the natural shape of the human foot, its toes stick out straight from the attached foot bones. The wearing of conventional shoes of the pointy-toed variety (and there are plenty of these still around, especially in boots and in women's shoes) gradually deforms the foot until the toes get curved and compressed. This makes the foot less efficient as a weight-bearing device, gives work to foot doctors, produces corns and calluses where the foot rubs the shoe, and makes the foot ugly when, at intimate moments, it is removed from its casing. You should, therefore, wear round-toed, square-toed, or open-toed shoes if you are going to wear shoes at all.

The next worst hazard is shoes that may cause falls or sprains. Shoes that fit loosely, like clogs, increase serious foot injuries; and the higher the heel, the greater likelihood of twists, sprains, and strain.

Unless you are the kind of person who is always working around things that may drop on or scrape your feet, or in mud or slime, sandals have many advantages for everyday life. They allow the skin of your feet to breathe normally; they allow your feet to function as feet evolved to function.

Sandals and sandal lacing lend themselves to inspired designs which you can work out for yourself—always better than a factory-standardized style. Their history goes back to Greek and Roman days; their elegance has been appreciated for millennia. You can also wear tabis (thongs), the Japanese rubber sandals which are the cheapest footwear yet devised by the mind of man.

Even in cities, some young people today experiment with going barefoot. In my country boyhood, nobody wore shoes from the time school was out until it opened again, except on compulsory formal occasions. City pavements are harder on the feet than country dirt, but many foot doctors believe it is far more harmful to wear shoes all the time. The real danger with bare feet in the cities is glass: there is so much broken glass around that you really have to keep alert, even if your soles are quite hardened. You will also be unwelcome in certain stores or restaurants, where managers will tell you that bare feet are dirty. You can offer to have your feet biologically tested along with their shoes (which would prove that their shoes have far more bacteria than your feet); it probably won't keep you from getting thrown out, but you'll have struck a small blow for the freedom of feet.

Do sandals give your feet support? Some foot doctors think "support" is necessary, considering modern conditions, and some don't. In a general way, you can assume that if your biological structure needed something, it's got it; your feet turned out to be feet rather than hooves or webs because that was most useful to your ancestors over a period of hundreds of thousands of years. Many people wear sandals because they like the feel of air on their feet, or because they don't like hot, smelly shoes (wearing sandals is a good way to get over athlete's foot, which thrives when the spaces between your toes are sweaty), or because they just like the looks of them. Hundreds of millions of people throughout Asia wear sandals —when they wear any shoes at all. In short, if you like the feel of sandals on your feet, and don't have any ill effects after you try them for a while, stop worrying about it.

There are various tricks by which the life of shoes can be stretched. One is the old newspaper or cardboard trick: when a hole wears in the sole, you lay a piece on the inside. This is good only as a stopgap, however, because the hole will continue to grow. Leather soles and some hard composition soles can be made to last longer by putting a layer of duct tape or Mystik cloth tape over the holes. Surprisingly, a double layer will often last for months, especially if you also lay paper or cardboard inside the shoe and don't wear the shoes when it's wet outside. There's not much you can do for crepe rubber or soft rubber soles.

You can re-heel your own shoes if you have patience and a moderate amount of skill with tools. You have to find a piece of old rubber tire, a knife sharp enough to cut it to shape, and some short, small nails. Remove the worn heel, before the sole under it begins to wear away, by prying it off (try to find the bent-over nail ends inside the shoe and straighten them out, which makes it easier). Carefully carve out a piece of tire rubber of the exact heel shape. Then putting the shoe upside down over a block of wood, nail the new heel on and crimp the nails inside; then replace the inner sole.

If you want to get a little more professional, which is always satisfying, you can glue on a new sole that will last something like a year. You may be able to find resoling kits at a big dime store, or you can just buy the sole material (Biltrite makes some that has pebbled texture) from a shoe-repair shop; it comes in sheets that give enough for two or three pairs of shoes, and costs about 20% of what a resoling job will cost you.

The trick is in gluing the sole material firmly onto the old sole. Best way: Clean the old sole carefully with a stiff suede brush or dry scrub brush. Cut off a piece of sole material bigger than the shoe. Then slop on a layer of Barge or silicone glue, not too thick, not too thin, and press the sole and new material together, driving out the air bubbles. Then lay some small stones or other small heavy weights on top of the shoes, and if the soles still curl up at the toes or sides, lay the whole business on top of some heavy rags to support the new material near the edges. After the glue has dried (allow plenty of time) trim off the excess sole around the edges.

If the sewing that holds the top parts of a shoe together has begun to come apart, you may be able to sew it back. However, to do this by hand you've got to get some strong "button" type thread and get the needle to go through the old holes. This takes time, but the shoemaker will charge you a couple of dollars to sew a shoe back together.

It's impossible, without special shoemaker's equipment, to sew back soles that have separated from the uppers. When that happens, a shoe is beyond your powers of redemption and good only for puppies to chew on.

SHOWERS

Although a lot of old houses have only bathtubs, with a little ingenuity you can always add a shower. You need two things: a spray for the water, and a curtain to keep it from going all over the bathroom. Here is the simplest and cheapest way to do it.

Find some kind of ring-shaped or squarish tubing for the shower-curtain rod. A hula-hoop will work; so will old water pipes. The opening needs to be at least thirty inches across so there's enough room inside. Now look around your bathroom and see how the rod can be suspended. The easiest way is usually to use wires running to screw eyes set into the ceiling and the wall next to the tub. That way you can usually suspend the rod at four points, which will make it hang firmly.

Now find or buy some kind of curtain. The plastic kind sold in dime stores work fine, and you need two of them to go all the way around. This is one use where nylon fabric is a good idea, because it sheds water and dries quickly. Be sure to make the curtain big enough to go entirely around you as you stand in the tub—you must keep the wall and floor from getting soaked.

Plumbing-supply stores, hardware stores, and variety stores sell different kinds of spray attachments. The main consideration is not appearance or even shape, but whether the attachment will fit the spout on your tub. The rubber press-on type will jump off some spouts. Take along a little drawing of your spout, and make sure you can return the attachment if it doesn't stay on.

Some sprays come with a bracket that screws into the wall at neck level—you can hang the spray head there for a shower, or take it down to spray yourself in the tub. Other kinds you'll need to suspend from a wire or a homemade bracket.

Of course you can also let your imagination run wilder in a shower. Since bathing is such a pleasant thing, you may want to make your shower curtain big enough for two people to get inside. You can embroider designs on the curtain. You can build a translucent portable shower stall of fiber-glass. The spray fitting can be a complicated water sculpture made of gracefully bent flexible copper tubing, or plastic transparent tubing, or who knows what. You can arrange it to spray you from above, below, and sideways. . . .

See also BATHS and PLUMBING.

SILVERWARE

These days "silverware" usually means either silver plate or stainless steel. There are two reasons why stainless steel is better: it is generally made in simpler designs, and it doesn't peel the way plate does. Secondhand stores usually have big boxes full of assorted cast-off knives, forks, and spoons. (Don't worry about uniformity or you'll get nowhere.) Learn to spot used stainless by its soft gray color and its hard feel (silver plate tends to be a bit yellower, and often you can see brass or rusty steel peeking out where the plate has begin to wear through or peel off). Then pick out items that have plain lines and a good heft to them. Watch out for knives with loose handles. Bent fork tines can usually be straightened, but they'll never be completely straight.

Very rarely, a thrift-shop clerk will miss a piece of genuine solid silver and put it in the general grab boxes. Old silver can be exquisitely beautiful, and if you like it and spend a lot of time in thrift shops, check your library to learn how to spot it.

New stainless steel in pleasant and sometimes elegant designs can now be bought fairly cheaply in import outlets and some hardware stores.

If you eat oriental style, you should have chopsticks. Bamboo ones (not plastic) are best, and can be bought very cheaply in Chinatowns. They simplify table setting, not to mention dishwashing, and are fun to eat with.

Incidentally, when spoons or forks slip down the sink drain, you can often fish them up with a pair of chopsticks.

SLEEPING BAGS

The sleeping bag or bedroll is an invention of far greater implications than you might guess. It liberates you from the idea of the bed, the nest, as a permanent structure to which you must return every night; it makes the whole world a possible sleeping place. With your bag strapped to your back, on your bicycle rack, or thrown into the trunk of your car, you can camp anywhere: at friends' houses, in parks, in the country, in your car, at the beach—in short, anyplace where police leave you alone.

Moreover, getting children used to sleeping bags makes them far more portable than children used to sleeping only in cribs or beds. You can take them with you to parties, on visits, on long drives: so long as they're in their familiar bag, they'll be able to sleep cozily.

There are many forms and qualities of sleeping bag: the "mummy" bag—GI and other; the standard bag—which can be zipped onto another one to make a bag big enough for two people, and can also be used unzipped as a quilt; the double-size bag. The cheapest and easiest to get are made of heavy cotton and filled with dacron stuffing. These cost less than a good quilt. They are all right for indoor use or warm, dry weather. But if the temperature goes much below fifty degrees you'll be cold, and if they get wet and soggy, you'll really be uncomfortable. Any bag you plan to use outdoors should have an inner weather flap along the zipper to keep out drafts.

The best sleeping bags are filled with goose down and covered with (very light) nylon or (heavier but sturdier) a super-tight-weave cotton cloth. Some good bags also now have a thin sheet of plastic foam, whose air bubbles make excellent insulation. Because a down bag loses its insulating value when wet (and can be quite hard to dry out), some people prefer Polarguard-filled bags, even though they are not quite so warm; they maintain their insulating qualities even when soaked, and dry out readily. You can find descriptions of really good bags in the catalogs of expedition outfitters such as Recreational Equipment, Inc. (a co-op that gives out straight information and also a dividend at year's end—Box C-88125, Seattle, WA 98188), the Eddie Bauer Company (Box 3700, Seattle, WA 98124), the Herter Company (Waseca, MN 56093), and Sierra Designs (Fourth and Addison Streets, Berkeley CA 94710). A good bag costs money, but if you can afford a down bag, it's a smart investment and should last a long time if you take decent care of it. Most kinds of bags need to be dry-cleaned, not washed, but you can cut down the frequency of cleaning if you use a detachable liner, or pin (or tie) a sheet into the bag.

A down bag "breathes" especially well: as you sleep you give off a lot of water vapor as well as heat, and the down lets this escape. (Don't throw a waterproof tarp over your bag at night—it traps the vapor and will make you colder, not warmer. If it's raining, string the tarp a few inches above the bag, with an air space between. Otherwise you will get drippy and thus clammy.) Remember that sleeping on the ground requires a watertight ground cloth under your bag—without one your bag will suck up moisture from the earth. An inch-and-a-half thick foam rubber pad makes a good mattress, but a camping pad of Ensolite is warmer, and waterproof besides.

The best down bags have their seams sewn so that there are no thin patches, and if you're going to spend money on a down bag, get one that's made properly.

Camping out in deep snow or very low temperatures is a special problem. Don't try it unless you have proper gear and you're with people who really know what they're doing.

SMALL CLAIMS COURT

This is a special court (sometimes called by other names) where claims involving small amounts (generally less than an average month's wages) can be decided. You probably can't have a lawyer represent you and you can't appeal if you lose—though the person sued can appeal if he loses and in some states can have your suit transferred to another court where you *will* need a lawyer if you pursue the matter. The virtue of small claims court is that it is cheap, relatively easy, and relatively prompt. If you have a good case, and especially if you have good witnesses, you are likely to win.

In case of a dispute that may go into court, it is always wise to seek a lawyer's advice as early as possible, for instance from a Neighborhood Legal Service office. If you decide on small claims court, you should then send a registered letter to the person or company you plan to sue, stating your case and informing them of your plan to sue if they don't give you satisfaction by such and such a date.

If they don't come across, you must go to the courthouse to ask the clerk for advice and to file your suit. (There is sometimes a special clerk office for small claims cases.) You have to fill out a form giving the exact business name and address of whomever you're suing and pay a filing fee of several dollars. Usually you must also pay a small fee to have a marshall "serve the papers" notifying the people you are suing and requiring them to appear if they want to defend themselves. A date will be set on which you must appear in court to personally state your case.

Prepare for your appearance by getting together whatever documents you possess that are relevant: work orders, purchase orders, canceled checks, written estimates. Jot down an outline of your story, with dates in order, so you don't get mixed up in telling it. Bring along any objects that might be useful in making your case (damaged items, etc.) and also any witnesses who can support your story. A person with some expertise on auto repair makes the best witness in suing a repair shop, for example, so long as he or she is not your friend or relative.

The judge will ask you to describe your side of the argument and why you think you are entitled to "damages"—payment by the other party. State your case factually, without making emotional accusations. It usually helps not even to look at your opponent while you're talking. Try to present your story logically and as briefly as possible. Then the other side will have the chance to answer your case. Sometimes the judge will give you the chance to question each other, or make additional arguments. Then usually he or she will send the decision to you by mail.

If you win, the judge's decision normally causes the losing party to pay up immediately. At the worst, you might have to pay another couple of dollars to get a court "writ"—a paper which forces the loser to pay.

Pushing a case in small claims court will cost you about $10 and time away from work. But that is far less than a lawyer would charge.

Landlords and storekeepers can also sue you in small claims court, and you must then show up on the appointed day in court or you will lose the case automatically by forfeit.

Everybody's Guide to Small Claims Court, by Ralph Warner. Nolo Press, 1978.

SMOKING

It is now solidly established that cigarette smoking is self-destructive behavior, leading not only to lung cancer but to heart disease and other maladies. It increases skin wrinkling and reduces blood circulation in the skin, probably leading not only to smoker's pallor but to reduced sensitivity, including that of sexual organs. It costs society, not to mention the 50 million individuals involved, huge sums in medical bills, lost work, etc. Each year, almost 100,000 people die from lung cancer, 80% of which is due to smoking; only 10% of lung cancer patients are saved. Smokers of low-nicotine cigarettes have only very slightly lower death rates. And, new evidence indicates, it harms non-smokers exposed to "side-stream" smoke from other people's lighted cigarettes, and may pose genetic dangers to smokers' offspring. (Cigar and pipe smoking cause cancer of the lips and mouth, rather than lung cancer.)

Most of these facts are widely known. Yet the total number of cigarettes smoked annually has risen sharply—chiefly due to the spread of smoking among female teenagers, while other groups in the population (above all, middle-class professionals) have greatly cut down on smoking.

Nicotine is a mildly addictive drug, and it is unlikely that its use will ever be completely eliminated. But the extent of its use, and the fact that it is capturing large numbers of adolescent users, must be laid to two major factors: the heavily financed advertising campaigns of the tobacco companies (which are also able to fight off most governmental restrictions or even warnings about the demon weed) and, paradoxically, the very fact that smoking *is* dangerous. Smokers, a good deal of evidence suggests, tend to be rebellious sorts who do not enjoy being told what to do, even when it means their own survival. (Some of them also simply manage to disbelieve the overwhelming evidence.) Many people seem to smoke to assert their independence, their belief in their own physiological immunity, and their determination to continue their own gratification no matter what anybody says about it. Smoking for such people plays somewhat the same role as dangerous sports like skiing or hang-gliding. There is also a strong economic factor: lower-class people, whose lives are severely deprived, may literally feel they have less to live for than middle-class people, and are thus less motivated to try to extend their lives if it means giving up immediate pleasure.

In an ultimate moral sense, people have as much right to kill themselves with cigarettes as with sleeping pills or guns, and nobody should weep for smokers, who presumably know perfectly well what they are doing. The smoker's habit, however, blows irritating and harmful smoke into the common atmosphere and affects many other people. (A single cigar can spoil the dinners of a hundred other diners in a restaurant, for instance.) For many decades, nonsmokers suffered in silence and smokers assumed they had a god-given right to pollute. In the seventies, however, the tables turned. Led by militant organizations such as GASP (Group Against Smoking Pollution), the nonsmokers assumed the offensive. They pointed out that about 34 million people are "clinically sensitive" to other people's smoke and get watery eyes, headaches, or lung problems from it; while another huge segment of the population, even though not so sensitive, would rather not be exposed to smoke-filled rooms, especially now that these are proven to be dangerous to health. Though some smokers have always remembered to ask if smoking is disagreeable in social situations, the number of defiantly inconsiderate smokers is large enough to make most public places unpleasant if no regulations to control them are in force. Since nonsmokers greatly outnumber smokers, legislation restricting smoking was passed in 30 states and hundreds of cities.

What such laws do, in fact, is mainly to reinforce manners, by putting smokers on public notice that their vice is offensive. Generally they require restaurants and other public facilities either to prohibit smoking or to provide separate sections where smokers can smoke without bothering nonsmokers. In the communities where such laws exist, most smokers have become a good deal more conscious of their impact on others; nonsmokers have become more assertive of their rights; "no-smoking households," with signs at the front door, have proliferated; and smoking has tended to become "socially unacceptable." Although

smokers who scoff at the laws are virtually never prosecuted, they are definitely discouraged from reckless smoking; sometimes they even develop enough guilt to attempt to stop smoking. (Nicotine addiction requires professional assistance to kick, in most cases; organizations and services exist in most cities.)

It is sometimes argued that anti-smoking ordinances are, like anti-marijuana ordinances, primarily "moral," and thus ultimately unconstitutional. This would be true of legislation prohibiting smoking entirely; but no one has proposed such legislation since 1914, as far as I can determine. Nicotine should, like marijuana and other presently illegal mind-altering substances, be freely available and consumable without penalty wherever its consumption does not intrude on important rights of others—such as the right to breathe clean air. People have the right to injure themselves or even kill themselves, but society has the right to insulate itself from the side-effects of the process.

Most smokers come from families where the parents smoked. An additional motive for trying to stop, therefore, is to protect your children from coming to unconsciously feel the habit is natural and desirable.

The tobacco industry fights legislation limiting smoking and tobacco advertising by hiring expensive advertising and political campaign firms. Nonetheless, a substantial majority (even of smokers themselves) favor restriction of smoking in public places, and during the 80's legislation to control smoking will probably become virtually universal. For information on how to help, contact Action on Smoking and Health (ASH), 2000 H Street NW, Washington, DC 20006.

Cigarette smokers also harm themselves and often their children through the accidental starting of fires in beds, sofas, and easy chairs. These cigarette-caused fires do something like two billion dollars of damage every year and account for 45% of the 4,900 deaths caused in home fires. An abandoned cigarette may smoulder for 45 minutes, but can start a fire in 15. The strength of the tobacco lobby has so far stymied all moves to make cigarettes self-extinguishing, though a simple and proven way to do so has long existed. Instead, elaborate attempts are being made, at enormously greater expense, to fireproof furniture! Unfortunately, much furniture is constructed with polyurethane foam, which gives off toxic smoke when it burns. (Generally, smoke inhalation kills people in fires, not actual contact with the flames.)

There is some evidence that a vegetarian diet and the avoidance of alcohol give the body a more alkaline balance which somehow helps to counter the desire for nicotine. Especially alkaline foods are molasses, lima beans, raisins, dried figs, beet greens, spinach, yeast, almonds, carrots, soybeans, sweet potatoes, and tomatoes.

SOCIAL SECURITY

Until 1935, when the Great Depression had brought the country to the verge of revolution, the United States had no social insurance program of any kind—lagging behind most other industrial countries. It was strictly dog eat dog—and when old age came, die dog die.

Social insurance is like private profit-making insurance except that it is cheaper and democratically controlled by Congress. It operates by spreading the risks of life among a huge mass of people. During working years, employees and employers (and, through the IRS, self-employed people) pay Social Security a percentage of their paychecks. This money goes into a special trust fund. When earnings drop or stop, because of disability or death or retirement, monthly cash benefit payments go to the worker or the surviving family. Because benefits have been increased, and because a greater number of retired people are coming along, Social Security deductions have grown steadily, and in the 80's, employees will pay about 7% of their income, of which 1% is for Medicare.

Most older people have checked into Social Security and know what their benefit payments will be when they reach retirement. But actually, Social Security insurance covers many other situations, including those which can affect young people. Long before retirement, you or members of your family may become eligible for Social Security payments. To find the Social Security Administration office, look in the phone book or ask at the post office. Here are the times when you should go around to the local office:

To get a card. When you first get a regular job, the employer will ask you to get a Social Security number; employers are obliged to take Social Security deductions from your pay, and contribute an equal amount themselves. All your deductions, accounts, and benefits will be handled under this number, even if you marry, divorce, or change your name. (If you happen to get two cards, it will cut down your benefits; go to a Social Security office and get the situation straightened out.) Your account information is held under your number at the Social Security Administration, Baltimore, MD 21235, and you can write at any time to get an accounting from them. Your benefits will depend on how much and how long your contributions have been, so it's important to keep the record accurate; especially if you change jobs often, be sure none of your deductions go unrecorded, penalizing you later.

When there is a death in the family. Survivors' insurance payments are due to children, widows (and sometimes dependent parents and divorced wives), and dependent widowers of deceased workers who have had Social Security deductions from their pay in recent years. Recently, benefits became payable to ex-spouses in cases where marriages lasted ten years or more, even if the former spouse has remarried. Moreover, widows and widowers no longer forfeit their benefits if they remarry—which will probably decrease the number of unmarried elderly people who have been living together. Children are now eligible when either parent dies. Even if you think you may not be eligible, go and check on it; there's a lot of money at stake. First, there are outright death payments, which should cover burial expenses. Second, there are monthly benefits to the survivors—indefinitely for adults, and up to the age of eighteen for children—extended to twenty-two if you go to college (and remain unmarried).

When somebody is disabled (meaning they can't work or expect to work for twelve months). Not only the disabled person, but other members of the family may be eligible for payments. Disabled children become eligible if a parent dies or begins to receive retirement or disability payments. It is important to go to the Social Security office and apply for benefits as soon as it appears someone is disabled for a lengthy period; this will avoid the possible loss of benefits. Curiously, it's easier to qualify for disability benefits when you're young than when you're over thirty-one. Handicapped and mentally retarded people are often eligible for substantial benefits.

When you are nearing retirement. Men are eligible for full retirement benefits, and Medicare coverage, at age sixty-five. Women are eligible at sixty-two. If you postpone retirement, your benefits when you do retire will be somewhat larger. And if you return to work after retiring for a while, your added earnings will usually boost your retirement payments when you stop working. If they wish, men can retire at age sixty-two, and widows at sixty; but the monthly checks are somewhat smaller. Nevertheless, depending upon your circumstances and style of life, earlier retirement may be preferable. However, you should go to the Social Security office to apply for benefits several months before you actually reach retirement age. The precise date at which you officially begin retirement may raise or lower your benefits received in your first "retirement year" by several thousand dollars. It will save time and simplify the application procedure if you take along your Social Security card, proof of age (such as birth certificates) for yourself and children, and your last year's income-tax form.

People receiving retirement payments under Social Security can also work, but their payments will be reduced somewhat. You can earn up to a set amount per year (in 1979 it was $4,500, or about the price of a compact car, and it will rise as the years pass) without any reduction in Social Security payments. Above that, however, $1 of benefit payments is withheld for every $2 you earn. "Substantial" employment (more than 45 hours per month) can cut your benefits irrespective of what you actually earn. Income from savings, investments, pensions, royalties, or insurance does not count as work income, so the situation isn't quite as bad as it seems. Nonetheless, it clearly pays retired people to try whatever they can to avoid ordinary paid work and instead use time to produce things for themselves—or to make transactions by barter or other informal methods; since no money is involved, this will not cut down your Social Security checks.

The total sums involved in Social Security are often large, even though the payments, on a monthly basis, may sometimes seem meager. As of 1980, a young widow with two small children, whose husband had an average income would get about $854 per month. By the time the children reached eighteen, the total payments would amount to more than $112,000—far more than could be gotten from any insurance policy they could afford. Some 7½ million people are now receiving Social Security survivor benefits. Inflation has taken a heavy toll—especially on older people, whose benefits are often based on only a few years of covered work, back in the days when dollars were worth a great deal more. Nonetheless, Social Security is one of the few undeniable good things in American life. It gives huge numbers of workers a guarantee of minimal subsistence in old age, and under the pressure of inflation (and an increasing elderly population) it is constantly being liberalized.

It is to your advantage to make sure Social Security deductions are taken from your pay even for short, low-paid, or part-time jobs. Some benefits depend not on the total money deducted, but on whether any was deducted over a three-month period. Domestic workers, especially, often neglect to have Social Security deducted from their already pitiful wages. But you can be "currently insured," as the term goes, if you've earned as little as $50 in three months—so long as Social Security deductions were taken out by your employer. (This qualifies you for disability and survivor payments you may desperately need.)

Not only wage earners but also farmers and other self-employed people can get Social Security coverage. And self-employed people—which includes a lot of artists, musicians, writers, inventors, travelers, and other ingenious souls, as well as people with small farms and more or less regular businesses—can get credit for a whole year of coverage if they have a net income of only $400. Farm workers can also get a whole year of coverage if they make $400. You get to be "fully insured" when you've run up a total of covered years that depends on your age; the minimum is 1½ and the maximum is 10 years. You get maximum benefits if you've been working at high-paid covered jobs in recent years, so that your average covered income is high; but an averaging process is used, so that a couple of lean years can often be left out of the calculations. If you work partly for tips, it may not be wise, in the long run, to underreport them; you'll probably lose far more in later Social Security benefits (because your reported average wages will be lower) than you'll save from income tax.

If you are operating something that might qualify as a business, get all the information you can on income tax and Social Security. Often enterprises which show virtually no profit on paper can be very useful to their operators, and run up Social Security credit besides. The paperwork is not very difficult because for small incomes you don't have to itemize expenses. Social Security offices have a special booklet for farmers which might give you some interesting ideas.

It is now possible to receive Social Security payments abroad, but the decline of the dollar means that you must find a low-cost country; living expenses in most of Europe are now higher than ours. Make arrangements at your local Social Security office.

Children receiving survivor benefits because one of their natural parents has died will lose their payments only when they reach eighteen, or if they are adopted by someone who is not a stepparent, grandparent, or other close relative. They may receive such payments until twenty-two if they are in college and remain unmarried.

Service in the armed forces counts as covered employment.

Aged, blind, and disabled people may qualify for "supplemental security income" in addition to or in place of Social Security payments.

The present Social Security system favors wives who stay home over wives who work (and thus contribute to the Social Security fund, but get no more benefits). It also penalizes married couples in which both husband and wife work (since they pay double contributions, but actually get *less* benefits than one-earner couples).

Oddly enough, since getting Social Security cards is a simple matter that requires no proof of your identity, they are often used for identification. It is also no particular trouble to get a new card with your new name on it if, for some reason, you change your name. Once we are all computerized into some national foolproof photographic identification-card scheme, this rather delightful system will doubtless be changed.

See MEDICARE AND MEDICAID.

SOLAR ENERGY

All our energy but nuclear is solar: coal and oil were made from deposits of billions of plants in prehistoric ages. But we are learning now to use "current" solar input, which is indefinitely renewable. There are several ways to do this.

Direct heating can be used to provide domestic hot water and industrial process steam. The devices needed range from simple "breadbox" heaters, which are essentially just barrels painted black and put in an insulated glass-fronted box, to elaborate systems of receptor panels, pumps, heat exchangers, and so on. These are sometimes combined with reflecting or concentrating surfaces to increase the solar heat falling on them. And, by suitable design for adaptation, sunlight can be used to warm living spaces directly; a vast amount of architectural ingenuity is currently going in this direction (see also INSULATION). For information, call the National Solar Heating and Cooling hotline: 800-523-2929.

We can also tap the energy stored as heat in the oceans, by building what amount to giant refrigerators running in reverse. They suck up cool water from the depths and put it next to warm water from the surface; the thermal differential can be made to produce power. And we can, through wind generators and windmills, tap the heat energy available in the movements of the atmosphere. Windmills were formerly a normal feature of American rural life, and they are returning to the land. Small ones that generate enough power for a household can be set up in backyards, but they require a place with strong and steady winds. Power companies are beginning to build gigantic arrays of windmills on windy passes. The Hawaiian Islands could, by harnessing their steady trade winds (and their GEOTHERMAL ENERGY) become essentially self-sufficient in energy.

Biomass energy is solar energy stored in plants, which we can burn directly (see WOOD STOVES) as is increasingly done with wastes from farms and forests, or turn them into burnable alcohol through fermentation and distillation. We happen to have a substantial though underground source of expertise in low-cost distillation in this country—the whiskey makers of the South—and they are being pressed into service to perfect relatively small-scale plants to produce alcohol for adding to gasoline; about 10% in a "gasohol" mixture has the effect of raising the octane level and decreasing the pollution output. The oil companies do not like this development because, since alcohol production is an intermediate technology that almost anybody can do, it takes control of energy supplies out of their hands. Nonetheless, it seems certain to spread enormously during the 80's, both in the US and elsewhere. (Alcohol can also be burned in stoves, of course, though it is not a terribly efficient fuel for such purposes. Never drink fuel alcohol, by the way; it might make you blind or crazy or at least very sick.)

A great deal of work is being done on ways to convert solar energy into electricity. At grotesque expense, a federal "solar tower" has been constructed which is supposed to produce, if it ever works, power on the scale of a central power plant. "Solar farms" have been proposed which would be the size of a major airport and, through generating steam with concentrating mirrors, produce very large amounts of electricity. Despite a good deal of incompetence and bureaucracy, these devices will probably become economically feasible during the 80's.

Photovoltaic cells, which produce current simply by being exposed to sunlight have the real potential for solar electricity. Ultimately, thus, you should be able to run a modest household's refrigerator, lights, radios, and so on from a cell array tacked

A newly designed and just completed home in Berkeley, California, taking advantage of solar with a separate collector array.

An extremely large solar collector array being installed at a factory site.

onto your roof. Even with technology known by 1980, it was possible to bring the cost of such cells, and the electricity they produce, down to competitive levels if the government had been willing to institute a massive procurement program, as it did with nuclear energy and aircraft innovations. But here again, the implications are unpleasant to the utilities, who would lose control of major segments of their markets and experience severe financial difficulties as a result. It may very well be that in this area too, as in electronics and automobiles, we will have to wait for the Japanese to make the critical breakthrough on a massive scale.

Although the production of solar energy devices does involve some pollution, solar is generally much cleaner over-all than conventional energy sources, and especially as compared to coal. See AIR POLLUTION.

The Soft Energy Path, by Amory Lovins. Harper & Row, 1977.

SOUPS

In old farm kitchens a soup pot was simmering on the back of the stove almost constantly. Today, soups are still one of the best ways to provide nutritious and interesting eating at a low cost. A really hearty soup can be the mainstay of a meal, together with a salad and some good bread. And soups can be made from things that are tasty but also low in cost; neck bones, chicken backs, fish, protein-rich beans or lentils, vegetables such as leeks that are cheap but good. Moreover, a big soup can be one way of using up leftovers without calling attention to them; just toss them in! Soups will keep in the refrigerator for several days. You can vary them easily by adding spices and herbs.

One of the pleasures of soup making is that you can play infinite variations on the basic themes available:

Meat soups. You can make your basic broth by boiling soup bones (which a butcher may give you free if you ask for them "for my dog"), super-cheap oxtail pieces, or the carcass of yesterday's chicken. Skim off the unhealthy fat. Sometimes you may want to stop there—a clear thin soup may be just the thing if you're sick. Or you can add green vegetables, potatoes, carrots, and onions.

Fish soups. If you really want to make a cheap, nourishing soup, buy fish fragments (heads, tails, and odd small pieces), put them in a cheesecloth bag, and boil them. (Or else just toss them in and then strain the resulting broth.) There are many special kinds of fish soups, such as bouillabaisse, which contain several different kinds of seafood. And a fish soup may be turned into a chowder by adding skim or low-fat milk (for white) or tomato sauce (for red).

Vegetable soups. A wholesome and filling soup can be made simply from inexpensive vegetables: cabbage, turnips, potatoes, carrots, green beans, onions, and so on. Often you can get these free at supermarket back doors early in the morning. If you have a blender, you can make some really scrumptious chilled soups from potatoes (vichyssoise), broccoli, spinach, carrots, etc.; there is no real line between a drippy puree and a thick soup!

Fruit soups. Yes, there *are* such things, especially in Scandanavia, and absolutely delicious, too. The problem is to keep them from getting too sweet or sticky (which can happen if you boil them too long), and they are best eaten chilled.

Bean soups. Soybeans are the most nutritious beans, and can be made into many different soups; red beans, white beans, garbanzo beans, lentils, black-eyed peas, and a host of other bean-type things also make thick, rich soups.

To thicken a soup or make it more filling, add various kinds of pasta (macaroni, noodles, little rings, etc.) or rice or buckwheat groats or whatever you please.

Don't be intimidated by recipes that start out "To your stock, add...." Stock is simply water with juices in it. You produce your own stock when you boil bones in plain water with a little salt. You can also make stock by throwing in a couple of bouillon cubes or using a powder that comes in a jar, either beef or chicken type.

Because of the importance of soups in an interesting but inexpensive diet, you should get soup bowls that really please you; they should be sturdy and big enough for a meal-sized portion. (If you only want a little, use a cup.)

SPRAY CANS

Some states have already outlawed these as a menace to the ozone in the atmosphere. But they are also a menace to you, and you should keep them out of your house (and especially out of your car). They can explode like hand grenades if they get hot—as they will in a glove compartment, or just on a windowsill in the sun. They tempt kids to play with them for fun—so they may give themselves or each other a dose of deadly insect spray or paint. Even innocent-looking hair spray is a menace—if you use it in a small room or carelessly, you'll breathe it in and it may coat so much of the inside of your lungs that their oxygen-absorbing capacity is cut down. Several other kinds of lung damage have also been caused by aerosols.

When a liquid absolutely has to be sprayed (which is probably a lot less often than you've been told by the advertisers), get it in a spray bottle that you work with a finger-pump. Keep it well away from your face, and if possible use it quickly and get out of the room until the tiny droplets that will be suspended in the air have a chance to settle.

STABLE-STATE SYSTEMS. See RECYCLING.

STOCKING UP

It is often wise to buy standard necessities in bulk, since that way you can usually get quantity or case discounts. Besides, it saves gas and tedious trips to the store. Many people do this for a surprising number of items: toilet paper, soap, shampoo, canned foods they use regularly, rice, lentils, and other staples, cleaning materials, light bulbs, and so on. In an age of inflation, this ordinary argument of economy becomes even stronger. If you buy, say, a couple of cases of toilet paper now, you are in effect saving an extra ten to twenty percent on your purchase outlays over the period in which you use it—whereas if you put that money in an ordinary savings account, and bought your paper roll by roll, you would only earn five percent on it. Aside from maintaining an emergency fund, thus, you might in fact be wise to plow *all* your spare cash into stocks of future necessities.

But, of course, there's a limit—usually the limit of your storage space. And you only want to stock up on things that don't spoil, rot, or mildew under your storage conditions. Be careful, also, not to overestimate your consumption rate—most preserved foods lose much of their nutritive value if kept more than six months or so, and storing frozen food costs so much in electric consumption that keeping it very long eats up the original savings you made by finding something at a good price. What you need to concentrate on, thus, are mainly non-food items. Inventory your house and jot down the things to keep an eye out for at discounts: coffee, toothpaste (if you use it), paper supplies, durable goods like towels and sheets, etc.

STOVES, PORTABLE

If you do a lot of camping or are otherwise on the move, a portable stove can be a blessing and save you a lot of money. (I used to keep mine in a VW camper, but it was easily removable to take to campsites.) The new propane stoves are as easy to use as a stove in a house—but it only costs a few cents to cook a meal on a Coleman stove using white gas, and about eight or ten times as much to cook it with propane.

If you are going backpacking, you will need a really small, light stove. There is a Swedish model called the Svea which burns white gas, has a self-contained cooking pot, and is reliable. (Practice starting and cleaning it before you go out with it; it's tricky.) Primus makes a good alcohol-burning backpacker's stove. These tiny stoves generate a surprising amount of heat, but you would not want to do regular home cooking on one.

The Coleman brand name is one worth paying attention to; they make better car-camping stoves than anybody else and cheaper than most. However, don't be misled by their expensive "Coleman fuel." The stoves run perfectly well on ordinary white (unleaded) gas, also sometimes called naphtha. The procedure of pumping up the pressure in the tank may seem complicated at first, but it soon gets to be second nature. And unless you do something dumb like trying to pour new fuel into a hot tank attached to a hot stove, they are perfectly safe. (Cool all gas-burning appliances and take them to a safe place for refilling—away from people, tents, clothes, leaves, grass, or anything inflammable.)

White-gas lanterns are also the best kind of intense light where electicity is not available. Their disadvantage compared to kerosene is that they make a constant hissing noise.

STREET LIFE

After the mess made of our cities by redevelopment and "renewal," some planners have finally realized that lively street life is the essence of cities. You have to arrange things so that the streets are interesting and safe, or people won't go into them—when they get the chance they will move out to the suburbs, leaving their old neighborhoods to rot.

As it happens, interesting streets are also safe streets, because they bring a lot of people out onto them. No city can have enough police to patrol everywhere; in the end, a citizen's safety depends on fellow citizens being around, keeping an eye on things, taking a hand if somebody is getting roughed up or robbed, and so on.

In looking for a place to live, therefore, you should find out what the street life is like. Avoid neighborhoods where people turn the streets over to the hustlers and muggers at nightfall. The best streets tend to be a little noisy, a little crowded; you're always running into neighbors and passing the time of day as you go to the store or the bus or subway. Places where people are on foot a lot are better than places where everybody drives. Streets that are full of little shops are livelier and safer than streets occupied by huge stores or by office buildings. Streets with children on them tend to be occupied by people who care about the neighborhood. And streets with trees are generally cooler in summer and more pleasant all year round.

STRING BAGS

The standard European shopping trip is accomplished not with the aid of heavy double-thickness brown paper bags (for which many trees die daily) but the traditional string bag—which, these days, is also available in colorful and perhaps here excusable nylon. You can routinely carry a string bag in pocket or purse just in case you need it, since it folds up to practically nothing. It is a good idea, of course, to save and re-use brown bags; but you can't carry them with you very easily.

SUGARS

Americans still consume an inordinate amount of sugar (92 pounds per person per year in 1977—down from 103 pounds in 1965), with detrimental effects on weight, teeth, the blood-sugar regulating mechanism, and probably on psychological moods.

Your body transforms starchy foods into digestible sugars, and a certain intake of sugar, especially if it is the form known as fructose (from fruits), can properly provide some of your carbohydrate dietary energy supplies. But if you are eating both a high-sugar and a high-fat diet, you will probably be overweight, and should attempt to cut down on both.

Sugar sold in stores, whether called "brown," "raw," "white," or whatever, is all refined sugar, made from sugar cane or sugar beets. Honey, which seems to contain tiny amounts of non-sugar substances that are good for you and generally tastes more interesting than sugar, might well become your standard household sweetener—but you should still hold down your consumption of it.

It seems likely that our bodily systems evolved to utilize small amounts of fructose sugars from fruits nibbled more or less throughout the day, as our ancestors foraged about. This gives the pancreas (whose insulin output governs blood-sugar levels) a more or less constant amount of work to do. But the rigid time scheduling of industrial life leads us to gulp huge amounts of sugar at fixed meals and coffee breaks, and the pancreas must react to these assaults with massive defense measures which cause blood sugar levels to drop drastically, causing us to crave another sugar shot. This pattern of over-reaction, which is very widespread in our population, leads some researchers to believe that carbohydrate metabolism disorders (sometimes connected to full-scale diabetic symptoms but often not) are chronic among us, in both normal and obese people.

Consumption of sugar can be reduced by avoiding pre-sugared breakfast foods and processed foods in general (which are mostly high in sugar, salt, and fat), and by experimenting to see whether you might like some foods just as well, or better, without your usual sugar dose. Many people seem to lose their sugar cravings as they get older, luckily. Coffee is a good place to start, especially since the caffeine in unsugared coffee gives your pancreas a jolt equal to that of several teaspoons of sugar anyway. Bakery goods are also heavy in sugars (not to mention saturated fats); the doughnut you turn down today is not around your midriff tomorrow. And swear off soft drinks.

SURPLUS STORES

These can be another good source of non-new things. Originally, they dealt strictly with leftover war material: uniforms, tents, shovels, and so on. Nowadays many "surplus" stores sell very little government surplus; their chief merchandise is junk—seconds and rejects in clothing, stuff they pick up at fire sales, tools that are often priced as high (or higher) than in a hardware store. Some things, however, cannot be found elsewhere: beautiful orange-and-white parachutes, camouflage ponchos, old gyroscopes. Sometimes, if you're careful, you can pick up used mummy sleeping bags or GI clothing at reasonable prices. But in general, treat the surplus store cautiously. It's no place for impulse buying.

T

TABLES

Eating is the one activity that all the people in a
house usually do together, so in a way the table is
the real center of the household. Therefore it ought
not to be just some cheap piece of formica-covered
plywood with chrome-plated legs, but a true
"board," as in bed and board. The best, most
ceremonious tables are made of heavy solid planks,
honestly fastened together and mounted on stout
legs or a base. In general, veneered tables are to be
avoided; although sometimes elegant, they will
begin to peel in time. If you cannot find a good
solid table big enough to feed comfortably all the
people you like to feed, make one. Prefabricated
bases are available inexpensively in finish-it-your-
self furniture stores; that way you just have to
worry about the top.

Round tables have the great advantage of equally
integrating everyone into the conversation. Their
shape naturally tends to make people feel more
together. But it is hard to find round tables big
enough for more than six people, and they are
harder to build than square or rectangular tables.

A table should be of hard wood, and it should be
finished carefully with non-glossy varnish or oil to
bring out the natural beauty of the wood. If the
wood is attractive, you don't need tablecloths or
placemats. All that will be needed to preserve it is
wiping off with a damp cloth, and an occasional
re-oiling to keep it liquid-proof.

TAXES

Taxation is what government is all about—and
once the disgraceful state of the American tax
system becomes known to the people, it will
provide a major and revolutionary issue, rather
than the dry and depressing subject you may think
it, or the mere occasion of erratic "tax revolts."

Indeed, the impossibility of collecting a fair share
of taxes from the rich under capitalism is one of the
basic economic arguments against it.

Despite widespread moaning about taxes, few
people realize how unfair our tax system really is.
Rich Americans often pay proportionally less of
their income in taxes than you do, not more. Many
millionaires pay no taxes at all and the share of
taxes paid by corporations has been steadily whit-
tled away for decades. Our taxes as a whole are in
fact "regressive," not "progressive" (they soak the
poor, not the rich), partly because of loopholes in
the tax laws and partly because sales taxes, phone
taxes, and gas taxes all bear more heavily on poor
people—as do some taxes on non-necessities such
as booze and cigarettes.

Moreover, the rich benefit far more from government programs than poor people do. Nationally,
government programs are contrived to benefit and
protect corporations and the rich. Locally, it
mysteriously works out that city hall spends much
more on schools, streets, and parks in rich neighborhoods than it does in poor ones—especially
poor black ones. The children of the better-off go
to state universities subsidized by tax funds, while
poor and disadvantaged youth get into the community college or trade school. State departments
like finance, agriculture and public health somehow turn out to be sympathetic to the interests of
businessmen and big farmers, while their ears are
deaf to the appeals of poor people.

In the federal government, where the really big
money is, a major part of the national budget is
spent on "defense," which largely means buying
endless armaments and supplies from corporations. But even in non-military spending, the
government is generous to its business friends. Its
depreciation allowances give industries huge, regular gifts. Its agricultural subsidies assist small
farmers less than huge agricultural corporations.
Its foreign policy tries to preserve the greatest
possible sphere of operation for American capital
and to intimidate anybody who might question the
right of American corporations to dominate foreign
economic life.

In short, taxes are spent mostly to maintain the
profits and privileges of the ruling class and to
throw some sops (like insured mortgages) to their
middle-class supporters. Constant pressure from
below sometimes forces Congress to enact programs
designed to help poor people too: in the depths of
the depression Congress finally enacted Social
Security measures; more recently it added food
stamps. But these are emergency measures taken in

fear when the prospect of rebellion arises, and as little money is spent on them as possible. It does not change the general operation of the tax system, which is a means of taking money out of a lot of small pockets and concentrating it in a few big pockets. You can grasp the seriousness of so-called tax reformers by noticing their views on inheritance taxes. It is the lack of effective inheritance taxes that has enabled the descendants of the great nineteenth-century robber barons (the Rockefellers, DuPonts, and so on) to control America's economy in an ever tighter grip, concentrating ownership through family alliances and inter-marriages. Since there is no particular reason why people should be rich just because their parents were, drastic inheritance taxes could greatly democratize our society.

Even from the standpoint of efficient capitalism, the tax system is deranged, because its structure of loopholes leads people to put money into things which provide tax shelters or depreciation allowances rather than into things which contribute to our society's productivity.

We have been discouraged from attempting serious reform of this mess by the complexity of tax law, the intimidating power of the opposing interests, and by our own apathy—which, as Ralph Nader puts it, costs the average citizen—you—about 5% of your income in "non-participation tax"—the heavier taxes you pay because the system goes unreformed.

What would tax policy be in a just society? For one thing, it would be predominantly local: communities would raise money to manage their own affairs, and only a small amount would be siphoned off by central government for purposes of national defense, transportation, centralized research institutes, and other matters too massive for cities and their associated regions to handle.

For another, it would probably focus on economic activity as such, rather than on personal or corporate income. In a general way, personal income taxes are practically enforceable only on wage-earners whose incomes can be tapped at the paycheck level; middle-class people and corporate people have thousands of resources for evading personal tax payment. In recent decades "turnover" or "value-added" taxes, which are, roughly speaking, sales taxes levied against companies, have been adopted in some countries as one way for government to tap the society's productivity at its source (rather than after it has been diverted into millions of more or less untraceable personal incomes).

Third, taxation would not be used as a *sub rosa* means of producing economic privileges, as it often is with us, through depletion allowances, capital gains exemptions, depreciation allowances, and a host of other subterfuges. But it *would* be used as a means of persuading companies to act in the public interest in the planning and construction of buildings, factories, transportation systems, and so on; thereby producing public benefits that government would otherwise have to construct itself.

In time, thus, the entire existing tax system will have to be overhauled, or simply thrown out and a new start made. Meanwhile, what can you do, besides making tax policy and tax issues an important part of your general political thinking?

It is tempting to believe, since we live in a society whose tax laws are contrived for the advantage of business, that you can act like a business and take advantage of them. This is true only to a very minor degree. If you can operate some kind of small business, and have a good tax accountant, you may be able to shave some of your taxes; and if you work but also have self-employment income, the expenses deductible from it may be larger than you suspect. Both these types of activity are desirable in themselves and for the health and variety of society, of course. But their tax advantages are tiny compared to those of big business. In the end, fair and just individual taxes can only be achieved through fair and just taxation of corporations, which will mean a wholesale change in our economic institutions. It is impossible to foresee whether this will come about through slow evolution, or some cataclysmic outbreak of public rage, or some as yet unimaginable economic breakdown.

See also INCOME TAX.

Tax Politics: How They Make You Pay and What You Can Do About It, by Robert M. Brandon, Jonathan Rowe, and Thomas H. Stanton; preface by Ralph Nader. Pantheon, 1976.

TAXIS

There's only one city in America with taxi service that approaches the ideal, as Londoners know it, and that's Washington, D.C., which has more cars per square mile than any other US city. In central Washington, taxis are cheap and easy to get; they run on a zone system rather than per mile. But, being standard American cars, they are clumsy and inconvenient to get in and out of, and lack the baggage compartment and driving agility of London cabs. (The Museum of Modern Art held a competition to design a better taxicab for us, but none have yet appeared on the streets.) If our cities were intelligently managed, the city councils would spend on subsidized taxis at least half what they now spend on streets and parking lots, and everyone would be far better off. Taxis cut down congestion, decrease the need for parking space, and move people around faster than private cars since they don't need to find parking spots. In short, they eat up less of society's resources and produce less smog. Besides, they're fun to ride in. Let someone else do the driving and enjoy yourself with your friends in the back seat, or watch the world go by.

Taxis seem expensive. The question, however, if you're trying to develop a sane style of life, is whether they're really more expensive than other ways of getting around—in particular, whether you're better off using taxis or having your own car. Of course, if you drive around a lot on little trips all the time, you may find it hard to get cabs quickly enough to suit you, even in New York, which has more cabs than any other US city by far.

But let's consider a person who doesn't have to drive around all day. If you calculate what your car really costs you to operate (see AUTOMOBILES, COSTS OF), the amount per month would buy you a surprising number of taxi rides, even at today's rates per mile. And except in very spread-out cities like Los Angeles, taxis can also be cheaper than rental cars.

Of course, you could save still more by riding the bus instead (or riding it one way and taking a taxi back), or by bicycling on short trips, or by walking and doing your health a favor. Moreover, if you use taxis, you don't have to worry about whether your car is dependable for an important trip. And you're not worrying about $75 for a repair bill, or where to park. You're not worrying about the tires getting slick, the brakes jerking dangerously, or somebody stealing your mag wheels. You're not even worrying about whether there's enough gas to get to the store and back.

Taxi service might well be a public service as are the transit companies. If the government was serious about cutting unemployment, it could buy fleets of taxis and set unemployed youths to driving them. Even if they hardly made anything above tips, the fun of driving around would appeal to a lot of young car freaks. Or there could be self-driven taxis—city-owned small cars that were legal to drive only in a restricted area downtown, and that you would leave for the next user—that turned on when you inserted your credit card in the slot. (Later you would be billed for the mileage.)

Such short-haul taxi systems could readily use electric vehicles, cutting down on metropolitan smog production.

No other transportation system can do what taxis do, and we will have them with us as long as we have cities. We need more taxis and better taxis, in order to diminish our reliance on the smog-belching and resource-gobbling private automobile horde. We also need more small taxi companies which can operate as democratic driver-collectives (as Yellow Cab itself is now, in some cities) relating to their neighborhood or section of the city in a friendly, personal way.

See PUBLIC TRANSPORATION.

TEA

Tea, like COFFEE, is a mild central nervous system stimulant; their active ingredient, whether called caffeine or thein, is essentially the same. (Both also contain tannins.) As drugs go, both are safe—"overdoses" only make you jittery or upset your stomach—but neither is good in excess. Coffee has been implicated as a probable cause of heart disease and tea has not, but that may simply be because Americans are not yet heavy enough tea drinkers for the evidence to come to light. Neither drink has any known food value, aside from the sugar, cream, or milk you may add to them, though both contain trace vitamins and other substances in very small quantities. (There is some medical evidence that tea aids digestion slightly; so does wine.)

One of the historical reasons for tea drinking in Asia seems to have been to make boiled and hence bacteria-free water more palatable. At any rate, tea is the cheapest drink there is, aside from plain water. (Milk combines chemically with the tannin, making the brew distinctly less astringent.) It is cheapest, of course, if you buy it loose by the pound—a pound makes well over two hundred cups of tea. Most teabags contain enough tea for two cups, so you waste tea if you make only one— save them. The handiest way to brew just one or two cups of loose tea is with a perforated spoon-with-a-lid which you can buy in good houseware stores. Tea should brew for three to five minutes; don't judge strength by the color—some leaves have more coloring in them.

For larger quantities of tea, use a crockery teapot. Heat it with hot tap water while you're boiling the tea water; that way the tea will stay warm. Bring some fresh cold water to a full boil and pour it over about a teaspoon of tea for each cup of water. Then let it brew in the pot for three to five minutes; then pour. For later cups, it's best to dilute the stronger tea by adding more hot water in your cup. Or you can suspend the tea in a little perforated metal tea ball, dangling inside the pot for three to five minutes.

There are three types of tea. Most tea sold in America is black tea—it gives a smooth flavor and bright color. Oolong tea is partly brownish and partly greenish; it has not been fermented as much as black tea and makes a lighter-colored tea. Green tea, which is drunk by the Asian folks whose ancestors discovered tea in the first place and probably know more about it than anybody else, is not fermented at all, and gives a very light, sometimes almost colorless tea. It often comes in attractive packages.

The designations "Orange Pekoe" and so on merely refer to sizes of leaf, not quality. Sometimes teas are labeled with the places they come from— (Darjeeling, Assam, etc.), but there is no infallible sign of quality in these names.

Most teas sold in supermarkets are blends, as are the coffees, made up by tasters whose job is to produce a uniform, drinkable, but not terribly special product. The real fun of tea, like coffee, is in experimenting with different types and finding those you really prefer. To do this you have to locate a store specializing in such matters. Such stores now exist all over and are usually delightfully aromatic and friendly places; some of them have bars where you can taste the different types before you buy. These teas have lovely names: Lapsang Souchong, Gunpowder, Jasmine, Keemun, Uva.

In my opinion, the only possible excuse for using instant tea is if you are a constant iced tea drinker. Sweeteened iced tea "mixes" have no excuse at all: they're ridiculously expensive combinations of artificial flavor, sugar, and a little tea powder. A healthier and tastier way to fix iced tea is to add a little orange juice to it.

Many interesting mint and herbal teas are now widely available, in health-food stores and supermarkets. Most of these do not contain thein or tannin, so they are rather easier on your system; some of them, like ginseng, are believed to have energizing or medicinal properties. It's fun to experiment and see which ones you like and which ones seem to affect your system in pleasant or desirable ways.

Fruit teas are also available, mainly in cube extract form.

TEETH, DENTAL CARE

Because so many parents bug their children about toothbrushing, a lot of people neglect their teeth when they finally get away from home. Young people today usually eat a great deal of soft, practically pre-chewed food (pizza, milk shakes, cake) and their diets when they start living on their own often lack essential nutrients. They also stop brushing their teeth and going to the dentist, feeling that such concerns are depressing to their newly liberated states. If they get hold of some money they'd rather spend it on records than on a dentist bill.

What happens is that they go along fine for a few years and then lose a couple of teeth, which shocks them back into toothbrushing and also flattens them with a huge dental bill.

Like eyes, ears, noses, breasts, penises, and other parts of the human body, teeth vary a lot. A few people have stupendously strong, beautiful teeth which will last until they're ninety with nothing more than a daily brushing. Others have teeth that rot away even under the finest dental care. Unfortunately, you never realize how wonderful it is to have good teeth until your teeth begin to go bad. Any kind of toothache or prolonged sensitivity to cold or hot is a sign of potential serious trouble—have a dentist check it out. And in any case, a twice-yearly visit to your dentist (for cleaning and checking your teeth) should be part of your life.

There are ways of getting dental work done for very little money—sometimes none at all. You may be located in a city where there's a dental school which has a clinic attached to it; check with the Dental Society office in your city.

Dental equipment and techniques are now virtually painless. But many parents still dread going to the dentist, and they transmit attitudes of fear and resistance to their children. It may help you feel better to have a friend go with you who doesn't mind dentistry. And certainly, when your child begins to go (a first preliminary checkup is needed around the age of two or three, to make sure the teeth are coming in correctly), make sure the person who takes him or her regards it as a tolerable experience. Kids have no innate distrust of dentistry, and rather enjoy all the machinery the dentist has to play with. A dentist who is kindly and sensible will always explain to the child just what is going to happen and why it's necessary. With novocaine, the worst discomfort you feel in the dentist's chair these days is the initial prick of the novocaine injection.

Your dentist probably has gruesome charts and pictures that can explain what tooth decay is and why it is important to fill cavities when they occur. Gum troubles, which are much better understood now than in earlier times, are especially important to watch for when you get to your thirties and forties (they can cause you to lose teeth, literally).

Teeth are an important part of archaeological study, incidentally, because by the study of teeth you can learn a lot about what ancient people ate and how they lived. American Indian skulls reveal that peoples who lived on acorns ground up with stone pestles often died young as a result, apparently, of tooth abscesses; chewing on acorn meal with stone particles mixed up in it literally ground away their teeth.

False teeth are expensive, hard to chew with, and a general mess; you should try to keep your own teeth as long as you can, even though it takes time and trouble. It is important to have tooth abscesses, especially, attended to. A rotten tooth just sitting there is a little infection factory that sends bacteria all through your system, and can cause a breakdown in your general health. If you have a serious toothache, don't try to kill the pain with medicines; see a dentist, for the pain is a biological signal warning you something is wrong.

The main things you should do to take care of your teeth are:

1. Get in the habit of using dental floss (or waxed dental tape) before you brush—it gets out food particles stuck between your teeth. Then brush regularly, after each meal if you can, but anyway in the morning after breakfast and at night after supper. Toothpaste is no particular necessity; it's the toothbrush that does the job. A brush with natural bristles is best—stiff enough to work, but not so stiff it scratches your gums. People spend a great deal of money on fancy-tasting toothpastes and powders whose sole advantage is that they may encourage you to do more brushing (a tiny dab is enough for this purpose). Stay away from toothpastes that claim to "whiten" your teeth— they are dangerously abrasive, especially for people over thirty-five.

Incidentally, it's surprising how many perfectly intelligent people don't really know how to brush their teeth. The most important part of it is the scouring, twisting wrist motion whereby you bring the bristles from the gum area sliding over the teeth—thus massaging the gums and digging out particles from between the teeth. Even if it makes you feel like an idiot, ask your dentist for a refresher course in toothbrushing.

2. See a dentist twice a year, and get your cavities fixed.

3. Eat a good diet, with plenty of nutritious foods and also chewy foods. Your teeth partly depend on your general state of health. And the reverse is also true: neglected teeth can cause medical trouble in your body generally.

4. For your small children, ask your dentist to give you a prescription for fluoride pills if the water in your city is not fluoridated. Taken while the teeth are developing (which they do until they actually come through the gums), fluoride markedly cuts down the tendency to cavities. The pills cost very little, and you will be repaid many times in lower dental bills, even during childhood. Women should take fluoride pills during pregnancy in unfluoridated areas, since some tooth enamel is laid down before birth.

TELEGRAMS (WESTERN UNION)

In the old days, telegrams usually brought bad news, and they were delivered by boys on bicycles. Phones were rare then, so telegrams were the best and surest way of sending messages rapidly over a long distance. Today, long-distance phone rates are reasonable, so you are usually wisest to phone when you really must get a message somewhere in a hurry. But there are two occasions when you might consider Western Union. One is when the message is for somebody who doesn't have a phone. Since nowadays the Western Union offices chiefly deliver messages by phone themselves, you might include in the message a phrase like DELIVER BY HAND, NO PHONE AT ADDRESS. On interstate messages, hand delivery is supposed to be included in any case, should phone delivery fail, but you should specifically ask to pay the extra "physical delivery" charge to make sure it is sent out by messenger.

The other time to use Western Union is when you have to transmit money in a great hurry and for some reason cannot trust to the mail. If money is needed immediately to bail someone out, to pay off a pressing debt, or to seal a stupendous bargain, the sender shoud take it to the Western Union office in the form of cash, bank draft, traveler's checks, or something else that requires no clearing. It will normally reach the office in the city where the receiver is within just a few hours' time, and if he's waiting by the phone, he can go down to the office and get it quickly, in cash if the amount is small, or in a Western Union check if it's large;

naturally, good identification must be presented to get the money. One hitch in this process is that the Western Union office in your town or neighborhood may be closed on evenings or weekends. In that case, messages that aren't delivered, including messages stating that your money has arrived, are supposed to be held at the main Western Union office downtown, which is open twenty-four hours a day. If you are expecting money to come and it hasn't, that is the place to phone. If they can't find any record of it, give them your phone number and ask them to hunt for it and call you back.

TELEPHONE TREES

A phone tree is organized like this:

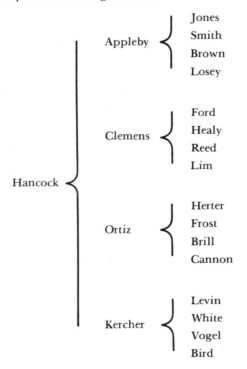

The telephone makes it possible to mobilize a group of people very rapidly for a demonstration, a meeting, or some neighborhood crisis—but you have to be organized in advance. Saying to a few people, "Everybody call around and get people together," won't do it.

Everybody in the organization gets a copy of this tree diagram with phone numbers after each name.

When Hancock sends out the word and everybody makes just four calls, a total of twenty people can be reached within a couple of minutes. You can reach even more people by having each one call five or six, but with four you can just make your calls and get moving.

TELEPHONES

Anyone who has lived for any length of time in any foreign country knows that American phone service is, by comparison, very good indeed. If you have the money to pay for it, you can get a phone installed (except in Manhattan and certain college towns during the fall influx) in a couple of days; generally you can get through to the number you want; and the cost of the service is not intolerably high. The telephone company has steadily dehumanized its system (as by dropping named exchanges and putting in the seven-digit dialing system) but at least the system usually works, except maybe in the case of pay phones in metropolitan areas which get smashed by thieves, and that's hardly the company's fault.

Here's what to watch for in dealing with the phone company. First, if you are new in the area and haven't had a phone before, or if you live in certain black, student, or poor areas, you will be asked to pay a deposit, often $25, on which you receive no interest. The rationale for this is that if you run up a big bill and don't pay it, the company will at least have your $25. Besides, they will charge you an actual installing fee. (By taking your old phone around to the office and picking up the new intrument yourself, you can get a $5 credit.) And the "business representative" you talk to in the office or on the phone will try to sell you a Princess phone or some other newfangled model. If you get pressured, just tell the rep that you are "sorry she (or he) feels that way," which is standard telephone company soft-soap talk used on complaining customers, and say you want the cheapest possible service and installation. Phone companies soft-pedal the fact that they have cheap limited-service deals available: "Lifeline" service with limited outgoing calls, and measured service for people who don't use the phone much except in the evenings.

Be sure you know what towns are included within your free-calls area; it may not include places you want to call a lot, so you'll be running up unexpected extra charges. In that case, you're wiser to switch to a billing that gives you a larger number of out-of-area calls before extra charges begin.

Once your phone is installed, you may think nothing can possibly go wrong. However, there are numerous possibilities. First, you may get a party line with someone who talks constantly, leaves the phone off the hook, or otherwise disrupts your service. Complain to the company immediately and ask them to switch you to another circuit, even if it means changing your number. Second, if you don't pay your bill for two months running, the company may disconnect your service. (They may do this even though they sent your bill to the wrong address through their own error.) Then if you want to get it hooked up again, they will stick you for the amount of the bill plus another installation fee. You can complain to the Public Utilities Commission, but usually these commissions are in the pocket of the utilities companies and you'll get nowhere.

In revenge, many people spend large amounts of talent and energy figuring out ways to defraud the telephone company. Most of these are soon discovered by the company, and its enormously sophisticated research laboratory figures out a method to stop it. However, there are still some ways in which you can save money on phones. One is to install extra instruments through homemade extensions. Don't connect the bell wire, otherwise it shows on the central testing board and they may come around to check on you; but you can still dial and talk.) Another is to share phones, either through extra extensions or through hallway pay phones or phones with dial locks so only some people can use them to call out. You can also have your phone put on "vacation service" which cuts your bill in half; then you can still dial out on it, but callers will be told that it is "temporarily disconnected at your request." There are many clever devices, most of them illegal bugging contraptions, for hooking on to existing lines, but as far as I know nobody has ever invented a way of really getting telephone service free.

Actually, you can have fun with phones if you don't take them seriously. You can paint them, put them in fanciful cases, and so on. One friend of mine achieved the ultimate in this direction. He had seven instruments scattered around his house, which he had found in junk shops, picked up from vacant apartments, or otherwise scrounged. But this didn't satisfy him; he wanted something really unusual. He didn't even consider spending money—say for a fancy European phone with the dial on the bottom, or a phony antique gold-plated French phone. Instead, he went to the butcher and got an enormous leg bone, about two inches thick

and several feet long. With great care he shortened it by taking out a middle section, and then hollowed out the ends, into which he carefully installed the working parts of one of his extra phones. He drilled a lot of little holes for the sound to pass through, inserted the necessary wires, glued everything back together, and polished the bone to a high gloss. All this, of course, was so that he could announce, "Excuse me, I've got to make a telebone call." Then he took the rest of the works, built a birdhouse-sized wall box for them, with a special door to conceal the dial and a hook to suspend the bone from, cutting off the circuit when the bone wasn't in use. When you talked to him, it sounded like he was hollering down a long tunnel. But it certainly had style.

In some parts of the country the phone company will give you a cutoff switch so that your phone won't ring if you don't want it to. In other parts they take the view that it would be a terrible loss to humanity if you couldn't be awakened or disturbed every time some salesperson or friend thinks of you. If your phone company won't give you a switch, you can open up your phone and achieve the same result. If it's a phone with a loud-soft adjustment, bend the ringing parts enough so that when it's turned to "soft" it won't ring but will just make a little purring sound. If it has no adjustment, you'll have to figure out a way of inserting some small lever or slide between the hammer and the bell. The phone company maintains that the phone instrument belongs to them, and they may give you a hard time if they find out you've been "tampering" with the phone, even if, as in this kind of case, it's their own fault that you had to. Some phone installers these days, especially in the metropolitan areas, are loose and amenable people. But a service call may bring some hard-nosed type, so better pull off any little "attachments" you have contrived before you call for help.

If the phone company had more of a sense of humor, they'd get less trouble from their customers. In the San Francisco area, to find out what time it is, you dial "POPCORN." In New York, it's "NERVOUS." Until the phone company does away with dial letters altogether, that can make you feel a little better about the whole thing. If you're lucky, your number may actually spell something pronounceable, like "DANKPUP" or "MIAMEE."

And if the company were less monopolistic, there would be less temptation to nationalize it and be done with it. The inside story of AT&T is a classic capitalist case: they own a subsidiary, Western Electric, so they can sell themselves phones and take double profits; they operate in open defiance of a Federal Communications Commission rates decision (connived at by the FCC); they refused, until compelled by a lawsuit, to install anybody else's phones but their own (despite the fact that phones work the same all over the world, and some European ones happen to be much more attractive than ours); they spend a lot of your phone-bill money on expensive ads designed to get people to install pastel-colored phones and other costly gimmicks; they are prime contractors for missiles and other gravy-train war toys.

Under all the presidential administrations of recent decades, quasi-legal and illegal telephone "bugging" has been carried out by the FBI and other agencies on a massive scale. Local police also seem to engage in a great deal of illegal wiretapping, as do companies seeking to steal each others' business secrets or plans. (Expensive anti-bugging kits are available to business people, enabling them to detect and defeat each others' dastardly plots.) You should *never* say anything on any phone that you would not wish to have known to some government agency. In fact, even without the nicety of a warrant, police can legally get a record of all the numbers you call.

Many government agencies and corporations have toll-free "800" numbers. Directories listing these numbers can be obtained, though not easily; such numbers are also often advertised, listed in the phone book yellow pages, etc. (If you know what to ask for, you can also dial 800-555-1212 for information.) Usually a few inquiries to the right people will locate a number you need.

TELEVISION

One of the bad things about a television set is that it can displace human relationships: it can become a "person" in the household, and individuals relate to it as much as they do to other human beings. This isn't entirely or always a bad thing; as it happens, some human beings aren't as interesting, or as wholesome to be with, as the idiot box. But it can deprive children, especially, of human contact. It sets deep patterns of dependence on machines for stimulation, education, entertainment. And it often encourages parents to let the machine amuse the children, so they don't have to "bother" with them.

A way to cut down on the TV set's dominance of the household is simply to put it away or give it away. The great advantage of portable sets (nine- or twelve-inch screens) is that they easily can be put away in a closet or drawer and only gotten out when you want to watch a specific program. That way the TV isn't a piece of furniture, available like a mental wheelchair to flop your mind down on at any time.

Another way, which works even for big heavy sets, is to sew up a cloth cover from some bright scraps of cloth, similar to the tea cozy that keeps teapots warm, or the covers some people use over sewing machines. For that matter, any attractive old piece of cloth can be draped over the set. You'll find that children don't try to snap it on quite so fast. Also, burglars won't notice it.

Statistics vary and can't be depended upon exactly; still, we know that most children in the United States watch television a great deal of the time. One study of preschool children said fifty-four hours per week, which is hard to believe since most preschool children are only awake a few hours more than that. On the other hand, in many households the TV is left on all day. It seems a fair conclusion, at any rate, that the average American child sees a great deal more of the TV than of either parents or friends. He or she has spent far more hours in front of the box, by age eighteen, than in school. In short, television is our chief national educational force—it is TV, above all, which is teaching us how to be human beings: how to eat, how to dress, how to talk, how to think. *If you don't want to be told, don't watch.*

Television programs obviously embody the attitudes current in our society, especially sexism. Our commercials and even the actual programs focus on bodily ills and defects, training viewers to worry about headaches, bad breath, acid indigestion, dirty clothes, lack of sex appeal, and so on—life-denying, anxious, neurotic fears about personal well-being. By watching TV we allow the advertisers to strengthen and deepen these fears in ourselves and to instill them in our children. We also encourage a primitive, superstitious, magical way of thinking: that by popping some pill, or spreading on some cream, or buying some object, our lives will suddenly be greatly improved.

Under the American advertiser-dominated TV system, the commercials are the most carefully made and expensively produced part of TV fare; hence in their surrealist, absurdist way, they are often more entertaining than the programs. They are a kind of running slapstick self-satire on American life, and if you like comedy, they can provide you much free entertainment—something like six hundred "brief messages" every day, up to sixteen minutes per hour. Needless to say, most commercials are outright lies, filmed with every kind of ingenious fakery that high-paid filmmakers can contrive, and anybody who takes them seriously must be some kind of idiot.

The programs themselves are, of course, another story. They were never terribly good, and they seem to be getting worse. Hollywood used to put out endless runs of faintly decadent but passably well-made standard TV entertainment. Its westerns and crime dramas and "family comedies" appealed to the conformist American suburbanite. More recently, TV sponsors have discovered that such individuals are not actually very good customers, and TV has been trying to change its image to appeal to the young and swinging who supposedly have more money to spend. This seems a suicidal course, because young and swinging people do not sit around watching TV, except maybe for some news and an occasional movie; they have heard that the average American adult spends a total of fifteen years of his life watching TV and they don't want it to happen to them.

News on TV is painless but (like radio) very brief; if you really want to have any idea of what's going on, you ought to read a newspaper. Many decent old movies can be seen on TV, and paperback guides to them are useful to have around, so you can plan your viewing.

The really interesting thing about TV is that under new regulations of the FCC (normally a conservative and broadcaster-dominated body), cable-TV franchise operators must now begin to originate local programs. Since these companies (which send out programs by wires and bill their subscribers) cover only a small geographical area, a vast proliferation of local programming must somehow be provided. With popular pressure and organization, much of this programming could be provided by and for local groups with special information needs: consumers, blacks and other minorities, young people, and so on. Otherwise the programming will be endless reruns of "I Love Lucy" and other cheap old programs. Since franchises are granted by city councils (as are franchises for streetcar operation or other public services), local groups have an opportunity to influence programming or revoke franchises by public exposure of corrupt deals with city councils.

Public TV channels continue to improve, and you might be surprised to find that their news coverage is about as full as that of a newspaper and probably less reactionary; their drama programs are consistently better than those on the commercial networks; their children's programs are intriguing. Unfortunately, as the CPB/PBS system has received more government funds, it has become more cautious politically, and no longer runs documentaries that name names and make strong charges (not that commercial TV does so very often either).

A "Blab-Off" for your TV. As it happens, there is an easy way to cut off bothersome TV commercials—at least to cut off their sound. You can attach a simple wire and a switch to your TV's speaker. Whenever a commercial comes on, you snap the switch and the sound cuts off. When the program resumes, snap the switch again and the sound returns. The Blab-Off will take about fifteen minutes to install and will cost you almost nothing. Here's how to do it.

If you don't have one lying around somewhere, buy a small enclosed switch; it should cost about a dollar. (The only kind of switch you *can't* use is a wall-type switch, which needs to sit in a wall box.) Buy as much wire as you need—if you have a big set, you probably sit back farther and need a little more wire. Get ordinary two-strand electric-light wire.

Here's how you attach it, step-by-step: (1) Unplug your TV. Move it to a table where you can see clearly to work. If possible work on the TV after it has been turned off for a day or so—certain parts of a TV hold high voltage for some time even after it has been turned off and can give you a worse shock than house current, so don't take any chances. (2) Unscrew the back and remove it. (3) Find the speaker. It will have two wires leading off into the works. Keeping your fingers away from the back of the picture tube and the parts that are connected to the tube, pull the wires out a little so you can cut one of them—make your cut a few inches away from the speaker so you have two ends you can work with. (4) Pare away three-quarters of an inch of the insulation on your wires and on the speaker wires, and join each strand of your wire to one end of the speaker wire. (5) Twist the ends of the wires together as firmly as you can. (6) Bend the twisted ends back alongside the speaker wires. Then cover each twisted part separately with adhesive tape or electrician's tape. (7) If possible, tape or tie your wire to something solid inside the set, so that if children yank on it later, it won't pull out. Better still, if you can find a small hole in the back of the set, slide the wire through that, after tying a knot in it on the inside side. (8) Carefully put the back on, making sure the speaker wire and your wire keep well away from the picture tube and other parts. (9)

Pare away the insulation on the other end of your wires, and attach to the switch. (10) Plug the set back in and try it out.

This simple device will save you endless aggravation. It will help you protect yourself and your children from the lies and enticements of the advertisers. And it will last as long as the TV itself. You can also play games with it. If the dialogue in a program bores you, switching it rapidly on and off will turn it into surrealistic "poetry." On some sets, the Blab-Off momentarily upsets the picture, and you can get it to do weird things by snapping the switch rapidly. And of course if you get fed up with sound entirely, you can just switch it off and watch the pictures in silence.

TEMPORARY HELP AGENCIES

For anybody who wants to work less than a steady, full-time, year-in-year-out grind, temporary job placement agencies can be very useful. Working through such agencies can be especially attractive to older people, who may have top abilities but find employers unwilling to hire them on a regular full-time, long-term basis. Some agencies specialize in providing accounting services or other special skills, but most deal in a wide range of office jobs for both men and women; they also offer manual and laboring jobs, mainly for men but occasionally for women too. Manpower Inc., Employers Overload, Kelly Girl, and small agencies exist in every city. The pay is about equal to that for jobs you could get directly yourself—but you don't get tied down to one job.

When you work through one of these agencies, you are actually an employee of the agency, and they rent you out to businesses—for a day, for a week, for a couple of months; when that job is done, they will send you on to something else. Considering how boring most jobs are, this gives you some delightful variety. And somehow it's not so bad doing menial work if you're not the boss's regular "property." You can tell the agency approximately how much of the time you want to work (be careful in thinking about this, and settle on a realistic figure), and they won't consider you suspect if it's only half-time, or only the first six months of the year, or only the summers.

Your pay, withholding and Social Security taxes, unemployment taxes, and so on are all handled by the agency. When you go on a job for them, you are not required to fill out forms, wring your hands in an interview, or worry—you just go to work. (Avoid temporary help agencies that charge you a fee. A legitimate one makes its money out of renting your services—they pay you.)

Shop around to find the best agency in town. The agency should pay once a week and should have an upwardly sliding scale depending on your skills. Frequently the smaller, local temporary agencies pay better than mammoth chains like Kelly Girl or Employers Overload.

Radical groups such as Women Organized for Employment are against temporary agencies, saying that they are an arm of the corporate structure and function to keep clerical workers from unionizing and being paid the wages they deserve. Agencies sometimes try to offer jobs in a category below your competency. If you are a senior typist (usually 60 words per minute) and you take a temporary junior typist job, the company gets a senior typist and you get junior pay. (And who knows—the agency might be charging the company for a senior typist.)

Since the agencies are now highly competitive for workers, they are all offering benefits of different types. You can opt for health insurance at certain agencies. Others give vacation time after you've worked a set number of hours for them within any given year. One agency has a "three-day weekend" bonus, where, if you work the Friday before and Tuesday after a three-day weekend you get paid for Monday.

TESTS

Because our schools are organized so that it is practically impossible for teachers to deal seriously with each student as an individual, the importance of tests is increasing despite the many and well-known drawbacks and distortions of both IQ and "achievement" tests. Companies and government also rely a great deal on tests for employment screening. Test taking, though largely utterly unscientific, is thus an important game to know how to play.

Here is how you can raise your score, whether you actually know more about the subject or not:

Survey the test before you begin work. Take a look at the different sections and get some idea of how much time you should ideally spend on each one. Also, find out which parts are easiest for you—do them first. If some parts count for more in the total score than others, it may be wise to spend more time on them.

Read all directions carefully. Many people lose points needlessly because they don't pay enough attention to the directions, and either misunderstand them or don't read them through to the end. After you've read the directions for a section, try one item, and see if you are absolutely clear on how to do it. If not, go back and look at the directions again. If anything remains unclear, ask for an explanation.

Pace your work. Work as rapidly as you can without making mistakes. If you come to a difficult problem, skip it and mark it—you can come back to it later if you have time. Never get stuck on one problem; if it doesn't come easily, leave it—later on, when you return to it, your mind may have worked it out for you. And no single problem deserves more than its reasonable share of your time.

Rest. Even in a test that lasts only a half hour, it will help to stop work occasionally, close your eyes, stretch your muscles, think of something different, and generally give your mind a rest.

Guess. If the directions do not tell you, ask whether the scoring will deduct wrong answers from right ones. When the score simply depends on how many you get right, you raise your score by guessing rather than by leaving items blank. If you are penalized severely for wrong guesses, you should be more cautious.

Eliminate. Many tests give you a number of choices to pick from. Even if you are not certain you know the right answer, you can often still pick the correct answer if you study the alternatives, because some of them will be obviously wrong and can be eliminated immediately. Each answer you eliminate improves the guessing odds in your favor.

Clues. In tests made up by your own teacher, you may be able to spot clues after a few tests—but it is dangerous to rely on these, except as a last resort. Some teachers make wrong answers simpler and less qualified than the correct ones, or longer or shorter. Some give more true items than false, in a true-false test (or the other way around).

Don't waste your energy in mental arguing with the person who made up the test. This will only decrease your score. Try to identify the level of sophistication the test asks you to display—and then stick to it. Later, when you've finished, you can always go back and scribble notes in the margin about how dumb the questions are.

Check. If you have kept to your schedule, you will probably have some time for re-checking your work. Check a couple of easy items, to make sure you were doing them right, as well as the hard ones. It is easy to overlook promising answers in a

multiple-choice test. There are, of course, tests which are deliberately so long that virtually no one can complete them in the alloted time. In such tests, it is even more important than usual to work rapidly and to concentrate your energy on the easy items, skipping any that hold you up.

It is important for children to become familiar with the mechanics of tests as early as possible, since test scores are much lower if the kids don't know what tests look like or how they will be asked to mark answers. When your child gets into school, go around to the school office and ask to see what kinds of tests the school uses. Then help your child to understand how the tests work, and pass on some of the above tips.

Books are available to help you prepare for college entrance tests, graduate and professional school admissions test, civil service tests, and exams in specialized fields. Look for them in your library or in a good college bookstore.

American College Testing Program for College Entrance, by Gary R. Gruber. Monarch Press, 1979.

TEXTBOOKS

There is nothing like a textbook to take all the life out of a subject. One of the greatest and simplest reforms that could be undertaken in our schools (and in our colleges and universities) would be to abolish texts entirely. This would throw teachers back on their own ingenuity and intelligence in organizing and presenting their material. Many teachers would develop new and ingenious approaches to things students need to know.

If you're a parent and your child has trouble in class, take a look at the textbook. Mark the passages that are dull, unclear, inaccurate, biased, prejudiced, sexist, or just plain impossible for an average rational reader to understand. Take it in and talk to the teacher about it; or write a letter about it to the state superintendent of schools, whose office is probably responsible for approving the texts your local school is forced to use. And if your child happens to get a good text once in a while, make a point of praising it to the same people.

But the main problem for students is to get out from under these pseudo-books. The way to do this is to learn how to use LIBRARIES—where the real books are. If a history text raves about what a great hero Cortez was, you can find books that tell what Cortez actually did—which might lead you to conclude that he was a white European imperialist interested in nothing but gold and power. If your civics textbooks tell you how governments are supposed to operate, there are many books that tell you how they operate in fact. And if the attitudes expressed in your texts seem outdated or just plain stupid, you can find many books in your library that can open up your mind instead of closing it off.

TOASTERS

Almost all toasters fall into the class of Needlessly Shiny Objects and they take a lot of useless attention to keep clean. Some are now made of stainless steel or aluminum or enameled like old-fashioned pots. But you can always cover up chrome plating—especially if it's begun to flake off or rust through—with some bright-colored enamel. Unplug the toaster, get all the grease off before you paint, and be careful not to let drips of paint go down inside.

If you're buying a toaster secondhand, insist on plugging it in to see if it works. The handle should stay down, then pop up briskly. All the heating element wires (the flat wires inside that turn red) should heat up on both sides of each piece of bread. Check for a dangerously worn or frayed cord, and see if the adjustment for darker or lighter toast works. (For darker toast, the bread stays down longer.) The bottom should open so you can clean out crumbs that collect. When you clean a toaster, unplug it and use a small rag—never put a toaster under water to clean it, because the electric wires will get wet and may short out or give you a shock.

Some recent toasters don't have a push-down handle; you put the bread in the slot and the toaster lowers it automatically. This fancy feature, like most extras, is likely to break down and cause expensive repairs. The same goes for "humidity-control" features. A toaster is a simple machine designed to do only one thing but do it reliably. Get a simple one.

Even simple toasters are not always worth repairing, since the repairs may cost more than a new toaster (or another secondhand one). If you're good at repairing, or have a handy friend, it's worth opening up the toaster to see what's wrong. But first just hold it over the sink with the bottom open and give it a good shaking: the most common troubles are due to crumbs or raisins clogging the works. Other likely troubles are loose electrical connections and misadjustment or failure of the bimetallic strip which moves in response to the heat and lets the toast pop up.

A safety note: if a piece of bread sticks down in the toaster, unplug the machine before you poke anything down the slot to pry it out. You can get a nasty shock if you touch the heating elements with a metal knife or fork.

TOOL RENTAL

Most cities now have many rental companies which will rent you anything from a small electric drill to heavy equipment such as a cement mixer. Their prices vary a good deal, so try phoning a couple from the Yellow Pages to locate what you want. (Most items require a deposit; ask how much.)

In many cases being able to get the right kind of heavy tool will make the difference between being able to do a job yourself or having to hire a professional. Sanding and refinishing a floor is a good example—you can rent a heavy sander for a day and do a job that would literally be impossible without it.

Renting tools is not second best to owning them unless they are tools you use constantly. Even contractors seldom own all the tools they need; they rent them occasionally, so when they're not using them they don't need to worry about theft, repairs, upkeep, or paying off the purchase price. The more expensive the tool, the more advantageous is renting.

When you are checking out something from a rental outfit, be sure you know how to work it. Also verify that it's in working condition—otherwise you may be liable for repair costs. A good way to make sure of this is to ask them to "show you how to use it."

Rentals usually go on a twenty-four hour basis, but some items can be gotten for a shorter time at a cheaper rate. You can also rent things by the week—even vacation trailers.

A few public libraries have now begun to loan tools, believe it or not, and the city of Portland has set up a public tool rental service. Check to see if your city has one.

TOXIC SUBSTANCES

By a classification made at the end of the 70's, about 129 dangerously toxic substances were sufficiently present in the environment to make it desirable to monitor them as health hazards. Many of these are industrial solvents and other chemicals. Others are residues of pesticides, herbicides, or poisons used in agriculture. Some, like PCBs, are illegal to manufacture any more in this country because they're carcinogenic—but 440 million pounds of the stuff are floating around in rivers, lakes, dumps, and coastal waters. (It is impossible to get allowable limits in seafood down to reasonable levels, says the FDA, "without significantly disrupting the food supply.")

Many industrial processes emit toxic fumes, such as silver soldering and brass welding. Acids and solvents give off toxic fumes. Even the materials used in artists' supplies and craft materials—used by a half-million professionals and almost 60 million other people—include many dangerous substances, but are sold without warning labels. (At one art school, 40% of the students were found to suffer from art-related health problems. Many small children are exposed to art supplies in schools, day-care centers, and summer camps.) For further information on art material hazards, send a self-addressed stamped envelope to Art Hazards Information Center, 5 Beekman St., New York, NY 10038.

Industries faced with the problem of disposing of the toxic by-products of their manufacturing processes sometimes hire "midnight movers" who haul the stuff away and dump it in public sewers, along public rights of way, or in remote spots. From such locations it disperses through the environment. At last, persons guilty of such actions have begun to be subjected to criminal prosecution (see ECO-CRIME). However, about 600 chemical dumps around the country which were created more or less legally pose immediate threats of leakage into water supplies, or worse.

See CANCER; CARCINOGENS AND MUTAGENS.

Toys

Going into a toy store gives me a headache, and I think I know why; so few of the toys there are any fun, either for me or for children. During the past few years there has been a great outpouring of "spectator toys"—battery-driven cars and spacecraft and so on—which are fine to watch for five minutes, but then what do you do? Single-purpose toys of this kind are an offshoot of television: you watch them zoom or whirl or whatever on TV, and if you spend the money you can watch them do the same thing in your own house—until the batteries wear out. But there's little you can actually *do* with them. So a child quickly begins to crave another model. By this type of insatiable consumption the child is being

"trained" to buy and buy and buy when he or she becomes an adult.

In addition, most toys are designed in hideous plastic shapes; their parts crack and break off with the slightest use; they make scraping, scratching, grinding noises; their switches fail and their wheels fall off. What "fun!"

The canny parent has observed, however, that children follow a very simple rule about playthings: they like to play with the same things you play with. They are programmed to imitate you, in big things and in small—that's how they learn to be human. And that's why babies get into your pots and pans, and fiddle with your radio and records, and pull your books off the shelves. Your response ought to be: Fine! Get them an old radio, and give them books, yours or the library's. Keep your pans down on the lowest shelf where a baby can easily reach them, together with a lot of other household utensils—you'll occasionally have to spend a minute hunting for something, but you'll save lots of minutes through having the child amused without special planning or attention. Give older children free access to the ordinary objects of the household; they'll invent plenty of fantasy things to do with them, and get a big kick out of imitating whatever it is you do with them.

The basic stock of toys that children need is simple, and you can improvise most of them or pick them up secondhand.

Balls. The simple fact that a ball rolls makes it entrancing to a baby. It makes little games possible for a two-year-old. And older kids can play a thousand games with a ball, any ball—a tennis ball, a ping-pong ball, a golf ball, rubber balls small or large, blow-up plastic balls. Big ball bearings make interesting noises as they roll.

Dolls. Actually "dolls" is a bad word, for it has tended to mean only pretty little female dolls with wigs, made for girl children to play mama with, although today both boys and girls can play with both male and female "anatomically correct" dolls. In most cultures, dolls come in a huge variety of types. There are hunger dolls, demon dolls, protector dolls; parent dolls and children dolls and ancestor dolls; the child's mind is the home of many fantastic figures besides mommy and daddy! If you are handy with sewing, you can make rag dolls and rag animals that will give your child a greater range of play fantasy than store-bought dolls. Some people are good at wood carving, and can make special heads for dolls. Remember that children are "savage," compared to adults—their minds have not been cramped and confined by a lifetime of "education" and training for routine jobs. They regard life in a much more direct and human way than most adults—they deal with its joys and its terrors in a far more immediate sense. Don't restrict your child's doll play to those cutesy miniature-adult dolls sold in stores.

When children get older, they are sometimes interested in puppets (the hand or string variety) or in putting on dramatic shows with costumes. It helps in such play if you can string a curtain across a corner of the room to make a stage area. Then watch the shows they put on. Two kids who really enjoy this can do things that will astonish you. Thrift shops are an excellent source of dress-up clothes, costume jewelry, feathers, bits of fur.

Blocks. The best blocks my daughter had were a set I made out of hardwood scraps from the saw table of a nearby lumberyard that specialized in exotic hardwoods—mahoganies, walnut, birch, ash, maple, and so on. I left them in curious irregular shapes, and just sanded off the sharp corners. Each block was different, and just right for some special purpose in a child's imagination. And I liked them too, because the wood was beautiful; it felt and smelled good; and the blocks made a good sound when my daughter banged them together. There's no need to spend money for blocks; any lumberyard or millwork shop should be willing to give you a boxful of scraps for nothing, especially if you tell them what you want them for. Besides being more fun to build with than standardized blocks, they begin to give your child a sense of the variety and subtlety of natural materials.

Play shelters. Children of all ages like to make little houses and tents for themselves—a kind of imitation of adult houses. They can drape sheets or blankets over chairs and tables; they can lean things against ropes you run across the room at their head height. Later on, when they can handle a hammer and nails, make sure there is scrap lumber around so they can build more substantial huts, outdoors. (In Scandinavia they have "junk playgrounds" where children, when given lots of stuff to work with, build entire miniature villages.) Tree houses, if you have a good tree, are one of the best parts of childhood, and some parents build big play sculptures in their yards out of driftwood or salvaged timbers—you can let your imagination go, and the result will serve as a castle, a tower, a house, a store....

Tools and utensils. Children as young as two-years-old can use simple tools, and toy stores sell sets of simple wrenches and nuts-and-bolts which

can be a lot of fun. A child of four or five begins to be able to use real tools—hammer, pliers, saw, though probably not a screwdriver. Make sure both boys and girls learn how to use tools. It's a good rule never to buy kids junky tools or utensils that you would never use yourself; buy decent tools that really work, provide a good place to store them, and begin to teach your child how to care for them. An old wooden crate makes a good workbench, and a small vise can be attached to it.

Art and craft materials. Children like to make things, and it gives them a sense of pride and competence. So you should help them learn how to cut and paste and draw and paint, and work with materials that are easy to handle: paper, cardboard, styrofoam, soft wood. Here are some basic materials that are useful: a good scissors (if you worry about the pointed ends, file them round—those little "children's scissors" won't cut worth a damn); white glue; odd pieces of paper and cardboard (save grocery bags, shoe boxes, and anything else that looks like fun); three or four tempera (poster paint) colors and brushes; a big set of crayons; cellophane tape and mending tape; and a big sheet of oilcloth or plastic to lay over a table or on the floor for kids to work on. (Remember that getting messy is half the fun of artwork.) Modeling clay is rather expensive; you can make dough clay for practically nothing, and it can be dried and then painted: just mix flour and water and a little salt. When kids get big enough to handle them, probably around five or six, buy some good watercolors (Pelikan paints have beautiful, intense colors, though they are expensive); crayon coloring is never very satisfying because it's hard to get really bright colors from crayons. Oil-tempera stick colors, though they are brighter, break very easily.

Games. There are many expensive board games in the stores, but most of them don't interest children for long and don't interest adults at all. You should find games that *you* like to play too—otherwise playing them with children is just a duty. Most of the games listed under GAMES are good for children, depending on their ages. Children learn to play active neighborhood games without any instruction from you (football, baseball, soccer, and so on), but it's nice to develop "family" games.

Incidentally, many store-bought toys are dangerous for young children. Toy ovens and plastic- or lead-casting devices get tremendously hot and also pose shock hazards. Dolls and stuffed animals contain pins. Putties and glowing substances may be toxic. Noisemaking rattles have sharp inside parts. Toys with glass parts may break.

TRADE-OFFS

There is no such thing as an unmitigated advantage, or pure Good Thing, or free lunch. (It is one of Barry Commoner's principles of ecology that you never get anything for nothing.) Any course of action entails sacrifices as well as benefits; this is simply in the nature of things. If you choose to become an expert typist, your handwriting will suffer through reduced use; if you drive, your legs will be less strong than if you walked. In the course of a day, we all make hundreds of conscious or unconscious trade-off judgments, deciding to do one thing rather than another (or nothing) because we have assessed in some manner the relative advantages and disadvantages, and decided to trade some off against others. Living a sane life is largely a matter of making these trade-offs sensibly, either through tradition or personal judgment.

One of the critical trade-offs we all make, and which influences a great many other aspects of our life, is between time and money. In a period of inflation, it is tempting to think of working longer hours and thus making more money. But this is seldom wise except as a temporary measure. For one thing, by sacrificing even more of your time to your job, you put yourself under greater emotional pressure, and probably cut down on the health of your relationships with friends and family. For another, by working more you are making your "terms of trade" with the world as a whole less favorable. By increasing your dollar income, you will increase the proportion of it you pay in income tax; you will probably need to spend money on things and services you could provide for yourself if you had more time (thus incurring sales or other taxes you'd otherwise avoid); the things you buy will mainly be "finished goods" rather than the wood, nails, and other component parts you'd buy if you were doing things for yourself. And, because you would probably not have so much garden produce or other things to BARTER, you would find yourself paying for everything you consumed, in taxable dollars.

One of the good things about barter is that it occurs outside the money economy and is thus not feasible to tax. But there are also other ways of emphasizing your private-life productivity, which is not taxed, rather than your job-time productivity, which is. The principle here is that "private" productivity, being untaxed, is actually "paid" at a higher rate.

To obtain a sofa that sells for, let's say, $1,000, you have two choices. If you buy it, you spend $1,000 + sales tax, perhaps a total of $1,060. But to get that $1,060, you have had to *earn* something like $1,300 to 1,500, depending on your tax bracket. The materials in the sofa, however, are probably worth $300. Thus, if you build it yourself, even if it takes you a lot longer to build the sofa than it would take in the furniture factory, you are probably being "paid" in savings at a much higher hourly rate than you would receive at your job if you simply work and save your money for the sofa. And you would have performed an enjoyable, productive, satisfying task, and provided yourself with a sofa precisely to *your* tastes, not those of some furniture designer in Grand Rapids.

Some people, carrying this logic to its ultimate conclusion, decide to move to the country where they have a better chance of doing a large number of things for themselves—from building their house to keeping a horse for local transportation. City dwellers are more restricted, but most of us can locate areas of our lives where we could, if we wished, secure more favorable trade-offs both economically and emotionally. Obviously people vary a great deal in their preferences, tastes, abilities, and needs. The person who always cooks at home, vegetarian-style, and eats on about half of what most of us spend for food, may have absolutely no inclination to have a sofa, much less build one, no matter how much could be saved. But you can find applications for the underlying principle somewhere in your life: the principle being that withdrawal from the money economy generally saves you money. The trick, of course, is to find the areas where it will *also* give you a better life—a more relaxed, secure, healthy way of being. The object is *not* simply to pare down your expenses, though that will be a by-product of the process.

It is necessary here to enter an aside concerning higher-income people. Most Americans don't make terribly much money now, and a continuing decline in real income (purchasing power) is in store for us as a nation. For the vast majority of Americans, therefore, a strategy of minimizing paid employment and maximizing "private" productivity is sound. (It is also good to keep in mind that almost 90% of Americans say they do not find their jobs very appealing.)

But there are Americans, sizable numbers of them, who manage to get high-paid jobs, inherit a house or other assets, or otherwise come into possession of money considerably beyond the average income. Does this change the trade-off principle's application? Indeed it does. People with significant disposable capital are in a fundamentally different position from people who are simply trying to get by. They face the problem of trying to find either profitable investments (as real estate has been) or "tax shelters" for their extra money, or at least to store it where inflation will eat it away as slowly as possible. (See MONEY.) People who have gotten into a position where they have enough free capital to make investments are often also, by that fact, able to put any extra cash to work multiplying itself at a rate greater than the savings they could achieve through the "minimizing" strategy outlined above. For them, therefore, ever deeper immersion in jobs or other cash-producing activities makes sense economically. Whether it makes sense psychologically, spiritually, or politically is another question, of course—and in my opinion it is easy to spend your life making money, until you wake up, at 50 or 60, and realize that you have only one life to live, and that you'd better get on with it, regardless of the economic cost. It is at this point, or course, that many people "drop out"—undergoing an almost religious conversion, often abandoning lifelong marriages and associations. They find to their astonishment that they can get along very happily without most of the goods they formerly strove so hard to buy; they put their energy into new, energy-filled personal relationships with new friends, new lovers, or formerly estranged children; they begin to take risks they would have passed by before, and generally find new excitement and vitality in their lives.

Taking Charge: Personal and Political Change Through Simple Living, by The Simple Living Collective. Bantam Books, 1977.

TRAVEL

Getting out of town once in a while is refreshing to the spirit; even if you don't have any money, you don't have to feel permanently stuck where you are. You can't expect to travel in the middle-class way without a great deal of cash. But—especially if you're by yourself—you can travel light and travel far. The secret is to provide for your necessities outside of hotels, motels, restaurants, and so on. If you are traveling by car or truck or camper, arrange to sleep in it. Take along a stove to cook on and try to eat in restaurants only for special occasions. Use state and national park campgrounds occasionally—plan your route so you hit one when you need to take a bath and do the wash. You should also plan your route to avoid interstate highways as much as possible—find the old roads that wind around through interesting little towns.

Air travel is heavily subsidized and is, unfortunately, more convenient for long trips than the train. In time, our train system will have to be restored, because trains consume far less energy and money for all except very long trips. Amtrak is a feeble attempt in this direction, hamstrung by foot-dragging incompetence from the railroads that actually operate the trains. Probably a whole new train system, using novel technology such as the magnetic-suspension, linear-motor trains now being built in Japan, will ultimately be adopted. Meanwhile, you can sometimes find a train going where you want to go, and if getting there on time is not too important to you, give it a try. The Canadians have very good trains, as do the Europeans. If you have to cross the continent, it's sometimes worth going up into Canada to take their crack trans-Canada trains, which are surprisingly inexpensive; be sure to bring along sandwich makings, fruit, and other food to keep eating expenses down.

Greyhound and other bus lines reach most places in the country, and they are cheap. Long-line buses now have more spacious seating than airplanes, clean restrooms, and non-smoking sections; they provide a soft, comfortable ride, and bus stations are located in convenient central locations. Take along food for a bus ride too, since most places where buses stop are greasy spoons. In planning a bus trip, make sure you find out whether there are express buses to where you want to go—they make far fewer stops and are usually bigger. You can stop off repeatedly on a bus ticket, so it can be a fun kind of travel if you want to see some places along the way.

Hitchhiking is, of course, the cheapest and in some ways the most interesting way to travel, though it has gotten increasingly dangerous in the US. With a pack on your back and a sleeping bag, you can be as footloose and fancy-free as it's possible for a human being to be. And if you have time, walking or bicycling are not bad ways to travel either; you won't go so far, but you'll see more and learn more. In the words of a wise old geographer, Carl Sauer, "Locomotion should be slow, the slower the better; and should be often interrupted by leisurely halts to sit on vantage points and stop at question marks."

If you have a driver's license and seem responsible, you can often get cars from a drive-away agency (see the Yellow Pages or ads in the newspapers). Sometimes you have to pay for the gas, but often not. Ask about the insurance situation. This can be the fastest cheap way to get from one major city to another.

TREES IN THE CITY

Wood for habitations and furniture is one of our most beautiful and satisfying materials. Trees are also a major force in making the earth a habitable planet. A decently Ecotopian society would engage in vast reforestation projects as a first priority. But trees in cities have an important role to play in helping to make them healthy and pleasant, and a new field of "urban forestry" has been developing in response to this need. City governments, conscious of the fact that a neighborhood proud of its trees will not only be more stable but also use less energy for heating and air conditioning, have begun tree-planting programs. Scientists have discovered that a treeless suburban tract is something like 15% hotter than an old neighborhood with big trees. (It's even hotter if, as is common, the tract devotes a larger proportion of its surface area to asphalt.) Trees increase property values in residential areas. And they are due to become an ever more important source of fuel wood; eventually urban woodlots may serve dual park and energy-production purposes. Wasteland areas of cities slated for later development can be put into quick-growing tree species so that they don't simply remain totally unproductive. And most city backyards could support an extra fruit tree or two. (Dwarf or miniature varieties are readily available if your yard is small.)

Trees help provide oxygen for the atmosphere. They absorb and diffuse sound and thus cut down on NOISE POLLUTION. Their decaying leaves add humus to the soil (don't burn them—compost them!). In alpine areas near treeline, it is dramatic to see how a tree somehow gains a foothold in the rocks and then, through the beneficient dropping of its needles, gradually makes habitable for other trees or bushes the crannies around it. The same process goes on, less visibly, wherever trees grow. Trees are indeed a chief ally in the process of resisting erosion by wind and water. Their beauty and peace, their very stolidity, give comfort in a world where everything else seems to move too fast. Planting a tree is not only good for the earth, it will be good for your soul. And, since trees usually grow slowly, seeing your tree grow will give you a link to the next generation, which will enjoy its shade and beauty long after you are gone.

In some situations you can obtain tree seedlings free; check with your city or county. But even if you have to buy them at a nursery, small trees are surprisingly inexpensive. Go to your library first and check out a guide to the tree species which grow in your region. If you are thinking of a tree on the street, check with your city street department; it probably has restrictions on what trees you may plant, but it may also have free or low-cost trees available, and may give you advice or even assitance in digging the hole.

Digging a big enough hole is the major problem in tree-planting. Allow plenty of time for the job, and get a good shovel. The hole needs to be about *twice* as far across and deep as the tree's root ball or can, so that you can surround its roots with good, soft earth. (Be prepared to mix some compost material in with the dirt you dig from the hole.) Then water the tree strictly according to instructions. A tree's first days and weeks in its new home are perilous—though once their roots have become well established, most trees fend for themselves with very little further care.

Always consider carefully the impact the tree will have, when full grown, on the sunlight situation. Though trees can be pruned and shaped, you don't want a dense evergreen to shade your sunny balcony where you take sun baths; if your yard is small, you won't want a tree that ultimately will occupy all of it. Generally, deciduous trees are best on the south side of a dwelling, since they provide shade in summer but let sunlight reach the building and warm it in winter. If you are in doubt where you want your tree, remember that a tub three feet square and two feet deep can, with proper care, support a tree twenty feet high; you can enjoy the tree while it grows, and plant it permanently later.

Acre for acre, trees produce more useful food or fuel than any other use of the land (as Native Americans knew who lived basically on acorns). Don't neglect the possibility of planting nut-bearing trees (or olives, if your climate permits) that will produce food as they beautify your environment.

Tree Crops: A Permanent Agriculture, by J. Russell Smith. Harper & Row, 1978.

Trucks, Live-In

The modern equivalent of the Gypsy wagon is the converted bread or mail truck or school bus, painted in cheerful colors and sporting chimney pipes, stained-glass windows, decorative carved woodwork, carpets, hangings, and all the comforts of home.

Some people just do not like living in one fixed place. They consider that to be vegetable existence, and prefer to keep on the move—especially if they can find a few congenial souls to share their wanderings. This is an attitude especially common today among young people, who feel a natural desire to get out and explore the world. And as our cities and suburbs have become more dismal and uncomfortable to live in, it's small wonder that ingenious and restless souls have discovered anew that a moveable house has its advantages.

For one thing, it makes it easy to get out into the country for indefinite periods; you aren't hung up with paying a steady city rent. You can rove around visiting your friends, in the country or in the city, without necessarily having to ask them to put you up. (They might like to come out and sleep over in your truck instead.) You're never forced to eat out—your kitchen is always with you. If you find a spot you like—and can find a place to park your rig where the locals won't bother you—you can just stay there for a while. (Offering to pay a little, like a dollar a day, and a friendly attitude will soften most country suspicions.) When you feel like moving on, you move on.

If you're actually going to live in your rig, you have to make it tolerably comfortable and appealing. Otherwise you'll soon find yourself retreating into a house existence. This means the basic essentials: heat, sleeping place, food-preparing place, washing place, and toilet. Most van-type vehicles are simply tin boxes. They need insulation: line the inside with insulating board, insulation batting covered with old carpets, or something similar. Then you need to install a stove—the best is a gas space heater that runs on bottled gas; vent the heater exhaust out the roof or side to get rid of fumes. (A cheap kerosene heater isn't much fun in such a small space.) Trailer supply houses sell bottled-gas equipment and other things you may not be able to build or find in junked vehicles. Put shutters on the windows; this may avoid calling attention to your presence in situations where sleeping in campers or trucks is prohibited.

One sizable bottled gas tank can feed a heater, a gas hot plate (though a Coleman or even Sterno will do for light cooking), and a "flash heater" to heat water. Such a heater is, admittedly, a luxury —but it will probably mean the difference between living in your truck and just camping in it. You won't always be parked outside a friend's apartment and able to use their shower.

Your water tank needs to be mounted sturdily at the highest point on the vehicle so the water will flow into heater and faucets. The gas tank can be mounted anywhere outside the living quarters. You'll need a convenient way to climb up to attend to both tanks.

There are many kinds of portable toilets designed for campers and trailers. Aside from the ordinary bucket, the cheapest and simplest are just toilet seats with plastic bags hanging underneath. You seal them up tightly after use, and dispose of them in a garbage can. But there are nowadays various portable toilets which are relatively inexpensive and hold the excrement in a compartment that unhooks and can be carried unobtrusively to a toilet and dumped. (They use a chemical disinfectant and deodorant fluid.) Fancy recreational vehicles, of course, have built-in holding tanks for their toilets, which you have to find a camper discharge connection to empty.

You may want to wire in electric lights from the truck's electric system. But these run down your battery, so kerosene or butane lights are better. You can even get refrigerators that run on butane. For obvious reasons, make sure you have a fire extinguisher.

There's no essential reason, of course, why you can't live in smaller vehicles, so long as you arrange them right. People have lived in VW campers for months, and in delivery trucks and station wagons too. A friend of mine (and his big dog) once lived in a VW sedan; he took out the passenger seat and the rear seat, and laid a padded sleeping board the length of the car. (To remove a front seat, you generally must detach some kind of sliding device under it. The back of a rear seat usually comes loose by sliding it up toward the roof, which unhooks it; the seat itself then just pops upward.) By taking out the rear seats in ordinary American cars, you usually get full-length sleeping room, with your legs stretching back into the trunk.

An alternative to curtains (which require rods or strings or wires) is to paint the inside of the glass in back with thinned white paint. This gives a nice glowing light during the daytime and privacy both day and night. Then you need to string just one curtain across at the back of the front seat.

In a really small space you have to keep everything super-compact: a sealable coffee can for a toilet, a Sterno or other small stove, only one pan and bowl, and so on. But it is amazing how much gear you can cram even into a VW if you have to. Regard it as a challenge to your ingenuity.

See VANS.

U

UNEMPLOYMENT

It is not just a loser's illusion that "there are never enough jobs." Under our kind of capitalism it is essential that a substantial pool of unemployed persons exist; otherwise, unless there are strict government controls as in wartime (or in welfare-state Scandinavia), wages and prices rise in an uncontrollable inflation and sooner or later the whole system crashes. It is thus the poor and unemployed who literally pay, with their bodies and souls, for the stability of the capitalist system. The old myth that everybody can get a job if they'll only be determined and hardworking and careful and clever is just a myth. No matter how determined people are, at least four or five percent of them must be kept unemployed, and government money policies deliberately aim at this. In America, this means unemployment for several million able-bodied and able-minded men and women. Plus, of course, several more millions who would work if there were more jobs, but who don't appear in the statistics because they have given up and are not actively looking for work.

To avoid the growth of dangerously massive discontent, the government has set up the unemployment system, run by state departments of employment, which provides compensation for people who are laid off; and the welfare system, which provides survival payments for people who have never found jobs in the first place. These programs are restrictive, limited, and subject to political cut-backs, so they meet only a part of the need. In most of our cities, thus, tens of thousands of people are out of work and unlikely to find any legal means of survival. The price they exact from society at large, in crime and other social pathology, is one of the costs of capitalism, and must be recognized as such.

Unemployment programs vary widely in their payments, but in the major industrial states they usually provide a subsistence income and sometimes more for up to half a year. However, even a little money can be made to go a long way; and your benefits are not affected by any other family or group income that may be available.

Since employers help finance the fund which pays these benefits (by a tax they have to pay on your earnings while you work for them), bosses are not eager to lay you off—they would rather make things difficult so that you quit instead. If you suspect such a plan is afoot, and layoffs are in the wind, be careful not to give them any excuses for firing you, and don't quit. A goodhearted boss, however, can usually be counted on to certify that you were indeed laid off—which he or she will have to do after you go around to apply for benefits.

Apply at the state department of employment; do so as soon as you are laid off, because it takes several weeks to begin getting checks. You will be expected to continue actively looking for work; find out exactly what this means—sometimes just phoning five companies a week to ask about job openings will suffice. You may have to go into the office for an interview every few weeks to prove you are still around and looking. If they line up a job appointment for you somewhere, you must go to it.

Obviously, however, when jobs are so scarce, it is unlikely that the employment people will find you a job during the twenty-six week eligibility period unless you do some kind of work that does have openings, like clerical jobs. If you possess a skill in a category where jobs are scarce, it is almost impossible for them to place you. (In most states they cannot force you to take a job outside your category or at a lower salary than you got before.)

One of the advantages of working intermittently, rather than part-time all the time, is that you may be able to find some jobs which you can tell will not last long. You can then count on a cushioned period after you get laid off if you arrange your life right—and save some money during the period you're working.

Most states also have some kind of disability insurance, which provides benefits if you get sick or injured and cannot work. (Worker's compensation provides only for disabilities that arise from your job, but the state programs often go beyond that.) A doctor's certificate of disability is required, and periodic checks are made to see if your condition is continuing. Sometimes applications for disability payments can be made by mail from the hospital or from home; call the employment department to find out.

USED CARS

Before wandering into any dealer lots, check in your library for the latest *Consumer Reports Buying Guide* which each year gives a rundown on commonly available used cars, including repair records. Also, unless you're really experienced with cars, it pays to have a mechanic look over any used car you're thinking of paying more than $100 for. It's hard to find a good or totally honest mechanic these days, but most mechanics will give you a reasonably accurate opinion for a modest fee. Don't even consider buying a used car whose present owner won't let you consult a mechanic. (If the owner or dealer is afraid to let you take the car yourself, ask him or her to go along.) A mechanic can make tests you can't do yourself. A compression test will show how much power is being wasted by worn valves or rings. The condition of the spark plugs and oil will give clues to the motor's condition (water globules in the oil mean real trouble). The mechanic can check the brake linings and wheel bearings and spot frame welding or other signs that the car has been in a crash. If some repairs are needed but you're still interested in the car, get the mechanic to write down exactly what they are. A dealer may offer to fix them, or you can use such a list to beat down an owner's price.

If you are an AAA member you can also use the AAA diagnostic service in major cities. However, it's doubtful if this checkup, despite the fancy electronic equipment used, is as practically useful as a checkup by a good mechanic who really knows the kind of car you're considering. And stay away from other "auto diagnosis" shops—they may try to sell you a new motor when your old one is fine.

Naturally, you should only spend money on expert advice after you've narrowed down the possibilities to one car that seems your best bet. Before that, check out all the lots to make sure you know what's available. There are lots of things you can check yourself, and many of them will remove a car from serious consideration—unless you can get it at a rock-bottom price:

Transmission. It's wise to avoid cars with automatic transmission. They eat more gas and wear out brakes faster (especially in city driving) than cars you shift yourself. They have more costly repair jobs, can get wrecked by being carelessly towed, and can't be started by pushing or rolling downhill when the battery is dead. Also, they're less fun to drive—they put a mechanical decision-making system between you and the road, decrease the "feel" you have for what the car is doing, and prevent certain kinds of quick actions (like downshifting in case of brake failure) that might save your life.

Tires and wheels. There should be enough tread on the tires to last you a year or two. That means the tread depressions should still be at least an eighth-of-an-inch deep. Check for spotty wear patterns, or wear that's worse on one side than the other. (Except on VW beetles and older buses—they're built to wear that way.) Make sure there is a spare tire, and that it holds air; it doesn't have to have much tread. There should be a jack and a lug wrench for changing tires. Grab the tires at the sides and twist them; if they move more than a little, the steering tie rods or other parts may be worn. Look for oil and grease leaks around the rear-wheel hubs.

Shock absorbers. Jump on the bumpers, then off. If the car bounces up and down, the shocks are gone. This means the wheels won't hold the road properly. (Shocks only last about twenty-five thousand miles.)

Doors and windows. Open and shut all the doors and run the windows up and down. Damage to doors may mean the car has been wrecked. Anyway, you need to know if the doors work. You don't necessarily have to have them *all* working: it's a bargaining point if they don't. Some states make you replace broken, cracked, or pitted window glass, which is *very* expensive. (You can, for rear-door windows not essential for driving safely, put in a piece of plastic sheet or plywood.)

Lights, etc. Turn on the lights and walk around the car to see if they all work; try both low and high beams. Have someone push the brake pedal and see if the brake lights work on both sides. Check turn signals, dome light, defroster fan. Try the windshield wipers. If there's a washer button, try it. Does the horn work?

Starter. Does the starter turn the engine over briskly? If it doesn't, the battery may be weak, or connections may be loose, or the starting motor may be developing trouble.

Motor. An engine naturally has some oil on it, which doesn't mean anything, but is there any oil on the ground where the car has been standing? This might indicate oil leaks. Does the motor run smoothly at a fast idle just after it's been started? If it doesn't, there may be ignition, choke, or carburetor trouble. At moderate idle, do you hear fairly loud clicking from the valve action? Does the car make a big cloud of blue smoke just after being started, or when you give it a shot of the accelerator? If so, it's probably burning a lot of oil and may need engine work on the piston rings, cylinder walls, and valves—all of them expensive. Engines with fuel injection and electronic ignition tend to run cleaner and give better mileage.

Choke. Most recent American cars have an automatic choke, which is supposed to give the engine a richer mixture of gas and air when it's starting up cold in the morning. Then after the engine warms up, a normal mixture is supposed to return. Automatic chokes very often get out of adjustment, however. They interfere with starting, or they make the engine stall, or they keep it running too fast after it's warmed up. The automatic choke is one more device to make cars "simpler to drive"—and more expensive and troublesome to maintain. Count yourself lucky if you find a car with a manual choke—but learn to use it right, or you'll waste gas.

Clutch and bearings. Does the car move off smoothly, without chattering in the clutch? Does the pedal have to come all the way out before you begin to move? If it does, the clutch needs adjustment and may also need an expensive repair job. To test further, put the car in high gear, put the hand brake on tight, give it plenty of gas, and let the clutch out slowly; this should stall the engine right away if there's some clutch left. Also listen for rattling bearings when you accelerate on a hill and for grinding noises when you accelerate or decelerate—these mean transmission bearing trouble. Listen for knocks and clicks in the transmission.

Gears. Will the shift go smoothly into all gears? Do you hear funny noises when you're shifting? Does the car jump out of gear when you accelerate or decelerate? Does the reverse gear work OK? Can you shift down from higher to lower gears without any clashing noises? Any trouble with the gears may mean expensive transmission work.

Road tests. Does the car accelerate well? Try it at highway speeds as well as on the streets. Does it shimmy? (Tire trouble.) Does it tend to drift off to one side or the other if you lift your hands slightly off the wheel—probably indicating front-end misalignment? (This might be due to road slope or wind—try it going in several directions.) Does the car rattle a lot? Try the brakes gently—do they pull in one direction, indicating bad brakes on that side? Do they brake evenly at high speeds? Loud squeaks probably show the lining is worn down;

this can be serious if the drums get scratched, but most brake work isn't terribly expensive. You should never drive with faulty brakes, even just around your neighborhood. Most people who get killed in cars are within five miles of home.

Steering. Is there play (looseness) in the action of the steering wheel? If you can turn it more than an inch without resistance, the mechanism is probably worn or out of adjustment and may endanger your control of the car. Turn the wheel from one extreme position through to the other extreme position, feeling for "bumps" or hard-to-turn places. Avoid power steering; it wastes energy and gives poorer road "feel."

Instruments. Naturally, never believe the mileage shown on a car! (And lube stickers may be phonies stuck on by a dishonest dealer.) But check the speedometer to see that it operates and also the fuel gauge and any other instruments. Unfortunately, the "idiot light" trouble indicators of many modern cars can make it impossible to tell whether the gauge is really working—the absence of a danger light may only mean the bulb is burned out, the sensor is defective, or a wire is loose. But most cars have their idiot lights wired so that when you first turn on the switch but haven't yet started the engine, all the trouble lights go on. Make sure this happens; if it doesn't, there may be something seriously wrong (such as no oil circulation).

Since most newer American cars don't have full instrument panels, you may have to do without some useful gauges. But you *can* install them yourself; auto parts stores sell kits which contain: (1) a temperature gauge, so you can tell if the engine is overheating—a common problem of old cars whose radiators have slowly clogged up over the years; (2) an ammeter, so you can tell if the generator is charging the battery, or if some unexpected short circuit has occurred; (3) an oil-pressure gauge, to warn you if the engine oil pressure fails—which is about the worst thing that can happen to your engine, as it will ruin itself quickly without oil.

Safety belts. For many people, driving a car is the most dangerous thing they do, and every car ought to have safety belts—all around if possible, but certainly in the front seats. Safety harnesses (across the shoulder and lap both) are better still, because they keep your head from banging into the car in case of an accident. Wearing a shoulder belt in combination with a lap belt at least doubles your chances of surviving an accident.

Alignment and balance of wheels. Wheels that aren't aligned properly cause tires to wear unevenly. Look for flat spots or tires where one side is worn down much more than the other. Correcting alignment isn't expensive, and is usually worth it for the money you save on tire wear. If the car shimmies, especially at speeds around fifty to sixty miles per hour, it probably means one or more tires are unbalanced—that is, heavier on one side than another. This is easily fixed by adding balance weights; most service stations can do it.

Direction of travel and levelness. A car that's been wrecked may have its whole frame bent out of line so that the rear wheels don't exactly follow the front wheels, but run off to one side a little. This makes the car unsafe and also causes terrible tire wear. You can spot this by having someone drive the car straight away from you, or by following it in another car. A car that doesn't set level probably has a broken spring—a dangerous condition.

Radiator. When you get back to the lot after your test drive, check the radiator with the motor still running. Can you spot any water leaks anywhere on the radiator surface? Any bubbles coming to the top inside the radiator—which probably means a blown head gasket? Has the radiator lost water since you started out?

Does the heater give heat? Does the car now idle pretty smoothly and not too fast? If not, it probably has ignition or carburetor trouble, or its automatic choke may be out of order.

Mufflers and tailpipe. Hold a heavy rag over the end of the tailpipe and see if any smoke comes through the walls or seams of the muffler, or through cracks in the exhaust pipe. Leaks cause the engine to make more exhaust noise, and they can poison you with carbon monoxide (a deadly gas) if engine fumes get into the passenger compartment. If you can't check this yourself, ask the mechanic to do it. A new muffler and pipe isn't expensive on most cars.

Body. The condition of the body is the last thing to worry about on an old car, but you should take a look at it anyway. Repainted parts tell you the car has been in at least one wreck. Are there rusted-out parts around the lower edge of the body, where winter road salt has eaten it away? This can get so bad that air—and exhaust fumes—will leak into the car. Are the fenders on tight so they don't squeak and wiggle if you shake them? Are the bumpers still intact? The bumper on most cars is a joke—a butter-soft, over-complicated chrome-plated affair that costs a fortune to replace. If you have to do something to it, why not replace it with a bolted-on piece of two-by-ten lumber instead?

A dirty old auto body may be some insurance against both car theft and people banging into

you; for some reason they figure it will scratch them more than it will you. Besides, if your car's looks aren't worth worrying about you can put your mind on more interesting matters. If you do want to make an old car look better, there's no limit to what you can do. The idea that a car has to be painted a uniform color is strictly a middle-class notion. You can paint every fender and door a different color; you can paint flowers, landscapes, cartoons, slogans, symbols, arabesques, stripes, bull's-eyes, whatever. Ordinary exterior enamel works fine on cars. If you want an even coat, clean the surface very carefully (with acetone), a section at a time, just before putting on the paint. Use a good soft brush and not too much paint, or it'll tend to drip and run. Paint in the shade; if the metal is hot, you can't get the paint on smoothly. Light colors are more visible in traffic, especially at night; white is best if your want to keep the car as cool as possible in sunlight.

For people who don't like painted or shiny objects, really weird possibilities exist. I have seen one ugly old Pontiac completely pasted over with furs, with deer horns mounted on the grille, and a tail. And somewhere there is a Volkswagen bug painted with bubbly crusty undercoating so that it looks as if it's been dipped in shit. To a police officer, a suggestion that cars are not to be taken seriously is blasphemy, so if you have a really funky car you can count on a certain amount of harassment. (If you want to avoid calling attention to your vehicle, buy a standard "intermediate" sedan in black.)

Cars will be harder to sell if they're hand-painted. One of the joys of having a really cheap car, therefore, is that you can do any damned thing to it you want, once you're planning to run it till it dies.

Upholstery and interior. You'll have trouble if springs are beginning to pop through, but otherwise worn seats can always be covered with an old blanket. Make sure you feel comfortable in the car. Does it have enough leg- and headroom for you? Can you see well enough? Are the seats at a comfortable height and tilt? Surprisingly, many large and expensive cars are more cramped inside than smaller, cheaper models.

As a general rule, you're likely to be better off buying from a private party, at least if you know anything at all about cars. You won't be taken in by guarantee promises, because there aren't any. You won't be up against a stream of fast talk and fancy figuring. And there's seldom any difficulty about taking a test ride and getting the car checked by a mechanic.

VACATIONS

Taking a conventional vacation may cost so much that you spend the rest of the year recovering from it financially. This tends to cast a pall over the whole operation. So the problem for most people is to find ways to get out of their usual surroundings and still spend no more money than they would if they stayed home—or maybe even less. Well, there are ways:

Camping. There are many public camp-grounds in this country, especially in the West. Those in the state and national parks have two disadvantages: they cost money and they are crowded, with the camping spots strictly regulated and jammed together. In many, advanced reservations are essential, and in some especially popular places, such as the Grand Canyon, these are given out by lottery! There is actually less privacy in such campgrounds than at home. And they are sometimes noisier because people run transistor radios, get drunk and boisterous, and generally ruin any wilderness feeling in the park.

Your best bet, therefore, is in the national forests where camping away from the roads is usually permitted anywhere you can find a suitable site, and the only regulations concern fire permits—which are altogether reasonable and may help keep some inexperienced camper from burning down half a county. (You'll do your cooking on a portable stove anyway, and burning scarce down wood is not advisable ecologically, so you'll seldom want a fire permit.) Detailed maps showing established campsites with toilet and water facilities are available from National Forest Service offices in Washington and in many other cities, and at the forests' headquarters. These maps also show the many dirt roads and trails that lead off into remote regions where only hardier backpackers penetrate —and where you will be free of the clusters of pickup campers, generator rigs, and other perils that infect popular campgrounds.

Astonishingly enough, walking about a mile is plenty to get away from such "campers," and may well bring you to some idyllic lake, meadow, streambank, or other pleasant spot. Your best plan is to buy the US Geological Survey 'quadrangle' map of the general area you're interested in; study the dirt roads that lead off into the wilderness in interesting directions. Be willing to use up some time exploring an area; if you get to know it, you may find places you want to come back to next year, and the year after that. Your map (see MAPS) will also enable you to strike out across country to campsites further away from the roads, and to other points of interest—lookouts, hot springs, etc.

There is something exhilarating about carrying everything you need for a week on your own back and being free to go wherever your feet take you. But for such a venture you need proper equipment and some experience in overnight camping. It's best to borrow the equipment for your first try: you may not like it. The minimum you need for fair weather is a backpack to carry stuff in, sleeping bag and waterproof ground cloth for under it, food (sporting-goods stores or mountain shops carry dehydrated types), a cooking pot and spoon, compact portable stove, matches, compass and map, a canteen, insect repellent, and a strong knife. You may also want to take along some luxuries like fishing line and hooks, a few band-aids, a fork. Take a complete change of clothes, including fresh socks. A broad-brimmed hat and sun-screen preparations will prevent sunburn. Remember that temperatures outdoors can plummet at night and get very high at midday. If showers are likely, a thin poncho can cover you and your gear. If rain is possible at night, take a tarpaulin to suspend over your sleeping bag. (A backpacking-weight tent is, of course, a lovely luxury in bad weather.)

It is surprisingly easy to get lost when you are a beginning hiker. Learn to rely on your map and check your bearings frequently. Better yet, go with experienced hikers and learn their tricks. Living outdoors is invigorating, but if you don't learn how to do it right you will wear yourself out and irritate everybody around you. The great thing about camping is the utter lassitude that settles over you once you have laid out your camp—and you want to be able to enjoy that to the fullest.

A pleasant variation on camping by car or on foot is the boat trip, which can take you through country literally inaccessible by any other means and often extraordinarily lovely. (Sometimes, too,

253

horribly polluted.) For this, of course, you have to build or rent or borrow or buy some kind of small boat and make sure (by talking with experienced boaters) that it will serve on the waters you plan to travel on—some small lakes can get very rough and even small rivers can have tricky rapids. Special needs for boat living are: ways to keep sleeping bags and other gear dry despite splashing; cover from the sun's heat (big hats, tarps); a waterproof container for matches; life preservers. On some riverbanks, it's very hard to find sleeping spots; it helps to have a boat large enough to sleep on comfortably if need be. Tie up along the bank; don't count on just drifting. You'll also need paddles, oars, sail, or motor. Learn the essentials of water safety, and abide by them. On navigated bodies of water, learn the routes of the barges, freighters, or other heavy traffic before you get into any situation that could be disastrous.

Exchanging your car for a van. Since vans get low mileage, you might be able to make a deal with a friend for a couple of weeks. Few restrictions now exist to prevent you from stopping and sleeping in a van near beaches, lakes, and other attractive spots.

Exchanging houses. You can sometimes arrange to switch houses with friends who live in nearby towns or in the country, thus giving both sides a change of environment. It's also possible to do this with strangers, usually by placing an ad in some

publication read by the kind of people you'd like to exchange with, or in the local paper of the place you want to go. Be prepared to furnish good references.

In an exchange vacation you may be able to get near a beach, river, forest, or some other naturally pleasant place; you might get to live in a city you've always wanted to visit; you might live in a houseboat, or just on the other side of town. In any case, it's a change—but without all the hassle of picking up household bag and baggage, and without the expenditure of energy involved in keeping a pack of children on the move. It's the next best thing to the old pattern of a family cabin owned by rich relatives.

Work vacations. Young people, especially, can sometimes arrange to work at ranches, orchards, resorts, and other establishments that have a heavy need for seasonal help. The best way to find such possibilities is through personal contacts—parents, friends, relatives—but employment agencies and ads sometimes help, and you can also talk to people in ski-equipment stores, for example, if you want to spend some time working in the mountains during the ski season. If such inquiries don't turn up anything, just go to the area well before the season you're interested in, and nose around, asking advice from the permanent residents.

When you drive, especially on vacations or other leisurely trips, try to explore back roads rather than sticking to interstate highways. You will discover interesting little towns, see a lot of scenery that's usually far more interesting than the built-up areas along major routes, and get some sense of how people live in non-urban settings. You will also find eating and lodging cheaper off the main routes.

VACUUM CLEANERS

Probably the easiest way to keep house floors clean is to have no rugs and vacuum every couple of days. A lightweight upright or "vacuum broom" cleaner will usually serve such purposes, though it won't clean rugs as well as a regular heavy cleaner. However, there's not much that can go wrong with a vacuum; you're likely to get a fairly good deal on a secondhand vacuum as long as you let it run awhile when you try it out and make sure it really picks up dust. (Try it on a little sand—that takes good suction.) Holding your hand over the hose isn't a good test—it's how well the nozzle sucks stuff up from the floor that counts. Don't be impressed by "attachments," which just clutter up

your closet. You can vacuum anything except tight corners with the basic nozzle. If you have rugs or carpets, a heavy upright vacuum with a rotating brush will beat the most dust out of them. If your nozzle scratches things, put a little adhesive tape on the bottom edges.

No vacuum will work right unless you keep emptying the bag or dirt collector. So when you buy one, try emptying it to see how much trouble it is. "Disposable" bags add substantially to the cost of operating a vacuum; try to find a model where you simply dump the dirt onto a piece of newspaper and wrap it up. Also check to see whether there is a narrow neck that will clog up easily. (A clogged hose can usually be poked clean with a broom handle.)

If you do carpentry or other messy work, you may want a heavy duty or "shop" vacuum with heavy motor and bigger pickup tube. It costs no more than the ordinary vacuum, but takes up a little more space. Sears or Wards is the best place to find it.

Vacuum cleaners are among the noisiest of common appliances, and responsible for a good deal of noise pollution. Ironically, companies that built quieter machines found that most people wouldn't buy them because they associated loud noise with good suction; so the companies built them noisier again. But you may still be able to find a relatively quiet model secondhand. Pay attention to its cleaning ability, not its sound!

VANS

In the seventies, small vans with large engines became popular as mobile living quarters. Being classified legally as trucks, they escaped smog regulations for a time; but being gas hogs, their appeal declined sharply as gas prices rose. It is still possible to live rather comfortably in a van for short periods (especially in beautiful surroundings) and of course they use far less gas than pick-up campers or full-scale "recreational vehicle" live-in units. For extended residence, however, you need enough headroom to stand upright, and space enough to provide some kind of shower and toilet. See TRUCKS, LIVE-IN.

VEGETARIANISM

Many people live as vegetarians to advanced old ages. The widespread American belief that you need "red meat" for good health is totally without basis. In fact, in recent decades, with the growth in public consciousness of health issues, more Americans have moved toward vegetarianism, either wholly or partly.

Any dietary change is emotionally threatening, and people generally alter their eating habits slowly and cautiously. Many foods in the standard vegetarian cuisine at first seem strange or even bad-tasting to people accustomed to the standard American diet. Bean curd (tofu) happens to be a superb source of almost "complete" protein, since it's made from soy beans; but unless you have encountered it in Japanese and Chinese restaurants, it may seem formless and alien. The first time Americans encounter alfalfa sprouts in a sandwich or salad they may suspect something has gone terribly wrong in the kitchen—until they learn that sprouts, almost magically, have even greater food value than the seeds of beans they come from.

But during the 80's we will have strong economic as well as nutritional motives for moving toward vegetarianism. As Frances Moore Lappe explained in her path-breaking book, *Diet for a Small Planet*, consumption of much of our protein in animal form puts a severe burden on our resources and diretly results in high food costs: a pound of beef protein requires many pounds of plant nutrients to produce. But, by eating plant proteins directly, we can "eat lower on the food chain." And because our high consumption of animal (saturated) fats is a major cause of cardiac disease, we would do our health a great favor besides. (The average vegetarian's cholesterol level is 150.)

Vegetarians differ in their views and you should explore the different positions as you experiment with your own diet. Most of them emphasize soy and other beans as well as brown rice, low-fat milk and cheese, and yogurt. But some vegetarians refuse to eat meat or animal foods such as milk or eggs out of religious or moral convictions: they regard it as wrong to kill other animals, and also wrong to pen them up during their lives. Others believe that humans evolved as vegetarian creatures and that our systems function best on a no-meat diet. There are also quasi-vegetarians who will eat meat or fish but only if they catch it themselves, as primitive hunters or Native Americans had to do. Many vegetarians claim that eating a purely vegetarian diet clears the head and complexion, gives the body a more wholesome smell, and reduces aggressiveness.

Many excellent vegetarian cookbooks are available; a few are listed below. Practically the whole of the enormous population of India is vegetarian,

and they enjoy a delicious and complex cuisine which we might well learn from. Incidentally, the sole essential nutrient you cannot obtain from a vegetarian diet is vitamin B_{12}, which you should take in pill form. In terms of nutrition, vegetables are a better buy than fruits, though of course you should eat plenty of fruit too. Collard greens, sweet corn, blackeye peas, kale, green peas, turnip greens, parsley, and spinach top the list, followed by asparagus, lima beans, broccoli, mustard greens, okra, and—red peppers!

See also FOOD FADS.

A Vegetarian Diet, by Shirley T. Moore, Ph.D., and Mary P. Buers. Woodbridge Press, Box 6189, Santa Barbara, CA 93111.

Diet for a Small Planet, by Frances Moore Lappe. Ballantine, 1975. Includes many recipes.

International Vegetarian Cuisine, by Marie Lovejoy. Quest, 1978.

The Book of Tofu, by William Shurtleff and Akiko Aoyagi. Autumn Press, 7 Littell Rd., Brookline, MA 02146.

Laurel's Kitchen, by Laurel Robertson, *et al.* Nilgiri Press, 1976.

Protein for Vegetarians, by Gary Null. Jove Books, 1978.

VD (VENEREAL DISEASE)

Although most types of VD can be combated fairly easily with drugs in the majority of cases, VD is still a widespread problem. There are three kinds:

Gonorrhea in males causes a discharge from the sex organs, itching, burning during urination, etc. I. is unpleasant and worrisome; because it is hard to spot in females, it may linger and damage reproductive organs. Too many people let it go, hoping it may not be real or that it will just go away. It won't. Drop in at a clinic and get the necessary pills, which will cure it in a few days, and notify any persons with whom you have had sexual contact in the past three weeks.

Syphilis causes sores, either on the sex organs or at other places on the body. Syphilis can be cured readily with proper treatment, and it can be a very serious disease if not treated—leading in its last stages years later to a nasty kind of insanity and death. Again, alert anyone with whom you have been sexually involved recently.

Herpes was formerly rare, but now accounts for 13% of all VD infections, and has now reached epidemic status in some metropolitan areas. It is related to the virus that causes cold sores, and its small, fluid-filled blisters resemble cold sores. They develop into shallow, moist sores, generally around the neck of the penis, on the lips of the vagina, or on the skin between the genitals and anus. They can also occur unnoticed on the cervix. Sometimes there is swelling in the genital or groin area, painful irritation, or vaginal discharge. Some persons experience hypersensitivity, itching, or burning on the skin of their buttocks, thighs, legs and heels before blisters appear.

The first outbreak of herpes is generally the worst; it may last from three to six weeks, but recurrences usually last less than ten days. The herpes virus remains in the body after the blisters have healed, and can break out again because of various factors, including stress and fatigue.

Herpes is highly contagious and may be transmitted by oral, anal, or genital contact. Various unsuccessful treatment methods for herpes were tried in the past, but only in 1979 was one found that showed real promise: a cream containing a special type of sugar, which cleared up 90% of women's and men's first-infection symptoms in four days and also healed recurring infections.

The discomfort from herpes can be minimized by cool baths, local anesthetic ointments, and pain medication. Keeping the infected area clean and dry is necessary to prevent secondary infection.

Herpes is especially unpleasant and dangerous for women. It increases their risk of cervical cancer and can cause miscarriage or premature delivery; if a woman has sores at the time of giving birth, a Caesarean delivery is necessary.

To avoid getting herpes, avoid sexual contact with anyone who has blisters or sores, or who has had them recently. It can, of course, be embarrassing to discuss such things at tender moments, but the risks of infection are far worse than even a great deal of embarrassment. The use of a condom provides protection only if the sores are located on the penis and completely covered by the condom, or if they are inside the vagina; and even then, great care is required; the virus can live on hands and mouth long enough to be passed from one person to another. It is dangerous and irresponsible to engage in sexual activity with someone when you are having an outbreak of herpes.

If you do contract herpes, get to know what triggers recurrences for you and try to avoid them. Also, avoid tight pants and nylon underwear, which keep the genital area overly warm and moist.

The latest information on herpes treatment can be obtained by sending a stamped, self-addressed envelope to HELP, Box 100, Palo Alto, CA 94320.

Venereal disease is transmitted through sexual contact—genital, oral, or anal. There are very rare cases of people catching it through kissing (obviously scientific research in this area is done under drastic limitations). Teenagers worry about catching it from toilet seats but this seems to be extremely rare.

The symptoms of VD are harder for a woman to spot than for a man. This means that early detection of it is primarily men's responsibility. If you find you have it, be sure to tell all the people you have recently had sexual contact with, since one or more of them probably gave it to you, or you may have given it to them, and you all ought to visit a clinic for tests and treatment. Otherwise they will give it to you (and anybody else they sleep with) again. Detection of VD, by the way, may require several tests.

Although not a disease but rather a small parasite, "crabs" can be treated at a VD clinic. The symptom is intense and persistent itching in the hair of the pubic area; if you are sharp-eyed you can spot the beasties themselves. A related skin parasite, scabies, is caused by a mite so small as to be invisible. They live only *outside* the pubic area, and causes persistent itching on stomach, legs, hands. Like crabs, they are readily dealt with through use of an ointment.

If you are a teenager and can't find a VD clinic or are embarrassed to go to one, you can get counseling by phone from the federal VD toll-free hotline number: 800-523-1885. (Such long-distance calls do not appear on your parents' telephone bill.)

VIDEOCASSETTES, VIDEODISCS AND MOVIES

A television set is not necessarily the captive of TV broadcasters; if you have sufficient capital to invest in a player, your TV can also play back movies, sports events, or previously recorded programs. "Betamax" and similar machines, introduced in the late 70's, first made it possible for the general public to *buy* movies instead of going out to see them in theaters. Not only that, the tape machines could also record your own material; suddenly it was possible to see yourself on the tube, and fertile imaginations soon devised plenty of private material.

However, the technology of videotape is such that taped versions of films are inherently fairly expensive, whether you buy them prerecorded or tape them off the air, attempting to edit out the commercials. Thus videodisc, a means of recording a film's images on a plastic disc the size of a phonograph record, has an inherent cost advantage—as well as some quality advantages.

During the 80's, thousands of new films and hopefully thousands of oldies and goodies (including experimental and other unorthodox work) will be released on videodisc, so that you can accumulate a library of favorites the way you do with books and music. Videodisc, however, cannot be used for recording; it is purely a playback device. In compensation, it enables you to slow down, freeze frame, reverse action, and run forward almost instantly to a scene of your choice; in short, it makes it possible to study the filmmaker's art in a close way heretofore possible only for people with expensive editing tables. It should also make it possible to see films that somehow refuse to turn up in your local repertory cinema.

Although the number of new films produced each year has declined sharply from the movie heyday of the forties, movies still offer enough in the way of stronger fare to lure many people away from the tube—at least for the occasional blockbuster—in spite of inflated ticket prices. The number of theaters has also declined sharply, especially in smaller communities; but, in compensation, some of the remaining ones have been split into several auditoriums. Many cities now also have repertory cinemas which show films from the past or recent past; so the total number of good films available is thus probably really only slightly less than it has ever been. (Seeing an old, good movie on TV—butchered to make room for commercials, and with only about half of the original image visible—is generally worse than never seeing it at all.) You should get on the mailing list of your local repertory house, so that you know what they have coming up. Generally their prices are lower than those of houses showing new films.

On cable TV some films are shown without commercials, and if you only get to see two per month this should still cover the cost of the cable service. Cable also generally broadens your choice of regular station coverage, and provides certain kinds of informational programs and locally originated "open access" programs where fare too unorthodox for commercial TV is aired.

Many college communities also support film societies that show unusual films of many kinds. Two or three devotees can generally get such a society started, sometimes through the help of an art museum or other established institution. The history of film is rich in surprises for anybody who thinks movies began with Hollywood. There are stunning early comedies—by Keaton and Lloyd and Langdon as well as Chaplin. The revolutionary films that came out of Soviet Russia led to a whole new style of filmmaking. Short film making has a long tradition in itself. The documentary film has included passionately beautiful films as well as dreary reportage. Film is a subject that can be thought about and enjoyed endlessly. Your library probably has at least a few books on the subject; they range from introductory capsule paperback histories like Arthur Knight's *The Liveliest Art* to meditative philosophical discourses like Andre Bazin's *What is Cinema?*

Never buy candy or other confections at a movie theater. The prices on these goodies are sky-high, especially at "art houses"; often they're where the theater really makes its money. If you think you really need that sugar fix, buy a candy bar at a grocery or gas station or someplace—anyplace—before you go into the theater.

The idea of making movies yourself has spread in recent years from a well-heeled minority into much larger circles. Home movies of the snapshot variety we have always with us; I am talking here of serious movies made in the spirit in which you might write poetry or paint. Although 8-mm equipment has become delightfully cheap, this is not a hobby that can be recommended for people without a certain amount of surplus money: you will have to spend far more on film stock and processing and editing equipment than on the camera itself; and once you get into it you will probably want sound, which is very expensive. Anyone itchy to try movie-making should borrow a camera and shoot with it for a while. That way you can sink all your available money into experience instead of equipment. Or if you simply must have your own camera, buy a secondhand standard 8-mm camera; the advent of Super 8 has thrown these onto the market very cheaply. The basic differences between 8 and Super 8 are that the picture area is slightly larger in Super 8 and that in regular 8 you have more different kinds of film stock available.

W

WAITING

It seems altogether likely that our society will grow rather less "efficient" in the 80's—our public services will decline further and will involve slower operations at almost every level; shortages and cost problems will also affect private and corporate enterprises, slowing down their operations. In short, you will probably spend more time standing in line at banks, in stores, in public offices or waiting at gas stations and in doctors' and dentists' offices, waiting for parts to be delivered, waiting to get a parking spot, etc.

We usually think of time spent waiting as "lost." But in actuality, if you prepare for waiting time, you can put it to some kind of use, and will probably be less irritated as a result. Make a habit of carrying a paperback book with you; carry some paper to make notes on; learn some exercises that you can do unobtrusively. (Isometric exercises, which involve the pushing or pulling of one set of muscles against another, can be done without anybody noticing at all.) Don't be afraid to be talkative; strike up conversations with other people waiting who look interesting. Most of all, seize the occasion as a rare opportunity to *think*, away from the confusions and pressures of your interpersonal or job relationships. Standing in line can be almost as good for thinking as taking a long solitary walk. Address yourself to some problem or concern in your life. Examine it carefully and systematically, pros and cons and maybes. Consider whether there may be ways to approach it that you have been in too much of a rut to really think about. After a while, when the subject has gotten thoroughly established in your head, try to let your mind go blank about it, which might give new ideas the chance to surface.

WALKING

Public-health surveys have found that Americans get less exercise than any other people on earth. And we're getting less and less all the time, probably because of the increased time we spend in cars, in front of televisions, and working at desk jobs. A nation of people who drive to the corner store a block away are asking for heart attacks, hardening of the arteries, degeneration of muscle tone, and a host of illnesses and disorders that come from being in bad physical shape. Chief among these is heart disease, which makes Americans die younger than people in other Western nations; we now rank something like seventeenth in longevity. And if everybody with chronic backaches lined up, they'd probably stretch halfway across the country.

Walking is the means by which evolution equipped us to move around. Being able to walk on two legs is an extraordinary thing among mammals, and we ought to appreciate it more than we do. To permit it, our bodies had to develop a superb sense of balance, a pelvic structure slightly different from four-legged animals, and a different angle for our necks. But in return we gained the freedom to use our front paws as hands—and it is likely that this is the essential evolutionary step that set our ancestors out along the path that led to our present condition.

Despite all this, contemporary Americans seldom enjoy walking. They think of it only if all other means of getting somewhere have failed. If they end up having to walk, they feel tired, whether they are actually tired or not, just because they resent it. Oddly enough, New Yorkers seem to walk more than most other Americans, because few of them own cars, and they are thus used to walking five or six blocks to and from (and within) subway stations. Small-town and middle-class people with cars almost *never* walk more than a block. To the direct financial cost of cars, therefore, we must add the immense costs to families and society in early deaths, medical bills, and time lost from productive work. (We need to think of walking, running, and bicycling as "preventive transportation," as in "preventive medication.")

Unfortunately, the redesigning of our cities to provide facilities for cars has made them less convenient and attractive for pedestrians, as well as smog-ridden. In years past, it is reliably reported, Americans used to stroll around their streets greeting their friends, stopping to chat, telling stories about their families and children. With the spread of cars that social structure is breaking down and

of property to allow them to include such amenities in their plans. But they succeed rarely. They are up against decades of vilely inhuman construction which has nearly ruined most of our major cities as pedestrian environments.

Sooner or later, private automobiles must be barred from our downtown areas. This plan, once thought heretical or impractical, is steadily gaining ground among planners and even businesses, who realize that no scheme, however clever or expensive, can possibly get everybody downtown by car without creating intolerable conditions for all.

Once the car is gone, and the only vehicles allowed are taxis, buses, perhaps minibuses for short trips, and trucks (hopefully powered by engines that don't emit smog), then the walking human being will once again feel at home.

Meanwhile, there are still pleasant places to walk. Dedicated walkers comprise a kind of secret society, and if you meet some members they will tell you their favorite haunts. Meanwhile you can start out simply by walking to a few of the places you usually go by car or bus. Then the next time you go, try a slightly different route. Even if you live in a city which is not very interesting architecturally and which doesn't have much street life and which definitely has too damned many cars (and most of us live in such places), you'll probably be surprised at all the interesting things you notice. Don't be in a hurry. Do your first walking when you can afford to stroll and loll a little, so you don't resent the fact that it takes longer to "get somewhere" than if you were on wheels.

Check out your own "walking range." For most of us, spoiled by too much car driving, it's absurdly short—especially when you consider that human beings can in a "primitive" society outrun (by outlasting them) both horses and giraffes. If your present comfortable range is only a couple of blocks, extend it little by little. In countries with better public health (which means most of the industrialized world), people normally walk distances up to a mile every day.

Then look around to see if there aren't some really fascinating parts of your city where you've never been on foot before. Try to find a foreign neighborhood that has interesting stores and people. Or look in your parks for pleasant places you've never been. Is there an arboretum, or garden for exotic plants? Is there a lake you can walk around? Is there a beach or river you can walk along? Check out local newspaper columns or books that give pointers on interesting nearby walks.

spreading out; even if you *do* walk a lot, you seldom see anybody you know. (They're all zooming by in cars.) But an equally important factor is that our builders and designers, in their surrender to the "priorities" of auto traffic, have systematically made our cities unfit to walk in. Our streets are filled with foul air and dangerous traffic. They lack trees, bushes, flowers, fountains, benches, sidewalk cafes, alcoves, and miniparks where people can buy a paper, sit down, watch the world go by, wait for a friend. A few planners have begun to realize this, and are trying to persuade the owners

After a while, you'll probably realize that you have your own special style of walking. Some people walk fast, some walk slow. Some stop a lot, some keep going. Some walkers like best to walk in the rain, or at night, or with their dogs. Some only like to walk where there are trees or water. Some find "nature walks" dull and walk only on busy city streets. You'll never discover your own style unless you try out the different possibilities.

The point of walking is to give you pleasure. It's what a philosopher might call "activity in accord with true virtue"—the virtue of using your body for what it evolved for. With our American concentration of "practicality," we have come to think of walking only as a means to an end—the end being to get somewhere, whether we know why or not. But walking is also an end in itself: the enjoying of your body's potentialities.

And the medical fact is that brisk walking is one of the best forms there is of all-around exercise. It tones up your body, without putting severe strain on joints or ligaments as running can do, and it's especially good for tired backs. It improves your circulation (though not as much as jogging or running or swimming). It may help your appetite for wholesome foods and aids in weight control (see REDUCING). It develops your breathing. (Many city people take very shallow breaths—which is perhaps understandable considering the quality of their air.)

In short, even if you have a car, make a point of walking whenever and wherever you can.

WASHERS AND DRYERS

These are expensive appliances, and when breakdowns occur, they can cost half what a new machine does. Unless you have a great deal of washing to do, therefore, you may be better off to use the laundromats—or, even better, to share a washer and dryer with a couple of neighboring houses. (These machines are not harmed by being outdoors except when it's cold and water can freeze in their piping, so sometimes they can stand on a covered back porch or in a shed, for easy access by all. This also keeps the noise level down in your house.)

Try not to do small loads, which are wasteful of water and energy. If you have a washer which adjusts for larger or smaller loads, don't forget to adjust it. Under the impact of higher gas and electricity prices, the clothesline is making something of a comeback (solar-powered drying!). Sun drying disinfects diapers, incidentally.

Watch out for expensive bleaches, fabric softeners, and other laundry gimmicks. Clorox, in particular, is far more expensive than identical products under other names. Dry bleaches are also expensive, including the (weaker) oxygen bleaches.

WATER BEDS

Water beds are interesting, whether you are concerned with backaches, the floating sleep-inducing gentle rocking they give you, or sex. (They are not to everybody's taste in any of these departments; try to get invited to sleep on one for a series of nights before you contemplate buying one, or rent one for a month.) Very expensive, guaranteed deluxe water beds are being made, but here are the minimum requirements: a strong floor (a water bed weighs up to a ton or ton and a half); a sturdy frame of two-inch lumber, smooth inside and reinforced at the corners (to keep the vinyl bag from stretching and breaking); a thin plastic liner to catch water if the bag itself should be punctured or spring a leak; and either an insulating pad on top of the bed or an electric heater under it.

Heaters are still the main problems with water beds. Cheap ones are not safe against possibly dangerous short circuits, and they all use a lot of electricity; keeping a ton of water heated up to eight-five or ninety degrees will add several dollars a month to your electric bill. If you want simplicity, safety, and minimum cost in money and energy, sacrifice a little oceanic feeling and use an Ensolite or foam-rubber insulating pad instead of a heater.

A few suppliers offering super-cheap water beds are using too thin vinyl; it should be twenty mils thick (twenty thousandths of an inch, that is). Fixing a leak caused by a puncture is possible with repair kits sold by dealers.

Water beds are hardly adapted to a mobile life, but for many people who stay put they have become a standard form of bed. They are cheaper new (if you look around, and build your own frame) than an ordinary bed.

If a water bed is too wavy for you, filling it more tightly with water may help. Some beds are also being filled with a gel which floats you like water but doesn't slosh around.

WATER CONSERVATION

As the American population has increased and concentrated more and more in huge cities, its drain upon natural water supplies has multiplied even faster. Many industries, such as chemical, paper, and plastics, use immense quantities of water. The flush toilet system uses huge amounts of water to move very small amounts of excrement. Agriculture, especially in the arid West, uses quantities of water so large as to be impossible to visualize: in some areas virtually the entire run-off capacities of major rivers are used in irrigation so that only a trickle reaches the sea. New technologies of pumped irrigation are steadily draining water from underground water-table reservoirs that will require centuries to recharge. And all of these uses are single-purpose; planned water re-use is at present virtually unknown, though the chemical effluents of industries along the Mississippi and Ohio form part of the drinking supplies of St. Louis and New Orleans—and have made them literally carcinogenic for many years. (Fertilizer and pesticide applications are another major source of water-supply contamination.)

Our cities have reached out into nearby mountain areas for their water supplies, but these supplies have now been entirely spoken for. Thus, if our population continues to increase, and our agriculture and industries do not find ways to make do with less water, droughts such as that which afflicted the West in 1976-77 will cause considerable hardship. During that drought, the preciousness of water resources was recognized by many people who had never previously given it a thought. They began taking conservation measures which cut public water consumption to around half of its previous levels: they stopped watering lawns, planted drought-resistant native plants, washed their cars less, took short showers and installed flow-restricters in faucets, didn't flush toilets just for urine, and put dams or bottles in their toilets (and bent down the float rods so they filled to lower levels) so that each flush used less water. They put pressure on golf courses, cities, and other public agencies to use recycled water for irrigation; indeed, golf courses began to compete to have sewage plants located next door so they could utilize the sewage effluent water (which also has fertilizing effects).

Such practices, it was found, can reduce domestic consumption to the point where communities can withstand all but a very prolonged drought. And some reductions were achieved in industrial use, which should be continued, especially if public water supply agencies charge companies for water at realistic costs. It is in agriculture, however, that really major changes are needed—especially the switch to drip methods of irrigation, which not only use far less water (and allow far less evaporation) but also minimize the salting-up of the productive soil which irrigation tends to bring about in regions of low rainfall.

In some areas, such as the Great Plains where corn is now being grown by water pumped from underground, huge new desert regions will ultimately be produced when the water table reserves have been "mined out." Nature does not accept the excuse that we didn't know what we were doing. If we destroy the balance of soil and water resources that a region's natural productive capacities can reliably support, agriculture and the towns dependent upon it will not survive. We have created a Dust Bowl once in our history, and it appears we are doing it again.

Even in the relatively well-watered East and Southeast, water conservation will be a problem for some metropolitan areas. In time, methods of handling excrement and returning it to the land as fertilizer will take some of the burden of water consumption off our sewage systems. For the present, a concern for water conservation dictates such simple but effective steps as:

- During such processes as shaving, brushing teeth, washing dishes, etc., turn off faucets when you don't actually need them running.
- Fix leaky faucet washers promptly; a slow drip can waste hundreds of gallons (besides making an annoying noise!)
- If you have a single-handle shower faucet that is unable to control water volume, install a little disc called a flow-restrictor in the shower head (hardware or plumbing-supply stores sell them— they cost very little).
- For decorative plantings, choose species with low watering needs.
- For vegetables, plant closely in raised beds, and use a drip watering system rather than over-all spray watering. Cover exposed soil with mulch (which also minimizes pests).
- For lawns, minimize evaporation losses (and do your grass a favor) by infrequent deep, long watering. Water in the evening.
- In washing your car (if you really feel you *have* to!) use a bucket of soapy water and only hose the car off after you've scrubbed it.

These measures will be, in the long run, especially needed in the West and arid Southwest— where population growth is taking place that cannot be supported by the available water resources of the region, no matter what monster boondoggle water-diversion schemes may be proposed or even carried out.

To survive in the long run, we will need to learn to live within the water supplies available in the different bioregions of our wonderful little green planet. But hungry people, often accompanied by their hungry goats, are cutting trees, digging deep wells, and generally creating new deserts in many parts of the world at an alarming pace. It is an open and terrible question whether this process can be reversed.

WATER HEATERS

Your domestic water heater accounts for a larger part of your home energy consumption than anything but your furnace. Wrap it with an insulation jacket (which many hardware stores can now supply) or use ordinary fiberglass wall insulation, taping it loosely around the tank (remember to wear a mask or handkerchief over your nose and mouth) and you will cut heat losses 30-40%.

An electric ignition system is no advantage for a hot water heater, since the pilot light does useful work in helping keep the hot water hot.

Your water heater will consume much less energy if you use less hot water—by not letting it run while you wash dishes, by installing flow restricters in shower heads, by washing clothes with cold or cool water (and washing things requiring hot water in a washer than can handle small loads with less water).

Gas appliances in general are and will remain through the 80's more economical to operate than electrical ones, since gas or oil have to be burned at the power plant to generate the electricity, with losses during generation and transmission; only when electricity from solar, wind, or other alternate sources competes in quantity and cost with gas could electricity gain an advantage.

Especially where state tax credits apply, the installation of a solar water heater will generally pay for itself in a few years. The possibilities range from very simple pre-heaters suitable for warm climates to relatively sophisticated designs involving heat-exchangers, non-freezable collecting fluids, and small pumps, which can provide your entire hot water supply in any climate.

WATERPROOF CLOTHING

Anybody who spends a lot of time outdoors (as all good Ecotopians do) knows that staying dry over long periods has not been easy to accomplish.

Airtight fabrics, rubberized or plastic, have the disadvantage of confining the large amounts of water vapor your body gives off (about a pint a day, even in cool weather). So this moisture condenses on the inside of garments and on the skin, resulting in the clammy condition familiar from impermeable raincoats and the foul-weather gear worn by sailors and construction workers. Perforations at the armpits, loose cuffs, and vents across the back have been tried and do allow some circulation of air.

One approach, unfortunately quite expensive, was to use fabric of super-close-woven cotton, which can sometimes be found in very costly hunting and arctic gear. In the parts that stay dry it breathes, but in the parts that get wet the fibers swell, closing off their pores so tightly that water cannot pass through.

But for general use the problem seemed basically insoluble—until the invention of Goretex fabric. This is a system of coating fabric with a film that has microscopic pores—pores so small, in fact, that air molecules can pass through them, but water can't. So the fabric breathes, and you stay dry and warm. Goretex is now used in camping equipment as well as garments. It requires careful handling, since the film is easily damaged.

Various water repellent finishes can be applied to outdoor garments, but most of them are not very effective, and also tend to increase the fabric's tendency to pick up and absorb stains.

WELFARE

Almost everybody who has been involved with it or studied it concludes that the welfare program of this country is a fearful mess. But, despite some ingenious social experiments that proved a "negative income tax" would not cause people to lie back and stop working, there is no strong constituency for welfare reform. Taxpayers clamor about the occasional welfare scandal but make not a peep about corporation boondoggles that cost them thousands of times as much. And so the welfare system muddles along; with our UNEMPLOYMENT programs, it sops up some of the casualties systematically produced by our type of economic system. Many of us will find ourselves such casualties from time to time, so it pays to know how welfare operates. Indeed, many single mothers who work full-time are paid so little that they qualify for welfare (and FOOD STAMPS) but don't know it.

The average time a family spends on welfare is 31 months; the average number of children is 2.4; more than half (and an increasing percentage) of welfare recipients are white. The national outlay is more than ten billion dollars a year for more than eleven million persons; but a vast army of administrators and social workers consumes almost a fifth of the money. A vigilant Parent Locator Service established by HEW has tracked down literally millions of fathers who disappeared or stopped providing child support, whether or not they are still married to the mother.

The commonest form of welfare is AFDC: Aid to Families with Dependent Children. In many areas it is in effect the only kind of welfare there is, except for a few occasional cases of desperate unemployed fathers who qualify for extremely small grants; GA (General Assistance) emergency relief may occasionally be granted (depending on the county regulations) to people who cannot get unemployment, "supplemental security income" through the Social Security system, or AFDC. However, by a familiar Catch-22, it is generally very hard to get an emergency grant unless you also qualify for AFDC. Recipients of emergency grants must report once or twice a day on their job-hunting efforts (unless they're disabled).

It is no longer illegal for a mother receiving AFDC to live with a man or have a man stay overnight, as was once the case (leading to dawn raids and other insanities). In fact, the only man she *cannot* live with is the father of her children. She must present the birth certificates of children who qualify her to receive welfare, and generally these carry the father's name, so he can then be tracked down; but if they don't, the mother cannot legally be compelled to supply it. A mother is not required to sue the father for support, though the state may do so.

Many mothers who qualify for AFDC have been married and divorced. Unless their ex-husbands are very well off and provide alimony as well as child support, they will be obliged to work, no matter the age of the children, unless they can get AFDC. And even if they do work, their wages may be so low that they are still entitled to welfare support.

States must now provide AFDC for anyone, without a residency requirement such as still applies to other forms of welfare. You can thus move to a different state and be eligible immediately. States vary widely in their welfare programs, and so do counties. Generally poor and backward areas are, as you would expect, less generous, but

the pattern is unpredictable and information has never been assembled into compact form; people pass tips among themselves. The one thing you can say with certainty is that it can easily be impossible to get welfare assistance unless you fall into the AFDC program; welfare programs, it has been estimated, touch only about ten percent of the population living below the poverty line. The unfortunate result is that for millions of Americans, the only route to survival is crime.

To receive welfare you must generally dispose of any substantial liquid assets you possess. You may be able to retain your house, and sometimes a car if it is not worth much. But you do not have to let welfare workers make uninvited visits to your home.

When you go in to apply for welfare, make sure you have the whole day free. Go in early and take a book along to read while you wait. The social worker will want to know whether you have any income or property at all, where the father of your children is, where you live and who else lives there, where your parents are, and other information. If you believe you are eligible and are refused welfare, you can ask to see a supervisor, or come back another day—with another worker you may have better luck, since some judgment is involved. Or you can consult a Neighborhood Legal Service office and see if they can help you. Welfare departments are under constant pressure to save money, and they will turn you down if they can. (Some states, in fact, have deliberately flouted federal welfare regulations.) It pays, therefore, to learn whatever you can from friends who have had contact with the local welfare program, from people in the waiting rooms, and from talking with sympathetic welfare workers.

WILLS AND PROBATE

When people die without a will, their property is passed on to their relatives according to state laws. Generally it goes to their spouse if he or she is still living; if not, it's divided up equally among the living children. This applies both to "real" property such as a house and to "personal" property such as a car or mobile home, boat, or clothes.

If for some reason you don't want your property to be given in the state's way, and many people do not, you can sometimes accomplish this through a will—though your spouse will get half of it, anyway, in community property states. (This is one reason why legal marriage agreements clarify your thinking and can prevent later trouble.) You can also provide for guardians other than grandparents for your children if you wouldn't want them to fall into your parents' hands.

A will can name an administrator (usually your lawyer or an old family friend) to manage or sell your property on behalf of your spouse or children.

A will can always be canceled just by burning the original; the copy you usually leave with the lawyer or court doesn't matter. Make a new will before burning the old.

When a relative dies and leaves you something, there is a court legal process called "probate" which verifies the will and sees that its provisions are carried out. Generally this requires the services of a lawyer in the place where the relative died. Most lawyers are glad to handle probate cases because there is a good deal of money in them—they are paid on a percentage. Some crooked lawyers will suck practically all the money out for themselves, so it is important that you or the family find an honest one. You may be able to get a little general advice from the Legal Aid or Neighborhood or Rural Legal Service, but they cannot actually handle such cases.

WOOD STOVES

Even in cities, wood for fuel is often available at prices that (per unit of heat) beat oil or gas—assuming, of course, that you have a really efficient stove, and aren't just using a fireplace or an open Franklin-type stove. (Generally a firplace is a net *loser* of heat—you suck more warm air out of the room and up the flue than the fire provides.)

A good stove is expensive. Moreover, it requires a commitment of energy and care, or it will not keep you warm and it may burn down your house. Nevertheless, wood stoves are spreading through the country very rapidly. (So rapidly that in some places they cause noticeable air pollution.) They appeal to people partly for economy's sake, partly because they use a renewable energy source, and partly to provide a secure back-up against future heating-oil shortages, which are likely to be severe and, in harsh climate areas, can be dangerous. A good wood stove will warm an average-sized house quite satisfactorily if it is used right and is equipped with a blower to circulate warm air to distant rooms (sometimes, but not always, ducting is a good idea for this purpose). Stove dealers will generally be willing to visit your house and recommend a stove appropriate to it. However, there is a wide range of experienced opinion about

wood stoves; do a lot of checking before you decide on one. People's recommendations vary wildly, depending on their expectations and habits. And there are great variations in the configurations and construction of stoves, which of course strongly affect price. Cast iron stoves are not necessarily superior to welded steel stoves; they are somewhat more fragile to impact and to temperature changes (for example when cold logs touch the hot sides) which can cause cracks.

To maintain a fire for a long period during the night, a stove must be of the airtight type, so that the draft can be closely controlled. Some airtight stoves have glass holes in their doors, so you can see the fire, but this is never like being in front of a fireplace. Some stoves have flat tops so you can cook on them. Some have water heater attachments, on the back or in the stovepipe, which preheat water going into your regular water heater. Some are designed to be used with a small motor-driven fan to increase the draft. Some have heat jackets to confine the air they heat, which can then be sent through ducts. Some will hold long logs, and some only short ones.

All wood stoves pose fire hazards and should only be installed in conformity with your local building codes and regulations, or your house fire insurance may become invalid. There are three main safety requirements for stoves. (1) They must stand on a fireproof base (ideally fire brick) and be a specified distance away from walls; if closer, the walls must be covered with a protective metal sheet set out from the wall surface. (2) They must have a properly designed stove pipe to insure smoke passage, maximize heat diffusion into the room, and minimize creosote deposits. (Creosote builds up from smoke particles, especially those from green wood; in time it becomes flammable, which can cause chimney and stove-pipe fires that are terrifying and dangerous. Stove pipes can be installed so they are easy to clean, with an openable T to catch creosote behind the stove as it runs down inside the pipe.) (3) Passage of the stove pipe through walls or ceiling or roof must be through fire-proof collars, the nature of which is prescribed by your local building code. In areas where wood stoves are common, building department personnel have much valuable experience with wood stove installations. They share your interest in not having your dwelling burn down, so you should follow their requirements.

A stove draws in a certain amount of air from the room, which it then sends up the stove pipe and/or chimney. New houses are sometimes so tightly sealed that a stove cannot get enough air, and will smoke. (The same can happen with a fireplace or Franklin-type stove.) You must then allow a little air to enter somewhere. Every stove has a certain number of idiosyncrasies, and it takes some weeks of breaking in before you and your stove will fully understand each other's performance requirements. But having a stove you know and love, especially if it saves you immense amounts of money, can be a most gratifying experience.

Before investing in a wood stove, explore the availability and price of firewood in your area. Laying in a supply of wood is something that needs to be done in the spring, so the wood can be well seasoned by the time you need it. It needs to be stored where rain or snow cannot dampen it, and you need to plan your delivery and storage to minimize the work of picking up logs and hauling them around; wood is heavy. The best stove wood is from modest-sized logs, so that the burning surfaces are at least half round (rather than split sides all around). Oak, hickory, and fruit woods burn the best and give the most heat. You need some soft wood around to use as kindling in starting fires, or course. But green wood and soft woods should be burned only as last resorts; they give relatively small amounts of heat, and large amounts of creosote—which, sooner or later, you must clean out of your stove pipe and chimney.

If you are near woodland areas, a chainsaw and pickup truck will enable you to gather your own fire wood. Don't underestimate the sheer labor this involves; but of course it can reduce your fuel costs to very little (unless you have to rent the truck). In national forests, with a proper permit, you can usually cut firewood for yourself; send for a brochure called *Firewood for Your Fireplace*, to Forest Services, US Department of Agriculture, Washington, DC 20013.

Tightly rolled newspapers can be used for fuel in fireplaces or stoves, though they're quick burning. You can buy a device to help, but a piece of broomstick will do fine. Fold sections of paper so they end up about 12 x 15" and a half-inch thick or less. Soak in water with a little detergent in it; this assists in wetting. Roll the papers onto the rod, squeezing out water; slide out the rod and stand your "log" on end to dry. It will take some weeks, even if you dry them on wire mesh to let air circulate. A daily paper makes a couple of logs, the Sunday paper maybe a half dozen, and they burn about a half hour.

The Woodburning Stove, by Geri Harrington. Collier Books, 1977.

WORK: SELF-EMPLOYMENT AND SUPPLEMENTAL JOBS

One of the drags of ordinary jobs is that you are at somebody else's beck and call. Even if your boss is a perfectly decent person, you may not like this aspect very much. And there are ways to create a job for yourself as an independent operator, even without having to find a lot of capital and "set up in business." The possibilities in every locality are different, but here are some kinds of work that are needed almost everywhere:

Typing A good free-lance typist can make the equivalent of normal wages, and can work at home any hours. Around universities and in big cities there are surprising amounts of typing to be done, and all you really need to get started is a good typewriter and some cards to stick up on bulletin boards or hand out to people. It's also useful to advertise in student newspapers.

Childcare. Since so many parent now work, there is a serious shortage of good CHILDCARE SERVICES. Operating government centers costs almost as much per child as paying the parents welfare to stay home, so it seems unlikely that government-run centers will expand to any significant extent. If you love children, therefore, you can certainly find children in your neighborhood who need care, and at going rates a half-dozen kids will bring in enough income to support you in a modest way. This is a kind of work that men are undertaking more often. Many American children living with their mothers have little contact with nurturing men, and such contact is extremely valuable. It's best to work with one or two other child-loving people you get along well with; you can then contemplate a better site, and perhaps develop into a full-scale nursery school. Be prepared to encounter hassles with city officials or neighbors; find a lawyer who knows the local situation to advise you and deal with trouble.

Juice stands and other refreshment places. You don't have to have a fixed place of business; you can rig up a truck or even a pushcart. By finding out where large crowds of people gather, you can do a brisk business if you offer a really fine product. People have especially good luck these days with good cold drinks—the ordinary food stands sell such chemically concocted junk that a good glass of real lemonade, orange juice, apple juice, or other cooling drink will sell fantastically at fairs, at outdoor concerts, in parks, and just on hot city streets. Ice-cream wagons, of course, are an old city standby. But you can sell hot pretzels, candy, fruit and a variety of other goodies—so long as you buy a business license from the city and scrupulously observe cleanliness requirements.

Teaching. If you know how to do something well, the chances are that you can find students who want to learn it. People live by teaching tennis, English, computer programming, music, swimming, reading, foreign languages, and so on.

Data processing. Because computerization has so many complexities, organizations often get into binds where they need outside help on an emergency or short-term basis. There are also many research projects and students who must use data processing but don't know how to handle it. If you happen to understand computer languages and like to be creative with them, you can make money by helping people who don't and aren't.

Caretaker and apartment manager jobs. There are many kinds of properties around the country, often located in remote places, which need watching: abandoned mines, summer estates, hunting or fishing clubs, unrented factory buildings, properties being contested in will settlements, and so on. Any property which is either economically valuable and might burn down or suffer other damage, or which is hazardous and might cause legal liabilities, is a candidate for a caretaker. Usually these jobs include live-in facilities, of course, but in some the conditions may be primitive. Metropolitan newspapers, and newspapers in the areas where the properties are, run caretaker ads in the classified sections. Some employment agencies occasionally have caretaker job listings too. When applying for such jobs, it pays to look responsible and carry along respectable references.

The urban counterpart is the apartment manager's job, where you get a free apartment (or reduced rent) and sometimes a part-time salary in return for taking care of a building. This chiefly means renting vacant apartments, fixing things that get out of order, keeping up the gardening, and so on—a pleasant and not very time-consuming sort of work. It can get a bit sticky if you have to collect the rent.

If people had basic security against starvation, as they would have under a guaranteed-income plan, they would be more free to improvise with their lives and come up with really interesting ways of making money. These would tend to be creative innovations—things that would help make life more cheerful and humane, rather than dull and machine-like. Young people from middle-class families have traditionally often had this advantage—they could go to college, look around

at leisure for interesting jobs, sometimes even start a small business of some kind. The ideal, obviously, is to invent some way of doing what you'd like to do anyway, but also to earn some money out of it!

WORKERS CONTROL. See EMPLOYEE OWNERSHIP.

WRITING AWAY FOR THINGS

One of the keys to enriching your life without spending much money is knowing how to reach out into the world and find out about or get things. For things that exist locally, you can do this by telephone (see INFORMATION, HOW TO FIND), but writing letters is often necessary too. Many people feel awkward about writing letters. There's no need to. Half the letters by which the nation's business is carried on are full of misspellings, bad phrasing, ambiguity, and so on. Don't worry, therefore, about getting everything perfect in order to write a letter. Just bat it out. The important thing is to write it so that it will work: bring back the information you want, or get the response you want.

The first thing you need to know is to whom to write. If what you're after is information about a product, most corporations have publicity departments to answer inquiries, or else their sales departments deal with inquiries. If you don't know who really ought to deal with your request, address it to "Office of the President"; executives have secretarial staffs who route letters to people who can deal with them. It's a good idea to send *all* complaints and letters of outrage (which can be great fun to write) to the president's office; that way they may conceivably do some good. In writing to government offices, all that matters is to get the name of the office right; no one can figure out exactly whom to send things to.

Make sure you phrase your question clearly. Generally your reply will be coming from a clerk of some kind, so try to write your question in a way that invites simple, clear answers. If you have a number of interconnected questions, put them in a numbered list. Whenever you're asking about something you may want to buy, ask for a price list and information about ordering. Most companies and organizations have a file of ready-made catalogs, booklets, flyers, and so on. Whenever you are after some information that is probably too precise to be included in that kind of scattershot publication, you'll have to ask for it very specifically. Companies have a nasty habit of only publicizing the expensive end of their product line—they may "forget" to send you the folders that describe their low-cost items.

Write your full name and address and zip code anywhere at the top of your letter. (Don't bother to put it on the envelope.) Otherwise no reply can be sent to you. If a quick reply is important, you may get one by enclosing a postcard on which you've written your own name and address—that way the clerk who answers you only has to jot down a reply on the card and toss it in the mail.

There are many things you may want to write for. Government agencies such as the departments of Agriculture, Health, Education, and Welfare, or Interior put out many free pamphlets, and some thicker ones that they charge a quarter or so for. Bureaus in your state and local governments also issue useful items. Companies sometimes offer free samples if you write to them enclosing a coupon from some ad. Publications will often send you a sample copy in hopes you will subscribe. Organizations offering services or seeking your support will often send you materials describing their work.

Yogurt

Yogurt is not the only cultured milk product you might enjoy—buttermilk and kefir are two others to try—but it has the great advantage of being easy to make yourself. It's a delicious and healthy dessert or snack, especially when a little fruit or jam is added.

Basic cookbooks such as *The Joy of Cooking* give easy-to-follow procedures for making yogurt. It's not necessary to buy an expensive yogurt-making rig, though a cooking thermometer will be a big help in getting the milk just hot enough. The essential is a place where the warm mixed yogurt can sit undisturbed for 7 or 8 hours while the culture "works." (Yogurt hates being jiggled. If you disturb it and it doesn't set, you have to do the whole process over again.) You can put a lightbulb and thermostat inside an old camp cooler; it should be kept warm but not hot. If you were lucky enough to live at a hot springs, like the Zen people at Tassajara, you could suspend your yogurt culture over the hot water. But simplest of all is to line a box with at least inch-thick insulating foam (including the bottom, and make a piece to lay on top of your yogurt cups or jars). Your yogurt is at 106-109°F when you finish mixing it, and this heat, if retained in such an insulated container, will be enough.

For "starter"—yogurt containing the micro-organisms that turns milk into yogurt—you can experiment with different commercial yogurts, or buy a package of culture from a health foods store. Save a little of your last batch for starter in the next one. But after ten batches or so, get some new starter.

Z

ZIPPERS

If zippers stick or don't run free, the tape on back may be binding in the slider; sometimes you can re-train it to stay out of the way. Dry cleaning can make a zipper run hard; sometimes a little soap on the teeth will lubricate it. Although the zipper is one of those rare modern inventions which is a real improvement over its predecessor (the button), zippers do jam, they do pull off in time, they do sometimes lose teeth; and then they need to be replaced. It is not as hard to replace a zipper as you may think. The chief thing is that you must get one which is the exact length of the old one. As you carefully remove the old one by clipping the threads with a small knife or scissors, pin the new one in as you go—that way it'll be in place and ready to be sewn on when you get rid of the old one.

Alternative to zippers is the VelCro sticky-strip kind of fastener which is sometimes used by commercial garment makers; you can buy it in sewing stores. It is especially useful for fastening things like headbands and bicycle-light straps that need to be adjustable.

ZONING

American society is the most rigidly segregated in the world in terms of zoning regulations, and many of our grievous transportation and energy problems stem from that fact, as well as much of our crime and other social disorder. For about seventy years now, it has been the official "wisdom" that different uses of land must be kept separate from each other: residential areas must contain nothing but residences, commercial areas only shops and businesses, and industrial areas only industry. There are, of course, aspects of zoning regulations which make sense and need to

be preserved: we need ways of controlling pollution and noise and traffic in *all* types of neighborhoods, not just the expensive residential ones that are the greatest beneficiaries of most zoning laws. But the rigidity of our zoning practices no longer serves our new urban needs.

In European and Asian cities that have been settled for millenia, an easy mixture of uses is normal and provides a standard of variety and amenity unknown in America. In Paris you are seldom more than a block from a bakery that offers fresh rolls in the morning, or a delicatessen, or a restaurant-cafe, or a bar, or a movie theater. In the densest parts of New York, San Francisco, and a few other US cities, this wholesome kind of mixture prevails—along with repair shops, groceries, small manufacturing operations, and other light industrial uses. The standard pattern for the car-dominated American city, however, puts a severe geographical distance between different uses. The consequence is that we all need cars: how, otherwise, will we get from our house or apartment to our job ten miles away (the local bus systems usually being so inadequate)? And how to get from the job to the supermarket two miles from the home? And how to visit friends who live halfway across town? Another consequence is that we consume vast amounts of time in moving around from place to place which might, if our neighborhoods were compact and multiple-use, be enjoyed in leisure pursuits, seeing friends, or conceivably even thinking.

Zoning has largely been sustained by the determination of the middle- and upper-classes to keep their residential areas secure and pleasant—at the cost of everybody else in the society. It is particularly overdeveloped in wealthy suburban areas where special regulations even require that home lots be huge, or that homes cost above a certain amount.

But in the end, America must develop a more efficient, urbane, and pleasantly urban type of mixed-use zoning for our neighborhoods. We will not much longer be able to use energy-guzzling cars to solve the problems caused by our dispersed zoning; we can't avoid confronting the nature of what goes on in our cities and trying to integrate it *all* into sensibly planned neighborhoods. People will need to have jobs—factory jobs as well as office and shop jobs—within walking or bicycling distance of their residences. They will need stores at which to purchase most of their daily necessities, and facilities for their amusement and education. Sprawl as a way of life is going to come to an end;

273

we can't go on avoiding problems by pushing them away into somebody else's neighborhood.

And behold, when you use what has been learned in the great cities of the past, it turns out that families and single people and communal groups *can* all co-exist quite happily in a neighborhood—that in fact they contribute different and valuable things to the neighborhood life. Small businesses add to the vitality and stability of a neighborhood, and their stores provide meeting places in which people encounter each other, discuss problems and exchange news. The shorter distances to work and shopping mean many people can get along without cars, saving themselves enormous amounts of money and conserving oil. When artists or small crafts shops move into an industrial area (especially if they manage to be allowed to live in or above their shops) they improve its appearance, its street liveliness, and its safety—even the industrial property then needs fewer guards and watchdogs.

A particularly nasty feature of contemporary zoning restricts who can live in a house. In many towns and cities only "families" (people related by marriage) are allowed to occupy houses, and unrelated persons wishing to share a house can get thrown out. As rents and house prices rise, such regulations become increasingly absurd: it is a rare couple with children who can afford a standard "family house" these days unless they share it with others, and many such houses are within the price range solely of couples with two incomes and no children. The "old-fashioned" family (with father working and mother home with the children) now comprises only 7 percent of our households. Our zoning laws are in flat conflict with this overwhelming sociological fact. In this area they don't just need revision, they need elimination, so that we can go on experimenting with EXTENDED FAMILIES of novel types to replace the declining nuclear family.

ABOUT THE AUTHOR

Ernest Callenbach grew up in a village in central Pennsylvania, on ten acres where his family raised chickens, ducks, and turkeys. He spent six years at the University of Chicago and then moved to California, becoming an editor at the University of California Press in Berkeley. In 1958 he founded *Film Quarterly*, an internationally respected journal of film criticism. He is the author of the contemporary classic *Ecotopia*, which has now appeared in eight languages, and is co-author (with Christine Leefeldt) of *The Art of Friendship*. He lectures regularly throughout the United States, urging the adoption of ecologically sane ways of living. His next book, a novel, will show how an Ecotopian society could come into existence.

Ecotopian Books
Available through AND/OR PRESS
ORIGINAL BANYAN TREE EDITIONS

Ecotopia
By Ernest Callenbach, $4.95

"The newest name after Wells, Verne, Huxley, and Orwell." —*Los Angeles Times*

A visit to a near-future ecologically sane society that really works — technologically, politically and on a human scale. *Ecotopia* is also a moving love story.

"The underground classic of a generation." —*Sipapu*

"None of the happy conditions in *Ecotopia* are beyond the technical or resource reach of our society." —*Ralph Nader*

"The first distinctively American utopia." —*Oregon Times*

Quality paperback, 5½ × 8, 167 pps.

The Ecotopian Sketchbook
By Judith Clancy, $4.25

Judith Clancy's drawings have been widely published, much exhibited, and are represented in numerous collections. Here she envisions fanciful scenes from *Ecotopian* life in a book inviting you to color, draw, write, collage, and create a new world — in the spirit of Ernest Callenbach's novel.

Quality paperback, 8½ × 11, 48 pps. Available June 1981.

Books on Health & Living Well from
AND/OR PRESS, INC.

Bestseller!
Holistic Health Handbook
Compiled by the Berkeley Holistic Health Center, $9.95

"The Handbook is a labor of love that deserves to become the workbook of the movement — a manual that is as wide and as deep as life itself." —*New Age Journal*

We are currently witnessing a revolution in ideas about health and disease. The Holistic Health Handbook is a comprehensive and multi-dimensional view of this growing movement.

Quality paperback, 8½ × 11, 480 pps.

Holistic Health Lifebook
Compiled by the Berkeley Holistic Health Center, $10.95

The *Holistic Health Lifebook* is designed to lead you to a healthier lifestyle. A companion volume to the best-selling Holistic Health Handbook.

This guide to personal and planetary well-being brings together the leading teachers and healers in the field, on such topics as: Body/Mind, Mind/Spirit, Relationships, Society/Environment, Overview and Future of Holistic Health.

Quality paperback, 8½ × 11, 384 pps.

Books on Health & Living Well from
AND/OR PRESS, INC.

Whole Foods:
Natural Foods Guide
Edited by Whole Foods Magazine, $8.95

Whole Foods is a guide to help consumers make informed choices about natural foods. Previously restricted to the trade, this information is publically available for the first time.
Whole Foods is the best of the good health and eating syndrome — read it cover to cover."
—*Co-Evolution Quarterly*
Quality paperback, 8½ × 11, 311 pps.

Cooking Naturally
By John Calella, $5.95

Cooking Naturally is a gourmet natural foods experience for vegetarians and non-vegetarians alike.
"Organic John takes time from his TV show to provide a somewhat eclectic range of 300 recipes using only natural vegetarian ingredients."
—*American Library Association Booklist*
Quality paperback, 8½ × 8½, 128 pps.

Joyous Childbirth:
Manual for Conscious Natural Childbirth
By Cybele and E.J. Gold, $8.95

"Highly recommended..." —*East West Journal*
Joyous Childbirth offers clear information for total physical, spiritual, and emotional preparation. Lavishly illustrated with diagrams, photographs and drawings.
Quality paperback, 5½ × 8½, 207 pps.